D1013580

ALASTAIR SAWDAY'S
SPECIAL PLACES TO STAY

FRENCH
HOTELS
CHÂTEAUX & OTHER PLACES

FRENCH
BED &
BREAKFAST

ALASTAIR SAWDAY'S
SPECIAL PLACES TO STAY

PARIS
HOTELS

ALASTAIR SAWDAY'S
SPECIAL PLACES TO STAY

ITALY

Alastair
Sawday's

Special Places to Stay

Fourth edition
Copyright © 2007 Alastair Sawday
Publishing Co. Ltd

Published in October 2007

Alastair Sawday Publishing Co. Ltd,
The Old Farmyard, Yanley Lane,
Long Ashton, Bristol BS41 9LR, UK
Tel: +44 (0)1275 395430
Fax: +44 (0)1275 393388
Email: info@sawdays.co.uk
Web: www.sawdays.co.uk

The Globe Pequot Press,
P. O. Box 480, Guilford,
Connecticut 06437, USA
Tel: +1 203 458 4500
Fax: +1 203 458 4601
Email: info@globepequot.com
Web: www.globepequot.com

Design concept: Company X, Bristol
Maps: Maidenhead Cartographic Services
Printing: Butler & Tanner, Frome
UK distribution: Penguin UK, London

ISBN-13: 978-1-901970-93-7

A responsible business: we are committed to being a green and socially responsible business. Here are a few things we already do: our pool cars run on recycled cooking oil and low-emission LPG; our award-winning eco-offices are equipped with solar-heated water, wood-pellet heating, and rainwater-fed loos and showers; and we were the world's first carbon-neutral publishing company. Find out more at www.sawdays.co.uk

Paper and print: we have sought the lowest possible ecological 'footprint' from the production of this book. Whenever possible, we use paper that is either recycled (with a high proportion of post-consumer waste) or FSC-certified, and give preference to local companies in order to foster our local economy and reduce our carbon footprint. Our printer is ISO 14001-registered.

Alastair Sawday's

Special Places
to Stay

French
Holiday Homes

4   Contents

6   Index by département

We are a small company, born in 1994 and growing slowly but surely every year – in 2007 we sold our millionth book. We have always published beautiful and immensely useful guide books, and we now also have a very successful website.

There are about 35 of us in the Company, producing the website, about 20 guide books and a growing series of environmental books under the Fragile Earth imprint. We think a lot about how we do it, how we behave, what our 'culture' is, and we are trying to be a little more than 'just a publishing company'.

Environmental & ethical policies

We have always had strong environmental policies. Our books are printed by a British company that is ISO14001 accredited, on recycled and/or FSC-certified paper, and we have been offsetting our carbon emissions since 2001. We now do so through an Indian NGO, which means that our money goes a long way. However, we are under no illusions about carbon-offsetting: it is part of a strong package of green measures including running company cars on gas or recycled cooking oil; composting or recycling waste; encouraging cycling and car-sharing; only buying organic or local food; not accepting web links with companies we consider unethical; and banking with the ethical Triodos Bank.

In 2005 we won a Business Commitment to the Environment Award and in 2006 a Queen's Award for Enterprise in the Sustainable Development category. All this has boosted our resolve to promote our green policies.

Eco offices

In January 2006 we moved into our new eco offices. With super-insulation, under-floor heating, a wood-pellet boiler, solar panels and a rainwater tank, we have a working environment kind to ourselves and to the environment. Lighting is low-energy, dark corners are lit by sun-pipes, materials are natural and one building is of green oak. Carpet tiles are from Herdwick sheep in the Lake District. The building is a delight to work in.

Ethics

We think that our role as a company is not much different from our role as the individuals within it: to play our part in the community, to reduce our ecological footprint, to be a benign influence, to foster good human relationships and to make a positive difference to the world around us.

Another phrase for the simple intentions above is Corporate Responsibility. It is a much-used buzz-phrase, but many of those adopting it as a policy are getting serious. A world-wide report by the think-tank Tomorrow's Company has revealed quite how convinced the world's major companies are that if they do not take on full responsibility for their impact, social and environmental, they will not survive.

The books – and a dilemma

So, we have created popular books and a handsome website that do good work. They promote authenticity, individuality and good local and organic food – a far cry from corporate culture. Rural economies, pubs, small farms, villages and hamlets all benefit. However, people use fossil fuel to get there. Should we aim to get our readers to offset their own carbon emissions, and the B&B and hotel owners too?

We are gradually introducing green ideas into the books: the Fine Breakfast Scheme that highlights British and Irish B&B owners who use local and organic food; celebrating those who make an extra environmental effort; gently encouraging the use of public transport, cycling and walking. We now give green and 'social' awards to pubs in our pub guide.

In 2006 we published the very successful *Green Places to Stay*, focusing on responsible travel and eco-properties around the globe. Bit by bit we will do more, and welcome ideas from all quarters. Our aim is to be a pioneering green publisher, and to be known as one. We hope one day to offer energy audits to our owners, to provide real help to those who want to 'go green'. And we will continue to champion the small-scale. We will also continue to oppose policies that encourage the growth of air traffic – however contradictory that might seem.

Our Fragile Earth series

The 'hard' side of our environmental publishing is the Fragile Earth series: *The Little Earth Book*, *The Little Food Book* and *The Little Money Book*. They consist of bite-sized essays, polemical, hard-hitting and well researched. They are a 'must have' for anyone who seeks clarity about some of the key issues of our time. We have also published *One Planet Living* with WWF.

A flagship project is the *The Big Earth Book*; it is packed with information and a stimulating and provocative read. It is being promoted, with remarkable generosity, by Yeo Valley Organic.

Lastly – what is special?

The notion of 'special' is at the heart of what we do, and highly subjective. We discuss this in the introduction to every book. We take huge pleasure in finding people and places that do their own thing – brilliantly; places that are unusual and follow no trends; places of peace and beauty; people who are kind and interesting – and genuine.

We seem to have touched a nerve with hundreds of thousands of readers; they obviously long for the independence that our books provide, for the warm human contact of Special Places, and to be able to avoid the banality and ugliness of so many other places.

A night in a Special Place can be a transforming experience.

Alastair Sawday

10   Acknowledgements

Ann Cooke-Yarborough began her publishing life as the *éminence grise* behind the French B&B book, and revelled in the relationships she was able to forge with their owners – such a rewarding collection of people. She has taken on the Herculean task of compiling and editing this book as a kindness to us and it has been a huge labour, less relieved by contact with owners because many of them are, by definition, absent when their houses are rented for self-catering. On top of that, she has had to struggle with computer connection problems that would have driven a less-motivated person to despair and beyond. We all salute her, and her indomitable loyalty and good humour.

At Ann's elbow have been Susan Herrick Luraschi in constant moral support in Paris, and Becci Stevens who bore the vast brunt of the adminstrative load in Bristol, acting as an anchor in choppy seas for Susan and Ann, our two French editors. But all these books are now team efforts so we mustn't forget Jo Boissevain, who as always was a tower of strength on the writing front, Jackie King, for her editorial expertise, and of course everyone else who contributed. The final trumpet should be blown for the heroic team of inspectors who have made this book possible. They are consistently loyal, perceptive and hardworking. We owe them a great deal.

Alastair Sawday

Heartfelt thanks to Brendan Flanagan for unflinching, loving support and to Susan Herrick Luraschi for tears and laughter shared on this roller-coaster.

Ann Cooke-Yarborough

Series Editor Alastair Sawday
Editor Ann Cooke-Yarborough
Editorial Director Annie Shillito
Writing Jo Boissevain,
Ann Cooke-Yarborough, Viv Cripps,
Matthew Hilton Dennis,
Susan Herrick Luraschi, Helen Pickles,
Janet Edsforth Stone
Inspections Katie Anderson,
Richard & Linda Armspach,
Andrew Bamford, Helen Barr,
Miranda Bell, Ann Cooke-Yarborough,
Jill Coyle, Meredith Dickinson,
Sue Edrich, John & Jane Edwards,
Valerie Foix, Georgina Gabriel,
Diana Sawday Harris, Judith Lott,
Susan Herrick Luraschi, Déirdre Mooney,
Annette Parker, Janet Edsforth Stone,
Elizabeth Yates
Accounts Bridget Bishop,
Rebecca Bebbington, Christine Buxton,
Sandra Hasell, Amy Lancastle,
Sally Ranahan
Editorial Sue Bourner,
Kate Ball, Jo Boissevain, Nicola Crosse,
Melanie Harrison, Jackie King,
Wendy Ogden, Florence Oldfield,
Maria Serrano, Kate Shepherd,
Becci Stevens, Danielle Williams
Production Julia Richardson,
Tom Germain, Rebecca Thomas,
Emma Wilson
Sales & Marketing & PR
Rob Richardson,
Thomas Caldwell, Sarah Bolton
Web & IT Russell Wilkinson,
Chris Banks, Isabelle Deakin,
Joe Green, Brian Kimberling
Previous Editor Emma Carey

The changes that sweep almost every area of human activity are sweeping France and its self-catering world too. One can assume that very little will remain stable from one year to the next. Fashions are built on sand, of course; but where once the word made one think of clothes, fashion now governs the inside of a house. Curtains, bedspreads, pots and pans, rugs and fans – they come and go, it seems, like songs at the top of the charts.

But I am a touch old-fashioned and have a special affection for places that nod only imperceptibly to the outside world – especially if this also includes enthusiasm for reducing the place's impact on the planet. We are happy to have found a lot of these. There is, for example, a tiny and most basic-but-lovely hut in the shrubbery with a nature-mad owner next door. The hut is just what I long to find for a quiet and basic escape from an overwhelming world – rather than a house filled with modern, perhaps electronic, reminders of our frenzy. We have also included a minutely planned and attentively greened estate with four or five gîtes around the lovely manor house. It has restored Italian gardens and spring water. There is, too, a couple who almost refuse to buy anything new and are brilliant at recycling, redefining and redirecting secondhand material of every description. Then there are those who have turned their land into a wildlife sanctuary. This list goes on, with one theme being a general passion for

wildlife and nature conservation and another being the conversion of buildings to reduce their energy output. This book is awash with interesting people and their houses and I feel a little guilty singling out individual places. But if you want somewhere merely beautiful, you will find it. If you want somewhere that combines beauty with a genuine engagement with the outside world – you will find it too.

France has always been a beacon to those whose passions are travel, culture, food, history and people. I am so glad to see that she still leads the way with her 'gîtes' – in all the new shapes and guises they take.

Alastair Sawday

Photo: Tom Germain

The making of this book has hugely expanded my experience of what are commonly known as gîtes in France. All I knew until this year was the odd little gatehouse or converted stable – basic-rustic in style and fittings but what matter when it's for a rare long weekend for two 'getting away from the family' – and a fine old presbytery for a big Christmas gathering which, coincidentally, has found its way into this new edition.

I am also glad to have found some highly qualified candidates for the first batch of Green Pages in *French Holiday Homes*, more than we have space for in this edition. So the selection is, as usual, subjective. Look for these green-tinged double-page spreads: each of them is going the extra sustainable mile and we are proud to salute them here.

Gîtes long suffered from a reputation for being unloved buildings and boring places to stay, rather like my basic-rustic boltholes of twenty years ago; so much so that the word came to be almost derogatory. But in French, before and after it became an English dictionary word for cheap self-catering place, 'gîte' has long had a sense of warm shelter, refuge even, so that the common expression *le gîte et le couvert* has far more welcome cosiness in it than its decidedly unpoetic English equivalent 'board and lodging'.

Over the last 15 years the number of gîtes has exploded and they are now far from being all French: owners have more competition, and 'foreigners' – mainly British and Dutch – are making that competition stiffer by their enlightened approach to renovating and furnishing old houses to rent. It's no longer enough to fix up an outbuilding, fling in a few cast-offs and dig out a pool. Owners need to find something to make their gîte stand out in the crowd.

Some have taken the luxury route: fully fitted kitchens with more mod cons than most of us have at home, heated pools, jacuzzis and spas, maid service and chefs to whip you up sumptuous dinners; one of the places in this book even has a mini-cinema. Others give you the opportunity to stay in a special building: a water mill, a fortified castle, a tiny tree house. Or they may offer simple treats: an organic kitchen garden where you may help yourselves, home-baked bread

Photo left: Chalet Gingerbread, entry 326
Photo right: Maison des Cerises, entry 312

delivered to the door, a bread and croissant bag with your completed order hung outside each morning, your own herb garden, cookery courses, writers' retreats, and delicious *table d'hôtes*. Yet others are developing the up-market holiday centre approach.

Stay in a special building: a water mill, a fortified castle, a tiny tree house

This mounting wave of gîte complexes is a conundrum for me as I am not the gregarious type. Their owners are doing a brilliant heritage-saving job by restoring superb and evocative places that their former French owners had left to disintegrate. One adventurous owner will do wonders turning an old barn into a walled swimming pool, another will kit out the former dairy as the kind of games room that parents and teenagers dream of, a third will build a sauna, a hot tub and a massage room in the wine press and book you an irresistible pamper session. Choose these places for gatherings of family and friends, for interesting encounters away from your normal stamping grounds – for socialising, in a nutshell. If you prefer the solitary retreat that allows you to live in splendid isolation for days on end, there are plenty of other enticing entries for you to choose from.

Bonnes vacances!

Ann Cooke-Yarborough

Photo: Mas Garrigue, entry 347

We look for houses that we like – and we are fiercely subjective in our choices. Those who are familiar with our Special Places series know that we look for comfort, originality, authenticity. Our Alpine inspector is not alone in hating "flush doors, cheap carpet and plastic wood flooring", though one or other of these may be the means of offering exceptionally good value. We reject the insincere, the anonymous and the banal.

Inspections

We visit every place in the guide to get a feel for how the place ticks. We don't take a clipboard and we don't have a list of what is acceptable and what is not. Instead, we chat with the owner or manager and then look carefully, sensitively round the house. It's all very informal, but it gives us an excellent idea of who would enjoy staying there. Once in the book, properties are re-inspected every three or four years so that we can keep things fresh and accurate.

We visit every place in the guide to get a feel for how the place ticks

Feedback

Do let us know how you get on in these houses, and get in touch if you stumble across others that deserve to be in our guide – we value your feedback enormously. Use the forms on our website at www.sawdays.co.uk, or later in this book (page 465). Any poor reports are

followed up with the owners in question, while praise is always a pleasure to pass on.

Subscriptions

Owners pay to appear in this guide. Their fee goes towards the costs of inspections, of producing an all-colour book and of maintaining our website. We only include places and owners that we find positively special. It is not possible for anyone to buy their way into our guides.

Disclaimer

We make no claims to pure objectivity in choosing our Special Places. They are here because we like them. Our opinions and tastes are ours alone and this book is a statement of them; we hope you will share them. We have done our utmost to get our facts right but apologise unreservedly for any mistakes that may have crept in.

You should know that we don't check such things as fire alarms, swimming pool security or any other regulation with which owners of properties receiving paying guests should comply. This is the responsibility of the owners.

Photo: Moreau – Le Pressoir, entry 175

Finding the right place for you

Do read our write-ups carefully — we want to guide you to a place where you'll feel happy. If you are staying on a farm don't be surprised to have tractors passing early in the morning, or the farmer rounding up his cattle, or a few flies, the inevitable companions of these rustic charms. Many of these properties have all mod cons but an ancient building may have temperamental plumbing and be less than hermetically sealed against draughts; a remote hilltop farmhouse may suffer the occasional power cut.

Use our descriptions as a taster of what is on offer and have a conversation with the owners about the finer details. Perhaps we've mentioned a pool and you want to check that it will be open at Easter; or you need to know whether the bikes will be available on your particular weekend. If you do find anything misleading in this or any of our books, please let us know. And do discuss any problem with your hosts at the time, however trivial. They are the ones who are most likely to be able to sort it out before the end of your holiday. Owners always say "if only we'd known" when we contact them on a reader's behalf after the event.

If the entry mentions other gîtes, or that the owners do B&B, note that you may not be in total isolation but will most probably be sharing the pool and garden with other guests and their families. This shouldn't spoil your holiday but, if absolute peace is vital to you, ask the owners how many others are likely to be around. Some of our properties have owners who live nearby; others live far away. If this matters to you, check when booking. There will usually be someone you can turn to should you lose your key!

The italics at the end of the write-up carry useful extra facts, some of which need explaining:
• Meals on request: the owners live on site and can provide *table d'hôtes* dinner or a barbecue for all their guests, by arrangement. In a few cases, a cook can be hired.
• Sawday B&B: also appears in our guide to *French Bed & Breakfast*.
• Sawday hotel: also appears in our guide to *French Hotels & Châteaux*.
• B&B also: offers B&B but we have not inspected that aspect of the property.
• Shared pool: where we have the information, we say when the swimming pool is shared.
• Unfenced water: there is an unfenced pond, river or lake on the property and young children require parental supervision.

Photo left: La Roque, entry 291
Photo right: Castelnau des Fieumarcon, entry 250

Maps

The general map of France is marked with the page numbers of the detailed maps, as are the individual entries. The entry numbers on the detailed maps show roughly where the holiday homes are. Our maps should be used in conjunction with a large-scale road map.

The address

We give only an abbreviated address for the property. Owners will supply complete addresses when you enquire or book.

Out of season you also have a better chance of seeing France going about its everyday business

Symbols

Below each entry in the book you will see some little black symbols, which are explained in a short table at the very back of the book. They are based on the information given to us by the owners. However, things do change: bikes may be under repair or a new pool may have been put in. Please use the symbols as a guide rather than an absolute statement of fact and double-check anything that is important to you.

Children – The ♟ symbol tells you that children of all ages are welcome. If there's no symbol, it may mean there is an unfenced pool, a large boisterous dog, fine things, steep stairs or that the owners are aiming to offer a child-free break. If you are convinced that your impeccably behaved five-year-old can cope, the owner may allow you to bring her – but at your own risk.

Pets – Our ▶ symbol tells you which houses generally welcome them but you must check whether this includes beasts the size and type of yours, whether the owner has one too (will they be compatible?) and whether you can bring it into the house or keep it in an outhouse. Your hosts will expect animals to be well-behaved and obviously you will be responsible for them at all times.

Quick reference indices

At the back of the book (page 466) you will find a number of quick-reference indices showing those places that offer a particular service. Scan these pages if you are looking for an intimate place for two or a big place to hold a family reunion, a wedding party or a workshop, if you want to connect to the internet, or swim in wild waters.

Green entries

We have chosen, very subjectively, seven places which are making a particular effort to be eco-friendly and have given them a double-page spread and extra photos to illustrate what they're up to. This does not mean there are no other places in the guide taking green initiatives – there are many – but we have highlighted just a few examples.

When to go

Families with school-age children will generally take their main holiday in July and August, which is when the French will be taking theirs. For these months it is essential to book well in advance. If you can holiday outside those busy months, do so: it'll be slightly cooler, it'll be cheaper and you'll be less likely to get snarled up in traffic jams, especially on arrival and departure.

Out of season you also have a better chance of seeing France going about its everyday business. May and June are the best months for flowers, for temperatures suitable for walking, and for visiting the Mediterranean coast. If mushrooms are your thing, September's the time, and temperatures in autumn can be ideal. The winter months, when you often get clear fine days, are well worth considering too.

Some holiday homes can be rented all year round, some close during the winter, others close during the winter but open for Christmas and New Year. Winter is often a good time to glimpse the real France; the weather in the south can be very pleasant and rates are normally more reasonable. In some cases, but not all, we tell you if winter lets are available, so please check with owners. A word of warning, though: some restaurants in rural areas only open in July and August. Some markets too, but they tend to be the touristy and less authentic ones. Many restaurants close for the winter.

Photo: Number One, entry 380

How many does it sleep?

In some instances we give two figures, separated by a hyphen. The first figure is the number of adults the house sleeps comfortably; the second is the number of people who can actually fit in. Some owners can provide extra beds, though there may be an additional charge, and where sofabeds or mezzanine levels are provided, privacy may be compromised. If you want to bring extra people, you absolutely must ask the owner first. Some places offer special rates if you are fewer people than the number shown, though this generally applies out of season only.

In this book a 'double' means one double bed, a 'twin' means two single beds. A 'triple' is three single beds. 'Family rooms' include at least one double bed. Extra beds and cots for children, sometimes at extra cost, can often be provided – do ask. We also give total numbers of bathrooms and shower rooms. We don't give details about which bathrooms are 'en suite' but many are, so check with the owners if this matters. We only mention wcs if they are separate from the bath and shower rooms which generally have their own.

Facilities

If it is important to you that your holiday home has a microwave, dishwasher, TV, CD-player, barbecue or central heating in winter, check with the owners first. Most properties will have a washing machine or shared laundry; we try to mention where they don't, but again, double-check. Electric kettles are still a rarity in French-owned homes so if you can't manage without bring your own. You may also want to consider bringing a portable fan as they can be a godsend in high summer. If you have your own electrical appliances bring an adaptor plug, as virtually all sockets are for two-pin plugs that run on 220/240 AC voltage.

Prices

Prices are in euros and/or sterling, according to the wishes of the owner.

All prices are per property per week, unless we say otherwise. We give a range from the cheapest, low-season price to the highest, high-season price. Check with the owner and confirm in writing

the price for the number in your party. Remember that in ski resorts, high season is February. Prices are for 2008 and may go up in 2009 so please check with the owner or on their website if they have one. A few properties offer a reduction if you stay for more than a week but don't expect any deals during peak season. Some places require you to stay a fortnight during these months.

The *taxe de séjour* is a small tax that local councils can levy on all visitors paying for accommodation. Some councils do, some don't: you may find your bill increased by a euro or two per person per day.

Do read our write-ups carefully – we want to guide you to a place where you'll feel happy

What's included?

Utilities – In most cases this covers electricity, gas and water. In some cases, the electricity meter will be read at the start and end of your stay and you will have to pay separately. In other cases, it will just be heating that's extra.

Linen – Where linen is not included, we say so alongside the price. You may need to bring your own or the owners may offer a hire service. Even where linen is included, towels often aren't, so check when booking.

Cleaning – Some owners charge for the cost of cleaning and you will have to pay this whether or not you are willing to clean the place yourself. At other places you can either clean up yourself or pay someone else to do it. In some cases the cleaning cost is deducted from the security deposit.

How to book

Our first advice is to **book early** and to check the owner's website to see if their place is available for your chosen dates. Once you have agreed on dates, the owner will normally send you a booking form or *contrat de location* (tenancy contract) which must be filled in and returned with the deposit and commits both sides. The owner will then send a written confirmation and invoice, which constitutes the formal acceptance of the booking. Contracts with British owners are normally governed by British law. Remember that Ireland and the UK are one hour behind the rest of Europe and people can be upset by enquiries coming through late in their evening.

One or two places in the guide can only be booked through the local Gîtes de France booking service but as most transactions are done by email nowadays the language problem, here or with non-English-speaking owners, should not arise.

Deposits

Owners usually ask for a non-refundable deposit to secure a booking. It makes sense to take out a travel insurance policy with a clause to enable you to recover a deposit if you are forced to cancel. Your policy should also cover you for personal belongings and public liability and, possibly, for taking part in adventurous sports. Many owners charge a refundable security/damage deposit, payable either in advance or on arrival.

Payment

The balance of the rent, and usually the security deposit, is normally payable at least eight weeks before the start of the holiday. (If you book within eight weeks of the holiday, you'll be required to make full payment when you book.) A few owners take credit cards, otherwise you will need to send a euro cheque, or a sterling cheque if the owner has a British bank account. The Paypal system of paying via the internet is being used by a few owners and will doubtless spread as it proves itself to be easy, secure and cheap.

Arrival day

Usually this is a Saturday. Where it is not we have tried to mention it under the booking details. Many owners are flexible outside the high season so, again, it is worth checking. Normally you must arrive after 4pm and leave by 10am. Don't arrive earlier as your house may not yet be ready and you will wrong-foot your busy owners.

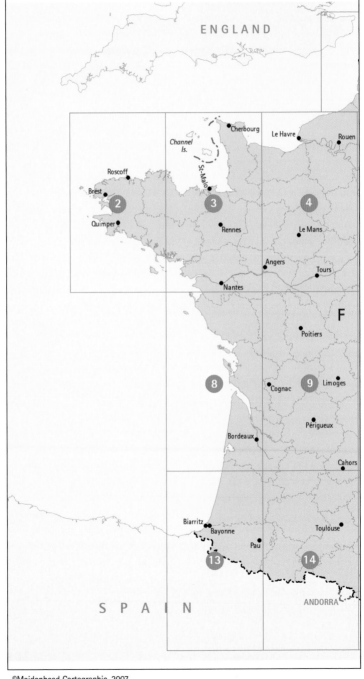

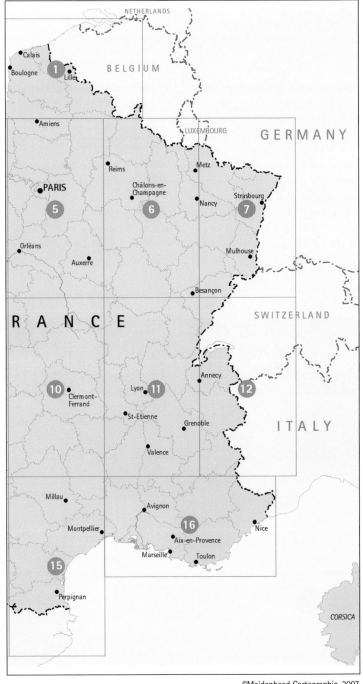

Medical & emergency procedures

If you are an EC citizen, it's a good idea to have a European Health Insurance Card with you in case you need any medical treatment. It may not cover all the costs so you may want to take out private insurance as well.

To contact the emergency services dial 112: this is an EU-wide number and you can be confident that the person who answers the phone will speak English as well as French, and can connect you to the police, ambulance and fire/rescue services.

Other insurance

If you are driving, it is probably wise to insure the contents of your car.

Roads & driving

Current speed limits are: motorways 130 kph (80 mph), RN national trunk roads 110 kph (68 mph), other open roads 90 kph (56 mph), in towns 50 kph (30 mph). The road police are very active and can demand on-the-spot payment of fines.

Directions in towns

The French drive towards a destination and use road numbers far less than we do. Thus, to find your way à la française, know the general direction you want to go, ie the towns your route goes through, and when you see *Autres Directions* or *Toutes Directions* in a town, forget road numbers, just continue towards the place name you're heading for or through.

Photo: istock.com

Map 1

25

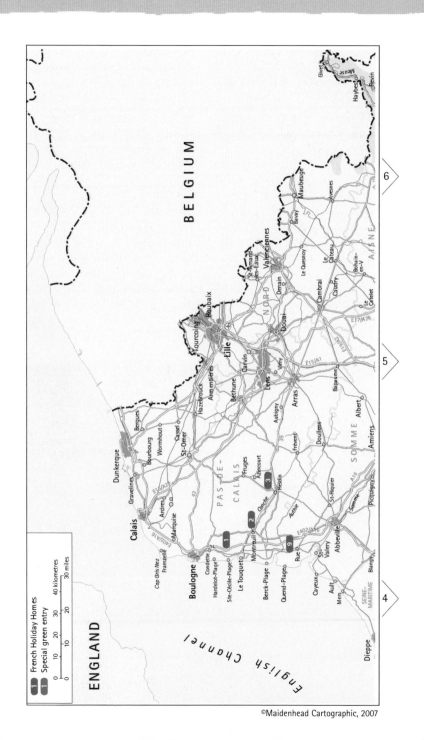

©Maidenhead Cartographic, 2007

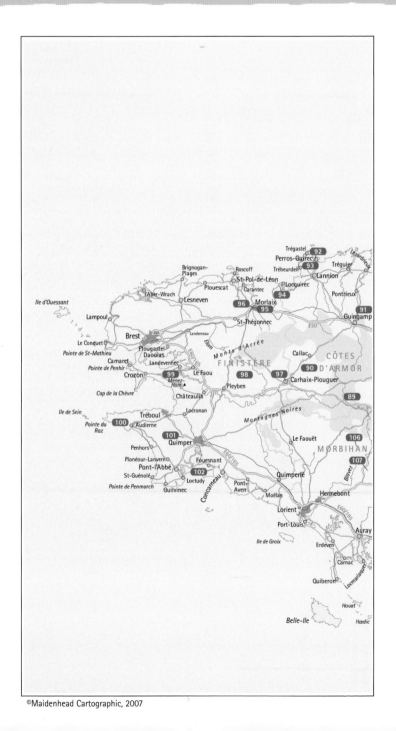

Map 3   27

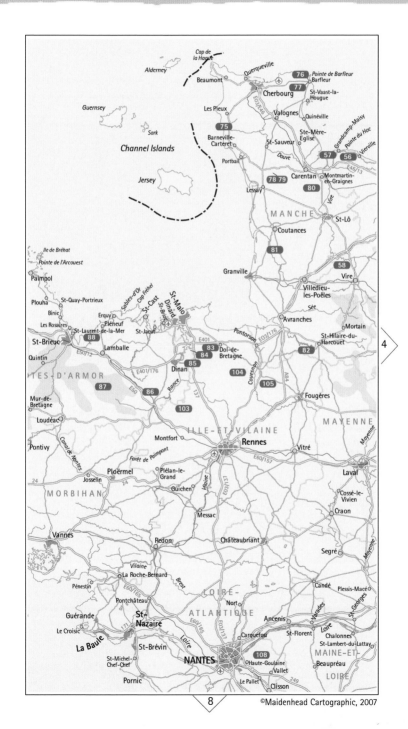

©Maidenhead Cartographic, 2007

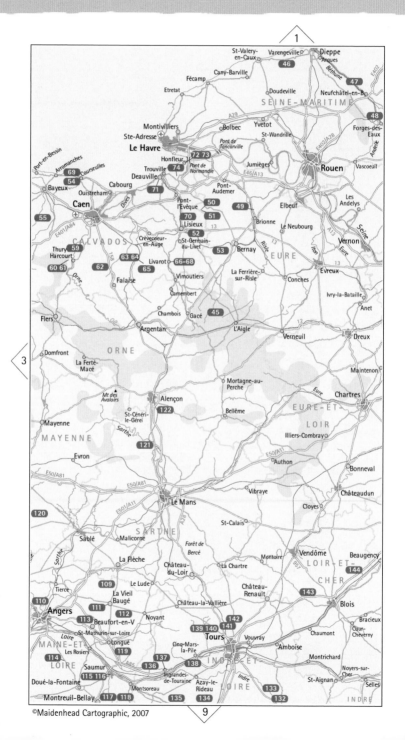

©Maidenhead Cartographic, 2007

Map 5　　　　　　　29

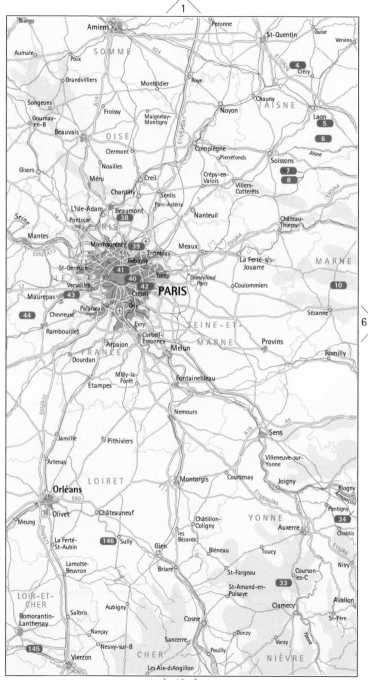

©Maidenhead Cartographic, 2007

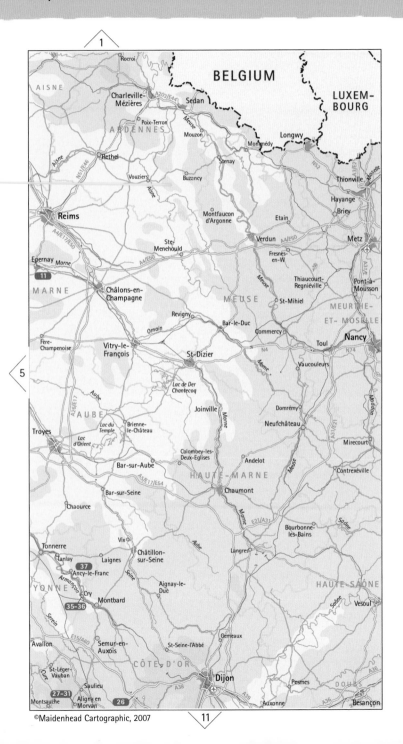

Map 7

31

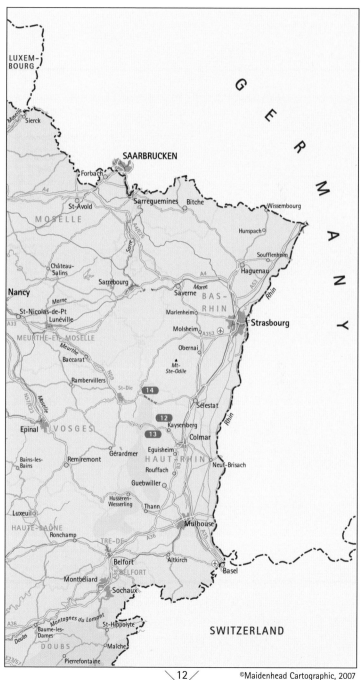

©Maidenhead Cartographic, 2007

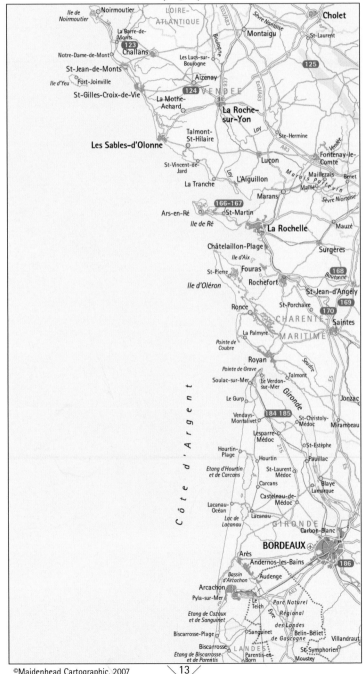

3

Ile de
Noirmoutier   Noirmoutier   LOIRE-
ATLANTIQUE   Sèvre Nantaise   Cholet
La Barre-de-
Monts   Montaigu   St-Laurent
Notre-Dame-de-Mont   123   Challans
Les Lucs-sur-
Boulogne   125
St-Jean-de-Monts
Ile d'Yeu   Port-Joinville   Aizenay
St-Gilles-Croix-de-Vie   124   VENDÉE
La Mothe-
Achard   La Roche-
sur-Yon
Talmont-
St-Hilaire   Loy   Ste-Hermine
Les Sables-d'Olonne   Luçon   Fontenay-le-
Comte
St-Vincent-de-
Jard   Loy   Maillezais   Benet
La Tranche   L'Aiguillon   Marais   Poitevin   Maillé
Marans   Sèvre Niortaise
Ars-en-Ré   166-167   St-Martin
Ile de Ré   St-Martin   La Rochelle   Mauzé
Châtelaillon-Plage   Surgères
Ile d'Aix   168
St-Pierre   Fouras   Boutonne
Ile d'Oléron   Rochefort
St-Jean-d'Angély
Ronce   St-Porchaire   170   169
La Palmyre   CHARENTE-   Saintes
Pointe de   MARITIME
Coubre
Royan
Pointe de Grave   Talmont
Soulac-sur-Mer   Le Verdon-   Gironde   Jonzac
sur-Mer
Le Gurp   184 185   St-Christoly-
Vendays-   Médoc   Mirambeau
Montalivet   Lesparre-
Médoc   St-Estèphe
Hourtin-
Plage   Hourtin   Pauillac
Etang d'Hourtin   St-Laurent
et de Carcans   Médoc   Blaye
Carcans   Lamarque
Castelnau-de-
Médoc
Lacanau-   GIRONDE
Océan   Lacanau
Lac de   Carbon-Blanc
Lacanau
BORDEAUX
Arès
Andernos-les-Bains   186
Bassin   Audenge
d'Arcachon
Arcachon
Pyla-sur-Mer   Le   Parc Naturel
Teich   Régional
Etang de Cazaux   des Landes
et de Sanguinet   Sanguinet   de Gascogne   Villandraut
Biscarrosse-Plage   Belin-Béliet
Biscarrosse   St-Symphorien
Etang de Biscarrosse   Parentis-en-   Moustey
et de Parentis   LANDES   Born

Côte d'Argent

13

Map 9   33

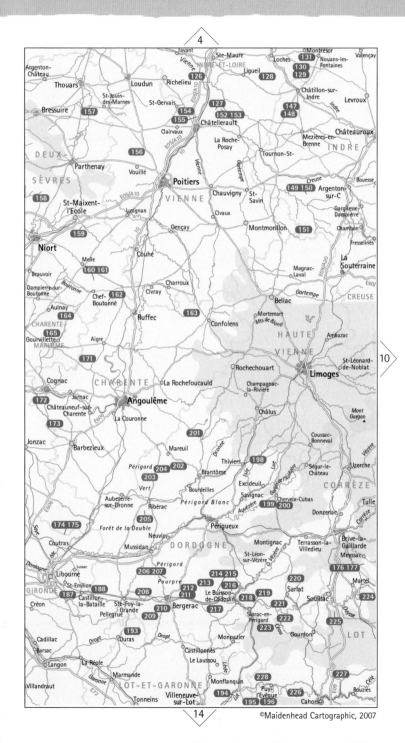

©Maidenhead Cartographic, 2007

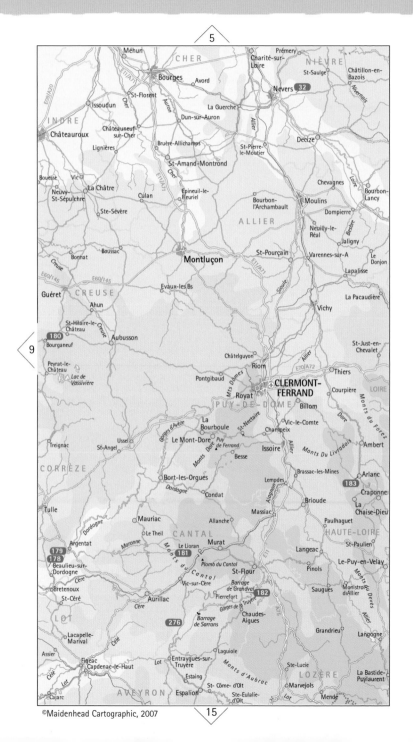

Map 11   35

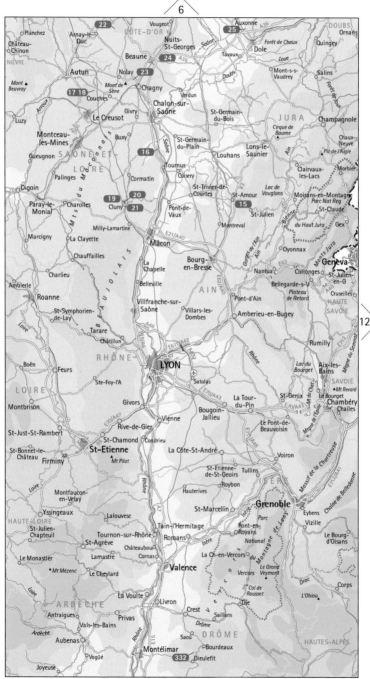

6

Map 13   37

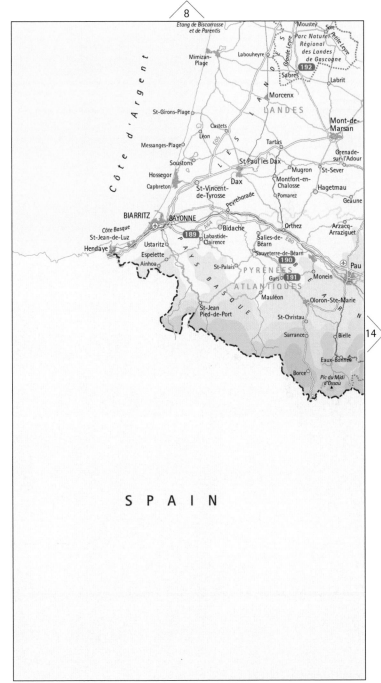

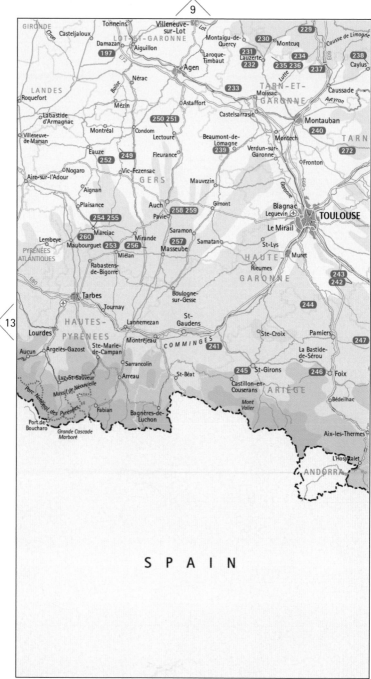

Map 15   39

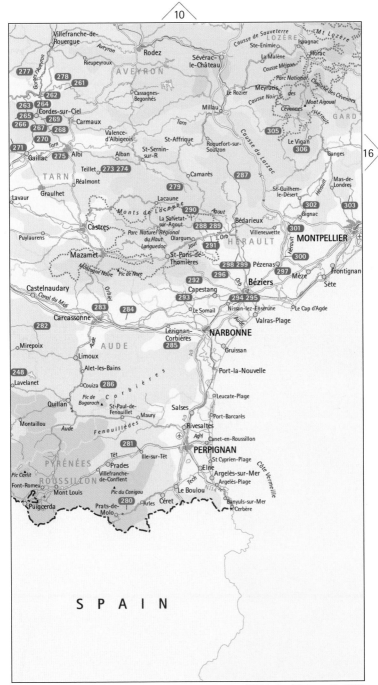

10

16

277
278
261
262
263 264
265
266 267 268
269
270
271
275
273 274
279
290
288 289
291
292
293
294 295
298 299
296
297
300
301
302
303
305
306
283
284
282
285
286
248
281
280

Villefranche-de-Rouergue
Rodez
Sévérac-le-Château
Ste-Énimie
Ispagnac
Florac
LOZÈRE
Mt Lozère
Causse de Sauveterre
Rieupeyroux
AVEYRON
Aveyron
La Malène
Causse Méjean
Parc National
Corniche des Cévennes
Cassagnes-Begonhés
Le Rozier
Meyrueis
des
Causse Noir
Cévennes
Mont Aigoual
Millau
GARD
Cordes-sur-Ciel
Carmaux
Tarn
Valence-d'Albigeois
St-Affrique
Roquefort-sur-Soulzon
Causse du Larzac
Le Vigan
Ganges
Gaillac
Albi
Alban
St-Sernin-sur-R
Hérault
Mas-de-Londres
Teillet
Réalmont
Camarès
St-Guilhem-le-Désert
Lavaur
Graulhet
Lacaune
Monts de Lacaune
Agout
Bédarieux
Gignac
Castres
La Salvetat-sur-Agout
Villeneuvette
Hérault
Puylaurens
Parc Naturel Régional du Haut Languedoc
Olargues
L'Orb
HÉRAULT
MONTPELLIER
Mazamet
St-Pons-de-Thomières
Jaur
Pézenas
Montagne Noire
Pic de Nore
Orb
Béziers
Mèze
Frontignan
Castelnaudary
Canal du Midi
Capestang
Sète
Carcassonne
Orbiel
Le Somail
Nissan-lez-Ensérune
Le Cap d'Agde
Mirepoix
Aude
AUDE
Lézignan-Corbières
NARBONNE
Valras-Plage
Limoux
Aude
Gruissan
Alet-les-Bains
Port-la-Nouvelle
Lavelanet
Couiza
Corbières
Quillan
Pic de Bugarach ▲
St-Paul-de-Fenouillet
Maury
Salses
Leucate-Plage
Montaillou
Aude
Fenouillèdes
Rivesaltes
Port-Barcarès
Agly
Canet-en-Roussillon
PYRÉNÉES
Têt
Ille-sur-Têt
PERPIGNAN
St Cyprien-Plage
Pic Carlit
Prades
ROUSSILLON
Villefranche-de-Conflent
Elne
Argelès-sur-Mer
Côte Vermeille
Font-Romeu
Mont Louis
Pic du Canigou
Tech
Argelès-Plage
Le Boulou
Puigcerda
Prats-de-Molo
Arles
Céret
Banyuls-sur-Mer
Cerbère

S P A I N

©Maidenhead Cartographic, 2007

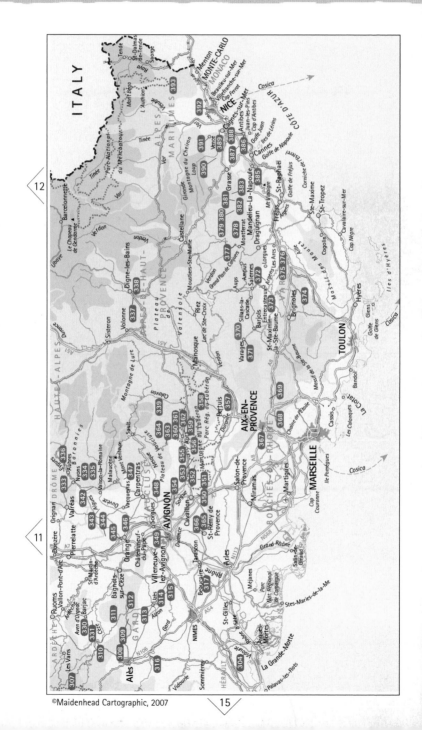

©Maidenhead Cartographic, 2007

15

The North • The East • Burgundy • Paris – Île de France

Halinghen Home

Just across the Channel – you could be here in time for lunch – Halinghen is a genuinely child-friendly holiday house, fine for two or more families. The huge garden and orchard have play space and swings; ping-pong, table football, snooker, games and toys should keep everyone happy on rainy days. The big light rooms have a homely English feel with their cosy medley of furniture. From the open-plan living area, French windows spill you onto the terrace, scented with honeysuckle on summer evenings. Beds are comfortable, bathrooms are carpeted, there are long country views from every window. Merelina swapped London for this gentle French village and lives in one self-contained side of the house. She is warm and helpful and will rustle up a celebration cake on request. Hardelot Plage is a 15-minute drive: its wide beaches, fringed with sand dunes and pines, have turned it into a popular sand-yachting centre, as is nearby Le Touquet. And there are over 100 kilometres of gorgeous sandy beaches on the Côte d'Opale. *Babysitting & hairdressing available. Flexible length of stay. B&B also.*

Price	€1,200 per week.
	€550 for three days in low season.
	Linen not included.
Sleeps	13-18.
Rooms	4: 1 double with bunks, 3 family
	rooms for 3; 2 shower rooms.
	Two extra double rooms on request.
Arrival	Flexible.
Closed	Rarely.

Merelina Ponsonby
Halinghen, Pas-de-Calais

Tel	+33 (0)3 21 83 04 80
Email	merelina@wanadoo.fr
Web	www.merelinasfrance.info

Rue du Général Potez

Pistachio ice cream or lime sorbet? This mouthwateringly pretty town cottage looks good enough to eat. Inside, everything is cute, colourful and cosy. And small. The downstairs space, with its exposed timber and brickwork, has a snug of navy-blue and striped chairs and sofa while tucked behind is the dining end: a floral-covered table and pale blue chairs. A slip of a kitchen, in sparkling white and blue, has all the essentials and you won't mind washing up by hand. Upstairs, a mixture of white walls, pitch pine, simple furniture and modern lighting lends a fresh cottage feel. The second double bed hides on a mezzanine level; a single bed is tucked into a corner. It is clean, tidy, inviting. From this raised cobbled terrace of 16th- and 17th-century houses, yards from the ancient ramparts, you step out of the door into history. Explore the marvellous medieval streets, browse the Saturday market and, in summer, catch the *son et lumière*. Then, after a pre-prandial drink on the tiny patio, set off for one of the town's many restaurants. *Sawday B&B. Ask owners about parking.*

Price	€350–€400 per week.
Sleeps	3-5.
Rooms	2: 1 family room for 3, 1 double on mezzanine; 1 bathroom.
Arrival	Flexible.
Closed	Rarely.

	Étienne & Véronique Bernard
	Montreuil sur Mer, Pas-de-Calais
Tel	+33 (0)3 21 06 09 41
Fax	+33 (0)3 21 06 09 41
Email	etienne.bernard6@wanadoo.fr
Web	gite.montreuil.online.fr

Le Verger

A stylishly restored 14th-century chapel offering perfect peace in its green acre, Le Verger has it all: three terraces, two barbecues, six bicycles, a duo of hammocks and a summer house in the garden. In the chapel is the sitting room – big and original-elm-beamed with three easy sofas on a honey-coloured oak floor before a raised open fire. New oak staircases lead to three bedrooms on two floors; Indian bedcovers, soft lights, pictures dotted here and there. In the 'west wing', more bedrooms and a snowy white bathroom. The huge farmhouse kitchen is a cook's dream, family-style: two dishwashers and fridges, a double porcelain sink, a stainless steel range, a chunky terracotta floor and a table that extends to 18. The master suite on the second floor – grand old beams, pure white walls – has a free-standing bath behind a partition and a chaise-longue for chats in the bubbles. Pastures flank the generous garden and the village church is across the lane. The nearest town, Hesdin, is ten kilometres away. Easy living, ancient peace.

Price	£1,000–£1,500 per week.
Sleeps	14–16.
Rooms	7: 2 doubles, 5 twins; 3 bathrooms, 1 shower room, 2 separate wcs.
Arrival	Friday, but flexible.
Closed	Rarely.

Peter & Moira McDermott
Wambercourt, Pas-de-Calais
Tel   +44 (0)20 8299 4099
Email   peter@mcdermottassociates.co.uk
Web   www.houseinnorthernfrance.com

Catillon du Temple

Deep in the country, high on a hill, an age-old redbrick house sits on giant granite blocks beneath slate roofs. Parts date from the 13th century when a fortified Templar settlement was raised on the ruins of a Roman camp. The massive 13th-century tithe barn still stands superb against the chilly blast. On this plain working farm there's space aplenty for a total of 18 guests; your part has its own small garden. All the living room walls are original fine-laid red brick, its beams are ancient, the squidgy pieces before the big open fireplace are modern, the good little kitchen shelters with the old bread oven behind a redbrick divider. With its ethnic wall hanging and massive old wooden trunk for logs, this is a splendid room. Up a steep narrow staircase you'll find two good-sized bedrooms with simple old and new furniture and cosy carpeting. The double bed looks up to some intricate and venerable overhead carpentry. A house of huge historical presence, soaring views and a delightful owner, here is a summer base for visiting those stirring Gothic cathedrals, picturesque villages and the lush countryside. *Sawday B&B.*

Price	€220-€300 per week. Weekend €150.
Sleeps	5-6.
Rooms	2: 1 double, 1 family: 2 singles, 1 single/pullout double; 1 bathroom.
Arrival	Saturday afternoon.
Closed	Mid-November to mid-March.

José-Marie Carette
Nouvion et Catillon, Aisne

Tel	+33 (0)3 23 56 51 28
Fax	+33 (0)3 23 56 50 14
Email	carette.jm@wanadoo.fr

Picardy

Le Clos

At the end of the château-like farmhouse, part of an 18th-century farming estate, is a big ground-floor gîte for two (or three). The owners, retired farmers, lovely people, live at the far end with their B&B guests. The sitting room occupies the full depth, its kitchen neatly set within a breakfast bar surround, its furniture generous and old-fashioned: golden velveteen sofa and chairs, sturdy antique sideboard, good sofabed. High windows are dressed in red and white striped fabric, floor tiles are beige and new and there's a white stone fireplace for logs in winter. In summer, doors open to the scent of grass and trees; you have your own gravelled entrance terrace and feel entirely private. The powder-blue bedroom is traditional and cosy with views to church tower and apple orchard. Bed quilts and mattresses are new, the shower room is simple and clean. Roam where you will, across the green pastures or to the large pond over the lane — take a picnic and a rod. There's a good little restaurant in the village and more in history-rich Laon. An authentic slice of old France. *Meals by arrangement. Sawday B&B.*

Price	€300 per week. €150 per weekend.
Sleeps	2-3.
Rooms	1 twin, 1 double sofabed; 1 shower room.
Arrival	Flexible.
Closed	Mid-December to March.

Madame Monique Simonnot
Chérêt, Aisne
Tel   +33 (0)3 23 24 80 64
Email   leclos.cheret@club-internet.fr
Web   www.lecloscheret.com

Verneuil - Gîte de Moussy

Deep in the country, surrounded by copses and fields, Moussy is a peaceful, isolated little farmhouse. After the devastation of the First World War, when all that remained of the village were the wash house and church, this farm was the only one to be rebuilt. So you gaze on grazing cattle and rolling acres of peas, sunflowers, barley and wheat. In the walled garden are swings, a barbecue, tables and chairs under the weeping willow; in the outbuildings, the farm equipment. Your house is bigger than it looks and, with immaculate white-walled rooms and just the right amount of furniture, the whole place has a new and spotless feel. One end of the living room has pretty, original tiling and rustic dining table; the other, dark polished boards, an inviting sofa and wicker chairs. Black and white floor tiles gleam on the hall floor and the square, airy kitchen is designed for whatever you need on holiday. Upstairs are simple, pleasant bedrooms and a plain bathroom. There's a Sunday morning market nearby, many war museums, monuments and cemeteries to visit, and some fabulous walks.

Price	€230–€390 per week. Linen not included.
Sleeps	6.
Rooms	3: 1 double, 2 twins; 1 bathroom, 1 separate wc.
Closed	Never.

Bruno & Blandine Cailliez
Vendresse-Beaulne, Aisne

Tel	+33 (0)3 23 24 41 44
Fax	+33 (0)3 23 24 43 55
Email	blandine.cailliez@wanadoo.fr
Web	www.gitedeverneuil.fr.st

Picardy

Ferme de Ressons

Come for soothing views of smooth pastures and arable expanses; feel the simple country lives which have been played out within these old walls. There's nothing fancy about this semi-detached farmworker's cottage; it has ancient beams, wood-burning stove in brick fireplace, almost secret access – and quiet neighbours. Gather round the old square table in your simple but very well-equipped kitchen with its incongruously grand Henri II dresser – or join Valérie and Jean-Paul and their B&B guests for excellent dinners in the farmhouse across the gardens; just book in advance. The cottage's rooms have an eclectic mix of antique and modern pieces and colourful soft furnishings. The double bedroom is downstairs, the twins up, all are cosily carpeted and share a bathroom on the ground floor. In sharp contrast to the flat vineyards, the hilly forests of the Montagne de Reims provide unexpectedly rich walking; the beech woods at Verzy are 500 years old. And if you fancy fishing on the lake, ask Valérie about permits and rods before you arrive. The market, restaurants and shops are two miles off. *Sawday B&B. Meals on request.*

Price	€305-€400 per week.
Sleeps	6.
Rooms	3: 1 double, 2 twins; 1 bathroom.
Closed	Never.

Valérie & Jean-Paul Ferry
Mont Saint Martin, Aisne

Tel	+33 (0)3 23 74 71 00
Fax	+33 (0)3 23 74 28 88

Le Point du Jour

Valérie, architect and mother, has left her creative stamp on this house's attractively simple, spacious rooms. And the long, rolling vistas stretch from the edge of the garden and over the arable fields to infinity.... just stride out into it all. A mile from the Ferrys' farm and B&B, the 19th-century village house exudes light, homeliness and sober good taste. The big living/dining room is generously furnished, a carved buffet holds white crockery and there are easy chairs, a piano and French windows that open onto a south-facing terrace. Upstairs, parquet floors, pretty cotton curtains, good mattresses, an ornately carved 19th-century Portuguese bed. One slopey-ceilinged twin has country-style beds, another has pine floorboards and oriental rugs; the bathroom has snowy-white tiles. Your friendly hosts are ready with help and advice; no doubt they will advise you on choosing one of the many champagne houses in Reims, a 20-minute drive, for a tasting of the bubbly stuff. Those of Mumm, Taittinger and Piper-Heidseick allow you to join (paying) tours without an appointment, including a *dégustation*. *Sawday B&B.*

Price	€350–€420 per week.
Sleeps	6.
Rooms	3: 1 double, 2 twins; 1 bathroom, 1 shower room, 2 separate wcs.
Closed	Never.

	Valérie & Jean-Paul Ferry
	Mont Saint Martin, Aisne
Tel	+33 (0)3 23 74 71 00
Fax	+33 (0)3 23 74 28 88

Picardy

Le Thurel

The exterior of the little pavilion, built to house a previous owner's mother, is 19th-century stately; inside, it is a minimalist's dream. This will delight all those who enjoy clutter-free living, sobriety and space. Scrubbed floorboards and perfect white walls are enriched by the odd splash of colour from ethnic rug or table cover. The huge sitting/dining room, with an open fire, is a symphony of ivory, white and cream in beautiful contrast with the elegant French-grey window frames, the antique dining table and chairs and the odd Flemish oil painting. There are views of the courtyard and a stunning redbrick barn to the front; behind is the large, leafy, gracious garden which you share with the Bree-Leclefs' B&B guests. And boules to play. Up steep stairs bedrooms are white (of course) with fabulously luxurious linen. Glamorous and welcoming, Patrick and Claudine go out of their way to initiate you into the local lore. He is an interior architect, she is a talented gardener and cook and her suppers are open to all guests; just book. *Cleaning charge. Sawday B&B. Meals on request.*

Price	€950 per week.
Sleeps	6.
Rooms	3: 2 doubles, 1 twin; 1 bathroom, 1 separate wc. Extra beds available.
Closed	January.

Claudine & Patrick van Bree-Leclef
Rue, Somme

Tel	+33 (0)3 22 25 04 44
Fax	+33 (0)3 22 25 79 69
Email	lethurel.relais@libertysurf.fr
Web	www.lethurel.com

Auprès de l'Église

New Zealanders Michael and Glenis first discovered Auprès de l'Église ten years ago. Now they own it, share it with guests, do excellent table d'hôtes and are planning a pool. Thanks to a previous artist owner, the 19th-century house has a very special atmosphere, is full of surprises – some walls are unadorned but for the mason's scribbles! – and has been gorgeously restored. The two upstairs bedrooms and bathroom are separated by a fabulous wall of bookcases and an attic stair, the ground floor has a French country feel and harmonious colours. Kitchen, dining and living rooms merge peacefully into one airy space that overlooks the courtyard and Oyes church. Sit out here in the sun and sip the wonderful local champagne as you watch the barbecue smoulder. Quirky brocante abounds yet the comforts are resolutely modern. Two more rooms and a shower lead off the hall, with crisp white cotton and huge beds. Charming Sézanne is a 20-minute drive and the marshlands (now drained but an unhappy surprise for the soldiers of the First World War) are a birdwatchers' paradise. *B&B also. Meals on request.*

Price	€1,000–€1,500 per week. Heating extra in winter.
Sleeps	8.
Rooms	4: 2 doubles, 1 twin/double, 1 twin; 1 bathroom, 1 shower room.
Arrival	Saturday, but flexible.
Closed	Rarely.

Glenis Foster
Oyes, Marne

Tel   +44 (0)7808 905 233
Email   enquiries@aupresdeleglise.com
Web   www.aupresdeleglise.com

Gîte de Cramant

A simple little cottage in a village in Champagne. It is distinctly homely, a little like a doll's house, one you can live in very comfortably. The Charbonniers, who do B&B on the spot, are a truly delightful couple and work hard to keep everyone happy (book yourself in for breakfast: it's a feast!). Cosy bedrooms are upstairs and share a neat little bathroom; the striped double has slanting ceilings and a couple of beams, the twin has small beds dressed in toile de Jouy duvets, perfect for children. Downstairs, an open-plan kitchen/living room with a tiled floor and neatly beamed ceiling – simply decorated, typically French. There's a round dining table, a fireplace (for decoration only) and lots of pretty china. Outside, a postage-stamp lawn is flanked charmingly on one side by an old stone wall up which creepers climb; iron-and-wood chairs, café table and barbecue invite meals outside. For restaurants and market you need to travel to Épernay (five kilometres). Sample the champagnes; if you overdo it, head for Reims and its cathedral to beg forgiveness. *Babysitting available. Sawday B&B. Meals on request.*

Price	€300 per week.
Sleeps	4–5.
Rooms	2: 1 double, 1 twin, 1 sofabed in sitting room; 1 bathroom.
Closed	Rarely.

Sylvie & Éric Charbonnier
Cramant, Marne
Tel   +33 (0)3 26 57 95 34
Email   eric-sylvie@wanadoo.fr
Web   www.ericsylvie.com

La Haute Grange

The views swoop down to the valley to Freland's distant church spire, the forest shimmers in the heat; up here is a haven of cool and peace. Back in 1834 a farmer built himself a chalet farmhouse up in the hills, inspired by the position. Not so very long ago Margaret and Philippe upped sticks from Normandy, renovated beautifully and moved in… they are thrilled to be here, caring for guests. Inside, all is spaciousness and light: parquet floors and warm friendly colours, king-size beds and luxury linens, a salon with leather sofas and a blazing fire, logs on the house, a library full of books, and the internet for those who must keep in touch. The kitchen has space for every modern thing – not that you have to be chef every night: the region teems with great restaurants and the nearest is in Freland, a drive down the hill. The terrace, furnished with barbecue and outdoor kitchen, is protected from the heat by a chestnut tree and breezes from the forest below; behind are sweet wildflower meadows. It's a blissful spot for a luxurious holiday – and with friendly hosts on tap should you need them.

Price	€1,500-€1,900 per week.
Sleeps	8.
Rooms	4: 3 doubles, 1 twin; 3 bathrooms, 1 shower.
Arrival	Flexible.
Closed	Never.

Margaret Love & Philippe Kalk
Freland, Haut-Rhin
Tel   +33 (0)3 89 71 90 06
Mobile   +33 (0)6 15 72 15 15
Email   lahautegrange@aol.com
Web   www.lahautegrange.fr

Alsace

Les Hirondelles

Swallows and redstarts nest in the eaves, deer populate the forests, breathtaking views stretch across the valley to the Black Forest beyond. Your whitewashed gîte – a former barn – is plainly furnished, spotless and peaceful and clad inside with pine. Floors are carpeted upstairs and wooden down, the kitchen sits in a corner, the bedrooms are under the eaves, and central heating guarantees warmth in the cold months. In summer, walk into the mountains from the front door, in winter don your skis... the non-sporty may follow the Route du Vin and discover the area's wines. The front-line trenches from the First World War are a ten-minute drive away; some of the fiercest fighting took place here and you can see bullet holes in the main house where the English owner lives. In summer, the locals compete for the best scarecrow and you'll see them in all shapes and sizes in the local villages. Orbey, just up the road, has all you need, even a cinema. Try Munster cheese – one of France's most pungent – from the farm shop opposite, and don't miss the stunning medieval walled village of Riquewihr.

Price	€462 per week.
Sleeps	5-8.
Rooms	2: 1 twin, 1 family room for 3; 1 shower; extra folding beds.
Closed	Never.

John Kennedy
Orbey, Haut-Rhin

Tel	+33 (0)3 89 71 34 96
Fax	+33 (0)3 89 71 34 96
Email	JhKen1@aol.com

L'Ancienne École

Down at the old village school... old world charm outside, modern decoration within. There are wide meadows opposite, forests behind and the murmur of the mountain stream. The owners live in Lusse but love coming out here for the views and the tranquillity – so will you. Céline, smiling, artistic, child-friendly, greets you and settles you in. Note the metal plates coating the exterior – weather-proofing Vosges style – and the original coat hooks in the hall. There are framed photographs of former pupils, now the seniors of the village! Few other vestiges of the school days remain; instead, you have a cosy, cheerful and comfortable home just right for a family or a group of walkers: two sofas with orange throws, a cupboard full of games, a spotless kitchen in white and yellow. Up the carpeted stairs are friendly bedrooms with artistic touches and a hand-painted linen cupboard; it is all most homely and welcoming. Small children will spend hours in the Wendy house on the patio, everyone will love the small, secret, shady garden, and the walking is superb. *Book via Gîtes de France: www.gite-ancienne-ecole.com.*

Price	€300–€500 per week.
Sleeps	6-10.
Rooms	3: 1 double, 1 triple, 1 single; 1 bathroom.
Closed	Never.

Stéphane & Céline Bastien
Lusse, Vosges

Tel	+33 (0)3 29 51 22 97
Fax	+33 (0)3 29 51 22 97
Email	celine-bastien@wanadoo.fr
Web	www.gite-ancienne-ecole.com

Franche Comté

Château Andelot

Winding narrow roads lead higher and higher, through woods and foothills, until you reach the top... a jaw-dropping sight. Conical towers, a mighty keep, thick-walled ramparts spread along a cliff top, the wooded valley falls sheer away. Pass through the monumental entrance portal and the adventure continues: the 12th-century castle is as dramatic inside as out. The bedrooms – main château or rampart buildings – are grand but beautifully uncluttered spaces for antiques, fine fabrics, cool tiles, rich rugs and lavish bedcovers. Bathrooms are as luxurious as a starry hotel. Most have million-dollar views over plunging valleys to the Jura mountains, the Swiss border – and Mont Blanc on a good day. Why rush to rise? Why, indeed. No need to make breakfast, or dinner; the château comes with staff – friendly and helpful. Eat in the vaulted dining room below the vast, beamed, tapestry-hung drawing room; retire to plump sofas, soft carpeting, old oils on the walls. Tennis court, swimming pool, formal garden and terrace, this is the place for celebrations and friends grandly reunited. Unforgettable. *Sawday hotel.*

Price	Whole château €6,400-€6,900. Part of château €3,000-€3,250. Prices per week, including breakfast & housekeeper.
Sleeps	12-14.
Rooms	7: 1 apartment with sofa bed, 1 suite with sofa bed, 4 doubles, 1 twin; 7 bathrooms.
Closed	Rarely.

Anne Drolet
Andelot lès Saint Amour, Jura
Tel	+33 (0)3 84 85 41 49
Fax	+33 (0)3 84 85 46 74
Email	info@chateauandelot.com
Web	www.chateauandelot.com

Abbaye de la Ferté - Le Moulin

The Thenards have been here since the French Revolution; they not only kept their heads but their château too, a jaw-dropper with its ornate windows and aristocratic feel. You are in the old mill; behind, water spills over the weir and into the lake. You can fish, swim or walk your socks off in the gorgeous grounds and discover the ancient abbey. An impossibly pretty setting with sunlight filtering through the graceful branches of tall trees and bouncing off water lilies at anchor on the lake. The gîte, attractive, uncluttered, welcoming, is a great little spot for a family stay (young children need supervision outside). You have exposed beams, gleaming tiles, generous windows; the double bedroom, nicely private via an outside stair, has an old armoire; the long, thin triple room is on the ground floor. No sitting room but a kitchen/dining room for eager cooks and a corner of the courtyard on which to sit and relish the results. Venture beyond the gates and you'll find horses and bikes to ride – or discover Beaune and a glass of something special. *Sawday B&B. Meals on request. Unfenced water.*

Price	€340-€640 per week.
Sleeps	4-5.
Rooms	2: 1 double, 1 triple; 1 bathroom, 1 shower room, 2 separate wcs.
Arrival	Saturday, but flexible.
Closed	Never.

Jacques & Virginie Thenard
Saint Ambreuil, Saône-et-Loire

Tel	+33 (0)3 85 44 17 96
Email	abbayedelaferte@aol.com
Web	www.abbayeferte.com

Burgundy

En La Marre - Pigeonnier, Chardonnay, Pinot Noir

It's like an oasis in the middle of the Burgundy hills and the picture-book views endlessly draw your eye. Gathered round a wide courtyard, a group of 19th-century farm buildings has been turned into six appealing apartments for couples wanting to share their holiday with neither children nor pets. Chris and Judith, your lively, charming hosts, love meeting new people and things will naturally become sociable as time goes by. Inside, there is a festival of exposed beams in bedrooms, sloping ceilings, some fine old tiled floors, lots of books, paintings and attention to comfort. Beneath a small forest of rafters, the old grain loft of the original farmhouse, now called Pinot Noir, is a great space to spend a quiet week. Chardonnay, underneath it on the ground floor, is ideal for the less agile whereas the Pigeonnier, standing somewhat apart and which Chris partly built himself (brilliantly – it looks as authentic as the rest), has steep stairs up to the bedroom and is favoured by honeymooners. Really well placed for excursions to Beaune, Dijon and the vineyards. *Shared pool. Owners' tennis 3km.*

Price	€600-€825 each per week.
Sleeps	Pigeonnier 2. Chardonnay 2. Pinot Noir 2.
Rooms	Each gîte: 1 double; 1 bathroom.
Closed	November-March.

Chris & Judith Mosedale
Andy & Wendy Price
Dracy lès Couches, Saône-et-Loire
Tel   +44 (0)1323 735 181
Email   france4two@hotmail.com
Web   www.france4two.org.uk

En La Marre - Pinot Blanc, Gamay, Aligoté

The other half of this enclave of retreats for couples wanting to combine independence and some quiet socialising – "no kids, no pets" is the motto – is three airy apartments in the converted barn, all identically neat, cosy and balconied. Indeed, they share the big balcony that runs, with all its geraniums, along the front of the barn, then each has its own second balcony and gas barbecue at the back with long country views. Inside, you find a generous living and dining area for two with lots of light, good-looking country furniture and the peaceful atmosphere of old timber-framed buildings. Comfortable big beds live up on mezzanines. It is all done in traditional French style with a touch of eccentricity and personal history: Chris and Judith have used many of their own pieces to give charm and individuality. Full of energy and fun, they may organise a communal barbecue one evening during your stay. Cows graze, birds sing, the beautiful countryside spreads peace and life feels good be you in your own nest or sharing the pool and garden with other quiet grown-ups. *Shared pool. Owners' tennis 3km.*

Price	€500–€700 per week.
Sleeps	3 apartments for 2.
Rooms	Pinot Blanc: 1 double; 1 bathroom. Gamay: 1 double; 1 bathroom. Aligoté: 1 twin/double; 1 bathroom.
Closed	November–March.

Chris & Judith Mosedale
Andy & Wendy Price
Dracy lès Couches, Saône-et-Loire
Tel   +44 (0)1323 735 181
Email   france4two@hotmail.com
Web   www.france4two.org.uk

Burgundy

Le Nid – Rouge-Gorge, Le Pinson, La Chouette, L'Hirondelle

An artist-owner in a dreamy place, an 18th-century Burgundian house divided neatly into three apartments plus the former stables. There is an understated elegance here, as if everything has been designed but quietly so, mixing old stone floors, limestone walls, high beamed ceilings, colour in small doses – a crisp sense of light and space. In the largest living room, cream sofas, blue armchairs, books, candles and a big fireplace. Apartments have kitchens or kitchenettes; Rouge-Gorge's kitchen has a table and chairs to serve a multitude, and every modern thing. A broad stone staircase leads from here to a hallway and delightful bedrooms. Good art hangs on the walls – sketches, prints, watercolours – while Karen's sculpture is dotted about the grounds. The pool, its loungers and its relaxing lawn bathe in sunlight. Beyond, fields and woodland stretch across the hills. This part of France has been compared to Tuscany, only it's less busy, and your hosts, who do B&B in the big house next door, will cheerfully help you discover the region. *B&B also. Shared pool. Yoga groups welcome.*

Price	RG €575–€820. LP €425–€645. LC €375–€535. Main house (RG, LP & LC) €1,250–€2,025. LH €645–€795. Prices per week.
Sleeps	RG 4. LP 2-4. LC 2-3. Main house (RG, LP & LC) sleeps 10-11 + 2 cots. LH(separate) 5 + 2 children.
Rooms	RG: 2 doubles; 1 bath, 1 shower. LP: 1 twin, 2 sofas; 1 shower. LC: 1 double, 1 sofa; 1 shower. LH: 2 doubles, 1 single, 1 twin on mezzanine; 2 shower rooms.
Closed	Never.

	Marc & Karen Keiser Château, Saône-et-Loire
Tel	+33 (0)3 85 59 18 02
Fax	+33 (0)3 85 59 86 98
Email	info@lenid-france.com
Web	www.lenid-france.com

La Maison Tupinier

A place of huge privilege: a charmingly grand apartment in a vastly civilised and venerable old town for those who love the fine things in life. Luc's antique shop has supplied these high 16th-century rooms with carved armoire and walnut dining table, the ground-floor baker makes the croissants, excellent restaurants beckon from your door, music festivals and superior vineyards abound, churches and cathedrals stand eternal. Spiral stone stairs lead up two floors (Luc lives on the first) to your stately quarters: lofty ceilings with decorated beams, a Louis XIV fireplace, a scalloped wash basin. A large, light hall opens to the living room, stunningly elegant with pale sofa on seagrass floor. The master bedroom's perfect proportions are painted the colour of corn; there are ornate tiles in the compact kitchen, a sublime new bathroom in stone and pebble, another with an *œil de bœuf* window. A door leads onto a delightfully secluded gallery then down to the green-smothered courtyard garden: ideal spots for those breakfast croissants. *Easy parking nearby. No washing machine. B&B also.*

Price	€650-€1,100 per week.
Sleeps	4-7.
Rooms	2 twins/doubles; 2 bathrooms.
Arrival	Flexible.
Closed	January-February.

Luc du Mesnil du Buisson
Cluny, Saône-et-Loire

Tel	+33 (0)3 85 59 27 67
Email	luc_dumesnil@hotmail.com
Web	www.lamaisontupinier.fr

Burgundy

La Musardière

An urban address – but what a delicious town in which to be urban! And it would be hard to find a more endearing place from which to explore. Built of stone and impeccably restored, the house stands at the end of the Roinés' small enchanting garden, with its own access from a side street. Walk straight into a beamed dining room where big handsome cupboards gleam richly and the corner kitchen is supplied with all the equipment you could ever need. Climb the stairs to the pretty little sitting room on one side and a fresh-painted white bedroom, furnished with antiques and ethnic rugs, on the other. Out in the passageway is a red-draped *lit en alcove*, acquired from the old hospital Hôtel Dieu in the town. Your gîte has its own tiny grass terrace with wooden table and chairs but you are also welcome to share the owners' walled garden, awash with herbs and old-fashioned flowers – irises, lavender, roses, clematis. Boisterous children may find the lack of outdoor space restrictive but would enjoy the three tortoises (authentic southern French) that creep gently and discreetly around. *B&B*.

Price	€600–€800 per week.
Sleeps	5 + cot.
Rooms	2: 1 double, 1 triple; 1 bath, 1 shower.
Closed	Six weeks at beginning of year.

René Roiné
Cluny, Saône-et-Loire

Tel	+33 (0)3 85 59 06 01
Fax	+33 (0)3 85 59 06 01
Email	lamusardierecluny@free.fr
Web	lamusardierecluny.free.fr

Rose Cottage

The best of Burgundy: vineyards, fine food and the Morvan National Park. Here, in the slumbering village of Painblanc ('white bread'), you get a taste of French village life – the main events of the week are the butcher's and baker's vans. Prettily draped in wisteria and roses, this 18th-century stone village house has been attractively restored by British owners Penny and Ben who live in a nearby village and will be here to settle you in. The centrepiece is the kitchen: sunny and homely, with a large wooden table to gather around for feasts in front of the wood-burner. The original hexagonal tomettes (softened with rugs), the handsome oak beams and the open fire are all intact, as are the endearingly sloping floors of the apricot and cream bedrooms. And, painted on the upstairs bathroom floor, the footprints of humans and geese! Take lazy long lunches under the enormous willow tree in the scented garden and orchard, replete with pond (dry in summer). Shop in pretty Bligny sur Ouche, a five-mile drive. Make time for some serious gastronomy – and for wine-tasting in the famous Côtes de Nuits vineyards.

Price	€500–€675 per week.
	Linen not included.
Sleeps	7 + cot.
Rooms	3: 1 double, 1 twin, 1 triple;
	1 bathroom, 1 shower room,
	2 separate wcs.
Closed	Never.

	Penny & Ben Martin
	Painblanc, Côte-d'Or
Tel	+33 (0)3 80 20 19 13
Fax	+33 (0)3 80 20 19 13
Email	benpenny.martin@club-internet.fr

Burgundy

La Brulardière

The old house used to form part of a wine-growing estate. The enchanting garden at the back, the work of a passionate gardener, still leads into vineyards. Madame spends hours on her roses, box hedges and shrubs, part of it just for gîte-dwellers. Your quarters in the old vaulted cellars are blissfully cool, your courtyard guarded by 17th-century buttresses and a rare octagonal pigeonnier. Enter from the street into a clear, calm space. The ceiling is lofty, the paintwork cream, the floor tiles terracotta, the spot-lighting diffuse – and there's natural light from front and back. Discreet furniture includes a small green-check sofa, a big old armoire in the corner, good prints on the walls, firm beds in the vaulted bedroom. There's a good, modern, well-equipped kitchen, too. Madame is charming, offering guests a welcome aperitif and a few words of English. All around you, vineyards stretching as far as the eye can see (those Burgundy wines will bewitch you), lashings of history and culture, two good restaurants in Santenay. Oh, and flawless cooking at the celebrated Lameloise in the very next village.

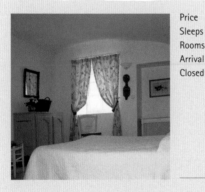

Price	€470 per week.
Sleeps	2.
Rooms	1 double; 1 bathroom.
Arrival	Monday.
Closed	Mid-September to mid-May.

Madame Claude Reny
Santenay, Côte-d'Or

Tel	+33 (0)3 80 20 64 51
Fax	+33 (0)3 80 20 64 59
Email	jacques.reny@wanadoo.fr
Web	www.brulardiere.com

Les Hêtres Rouges

The mood is quaint, the furniture antique, and the gardens full of flowers stretch serenely as far as the eye can see: little would seem to have changed since the Duke of Burgundy dropped by at weekends to hunt. Madame, who looks after her B&B guests in the hunting lodge next door, used to run an antique shop and the past is something in which she is well versed. Restoring old buildings is her passion and she has put her artistic talent to good use in renovating and decorating this lovely wisteria-draped outbuilding. Rooms downstairs are a festival of warm ochres, pinks and blues which enhance the lovely antique furniture – and there's a fine working fireplace. The upstairs bedroom has a handsome brass bed, rich colourful fabrics and interesting *objets*. Outside, antique watering cans separate your pretty patch from the owners'! If you're a wine buff you'll know the names of villages such as Nuits Saint Georges and Pommard already; visit their *caves* for a tasting if your purse allows. There are plenty of restaurants within a ten-minute drive. *Sawday B&B.*

Price	€590 per week.
Sleeps	2-3.
Rooms	1 double with extra single bed; 1 bathroom.
Arrival	Flexible.
Closed	Never.

Jean-François & Christiane Bugnet
Argilly, Côte-d'Or

Tel	+33 (0)3 80 62 53 98
Fax	+33 (0)3 80 62 54 85
Email	leshetresrouges@free.fr
Web	www.leshetresrouges.com

Burgundy

Château de Flammerans

'Glamorous' and 'gite' co-exist here: in the grounds of a Burgundian château is an old farm building whose plain stone face conceals a houseful of riches. Enter a large, airy hall with a living room to the left, a kitchen straight ahead, a bedroom to the right and a staircase to the first floor. The subtleties of stone grey, sand beige and oak buff speak out across these simply elegant rooms, with patches of pure white in contrast and muslin flowing at every window. Bedrooms have irresistible stitched quilts on mosquito-net draped beds, handsome fauteuils on limed and planked floors. Bathrooms are fabulous, with their distressed marble from Provence, and bathrobes white and fluffy. Catherine is the lady of the house and mother of a young family, Guy is passionate about cooking and gives lessons in the château kitchen. The gîte garden area is open-plan, the swimming pool and orangery (with chic lounge/bar) are shared with the B&B guests, and the farm outbuildings are in the process of being restored. There are walks in the forest and charming shops in Auxonne. *Shared pool. Sawday hotel.*

Price	€1,650–€1,950.
Sleeps	6-9.
Rooms	3 doubles; 3 bathrooms. Extra beds.
Arrival	Flexible.
Closed	Rarely.

Guy & Catherine Barrier
Flammerans, Côte-d'Or
Tel +33 (0)3 80 27 05 70
Fax +33 (0)3 80 31 12 12
Email info@chateaudeflammerans.com
Web www.flammerans.com

Château de Créancey

In the grounds of a breathtakingly beautiful château, with a listed 14th-century dovecote and a moat running past, stands this good-looking little house. Fiona and her French husband Bruno have restored it with passionate respect for the original materials and rustic character. An old wooden staircase twists its crooked way upwards; French country furniture, original tomettes and ochre walls create a mood of remote quaintness and almost medieval charm, though the two deep armchairs are new. There's a great open fireplace in the living room and ancient beams in the generous double room upstairs; the tiny twin is definitely for children. Your oak kitchen, atmospherically basic and hung with old country pots and pans, leads into the château yard where ducks stroll. Eat on the terrace by the moat to the sound of hoopoes or by candlelight indoors, then feel free to roam. Delightful Fiona does B&B in the château and will advise you on the region: discover the wine-tasting châteaux of the rugged Côte d'Or on foot or by bike, and Dijon, and Beaune. *Because of moat, children must be able to swim. Sawday hotel.*

Price	€600–€720 per week.
Sleeps	2-4.
Rooms	2: 1 double, 1 twin for children; 1 shower room.
Closed	Never.

Fiona de Wulf
Créancey, Côte-d'Or

Tel	+33 (0)3 80 90 57 50
Fax	+33 (0)3 80 90 57 51
Email	chateau@creancey.com
Web	www.creancey.com

Burgundy

Domaine de La Chaux - Le Château

La Chaux is more village than domaine. Rent a small part of it – or the whole place for an anniversary or wedding. Madame de Chambure lives in the middle of it all, sparkles with energy and exercises a benign rule, delighting in bringing families and friends together. The peace enfolds you and the magnolias and ancient trees of the award-winning *jardin remarquable* are stunning. The Château, an old hunting lodge, is where Madame herself once lived and its vast warren of rooms has barely changed over the years, in spite of the addition of a new kitchen, modern plumbing and some elegant wrought-iron furniture. Two dining rooms, two salons, all with open fires: a warm, ample place for a large party. It has that wonderful French feel, with stippled, faux-marble walls, fine furniture from Louis XV onwards, polished parquet – an old-fashioned elegance touched with eccentricity. Bedrooms, bathrooms and a dressing room share the top two storeys; views swoop over parkland and hills; you have all you could possibly need, a library full of books, TV, table tennis, loungers. Restaurants are five kilometres away.

Price	€2,415 per week.
Sleeps	15.
Rooms	11: 4 doubles, 7 singles; 3 bathrooms, 3 shower rooms, 3 separate wcs.
Closed	Never.

Alice de Chambure
Alligny en Morvan, Nièvre
Tel   +33 (0)3 86 76 10 10
Fax   +33 (0)3 86 76 10 10
Email   contact@gites-lachaux.fr
Web   www.gites-lachaux.fr

Domaine de La Chaux - Lavande & Vitis

The latest addition to the Domaine's stable is Lavande. It occupies one end of a long, low, L-shaped building at the far end of which lives Madame, the remarkable owner of La Chaux. The gardens, now listed among Burgundy's finest, are superb (gigantic sequoias, Lebanese cedars, banks of rhododendrons, four lakes) and the population of this rural enclave soars to 67 in summer, including Madame and her son. (He and his wife are new co-managers, brimming with plans.) Enter an open-plan living area, whiter than white, with a charming easy chair-ed mezzanine under super high rafters; step down to fresh bedrooms with vintage terracotta floors. The kitchen is compact; the terrace is charmingly flagged; everything sparkles. With sidelong glances to the château from its safe and secluded garden is Vitis – a dear little cottage. Expect a sitting room, a separate kitchen/diner, stairs down to bedrooms and a door to the garden. The fireplace has a carved pitch-pine surround, black and white tulips dominate a white wall, rush mats soften old terracotta and the kitchen is white and pristine. *Shared laundry.*

Price	€550 each per week.
	€100 each per day.
Sleeps	Lavande 4. Vitis 4.
Rooms	Lavande: 1 double, 1 twin; 1 bath,
	1 shower, separate wc.
	Vitis: 1 double, 1 twin; 1 bath,
	separate wc.
Arrival	Flexible.
Closed	Never.

Alice de Chambure
Alligny en Morvan, Nièvre

Tel	+33 (0)3 86 76 10 10
Fax	+33 (0)3 86 76 10 10
Email	contact@gites-lachaux.fr
Web	www.gites-lachaux.fr

Burgundy

Domaine de La Chaux - Moines & Roses

Moines is great fun and its monkish name is reflected in the décor of refreshing, monastic simplicity. Bedrooms on the second floor, in a row of monks' cells, have two wash rooms between them, each graced with three unmonastic designer basins set in granite. Showers are downstairs on the ground floor; the two main bedrooms have wcs and basins en suite. It's a big, delightful space where you could happily retreat for a week with friends. Warm colours, solid beams, terracotta floors, three staircases; you have a library and a living room with antique trestle tables and rush-seated ladderback chairs. A carved statue of the Virgin Mary stands in one corner, two cream-coloured fauteuils pull up by the fire. And what a hearth — it's big enough to fit a small tree and belts out quite a heat on winter days. Across a small meadow is Roses with four bedrooms (two in the attic) and another lovely fireplace. With its trestle table and wood-panelled walls it has a similarly medieval feel but is smaller and suitable for six. The gardens are *remarquables. Shared laundry.*

Price	Moines €1,680. Roses €690. Prices per week.
Sleeps	Moines 13-18. Roses 6.
Rooms	Moines: 3 doubles, 1 twin, 1 single, 1 family room for 3, 1 family room for 6; 2 shower rooms, 3 separate wcs. Roses: 1 double, 1 twin, 2 singles; 1 bathroom, 1 separate wc.
Closed	Never.

	Alice de Chambure
	Alligny en Morvan, Nièvre
Tel	+33 (0)3 86 76 10 10
Fax	+33 (0)3 86 76 10 10
Email	contact@gites-lachaux.fr
Web	www.gites-lachaux.fr

Domaine de La Chaux - Chèvrefeuille & Glycines

These two gîtes are a step apart – Chèvrefeuille (Honeysuckle) with its farmhouse feel, and the more modern Glycines (Wisteria), custom-made for wheelchairs: its rooms span the ground floor of the last stone cottage in a row of four. Chèvrefeuille has two storeys and a charming outside stone staircase; floors are new and tiled, furniture a mix of newish and old, and the kitchen is simple. Note, this is an outdoorsy place and the grounds are more beautifully tended than the gîtes. But there's masses to do: table tennis on the estate, trout-fishing in crystal-clear creeks beyond, kayaking on the River Cure. You are right in the middle of the miraculously unspoilt Morvan National Park, distinguished by vast forests of beech and oak, moorland and lakes. Criss-crossed by rapids, the area is a dream for white-water enthusiasts; the walking, too, is exceptional. Take maps, go off the beaten track and look out for red and roe deer, wild boar and badgers, buzzards and woodpeckers. In the gentler, more pastoral northern sector there are carpets of wild flowers in spring. *Shared laundry.*

Price	Chèvrefeuille €690. Glycines €700. Prices per week.
Sleeps	Chèvrefeuille 6. Glycines 6.
Rooms	Chèvrefeuille: 2 doubles, 1 twin; 1 bathroom. Glycines: 2 doubles, 2 singles; 1 shower room, 1 separate wc.
Closed	Never.

Alice de Chambure
Alligny en Morvan, Nièvre

Tel	+33 (0)3 86 76 10 10
Fax	+33 (0)3 86 76 10 10
Email	contact@gites-lachaux.fr
Web	www.gites-lachaux.fr

Burgundy

Domaine de La Chaux - Iris & Clématites

Every house in La Chaux has its own individual touch but there's one feature they all share (Lavande excepted): a huge fireplace stacked with logs. So winter stays are possible as well as summer ones; the wood is provided at extra charge. Ground-floor gîtes Iris and Clématites sit opposite each other, with a good stretch of grass in between – ideal for a family and grandparents on holiday together. Clématites' raised fireplace dominates the main bedroom, giving this pale-walled, red-tiled room an easy feel. The living area is open plan with the kitchen in the corner (with all you need, dishwasher included); the second, bigger bedroom has three beds. Iris, too, is terracotta-tiled, with russet-brown curtains and the odd bit of country furniture. Every house in the domaine has a barbecue and garden furniture, including loungers: summers are long and hot in the Haut Morvan. A visit to the Lac des Settons, the biggest man-made lake in Europe, will cool you down: sail, swim, waterski, windsurf or pedalo. And there's a magnificent *bateau mouche* for the less sporty. *Shared laundry.*

Price	Iris €250. Clématites €610. Prices per week.
Sleeps	Iris 2. Clématites 4–6.
Rooms	Iris: 1 sofabed; 1 shower room, 1 separate wc.
	Clématites: 1 double, 1 family room for 4; 1 bathroom, 1 separate wc.
Closed	Never.

Alice de Chambure
Alligny en Morvan, Nièvre

Tel	+33 (0)3 86 76 10 10
Fax	+33 (0)3 86 76 10 10
Email	contact@gites-lachaux.fr
Web	www.gites-lachaux.fr

Le Pavillon du Château de Prye

In a magical situation looking over age-old trees to copse-crested hills, and the madly moated neo-Gothic château just visible across the vast estate, this compact, sweet-turreted 18th-century gate house is ideal for those seeking real rural isolation: shops and all things 'civilised' are a fair drive away. Outside, the endless green grounds are yours to roam alongside the fine Charolais herd; inside, the tone is red and white with the odd burst of blue, good furnishings and nice old pieces such as a pair of carved wardrobe doors on a built-in cupboard and the deep-carved Henri IV sideboard that dominates the dining room. There is comfort and personality, wonderful original satin-finished terracotta flooring and decent crockery, a neat black and check sofa before the open hearth. In the bathroom you will find soft white towels, deep blue tiling and a leafy view. The walking is exceptional, the vineyards are not far and country pursuits abound. The open-minded young owners at the château are altogether charming. *Sawday hotel.*

Price	€355–€440 per week.
Sleeps	4.
Rooms	2: 1 double, 1 twin; 2 bathrooms, separate wc.
Closed	Rarely.

Magdalena & Antoine-Emmanuel
du Bourg de Bozas
La Fermeté, Nièvre

Tel/Fax	+33 (0)3 86 58 42 64
Email	info@chateaudeprye.com
Web	www.chateaudeprye.com

Entry 32 Map 10

Burgundy

The Cottage & Haven House

In a quiet village, watched over by the ancient church, a few steps up from the calm waters of the Canal du Nivernais where slow boats dawdle and geese guard the banks, the Cottage (main picture) is ideal for soft rolling Burgundy explorations (canals paths, riversides and woods), the serenity of Vézelay, wine tastings; the chablis vineyards are near. The prettily converted house is bigger than it looks. Enter to a convivial fireplace and open-plan living room, through the kitchen to the walled courtyard – a great suntrap and barbecue spot. Upstairs you find a super antique bed then down the raftered passage to the neat green bathroom and second bedroom. Haven House (smaller picture), over the river Yonne in the delightful backwater that is Crain, is decorated with the same gentle inspiration and just enough furniture, some old some new, good fabrics, the odd picture. You'll be comfortable in either, both instantly feel like home and Crain has a lovely big garden if you want more than a courtyard garden for those barbecues. *Cottage not suitable for small children.*

Price	Cottage £225-£275. Haven House £250-£295. Prices per week.
Sleeps	Cottage 4. Haven House 5.
Rooms	Cottage: 1 double, 1 twin; 1 bathroom, 1 shower room. Haven House: 1 double, 1 family; 1 bathroom, 1 shower room.
Arrival	Flexible.
Closed	Never.

Sheila Clifton
Lucy sur Yonne & Crain, Yonne

Tel	+44 (0)1237 459 588
Mobile	+44 (0)7771 550 252
Email	sheila@lucylettings.com
Web	www.lucylettings.com

Château de Percey

The 18th-century château oozes fabulousness yet has a singularly modern style. South African Pauwl and Dutch Lara spent five years restoring the acres of marble, the 101 windows, the pretty cornices – then added crisp colours, fine furniture, bold art. Tucked in one wing, with high-ceilinged sitting room and dusky dining room, the gîte mixes white leather sofa with glittering chandelier, 40s furnishings with modern art, cots for the babies with WiFi and TV while the magazine-sleek kitchen guards antique china. Spread over the top two floors, bedrooms are cool and restful with old touches – an Art Deco lamp, a 19th-century bed. Bathrooms are sculptural-smooth. Skip three floors down the curly-banister'd staircase into your 14-acre estate. At weekends it may be shared with the public (the château art gallery and tea room are open on summer weekends) but it's still lovely, with wildflower garden, maze, peony garden and mature woodland. Beyond is Burgundy: vineyards, cheese farms, châteaux, abbeys. Your well-travelled and welcoming hosts live in the other wing. Stunning place, surprising price. *Meals on request.*

Price	€900–€1,350 per week.
Sleeps	10 + cots.
Rooms	4: 1 double, 1 twin, 2 triples; 1 bathroom, 1 shower room, 2 separate wcs.
Closed	November–April.

	Lara Lunow
	Percey, Yonne
Tel	+33 (0)3 86 43 26 21
Email	info@chateaupercey.com
Web	www.chateaupercey.com

Burgundy

La Maison du Château

The charming 18th-century manor house on the edge of the quiet village seduces all who stay. Its English owners chanced upon it one day, fell in love with it and its 24 acres and took on the lot: chestnut avenue, grass tennis court, trout river and all. You could almost spend your entire holiday exploring the grounds; there's even a boat to row to your own small island. Large, luminous rooms have enchanting park or meadow views and captivating art on ochre walls. Floors are oak parquet or pale stone with slate inlay, curtains are linen and white, there's a gracious hall with an elegant staircase, the kitchen riches include two ovens and china for 30. A stone fireplace and an antique washstand grace one bathroom, beds are beautifully dressed, sofas are merry with throws. The barn houses two en suite bedrooms, a grand piano, a long period table, colourful rugs on a planked floor: as generously embracing as all the rest – and stone stairs to take you down to the enclosed pool with teak loungers, barbecue and fridge. *Ask about painting / wine / bridge courses. Two extra double rooms available in Gate House.*

Price	£1,750-£7,600 per week. Price includes cook's services.
Sleeps	17 + children's beds & cots.
Rooms	9: 6 twins/doubles, 2 doubles, 1 single; 7 bathrooms.
Closed	Rarely.

Lady Susanna Lyell
Cry, Yonne

Tel	+44 (0)1582 840 635
Fax	+44 (0)1582 842 389
Email	info@lmdc.co.uk
Web	www.lamaisonduchateau.co.uk

The Gate House

Adorable, white-shuttered, independent and with a secluded feel, the little gate house sits in a walled garden with a gate that leads to a boat and a river – will it be trout for dinner? From the apple-treed and rose-tossed garden you step into the hall, then the large and lovely kitchen and living area. There are simple white walls, rush matting on a flagged floor, four windows full of light, modern furniture, old country pieces, stacks of logs for the wood-burner and, in winter, a just-lit fire. On the same level are the bedrooms: duvets and linen on good new beds, bright wicker furniture, boat prints on fresh white walls, garden flowers. No access to pool or park – just a romantic, cosy and comforting little house on the edge of a honeysuckled village in the heart of Burgundy: one of the best. And you should go on at least one wine tour while you are here and sample some of the area's finest burgundies and chablis; the House Book comes with all the information. *Ask about painting / wine / walking / bridge courses.*

Price	£300–£510 per week.
Sleeps	4.
Rooms	2: 1 double, 1 twin/double; 1 bathroom.
Closed	Rarely.

Lady Susanna Lyell
Cry, Yonne

Tel	+44 (0)1582 840 635
Fax	+44 (0)1582 842 389
Email	info@lmdc.co.uk
Web	www.lamaisonduchateau.co.uk

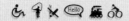

Burgundy

La Poterne

Old stone steps lead up to a farmhouse door. Step inside and this renovated cottage reveals itself, tardis-like, as an adorable little gîte of exposed stone walls, low beamed ceilings and polished floors. Furnished with rustic simplicity, the sitting room welcomes you with a bottle of wine, a large sofa (extra bed if pushed) and vast fireplace with logs for cool nights. Beyond, it opens onto a sheltered, sweet-smelling garden with lawn and barbecue. The bedrooms are timeless spaces of plain white walls and stripped wood floors. Quirkily, the bathroom is downstairs (the cottage is built into a slope) next to the low-beamed kitchen – not big but fine for holiday cooking – dominated by the original bread oven. The dining room is a delight; half-underground, a window peeping over the garden, it demands flickering candles. Outside, there are châteaux, chablis vineyards, medieval Vézelay, canoeing and cycling to discover. The Calderwoods, friendly Australians, live next door. They offer home-grown organic vegetables and invite you to join in authentic village life.

Price	€435–€515 per week.
Sleeps	4.
Rooms	2: 1 double, 1 twin; 1 shower room, 1 separate wc.
Closed	Never.

Karen Calderwood
Stigny, Yonne

Tel	+33 (0)3 86 75 03 36
Email	karen.calderwood@wanadoo.fr
Web	perso.wanadoo.fr/lapoterne/

La Forge

There's a riding school next door, tennis in the village, walks in the forest – and Paris just 30 minutes by train. What you have here is an exquisite little apartment for two, with an equally sweet garden corner laid to cobble and grass. The owners, cultured, delightful, the parents of three young boys, live in the orangery of their 17th-century domain; an old gate leads to their house and beautiful-beyond-words garden. Their office is in the creamy stoned old blacksmith's forge, your apartment is in the semi-basement below – and you enter a refined yet charming space. The paintwork glows, the floors are the original mellow terracotta and the furniture is elegant antique. There's a straw-coloured sofa, a bed dressed in fine linen and, most striking of all, oils, watercolours and prints in gilt frames on every white wall, including the bathroom's. The kitchen, small, neat, uncomplicated, would be pushed to cope with a three-course Sunday lunch, but there is an excellent restaurant at the 18-hole golf course down the road – a leisurely stroll. *Station 500m, 30-minute train to Paris.*

Price	€500-€600 for 2 per week.
Sleeps	2-4.
Rooms	1 double; 1 bathroom, sofabed.
Arrival	Flexible.
Closed	Rarely.

Marie de Biolley
Presles, Val-d'Oise
Tel +33 (0)1 34 70 06 56
Mobile +33 (0)6 11 78 03 82
Email mariedebiolley@aol.com

Entry 38 Map 5

Montparnasse district

Behind Montparnasse, beneath the chestnut tree that spreads over the cobbled alley, you will find what looks like a garden shed. Enter: the shed turns into a smart dark grass-papered hall, beyond it a blue-plush, white-walled double-height indoor 'garden' full of happy plants and northern light from the sloping glass roof, and generous living space for two. It is the nicest, most unexpected Parisian hideaway imaginable, totally sheltered from road noise, highly original and delighting in a tiny, pretty kitchen. Up a steep staircase, the bedroom looks into the living room: three cottage windows light its beige, green and brown quietness. The owner's oriental origins show discreetly through in Chinese prints and vases, in her taste for rich dark colours and unobtrusive class. After the bedroom comes the study – big glass writing table, single divan and... deep-freeze; then the laundry – useful washer/dryer – and the splendid black and white bathroom that gives onto a leafy courtyard straight from a provincial backwater. A secret cocoon, restaurants galore, the whole of Paris to hand.

Price	€1,000 per week; €3,000 per month.
Sleeps	2-3.
Rooms	1 double, 1 sofabed; 1 bathroom, 1 separate wc.
Closed	Never.

Alice de Chambure
Paris

Tel	+33 (0)3 86 76 10 10
Fax	+33 (0)3 86 76 10 10
Email	contact@gites-lachaux.fr

Montparnasse district

No, that little white-faced blue-shuttered terrace house in a stunningly quiet cobbled alley is not a country village dream, it's a most delectable intellectual place that can be yours for a decent long summer stay in sophisticated Left Bank Paris. The hall, which also leads to another flat upstairs, welcomes you with shelves of books. To the left, a good square bedroom with a pleasingly eclectic mix of warm fabrics, honeycomb tiles, old chest and contemporary paintings. The new white and pine bathroom has space, all mod cons and good cupboards. To the right is the pretty, wood-ceilinged and well-fitted kitchen/diner. Beyond lies the richly French sitting room – modern art alongside antiques and books, an alcove stuffed with music and more books – and the inestimable privilege of the little patio with its table, chairs and plants. The fine second bedroom is at the back with its smart bathroom. Public transport abounds, so do shops, restaurants and cafés. An ideal way to mix peace and quiet in a Parisian home with sightseeing and shopping, night life… or research… or business. *Sawday B&B only October-June.*

Price	€950-€1,000 per week.
	Discounts for longer stays.
Sleeps	4.
Rooms	2 doubles; 2 bathrooms.
Arrival	Flexible.
Closed	October-June.

	Janine Euvrard
	Paris
Tel	+33 (0)1 43 27 19 43
Fax	+33 (0)1 43 27 19 43
Email	euvrard@club-internet.fr

Entry 40 Map 5

Paris – Île de France

11 rue Duhesme

If you want a secret place for two with all mod cons in genuine old Paris – and who wouldn't – come to Rue Duhesme. The entrance, yard and stairs are authentically unprettified but when you reach the third floor you find a simple little gem with that 1920s Paris sparkle. Original dado panelling and polished floors set the warm tone; the old cast-iron fireplace sports a gaggle of new-style candles for evening glamour on the Récamier daybed, big letters on the wall spell out AMOUR. And the super-duper frothy white and soft blue bedroom is romantissimo. Really comfortable, too, it gives onto the quiet, aptly named Rue des Cottages. There's a pretty, pink and feminine shower room and the loo is a wonder of design art in dark blue with half a Greek head, a giant pink rose photograph and a bunch of silk tulips. And yet it feels simple and unkitsch – a skilful balance. The whole sweet place is deeply pleasing, has little luxuries such as Jo Malone smellies, bathrobes and a neat little kitchen. Modigliani, the quintessentially Parisian artist, is in favour here, as is Doisneau in black and white. Exceptional.

Price	£595 per week. Minimum 2 days.
Sleeps	2 + cot.
Rooms	1 double, 1 shower room; separate wc.
Arrival	Flexible.
Closed	Never.

Brendan Kirwan &
Amanda Swanwick-Aharoni
Paris
Tel   +44 (0)1332 232 844
Email   judith@swell-apartments.co.uk
Web   www.swell-apartments.co.uk

La Varenne - Pavillon Fond

Could this be the perfect mix? Your own 'country cottage' for quiet seclusion in a bushy bird-filled garden, the magnificent Marne river flowing broad at the bottom of the road for tree-lined walks and boating, the little town shops five minutes away – and Paris just a short train hop. Behind a typical 1890s gent's country res. (an actor, he used to come from his Châtelet theatre on horseback), the converted stablehands' rooms are now two sweet and modest bedrooms in mushroom and white with a superb new shower room, and the 1950s extension is a large friendly living space lit by three good windows, warmed by a generous fireplace and furnished for comfort but no clutter. In quiet, unflashy colours, all the fittings are new, the kitchen has everything, the top-quality convertible sofa is supremely comfortable. Make it your own for a week and you have the best of both worlds, town and country. The young owners, both professional musicians, are most attentive: toys in the cupboard if children are staying, advice, bikes on loan. *German spoken. 3-minute walk to station, 20-minute train to central Paris.*

Price	€100 for 2, €110 for 4, €120 for 6. Prices per day.
Sleeps	2-6.
Rooms	2: 1 double, 1 twin, 1 sofabed; 1 shower room, separate wc.
Arrival	Flexible.
Closed	Rarely.

Aurore & Olivier Doise
La Varenne Saint Hilaire, Val-de-Marne
Tel   +33 (0)1 48 89 34 47
Email olivier.doise@free.fr

L'Orangerie

Versailles, a lively, classy town, paid dearly for being a place of privilege in 1789 but nowadays no-one will begrudge you your share. Off the busy avenue that leads straight to the palace, a sober porch lets you into a bare yard, then up steps to a complete surprise: a bird-filled garden of lawn and trees and roses. At the back, an 18th-century orangery, a miniature Marie-Antoinette Trianon, divided into two super little luxury flats. Properly arched windows light a pale living area where a modern plush sofa stands on beautiful new Versailles parquet flanked by a couple of Louis XV armchairs. The cosy kitchen is fine for a short stay, the marble bathroom is high-luxe, the mezzanine bedroom generously comfortable. One flat has a strong fuchsia-flashed colour scheme, the other is soberly taupe and almond – a question of taste or mood. Two couples can easily share the terrace, the garden has several separate corners and your intelligent, interesting hosts love inviting guests and friends to a champagne aperitif. Extraordinarily civilised. *5-minute walk to station, 20-minute train to central Paris.*

Price	From €135 each per day. Minimum 2 days. Discounts for longer stays.
Sleeps	2 apartments for 2.
Rooms	Each apartment: 1 double; 1 bathroom. Extra double with bathroom available in main house.
Arrival	Flexible.
Closed	Rarely.

Patricia White-Palacio
Versailles, Yvelines

Tel	+33 (0)1 39 43 07 57 or +33 (0)1 53 61 07 57
Mobile	+33 (0)6 82 42 81 39
Email	mp.white@free.fr

Domaine des Basses Masures

There are riding stables nearby so you can saddle up and go deep into Rambouillet forest: it encircles this peaceful hamlet. Madame, who is friendly and informal, takes care of the fine horses that graze in the field behind the house – do introduce yourself. The house is an old stables: long, low and stone-fronted, built in 1725 and covered in Virginia creeper and ancient wisteria. Madame lives in one end and does B&B; the gîte is at the other end. It is a homely little place with a cottagey feel. Whitewashed bedrooms, carpeted, cosy and up under the eaves, have roof windows and the odd rafter, new beds dressed in crisp cotton and fat pillows. In the sitting room downstairs there's a cheerful blue sofa that opens to a bed, a big oriental rug, modern wicker armchairs, an open fireplace and white-painted beams. The back windows look over the surrounding fields. The kitchen, more functional than aesthetic, has a round dining table and is very well equipped; it leads into the garden, with outdoor furniture. Versailles is 20 minutes, Paris 45 and there's excellent walking from the door. *B&B also.*

Price	€750 per week.
Sleeps	4-6.
Rooms	2 doubles, 1 sofabed; 2 bathrooms.
Closed	Never.

Madame Walburg de Vernisy
Poigny la Forêt, Yvelines

Tel	+33 (0)1 34 84 73 44
Email	domainebassesmasures@wanadoo.fr
Web	www.domaine-des-basses-masures.com

Entry 44 Map 5

Normandy • Brittany

La Poterie

In the grounds is a dairy where camembert was once made. It evidently did rather well for the owner made enough money to build himself this big, mid-19th-century house. It stands by a quiet road, backing onto open countryside, with an airy and impressive interior. The long, inviting sitting room has windows on three sides and an abundance of books, videos and games; the immense oak table in the green-and-white dining room seats 14. Cooking for that number shouldn't be too daunting, given the superbly designed kitchen and a dresser packed with local organic produce – paté, honey, jam, cider (plus price lists and honesty box). White bedrooms have their original parquet floors, two windows and beds made up with pretty white linen. Sue and Dan have worked hard to make this a great place for families: there's an enticing selection of bicycles and tricycles, doll's prams, garden toys, a paddling pool – even a snooker table. The dairy is being converted into a separate gîte (serving as games room in the meantime) and there's an excellent fishing and swimming lake in the village (1km). *Meals on request.*

Price	£950–£1,600 per week.
Sleeps	14.
Rooms	7: 5 doubles, 2 twins; 1 bathroom, 1 shower room, separate wc.
Closed	Never.

Sue & Dan Gascoyne
Saint Evroult Notre Dame du Bois, Orne

Tel	+44 (0)1206 790 828
Fax	+44 (0)1206 790 828
Email	info@lapoterie.co.uk
Web	www.lapoterie.co.uk

Les Cerisiers

As soon as the church bells chime midday, locals pack the little grocery-restaurant outside for the popular 'plat du jour'. Village life lies at the door of this postcard-pretty 19th-century cottage. Between the irises, potted lavender, cherry trees and roses, the garden is a delight for children and adults alike — a sweet place to be. The cottage can be rented as two individual units, hence a brace of sitting rooms, each warmed by a wood-burning stove. One has three neutral coloured sofas with a dining area off to one end; two deep brown leather couches square up in the second, the dining area apart. Even demanding cooks will want for nothing in the heavily beamed kitchens. Bedrooms are reached by two staircases, one to a double and a triple, the other to three interconnecting rooms under sloping overheads, the cotton-quilted beds lying beneath skylights. Showers are upstairs; step downstairs for a soak in a tub. The Laws family moved here to do B&B in their nearby watermill. Historic Dieppe is ten minutes down the road: ferry port, good restaurants, fine coastal walks.

Price	£650-£950 per week.
Sleeps	Cottage for 10-12.
	Can be let as two separate units.
Rooms	5: 2 doubles, 1 twin, 2 triples;
	1 bathroom, 1 shower room,
	2 separate wcs.
Closed	Never.

Ann Laws
La Chapelle sur Dun, Seine-Maritime

Tel	+33 (0)2 35 84 45 56
Mobile	+33 (0)6 12 61 61 24
Email	interspanhomes@aol.com
Web	www.interspanhomes.com

Château Le Bourg

The 1860's *petit château* has tall windows, a grand position in the middle of a small village and was once owned by the mayor of Dieppe. You get the top floor to yourself and with it the best views – of the village, church and surrounding low hills. The interior comes in comfortable, homely-château style: high slanting ceilings (you are up under the eaves), stylish fabrics, vibrant quilts, polished floorboards. The odd timber runs from floor to ceiling and there are skylights and dormer windows. The master suite is vast, the other rooms smaller, one with a mural, and the beds are the best. A spacious sitting room has sunny yellow walls, comfy sofas and more colour. Leonora, a retired lawyer from Hereford, is a talented cook and you are welcome to join her for sumptuous dinners – *bistrot* or *gastronomique*. Relax in her dining room decorated in the grand style: old oils, period wallpaper, candelabra on a polished table. And there is a garden to share, with barbecue and trees for your children to climb. Beyond, cows graze the meadows and the market town of Neufchâtel is close. *Sawday B&B. Meals on request.*

Price	€525 per week.
Sleeps	6 + 1 child.
Rooms	4: 1 twin/double, 2 twins, 1 child's room; 1 bathroom, 1 shower room.
Closed	Never.

Leonora Macleod
Bures en Bray, Seine-Maritime
Tel +33 (0)2 35 94 09 35
Email leonora.macleod@wanadoo.fr

Normandy

Le Gaillon

Two hours from Calais, in deep countryside, a solid little farmhouse just right for a family or close friends. Red terracotta tiles run throughout the ground floor; there's a sitting room with fine oak ceiling beams, old-fashioned easy chairs, a brick fireplace with logs in winter, piles of videos, books and board games. In the dining room, a refectory table for eight, a patterned rug, a huge mirror; in the light, well-equipped kitchen, a table for six and a further fireplace. The master bedroom is also on this floor, with its feather-filled duvet and pretty patchwork quilt, and so is the one large shower room that the household shares. Then upstairs to a long, large, uncluttered sleeping space under the eaves — white, open, airy, all beautiful gnarled timbers and endless views. Stow most of the party up here and they'll be happy. Fencing keeps the frisky cows framed in their buttercup meadow, leaving you the run of the pleasing garden. As dusk falls, you can sit, chat and barbecue as the poplars rustle and the fairylights twinkle like fireflies. Good value, gorgeous views.

Price	£280–£700 per week.
Sleeps	6-8 + cot.
Rooms	3: 2 doubles, 1 triple, 1 sofabed on mezzanine; 1 shower room, 2 separate wcs.
Closed	Rarely.

Mr & Mrs P Slack
Forges les Eaux, Seine-Maritime
Tel   +44 (0)1435 866 688
Email   info@legaillon.com
Web   www.legaillon.com

La Maison Bleue

In one of the most beautiful villages of France, with evocative bedroom views onto the majestic Bec Hellouin Abbey – famous for ceramics, Gregorian chant and prayer – this ancient, half-timbered cottage has a gem of a garden. Perfectly delightful bedrooms look as if everything has just tumbled out of a glossy design mag: lime-green walls and garden-gate headboards, modern muslined four-poster and the odd white feather, contrasting antique, wicker and florals. Beds are beautifully dressed, it all fits together perfectly and the pink bathroom is one of the loveliest you are likely to see: a free-standing claw-foot bath set bang next to the window overlooking the abbey and a wicker armchair for that someone to chat to you in your bubbles. On original tiled floors, the hall and sitting room occupy the breadth of the house. Done in yet more lovely colour harmonies, low-lit and painting-hung, the sitting room will relax you instantly, until it's time to go to work at the fine black kitchen range and produce a meal in the wood-clad dining room overlooking that dear little garden and the village church spire.

Price	€585–€945 per week.
Sleeps	6.
Rooms	3: 2 doubles, 1 twin; 1 bathroom, 1 shower, 1 separate wc.
Closed	Christmas week.

Nathalie & Dominique Boyer
Le Bec Hellouin, Eure

Mobile	+33 (0)6 11 96 69 25
Email	paullouisboyer@wanadoo.fr
Web	www.holidayrentalnormandybluehouse.com

Clos Vorin – La Maison Verte & La Grange

Amid rustling poplar trees, fields of corn and cattle-grazed meadows is this charming ensemble of four timbered farm buildings, clustered round the owners' house, surrounded by greenness and space. Grange, with its decent-sized swoop of lawn in front and ample outdoor eating space, is the most sheltered of the gîtes; all have their own patch of private lawn, pretty garden furniture and screening shrubs. Indoors, Verte has a generous serving of ground-floor rooms, kitchen opening to dining room to living room to library, and steps down to a conservatory at the end; then up to a lovely large open-plan sleeping area sandwiched between two doubles. Grange is as gorgeous, its double room on the mezzanine overlooking the living room below (cream tiles, dark timbers, white wrought-iron seats stylishly cushioned), and leading – no doors – into the family room, palely, elegantly informal, with oatmeal carpeting and roof timbers painted pastel blue. The shower room is downstairs; the 'conservatory' is a stunningly converted farm treadmill. Normandy at its enchanting best.

Price	Verte: €680–€1,190 (€550 for four, €450 for two).
	Grange: €472–€840 (€450 for four, €380 for two).
	Prices per week.
Sleeps	Verte 8. Grange 6.
Rooms	Verte: 2 doubles, 1 family room for 4; 1 shower room, 1 separate wc.
	Grange: 1 double, 1 family room for 4; 1 shower room, 1 separate wc.
Arrival	Flexible.
Closed	Never.

Eddy & Delphine Cayeux
Triqueville, Eure

Tel	+33 (0)2 32 56 53 15
Mobile	+33 (0)6 14 78 66 41
Email	gite.closvorin@wanadoo.fr
Web	www.leclosvorin.com

Clos Vorin - La Maison Bleue & La Petite Maison Verte

The painted, timbered doll's house cottages are so pretty, the apple trees which surround them so lush, you have to pinch yourself to believe they're real. Even when you've crept inside, the fairytale continues: white plaster and painted beams, a simple kitchenette screened off by vertical timbers, fluttering voile... a piano in one, a Provençal-patterned wall in another. Furniture is a good mix of old and new, expensive and budget – Bleue has a wonderful baroque-style antique bed and an old trunk for a coffee table. Both are intimate, simple, delightful. Outside, a cobbled terrace safe for children, a barbecue, perhaps a hammock slung between nearby trees. This magical farm group (four gîtes plus the owners' house) is the creation of Eddy and Delphine, who have two small children and put on weekly drinks for all. In 20 minutes you can be in Honfleur for picturesque architecture, sea front, seafood restaurants, autumn shrimp festival, while Trouville and Deauville, for bathing beaches, casinos and period villas, are not much further.

Price	Bleue: €310–€490.
	Petite Verte: €250–€380.
	Prices per week.
Sleeps	Bleue 2-4. Petite Verte 2.
Rooms	Bleue: 1 double, 1 sofabed in living room; 1 shower room.
	Petite Verte: 1 double; 1 shower room.
Arrival	Flexible.
Closed	Never.

Eddy & Delphine Cayeux
Triqueville, Eure

Tel	+33 (0)2 32 56 53 15
Mobile	+33 (0)6 14 78 66 41
Email	gite.closvorin@wanadoo.fr
Web	www.leclosvorin.com

Normandy

La Baronnière

A 200-year-old barn in the grounds of a manor house; nine rambling acres and a forest to insulate you from the world. The barn once stood elsewhere; the Fleurys dismantled it piece by piece, then reassembled it 20 paces from the lake. It is a stunning timber and brick building, renovated with boundless verve and sublime style. Pristine white walls soak up the Normandy light, exposed beams and sandblasted timbers stand out like ribs. Uncluttered bedrooms have garden views, trim carpets, new wooden beds, maybe a hi-fi; outside are barbecue and terrace. The English owners run painting and cookery courses and you can gorge on a four-course feast at the manor house if you don't wish to cook. They'll do your shopping, too, before you arrive; just ask. Visit Monet's garden at Giverny or the tractor-pulling championships in Bernay in June! Or stay put and watch the geese on the lake. Later you will fall asleep to the sound of water: the stream that feeds the lake tumbles over a sluice gate close by. Too much camembert and calvados is inevitable — why resist? *Sawday B&B. Meals on request.*

Price	€500-€750 for 3 bedrooms; €750-€1,000 for 4 bedrooms. Prices per week.
Sleeps	6-8.
Rooms	3: 2 doubles, 1 twin; 1 bathroom, 1 shower room, separate wc. Extra en suite double available with separate entrance.
Closed	Never.

	Christine Gilliatt-Fleury Cordebugle, Calvados
Tel	+33 (0)2 32 46 41 74
Fax	+33 (0)2 32 44 26 09
Email	labaronniere@wanadoo.fr
Web	labaronniere.com

Entry 52 Map 4

Entry 52 Map 4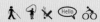

La Baronnière - La Petite Maison

It shares a boundary with La Baronniere (see entry 52) yet the two entrances are a kilometre apart. Here you have a typical Norman cottage set in a smallish square garden (not especially flowered but entirely safe for children), far from the madding crowd. The hamlet is surrounded by fields; hedging camouflages you from the property next door. The ground floor is a well-converted, open-plan affair: white walls, pale beams, terracotta floors, wood-burning stove, lace curtains at small windows. Sofa and armchairs are covered with dark throws and cream cushions, the well-fitted kitchen appears behind five crooked timbers, there's a downstairs shower that doubles as a laundry room, and good and varied pictures hang throughout. Upstairs are chocolate beams and bedrooms in the attic (cosy spaces but too low for wardrobes – there are hanging rails instead) and an agreeably large bathroom with shells round the bath and a prettily tiled floor. Book in for delicious dinner chez the owners; it's a meadow walk past black-headed sheep to the stream-fed lake and the charming old manor house. *Sawday B&B. Meals on request.*

Price	€600–€850.
Sleeps	5-6.
Rooms	3: 2 doubles, 1 single/twin on landing; 1 bathroom, 1 shower room.
Closed	Rarely.

Christine Gilliatt-Fleury
La Chapelle Hareng, Eure

Tel	+33 (0)2 32 46 41 74
Fax	+33 (0)2 32 44 26 09
Email	labaronniere@wanadoo.fr
Web	www.labaronniere.com

Le Clos St Bernard - Les Camélias & Les Fuchsias

The very first farmhouse built in this Normandy village – well placed for countryside and coast – has been transformed into two neat, spotless gîtes and sits in the walled courtyard opposite the owner's house. Les Camélias has a living/kitchen room on its ground floor with exposed stone and beams, cane armchairs, floral drapes, sofabed and dining table – and the equipment in the well-supplied kitchen stretches to a raclette machine and an electric mixer. An open-tread stair leads to carpeted blue and white bedrooms, the double with a fitted pine wardrobe and original stone sink and spout, now a display unit. Visitors can drive in to unload, then park safely outside; gates are securely locked at night. Les Fuchsias, on the first floor, is reached via a stone stair. It has a charmingly beamed kitchen/sitting room with pretty tiles and curtains and a white tiled floor. It, too, is well-equipped: try the fondue set! A corner of the gravelled courtyard has been set aside for both gîtes, each with loungers, parasol, table, chairs and barbecue. *Sawday B&B.*

Price	Camélias €270-€400. Fuchsias €250-€360. Prices per week. Linen & electricity not included.
Sleeps	Camélias 4. Fuchsias 2-4.
Rooms	Camélias: 1 double, 1 twin; 1 shower room. Fuchsias: 1 twin; 1 bathroom; sofabed.
Closed	Never.

Nicole Vandon
Reviers, Calvados

Tel	+33 (0)2 31 37 87 82
Fax	+33 (0)2 31 37 87 82
Email	leclosbernard@wanadoo.fr
Web	www.leclosbernard.com

8 rue Laitière

A gem! Hidden away on a quiet street in the centre of Bayeux, within sight of the great cathedral, this is one of those 19th-century stone-built cottages whose discreet entrance really does lead to a secret courtyard. The sun pours into the living room at midday, bouncing off mirrors and pictures, illuminating the red sofa, the rush armchair, the charming stone mantlepiece with its 'wood-burning' (electric) stove. A wide opening leads into a well-stocked kitchen and dining area where ornamental plates reside on a dresser, the perfect companions for a welcome pack of Normandy's finest. From here, curved stairs lead to the first floor and a brace of bedrooms. The twin has cane bed-heads, a blue fitted carpet and blue-spotted walls; the master room is elegantly wrapped in toile de Jouy wallpaper, matched by pretty white and blue cushions. Parting voile curtains at a tall window you look down onto a courtyard of shrubs, planter plots, your own garden table and chairs. Apart from the bells, it's impossible to believe that bustling Bayeux lies outside the door. *Ask owner about parking. B&B also.*

Price	€510–€870 per week.
	Shorter stays possible.
Sleeps	4.
Rooms	2: 1 double, 1 twin; 1 bathroom.
Arrival	Flexible.
Closed	Never.

Charlotte Liddell
Bayeux, Calvados
Tel   +33 (0)2 31 21 07 72
Email   charles.liddell@free.fr
Web   www.gites-in-normandy.co.uk

Normandy

La Commune

A great little two-person gite has been created from the former bakehouse that stood in the gardens of the owners' house. They are exceptionally welcoming, going so far as to include a packet of hand-made bonbons in their welcome pack. Even better, Monsieur has a 12-metre sailing boat and will happily take you out to view the landing beaches from the sea, or prepare a barbecue for you on the island of Saint Marcouf. La Commune is well named – there's an easy feel. The sitting area was the former bakehouse, an old stone manger and pretty floor tiles are intact, as is the original fireplace, with logs provided. It is not designer-decorated, preferring a low-key, easy-going style: a round dining table and four chairs, a sofa, a sideboard for the crockery. Up the open stairs to the mezzanine bedroom, full of light from big roof windows; back down to the shower. The setting is verdant, a magnificent and ancient pear tree gives shade in your own garden and the travelling baker passes by each morning at about 10.30, so late breakfasts are obligatory.

Price	€320–€430 per week.
Sleeps	2.
Rooms	1 double; 1 shower room.
Closed	Never.

Chantal Henkart
Cricqueville en Bessin, Calvados

Tel	+33 (0)2 31 22 66 82
Email	chantal.henkart@gmail.com
Web	lacommune.canalblog.com

Manoir de la Rivière

Isolated at the end of the manor's walled garden, this little gem is the cosiest lovers' retreat. Built into the high walls around the old manor, it was once the watchtower for the fortified farm and was probably also used by customs officers fighting the smuggling along this coast. All you'll spy today are the Leharivels' 80-odd dairy cows mowing the lush pastures of the Cotentin peninsula. Arrive in winter and Isabelle will have lit a fire for you in the wood-burner; come in summer and you have a sun-drenched terrace to lounge on. Pale stone walls and pretty toile de Jouy create a mood of light and calm for the bedroom, with its corner shower cubicle. A steep staircase leads down to the tiny beamed living room: darkly atmospheric, it's just big enough to squeeze in a sofa, a drop-leaf table and a corner kitchenette. The beach is a stroll away; restaurants and shops are a short drive. And you can visit the D-day landing beaches, including Pointe du Hoc on Omaha Beach where you'll still see German bunkers and shell-holes in the cliffs. *Second gîte in manor house. Sawday B&B.*

Price	€280–€420 per week. Linen not included.
Sleeps	2.
Rooms	1 double; 1 shower room, 1 separate wc.
Closed	Rarely.

Gérard & Isabelle Leharivel
Géfosse Fontenay, Calvados

Tel	+33 (0)2 31 22 64 45
Fax	+33 (0)2 31 22 01 18
Email	leharivel@wanadoo.fr
Web	www.chez.com/manoirdelariviere

Le Moulin l'Évêque - L'Île, Le Parc, Le Cadran Solaire

In a timeless setting of unsurpassed lushness and bucolic sensuality, this must be one of the most beautiful old water-mills ever. The buildings – owner's house and three stone gîtes, each with its own patch of delightful garden – fit their piece of paradise perfectly. So the contrast is even more startling when you step inside. These interiors are almost museum pieces, they are so dated: 1980s rental style in all its straightforward granny-type practicality. They are correctly fitted, functional and clean and have all the right bits. However, don't expect any frills, just the odd foreign costume doll, framed jigsaw or straw hat, good beds and bedding in bright colours, storage ranging from spartan hanging rail to rococo wardrobe, an open fireplace (logs sold on site) and some homely-comfy chairs. Right down by the water, l'Ile is one little cabin with big windows, a closet-kitchen and a shower for the nimble; the main bedroom in Parc is pleasing with its brass bed and mirrored wardrobe; Cadran Solaire (sundial) is a traditional-modern mix. And Johnny's organic veg patch is coming along.

Price	Cadran Solaire: £410-£635. Parc: £300-£450. L'Île: £240-£350. Prices per week. Linen not included.
Sleeps	Cadran Solaire 7. Parc 4. Ile 2.
Rooms	Cadran Solaire: 2 doubles, 1 triple; 2 showers, 2 separate wcs. Parc: 1 double, 1 twin; 1 shower room, separate wc. L'Île: 1 twin; 1 shower room, separate wc.
Arrival	Flexible in low season.
Closed	Never.

Johnny Carroll
Campeaux, Calvados

Tel	+33 (0)2 31 66 05 69
Fax	+33 (0)2 31 66 05 69
Email	johnnycarroll@wanadoo.fr
Web	www.gites-du-moulin.com

Les Fontaines

Just about impossible to fault this big elegant mansion with its lovely half-kempt garden and (unfenced) pond, its English antiques and polished parquet, its library and games room in the attic. Children can make dens among the palm trees and the laurels, teenagers can play drums or watch TV at the top, adults can rustle up barbecues on the covered terrace. Sitting and dining rooms, filled with light from tall windows, reveal interesting frescoes from the 1900s, wood panelling, sofas, armchairs, a piano and seriously big tables... the whole rambling house embraces 17 people and several babies. Up the lovely curved elm staircase is a long carpeted landing off which friendly bedrooms lie: wrought-iron beds and tub chairs, a pretty stone fireplace, a tall glass-fronted bookcase, a huge family suite in the attic. The kitchen, opening to an expanse of lawned garden at the back, has sufficient pots, pans, cutlery and crocks to feed a multitude. This is a superb place for family, friends and relations to stay – comfortable, civilised, easy. Bretteville's shops and market are two miles away. *Unfenced water.*

Price	€1,500-€2,500 per week.
Sleeps	18 + cots.
Rooms	6: 2 doubles, 1 twin, 2 family rooms for 4, 1 family room for 5; 1 bathroom, 5 shower rooms.
Arrival	Flexible.
Closed	Never.

Elizabeth & Andrew Bamford
Barbery, Calvados
Tel   +33 (0)4 79 59 79 60
Fax   +44 (0)207 7515736
Email information@lesfontaines.com
Web   www.lesfontaines.com

Normandy

Le Moulin du Pont

Nothing but the sound of rushing water and rustling trees. Despite its mature gardens and its graceful good looks, this luxurious house was built in the 1970s on the site of a mill. Everything is designed to capitalise on the setting. Water flows under the house (it's on stilts), a rose-clad Monet-style bridge crosses the mill race, gardens stretch along the river bank, windows drink in the views. Bedrooms reflect the hand of a de-luxe designer: French sleigh bed and slipper bath in one; sophisticated aubergine and cream colours with an alcove bath in another. The star has French windows to the garden and a super-duper bathroom. The open-plan living room wants for nothing – fireplace (logs provided), comfy sofas, elegant dining table, soft lamps, soft rugs and a fleet of windows leading to a marble terrace: perfect for suppers overlooking the floodlit garden. Cooking is no hardship in a kitchen where only the best will do. Everything is to hand, from binoculars for birdwatching to tumble-dryer to stocked larder. The charms of the Normandy coast are near, if you can tear yourself away from sybaritc indulgence. *B&B also.*

Price	£1,000–£1,600 per week.
Sleeps	6.
Rooms	3 doubles; 3 bathrooms.
Arrival	Flexible, but minimum stay 5 days.
Closed	Rarely.

David & Lesley Craven
Culey le Patry, Calvados
Tel   +33 (0)2 31 79 19 37
Fax   +33 (0)2 31 79 19 37
Email   info@chateaulacour.com
Web   www.chateaulacour.com

Château La Cour - Le Jardin

Up a stone staircase, through a small door and into an unexpected world of grand windows, oak-panelled doors and elegant rooms. Lesley and David, who have wisely chosen to settle in France, are the friendly lord and lady of this 13th-century château in deep countryside, with views stretching over the Suisse Normande. Your apartment, a private and discreet three-room suite, is light, spacious and gracious – from the parquet corridor with floor-to-ceiling windows to the oak-panelled doors and the richly coloured curtains falling in folds to the floor. If you think the bedroom is swish – king-size bed, stacks of cushions – just wait until you see the bathroom; gleaming white with brushed chrome, its roll top bath has space enough to perch a G&T. The living area, a soft, roomy space of sofas, hi-tech lights and natural linen with a dining table by the window to feed your daydreams, has a futuristic corner kitchen, a showpiece of stainless steel and gadgets. Flowers, welcome groceries, binoculars for birds, hosts who love to spoil... Sawday *grand cru. Sawday hotel.*

Price	£550 per week.
Sleeps	2.
Rooms	1 double; 1 bathroom.
Arrival	Flexible.
Closed	Rarely.

David & Lesley Craven
Culey le Patry, Calvados
Tel +33 (0)2 31 79 19 37
Fax +33 (0)2 31 79 19 37
Email info@chateaulacour.com
Web www.chateaulacour.com

Normandy

Manoir de Laize - Le Pressoir & La Grange

Apples used to be pressed for cider and calvados in the grandiose, medieval *pressoir*. Across the lawns, pretty with blossoming apple trees in the spring, is the 15th-century manor farmhouse where the owners live. Horses graze in the meadows, dogs and cats doze in the barns, and David and Emily are the friendliest, most thoughtful of hosts. Inside the Pressoir, much country charm: ceiling beams, tiled floors, soft colours, the odd antique and plenty of space. The lovely light living area is open plan, with a well equipped kitchen in the corner; French windows lead down a step to a walled suntrap patio with barbecue. Upstairs: new beds dressed in crisp white linen, a bathroom filled with soft towels. Books, toys, games – and central heating for winter cosiness. More open-plan living in the adjoining La Grange, new carpeting and harmonious colours. The place is brilliant for families: a superb games room, a fenced pool, a stream to dam. Soak up the setting, stock up at the weekly market in Falaise, cycle or canoe down the gorge of the Orne, pick wild flowers in spring. *Babysitting available.*

Price	£350–£900 each per week.
Sleeps	Pressoir 7 + cot. Grange 6 + cot.
Rooms	Pressoir: 2 twins, 1 family room for 3; 1 bathroom. Grange: 3: 1 double, 2 twins; 1 bathroom, 1 shower room.
Arrival	Saturday or Tuesday.
Closed	Never.

David & Emily Lloyd
Fontaine Le Pin, Calvados
Tel   +33 (0)2 31 20 93 74
Email   emlloy@aol.com
Web   www.manoirdelaize.com

La Ferme de l'Oudon - Les Tulipes

The Vesques' farmhouse has a dovecote and is partly 15th century. Although the days of farming have long gone, clucking hens survive, as do the ducks who sail upon their pond with highfaluting grace. Monsieur and Madame are the nicest people, keep horses, do B&B in the main house, cook brilliantly and provide picnic baskets on request. Madame is learning English with the local Chamber of Commerce, Monsieur runs an interior design company, and his work is on view in the old dairy to stunning effect. Les Tulipes is a charming, sunny, two-floor conversion that has been carried out with imagination and a consummate eye for detail. Enter to find an open-plan living area where contemporary furniture, warm fabrics and a luxurious tomato-red kitchen are off-set by ancient timbers, mellow tiles and creamy exposed stone. One bedroom is up, one down, there are terraces for summer, a wood-burner for winter, a bathroom with beautiful multi-coloured tiles, an enclosed garden with table tennis and barbecue, a potager to pluck from and bicycles to rent. *Superbe! Sawday B&B. Meals on request.*

Price	€700-€890 per week.
Sleeps	4-6.
Rooms	2 doubles, 2 single sofabeds; 2 bathrooms.
Closed	3-23 January.

Patrick & Dany Vesque
Berville l'Oudon, Calvados

Tel	+33 (0)2 31 20 77 96
Fax	+33 (0)2 31 20 67 13
Email	contact@fermedeloudon.com
Web	www.fermedeloudon.com

Entry 63 Map 4

Normandy

La Ferme de l'Oudon - Le Pressoir

Another enchanting farm building at L'Oudon, another fine restoration. This was the old cider press, its ground floor now a vast, light living space, comfortable and contemporary. You find big leather sofas, beautiful floor-to-ceiling curtains and an ultra-chic wood-burning stove. A gorgeous kitchen/diner leads to a private garden; there's a big, bold, sunny bedroom and the paved and furnished terrace is as inviting as all the rest. Walls are white plaster or light-gold stone, floors are pale-tiled, there are old beams and joists and new windows to pull in the light. Ascend the staircase with tiled treads to a mezzanine with sofa and two skylit bedrooms under the eaves, one large, both delightful. Bathrooms shine. The charming Vesques give you cider, homemade jam and farm eggs on arrival, and everything is included in the price, from linen to logs. Twice a week there's table d'hôtes – a chance to meet the B&B and other guests over a civilised meal. The orchards, rich pastures and half-timbered manor houses of the Pays d'Auge are yours to discover. *Sawday B&B. Meals on request.*

Price	€800-€990 per week.
Sleeps	6-8.
Rooms	3: 2 family rooms for 3, 1 twin; 2 bathrooms.
Closed	3-23 January.

Patrick & Dany Vesque
Berville l'Oudon, Calvados
Tel   +33 (0)2 31 20 77 96
Fax   +33 (0)2 31 20 67 13
Email   contact@fermedeloudon.com
Web   www.fermedeloudon.com

La Ferme de l'Oudon - Le Lavoir

The latest of Patrick and Dany's sparkling ventures is a restored wash house – a delicious bolthole for two. Its veranda laps at the edge of a lively pond where nature frolics and recycled water babbles: a delight to ear and eye. Trot down the new brick path and through the fenced garden to find an unexpectedly lofty, light-drenched room with a clean sweep of stone floor. A weaving hangs above a pale stone fireplace, a *chaise-hamac* is suspended from a beam, there are cream curtains at sliding glass doors, bright red towels in a chic shower, a kitchen that is a joy to use and a metal spiral stair winding up to a bed that tucks itself – and you – under the eaves. You get your own decked veranda with a Japanese feel, and seven hectares of fields, gardens, ponds, potager, horses and hens to share with the others. There is also table d'hôtes – delicious, twice-weekly, huge fun. Under construction are a large eco pond so you can swim with the frogs (purification ingeniously taken care of, thanks to special plants) and a hammam and fitness centre. Amazing! *Sawday B&B. Meals on request.*

Price	€650–€790 per week.
Sleeps	2.
Rooms	1 double; 1 shower.
Arrival	Flexible.
Closed	January.

Patrick & Dany Vesque
Berville l'Oudon, Calvados

Tel	+33 (0)2 31 20 77 96
Fax	+33 (0)2 31 20 67 13
Email	contact@fermedeloudon.com
Web	www.fermedeloudon.com

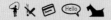

La Boursaie - Le Pressoir

You can almost smell the intoxicating aroma of fermenting apples as you dine in the groove where the great granite wheel of the old cider press turned. Apples have made this superb cluster of half-timbered buildings tick since medieval times, and English owner Peter and his German wife Anja have done a good job restoring them. The interiors of what are now five holiday cottages are decorated with 'ciderabilia' that Peter has bought over the years, and ancient cider barrels, wheelbarrows and apple baskets have been used in ingenious ways around the grounds. The whole of the ground floor is living space. The open-plan, terracotta-floored sitting, dining and kitchen area has the hugest beams, pink velvet armchairs, and butter churns for side tables. Up a ladder stair to cosy bedrooms (the master bedroom overlooks the press). Other guests are around but with 65 acres there's room to roam. Watch the buzzards from your private patch of garden, soak up valley views, join the apple harvest in autumn. The Davieses are happy to put up wedding or birthday parties, and can host dinners. *B&B also. Meals on request.*

Price	€700–€1,290 per week. Linen not included.
Sleeps	7.
Rooms	4: 2 doubles, 1 twin, 1 single; 1 bathroom, 1 shower room, 1 separate wc.
Arrival	Saturday July–August, flexible low season.
Closed	Rarely.

Anja & Peter Davies
Livarot, Calvados

Tel	+33 (0)2 31 63 14 20
Fax	+33 (0)2 31 63 14 20
Email	laboursaie@wanadoo.fr
Web	www.laboursaie.com

La Boursaie - La Grange

If you're lucky you'll spot deer in the early mornings; foxes, badgers and the occasional wild boar roam the magical woods. The hamlet takes its name from *bource*, the old Norman word for spring. Soak in the ancient beauty of this cider farm under the shade of the 300-year-old walnut tree which towers and protects like a friendly giant. Anja and Peter will bring walnuts, apples and pears to your door and you can buy their home-produced cider and calvados. La Grange, with its stupendous views over the courtyard and duck pond to the valley beyond, was once the hayloft and has been converted into a delightful split-level, first-floor living area. Ceilings slope and glorious old beams have been skilfully used to divide the space, blending atmospherically with old and new furniture and seagrass floors. Peter has his painting studio below — his work is displayed in several of the cottages — and there's a dining room where the couple entertain guests to a weekly feast: Norman cooking at its best. They also hold art courses in spring and autumn. *B&B also. Meals on request.*

Price	€590-€980 per week. Linen not included.
Sleeps	4.
Rooms	2 twins; 1 shower room, 1 bathroom.
Arrival	Saturday July-August, flexible low season.
Closed	Never.

Anja & Peter Davies
Livarot, Calvados

Tel	+33 (0)2 31 63 14 20
Fax	+33 (0)2 31 63 14 20
Email	laboursaie@wanadoo.fr
Web	www.laboursaie.com

La Boursaie - Le Trou Normand

Even the ducks and chickens live in a half-timbered cottage. No modern building disrupts the black and white beauty of this tranquil farmstead, clustered around a large grassy courtyard, set in a fold between rolling hills. Couples will love this most private of cottages where once calvados was distilled; now you may relax by the fire in winter tasting a glass of home-produced cider. It is a delicious nest for two: cream walls, tiled floors and pink toile de Jouy on the sofa downstairs; low cruck beams and minute windows in the bedroom up; views that sail over orchards of apple, cherry and pear. With a restaurant in the old cowshed and a play area for kids: a small community to join if you wish; or enjoy your own well-furnished piece of garden. If you love walking, the Tour du Pays d'Auge footpath runs almost from the door; there's riding on the beach at Deauville — a half-hour drive — and Camembert is not far either. The cheese's creator, Marie Harel, whose promotion campaign included sending free samples to Napoleon, is commemorated in the next-door village of Vimoutiers. *B&B also. Meals on request.*

Price	€390–€490 per week. Linen not included.
Sleeps	2.
Rooms	1 double; 1 shower room.
Arrival	Flexible.
Closed	Never.

Anja & Peter Davies
Livarot, Calvados

Tel	+33 (0)2 31 63 14 20
Fax	+33 (0)2 31 63 14 20
Email	laboursaie@wanadoo.fr
Web	www.laboursaie.com

2 impasse de l'Horizon - Three Apartments

A house which almost dangles its feet in the sea. A mere sea wall separates the garden wall from the sandy beach (part of D-Day landings Gold Beach) and the Mulberry Harbour (relic of brilliant D-Day engineering) lies offshore — what a position for this little post-war house. There's a tiny 'cottage' sleeping four, remarkable for its mezzanine bathroom with colourful curtains; the other two apartments have glorious sea views. Kitchens are well equipped, living rooms share similar features in the shape of dining tables, leather sofas, armchairs, books and TVs. There are patchwork quilts and cream brocade covers in friendly bedrooms that slope romantically under the eaves. In bath and shower rooms — one big enough for two in the lower apartment — you'll find an indulgent pile of coffee-coloured towels. The houses are cleaned and the linen changed every three days. Start the day with an early morning swim, kick a football around in the field next door, bask on a chaise-longue in the communal garden, swing on the swing. You're surrounded by D-Day history and the tide goes out for miles.

Price	€420-€840 per week. €60-€120 per day.	
Sleeps	Cottage for 2-4. Apartment for 2-3. Apartment for 2.	
Rooms	Cottage: 1 family room for 4; 1 bathroom. Apartment 1: 1 family room for 3; 1 bathroom. Apartment 2: 1 double; 1 bathroom.	
Arrival	Flexible.	
Closed	Never.	

Isabelle Sileghem
Asnelles, Calvados

Tel	+33 (0)2 31 22 21 73
Fax	+33 (0)2 31 22 98 39
Email	ranconniere@wanadoo.fr

Normandy

Le Manoir des Parcs

Come to party in the summer palace of the Bishops of Lisieux! Fleets of bedrooms and salons and a tree-studded park... 25 can stay in some style. Although vast in size and handsome in looks, this 18th-century manor house is furnished in a homely way... no danger of children breaking the Meissen. Old mixes with new; modern paintings and leopard print bedcovers rub easy shoulders with chesterfield sofas and stone fireplaces. Two ground-floor salons, scattered with tables, lamps and books, ask for fun and games yet still leave corners for book-reading and snoozing. A professional kitchen does the business (though meals can be requested). Bedrooms, over two floors, are a quirky mix of the grand and the dormitory, with single rooms tucked into corners, and there are heaps of bathrooms with some en suites open-plan. It is comfortable, colourful and furnished with more dash than style. Monsieur is energetic, charming, full of smiles and ideas, for golf and riding, châteaux and calvados. Back at the estate: a small pool, a barn for banquets and parkland for escape. *B&B also. Meals on request.*

Price	€1,500–€3,500 per week.
Sleeps	25.
Rooms	House: 4 doubles, 2 singles, 1 suite for 3; 4 bathrooms. Orangery: 1 apt for 3-4, 1 apt for 4-6, each with bath.
Closed	Never.

Arnaud & Frédérika Sintive
Ouilly le Vicomte, Calvados

Mobile	+33 (0)6 85 92 66 86, +33 (0)6 80 37 67 93
Fax	+33 (0)2 31 62 89 80
Email	contact@lemanoirdesparcs.com
Web	www.lemanoirdesparcs.com

Villa Caprice - Studio

So enchanting, so Marie-Antoinette in its mouldings and curly furniture, this is the perfect romantic nest. White and grey and gold with the occasional blushing flower, lacy, even racy (meet the naked lady in the garden), it is a place for grown-ups in search of glamour indoors and out. Since being founded in 1890 by the Duke of Morny, Deauville has been the ultimate smart seaside resort: casino and film festival, racecourse and polo, fine beaches and 'the boards' for making your latest fashion statement. In this superior urban setting (there will be some traffic), you have a super secluded garden with a rose-covered arbour and all the right furniture. Once inside the studio room, you find a festival of dramatic carved gilt headboard, antique tables and chests, softly draping muslin, all set on pale seagrass, all impeccable. Practical too, with excellent cupboards. The two antique painted panels over the bath are the perfect refinement. You also have a neat little kitchen with everything you'll need including, of course, a champagne bucket, though the choice of eating places within a short stroll is vast.

Price	£250–£550 per week.
Sleeps	2-4.
Rooms	1 double, 1 sofabed; 1 bathroom.
Closed	Never.

	Lyndia Shaw
	Deauville, Calvados
Tel	+44 (0)20 7263 3942
Email	avonpriestley@yahoo.co.uk

Entry 71 Map 4

Maison de Honfleur - Clos Massillon & Clos Vorin

The wonderful little medieval fishing port of Honfleur draws thousands of tourists in summer and a regular flow throughout the winter weekends. Come for cultural wanders and characterful architecture, shrimp sellers on the quayside and shops that brim with Normandy goodies, steep walks to the endearing fishermen's chapel on the cliff behind and the picturesquely set marina. A five-minute walk from the Vieux Bassin is this old shuttered townhouse and its fresh new holiday apartments. First-floor Clos Massillon has spaciousness, light and warm wooden floors, a pretty little bedroom painted mauve, a children's room with alphabet walls and a super-smart, open-plan kitchen. The dining and living rooms are panelled and painted in gentle greys, the windows are elegantly dressed, and there are sofabeds for extra people. Second-floor Clos Vorin exudes a simple young charm: an all-white living space with wooden floor and farmhouse table, sofabed and wicker chair, and a sweet bedroom with high views over the trees to patches of sea beyond. *Secure parking.*

Price	Massillon: €350-€690. Vorin: €310-€450. Prices per week. Linen not included.
Sleeps	Massillon 6. Vorin 2-4.
Rooms	Massillon: 1 double, 1 children's room with bunkbeds; 1 bathroom, 2 sofabeds. Vorin: 1 double; 1 bathroom; sofabed.
Closed	Never.

Eddy & Delphine Cayeux
Honfleur, Calvados
Tel +33 (0)2 32 56 53 15
Mobile +33 (0)6 14 78 66 41
Email gite.closvorin@wanadoo.fr
Web www.leclosvorin.com

Maison de Honfleur - Clos Berthot & Clos Jeanne

In a pale pink 19th-century townhouse 200 metres from Honfleur's heart are four apartments recently refurbished and prettily presented. Ground-floor Clos Berthot's living room has large modern floor tiles, two elegant windows and a wall of original panelling painted mushroom and cream. The bedroom is French-feminine with a draped bedhead and painted antique tables, the bathroom sparkles in white. Clos Jeanne, also on the ground floor, is a one-room studio (with sofabed not bed) whose grand wraparound panelling is strikingly mauve, mushroom and cream; the bathroom is impeccable in white and lime green. Corner kitchens are ideal for light spontaneous cooking and a bottle of cider waits on each dining table. You look onto the town's tennis courts, the public swimming pool and the pretty municipal gardens of Honfleur, shrouded by a tree-lined avenue on one side and old townhouses the other. Behind is the hiddledy-piggledy architectural charm of Honfleur's past, from medieval brick-and-beams to turn-of-the-century villas. *No washing machines. Secure parking.*

Price	Berthot: €290-€430. Jeanne: €250-€380. Prices per week. Linen not included.
Sleeps	Berthot 2-4. Jeanne 2.
Rooms	Berthot: 1 double; 1 bathroom; sofabed. Jeanne: 1 bed/sitting room for 2; 1 bathroom.
Arrival	Flexible.
Closed	Never

	Eddy & Delphine Cayeux Honfleur, Calvados
Tel	+33 (0)2 32 56 53 15
Mobile	+33 (0)6 14 78 66 41
Email	gite.closvorin@wanadoo.fr
Web	www.leclosvorin.com

Entry 73 Map 4

Normandy

L'Atelier

Through the Norman gateway into the sun-drenched courtyard: Liliane and history embrace you. One of the jewels of ancient Honfleur, the complex was first a convent, then fishermen's cottages, later a *cidrerie*. Now this quarter is a conservation area and all has been properly restored. On one side of the enclosed yard, the side where the apples used to be pressed, Liliane does B&B and above a small art gallery she has created an immaculate gîte. Privately off the street, up a steep narrow stair, is a charming light contemporary space with pure white walls, woodwork painted a soft grey, a sweep of pale parquet. There's an elegant blue sofabed, a suave leather armchair with footstool to match, walk-in cupboards, music, books, games, TV. At the far end, separated by pale grey standing timbers, is a well-kitted-out kitchen; a fig tree taps at the window from the courtyard below. The bathroom is next door; the bedrooms are on the second floor: good curtains, crisp white bedcovers on new wrought-iron beds. Honfleur is at your feet and charming Liliane knows the town intimately. *Sawday B&B.*

Price	€650 per week. Parking €8 per day.
Sleeps	4–6.
Rooms	2: 1 twin/double, 1 twin; 1 bathroom; sofabed.
Closed	Never.

Mélina Giaglis
Honfleur, Calvados
Tel +33 (0)2 31 89 42 40
Web www.giaglis.com

Les Sources

Peaceful narrow lanes between high banks and hedges bring you to Les Sources. Hydrangeas and old-fashioned roses surround the early 19th-century *longère* – restored, traditionally furnished and nicely equipped by Roger and Sandra. They used to own an award-winning hotel and restaurant in Wales so the kitchen brims over with every culinary aid you could want, from Le Creuset pots to seafood pans. Rooms are beamed, spotless and comfortable; in winter, curl up with books, games, puzzles before a crackling fire – logs are provided for the big granite fireplace. Open-tread stairs (with safety gate) lead to three carpeted bedrooms with sloping ceilings, roof windows, coordinated bedding, bedside lamps and pictures. The bathroom is on the ground floor. Such a lovely setting – nearly an acre of lawns, trees and shrubs and a stream to one side. There's a herb garden, too, and an orchard full of rich fruit-bearing trees. All around are fields and the sea is less than two miles, with deserted sandy beaches and a view of Jersey. *Babysitting available.*

Price	£250-£550 per week.
Sleeps	5-6 + cot.
Rooms	3: 2 doubles, 1 single; 1 bathroom, separate wc. Extra single bed.
Closed	Never.

Roger & Sandra Bates
Surtainville, Manche

Tel	+33 (0)2 33 52 12 89
Email	rogersandrabates@wanadoo.fr
Web	www.lessourcesgite.com

Entry 75 Map 3

Normandy

La Fèvrerie No 1

The creeper-clad 16th-century house was a farm labourer's cottage; the other half is also rented out (see opposite): each has its own private garden on either side of a high hedge. The owners are sheer delight: she charming, bubbly and elegant, he full of kindness; together they've grown vegetables on their farm near the sea for as long as they can remember. They're now retired and run an idyllic B&B 50 yards down the lane. Madame's passion is interior decoration, and it shows: ancient-beamed rooms are furnished with solid, comfortable sofas and chairs, beautiful country antiques, plain or checked curtains. The kitchen is both practical and pretty, and a wooden, open-tread stair leads from the large open-plan living room to charming bedrooms above. The tiny fishing village of Barfleur is just across the fields and the landing beaches a short drive to the south. In summer you can pop over to the nearby island of Tatihou for atmospheric concerts. Don't forget to taste the local oysters. *Supplement for cleaning at end of stay. Sawday B&B.*

Price	€330-€490 per week.
Sleeps	4-5.
Rooms	2: 1 twin, 1 triple; 1 bathroom.
Closed	Never.

Marie-France & Maurice Caillet
Sainte Geneviève, Manche
Tel   +33 (0)2 33 54 33 53
Fax   +33 (0)2 33 22 12 50
Email   caillet.manoirlafevrerie@wanadoo.fr

La Fèvrerie No 2

The old stone cottage is buffered from the rugged rocky Normandy coast by a swathe of dreamy fields where Monsieur Caillet's racehorses graze. The owners are a sparkling and cultivated couple who have given up vegetable farming and full-time stud farming to run a successful B&B, although Monsieur still breeds a few horses every year. Inside the large living room, that magnificent stone fireplace, exposed stone walls, some impressive beams, comfortable seating and French windows with yellow curtains that open to a small patio for dining out. A delicious retreat, whose pretty carpeted bedrooms have dark antique furniture, charming French wallpapers and tranquil views over surrounding fields. Explore the Cotentin peninsula on foot, visit the weekly markets at Barfleur and Saint Pierre Église, or stroll along the bay in attractive Saint Vaast la Hougue where Edward III landed on his way to Crécy. There are some excellent seafood restaurants in little Barfleur, a two-mile drive, and in Saint Vaast. And all that Franco-English history. *Supplement for cleaning at end of stay. Sawday B&B.*

Price	€330-€490 per week.
Sleeps	4-5.
Rooms	2: 1 twin, 1 family room for 3; 1 shower room, 1 separate wc.
Closed	Never.

Marie-France & Maurice Caillet
Sainte Geneviève, Manche

Tel	+33 (0)2 33 54 33 53
Fax	+33 (0)2 33 22 12 50
Email	caillet.manoirlafevrerie@wanadoo.fr

Normandy

La Merise

Another pretty little cottage with rambling pink roses by the front door. It basks on the sunny side of Mont Castre, an island of stone in a sea of green. You are in a national park: marshland, coastal dunes and woods burst with all sorts of birds; wild flowers flourish. Back at the ranch John and Valerie, two ex-pat Aussies who do B&B, have brought a colourful organic garden to life; you have your own piece of it, with barbecue, for outdoor dining. This tiny gîte, attached to the owners' home, is encased within 300-year-old walls: simple, cosy, good value for two. The front door opens to a sunny kitchen/living room and a dear little mezzanine bedroom, reached via a steepish stair. There are books and bicycles to borrow and old railway lines to cycle along. In summer, grab the boogie boards and head for the beach. You will find a local market for each day of the week, or try the fisherman's cooperatives for oysters, mussels, lobster, crab. Lessay with its abbey is well worth a visit; its September festival has been going for over 900 years – the oldest country fair in Europe. *Sawday B&B.*

Price	€250-€320 per week.
Sleeps	2.
Rooms	1 double; 1 shower room.
Arrival	Saturday, flexible out of season.
Closed	Never.

	Valerie & John Armstrong
	Gerville la Forêt, Manche
Tel	+33 (0)2 33 45 63 86
Mobile	+33 (0)6 30 74 42 49
Email	the.armstrong@free.fr

Normandy

La Campanule

The croissants brought fresh to your door are worth rousing yourself for. On a quiet, winding road this old farmworker's cottage has been smartly revived. Its fresh young face is softening with age and climbing plants. Inside this thoughtful renovation all is spanking new, with underfloor heating downstairs to keep you as warm as toast in winter. The soberly elegant sitting room has a lime-rendered fireplace for its wood-burner and French floral sofas; the dining room, sandwiched between the warm ochre kitchen and the sitting room, seats eight. A hardwood staircase leads you up to planked floors covered with rugs, a star-gazing bed in the double, a bathroom big enough for all. Australian owners Valerie and John, artist and historian, are as friendly as can be, offer you a welcome drink, introduce you to your new home and fill you in on the local history. Loving fingers have tackled the large garden where chirruping peace is a constant and the sun shines a lot. You are on an official cycle and walking route, so two free bikes come in handy. Mont St Michel and Bayeux are nearby. *Sawday B&B.*

Price	€430–€615 per week.
Sleeps	5.
Rooms	3:1 double, 1 twin, 1 single; 1 bathroom, separate wc.
Arrival	Saturday, flexible out of season.
Closed	Never.

Valerie & John Armstrong
Gerville la Forêt, Manche
Tel   +33 (0)2 33 45 63 86
Mobile   +33 (0)6 30 74 42 49
Email   the.armstrong@free.fr

Normandy

Gîte le Marais

This is a Jekyll and Hyde house. In winter, it's on an island, in summer, it sits high and dry as the waters disappear. Welcome to the magical marshlands of the Cotentin. Outdoor families will love staying at this stone and cob cottage, once the farm's cattle shed. There are boat trips, beaches a half-hour drive, footpath walks with heaps of birds to spot – herons, egrets, storks – and hedgehogs in the garden. Though modest, the house has been thoughtfully equipped with toys, high chair, baby bath, binoculars for the birds, and a generously equipped kitchen-diner. This sunny room, with its jolly rush seat chairs, leads to a patio and herb garden. Easy to relax out here with your wine while the children play in the little sitting room or scamper around the pretty garden and orchard (shared with your friendly host, Madame Berthe). Upstairs are three neat and simple, pine-furnished bedrooms, with teddy bears and pictures for the little ones. Madame Berthe will leave you a homemade dinner for those days when you're too tired to cook; the butcher and baker are a five-minute drive. *Meals on request.*

Price	€282-€470 per week.
	Linen not included.
Sleeps	5-7 + cot.
Rooms	3: 1 double, 1 twin, 1 single;
	1 bathroom, separate wc, sofabed.
Closed	Rarely

Yolande Berthe
Saint André de Bohon, Manche

Tel   +33 (0)2 33 71 13 62
Email   philippe.thiennaud@free.fr
Web   gitelemarais.free.fr

La Germainière

Find bucolic bliss at this grand old farmhouse behind high hedgerows. Past orchards and fields of quiet cows, down a private half-mile drive, the 300-year-old stone façade comes into view. This is a house that feels solid, loved and lived in – three floors of robust stone walls, characterful beams, tiled floors and a huge Normandy fireplace. The big modern kitchen – beech units and all the equipment – leads into a dining room with massive table and dresser. In the warm, low-beamed lounge, cocoon yourself before the fire on the occasional rainy day in velvet and leather sofas. Bedrooms are big, carpeted, personal: a 1920s' poster here, silk flowers there, the odd friendly antique. The twin room is a vision in shocking pink, there are yellows and golds in the master room and calming lavender and blue elsewhere. Outside, a vine-shaded veranda for leisurely meals, lovely views over the tree-fringed valley, glimpses of the fine big swimming pool, a lawn and hidden orchard to keep the children happy. There are five old bikes for free: you can be at the village bistro in five minutes. Peace, comfort and charm.

Price	£450–£1,950 per week.
Sleeps	12.
Rooms	6: 2 doubles, 4 twins; 1 bathroom, 2 shower rooms.
Closed	Never.

Brian & Sue Smart
Guéhébert, Manche
Tel   +44 (0)1747 812 019
Fax   +44 (0)1747 811 066
Email   hambye@hartgrovefarm.co.uk
Web   www.normandyfarmhouses.co.uk

Entry 81 Map 3

Normandy

La Cahudière - Coquelicot & Bleuet

The lane runs out at La Cahudière – into the peace and quiet of rolling folds and deep country. A family venture, this 100-year-old stone farmhouse with hay barn has been converted into two immaculate gîtes. Window boxes brim with colour, butterflies come for the peach trees, you may gather the fruit. There are white walls and new pine, shuttered windows, pastel fabrics and tiled floors. Wood-burners give winter warmth, thick walls keep you cool in summer, pretty bedrooms are spotless and have check curtains, cane furniture, good beds. There are big double rooms for adults and bunk rooms for children. Sit out in front and watch the cattle graze; spot deer in the woods. It's great for families: a new pool with decked area (all yours if you book both gites), tennis and fishing nearby, a video/DVD library for cosy nights in. Children have masses of space to run around in safely and there's a private patio for each gîte. The village, a mile away, has good little shops and a restaurant for lunch. Mont St Michel is within striking distance; Cancale, a pretty coastal town, is known for its oysters. *Shared laundry & pool.*

Price	£295–£1,200 per week. See website for details. Linen not included.
Sleeps	Coquelicot 4–7. Bleuet 10–14.
Rooms	Coquelicot: 1 double, 1 triple with bunks; 1 bathroom; 1 sofabed. Bleuet: 3 doubles, 2 twins, 1 adult bunks, 1 children's bunks; 2 bathrooms, 1 shower room.
Closed	Never.

Margaret Atherton
Saint Martin de Landelles, Manche
Tel +33 (0)2 33 49 30 45
Email enquiries@lacahudiere.co.uk
Web www.lacahudiere.co.uk

La Channais

A very comfortable 18th-century terraced cottage in a quiet back lane 500m from the river Rance. Guests are asked to mow the grass and clean the house before they go but this seems fair exchange for the use of four bikes and an eight-foot dinghy on the river. Inside, a well-equipped kitchen sits on a slate floor and cosy red sofas pull up around an impressive granite fireplace (logs on the house); there are interesting pictures, two oak ship's timbers in the ceiling and a stone spiral stair. A spliced and knotted rope handrail hauls you up to the landing and the pretty iron balcony on the front of the house. Bathrooms are spotless. Cottagey bedrooms, a good size, overlook the woods and delightful gardens at front and rear. The secluded back garden, part terrace (teak furniture and barbecue) and part large lawn (badminton equipment provided), brims over with flowers and shrubs. You will find plentiful instructions and advice for visitors; medieval Dinan is 20 minutes away by car and Plouër — shops, supermarket, two restaurants and several sports — is up the road. *Dinghy available.*

Price	£220–£475 per week.
Sleeps	5-8.
Rooms	3: 1 double, 1 twin, 1 room with bunks & single bed; 2 bathrooms.
Closed	In winter.

Juliet Evans & Ronnie Bryce
Plouër sur Rance, Côtes-d'Armor
Tel   +44 (0)20 7937 3777
Email   jeffandjuliet@hotmail.com

Brittany

La Rive

How soothing to watch the boats bobbing in the marina from your sofa. On the ground floor of a fine 19th-century stone farmhouse, right on the quay by the river Rance, is a prettily decorated apartment with a private garden. The open-plan sitting room and kitchen have a sweep of pale tiled floor and a contemporary feel, the main bedroom is floral, the single is all-white with dashes of bright colour, the well-laid-out shower room, in blue grey with a fish-design border, is beautifully done. And the beds are brand new. Jocelyne, who lives in the apartment upstairs, is charming and puts much energy into making your stay a joyous one. She also happens to run a lovely riverside restaurant in Plouër sur Rance if you fancy venturing a little further afield. In the garden, fronted by a stone wall and fringed by beds of flowers, are table, chairs and barbecue, and a little area tucked to one side for the washing. Tempting to stay here and indulge in those watery views, but there's some splendid sightseeing to be had, in Dinan, Dinard, Saint Malo and Mont Saint Michel.

Price	€500-€600 per week.
Sleeps	4-5.
Rooms	2: 1 double, 1 twin; 1 shower room; sofabed.
Arrival	Flexible.
Closed	Never.

	Jocelyne Tullou-Denisot
	La Vicomté sur Rance, Côtes-d'Armor
Tel	+33 (0)2 96 83 27 48
Email	gite.larive@wanadoo.fr
Web	perso.wanadoo.fr/gite.larive

La Julerie - Four Gîtes

Down a winding country lane, a sunny, tranquil hideaway. Converted from a Breton longère, the gîtes are close yet there's a feeling of space. Step outside to your private patio, relax by the pool (a barn conversion with sliding doors), leave the children to play (table tennis, ball games, sandpit, boules and swings). The Normans sourced original materials during the renovation, son Tim did all the conservation work, and the result is a blend of modern comfort and characterful rusticity. Open-plan living areas are cosy with beams, cottagey dressers, flowery sofas – easy spaces where you can chat with the cook or gather round the farmhouse table – La Vieille Ferme seats up to 22! Three have dishwashers, two have wood-burning stoves, bedrooms sport simple cottage or Breton-style furnishings, wooden floors and colourful bedcovers. The luxurious Grenier has a generous bedroom in the loft; Les Écuries is wheelchair friendly; take all four and have a party. Tim and his French-born wife Lydiane are lovely and live here, the owls will hoot you to sleep, the beaches are a 20-minute drive. *Pool unheated New Year to Easter.*

Price	€435–€1,290 per week.
Sleeps	Gites for 7-8; 4-6; 4-5; 4.
Rooms	Grenier: 2 doubles, 1 twin & sofabed; 3 baths.
	Vieille Ferme: 1 double, 1 twin, 1 room with bunks, sofabed; 1 bath, 1 shower.
	Écuries: 1 double, 1 twin; 1 bath, 1 shower. Extra bed.
	Étables: 1 double, 1 twin; 1 bath, 1 shower.
Arrival	Flexible in low season.
Closed	Never.

Robert Norman
Corseul, Côtes-d'Armor

Tel	+44 (0)1373 471 983
Email	robdnorman@hotmail.com
Web	www.lajulerie-gites.com

Launay Arot - Sabine, Hélène, Pascale, Germaine, Marguerite

A peaceful cluster of gîtes in beautiful countryside near Dinan, Saint Malo and lovely beaches — perfect for families or holiday chums. Blue paintwork decorates each quintessentially Breton granite cottage, three of which are converted farm cottages and two are in the former stables, attached to the house where your English hosts live. The Thains are the kindest people, proud of their enterprise and generous to guests: there's wood for open fires, fresh linen weekly, barbecues, cots, high chairs and stair gates, a welcome pack of goodies and a great information folder. Rooms are a good size, nothing feels poky, walls are whitewashed, electricity is included. Bedrooms, some at mezzanine level — ever popular with children! — are simply furnished with pale fabrics and new beds, modern kitchens hold all you need, sitting rooms are homely with real fires. There's not much that isn't within a half-hour drive, the countryside is open and pretty and there's a really special restaurant at Plélan le Petit (3km). All this plus boules, swings and two acres of gardens to roam. *Shared washing machines.*

Price	£350–£595 per week.
Sleeps	2 gîtes for 4; 3 gîtes for 6–8.
Rooms	Sabine, Hélène: 1 double, 1 twin; 1 bathroom.
	Pascale, Germaine, Marguerite: 1 double, 2 twins; 2 bathrooms.
Arrival	Wednesdays & Saturdays.
Closed	Never.

	Sue & Nick Thain
	La Landec, Côtes-d'Armor
Tel	+33 (0)2 96 84 54 44
Email	nick@bretoncottages.com
Web	www.bretoncottages.com

Ville Lieu de Fer - Manor House, Garden House, Artist's Studio

In the high summer months bring the extended family, a dozen friends, the cricket team to share these three luxurious houses round the garden courtyard (rented individually at other times). From smart barbecues to underfloor heating, you get the best. The Manor House has a vast 50-foot living room, a wood-burner, French windows to the patio and a table for 12. And the all-dancing kitchen has a brand new range (though you can call in a private chef). Fine oak stairs lead to grand bedrooms: beds are king-size, the singles are 'Breton' (larger than usual), there's fine French wallpaper... it's like walking into a friend's beautiful home. The Garden House conservatory-living room has an African theme, pale washes, lots of light. The Studio is a loft apartment with a sunny balcony. Add a superb communal laundry, a coach house with table tennis and games, a pool, encircled by lawns and loungers, that can be heated to 30 degrees. It's a gorgeous setting, the village has both bakery and bar, and medieval Lamballe, a 15-minute drive, has the rest. *'Manor' & 'Garden' connect via a central hall for combined rental.*

Price	Whole property: June & Sept £1,300; July & Aug £2,600. Other months separate rentals: Manor £700. Garden £500. Studio £300. Pool June-Sept, heated £125. Prices per week.
Sleeps	Manor 4-6. Garden 4. Studio 2.
Rooms	Manor: 1 double, 1 twin, 1 twin on mezzanine; 1 bath, 1 shower, separate wc. Garden: 1 double, 1 twin; 1 bath; 1 shower. Studio: 1 double; 1 shower.
Closed	Never.

Mike & Gaile Richardson
Le Gouray, Côtes-d'Armor

Tel	+33 (0)2 96 34 95 30
Fax	+33 (0)2 96 34 95 30
Email	richardson.michael@wanadoo.fr

Brittany

Château de Bonabry

This little gem used to house the archives of the château (built by the Vicomte's ancestors in 1373): the family discovered piles of musty parchment documents when they restored it. With the sea at the end of the drive, your own rose- and shrub-filled walled garden to spill out into in the summer, and two lively, loveable hosts who do B&B in the château, this is a wonderful place for a small family to stay. Downstairs rooms have stone vaulted ceilings, crimson-washed walls and age-old terracotta floors, a new sofa and a striped fauteuil; while the kitchen is fitted and white, with a round table and yellow chairs. Beamy bedrooms are beautiful: in the twin, a stripped floor and pink toile de Jouy; in the double, deep yellow fabric-clad walls – an enthusastic redecoration by the Vicomtesse. If they aren't out hunting, your hosts will be on hand to help, and the Vicomte may well bring offerings from his personal vegetable garden. Your 'English' garden is furnished with parasol, barbecue and wooden loungers. This is a dear little place in which to unwind. *Sawday B&B.*

Price	€450–€1,150 per week. Linen not included.
Sleeps	4.
Rooms	2: 1 double, 1 twin; 1 shower room.
Closed	Never.

Vicomtesse Louis du Fou de Kerdaniel
Hillion, Côtes-d'Armor
Tel   +33 (0)2 96 32 21 06
Fax   +33 (0)2 96 32 21 06
Email   bonabry@wanadoo.fr
Web   bonabry.fr.st

Entry 88 Map 3

Kerpoence

Pretend you're playing doll's houses! This is an entrancing place, a one-up, one-down cottage in a quiet street in the village of Laniscat. And it doesn't feel the least cramped; every inch of space has been used to simple, stylish effect. Ceramic tiles cover the open-plan ground floor, a Moroccan rug and bright armchairs add colour; diminutive windows are hung with cream cotton tatting done by Julie's great aunt; a tiny, perfect kitchen is tucked under the stairs. Bedroom and bathroom are up in the beamed roof space where Julie's paintings decorate the walls and the low bed, flanked by niche lights, is covered with gingham. Admire Jez's expert carpentry on the bath panelling (but don't expect to lie full stretch in the bath: it's three-quarter size). You'll like Julie and Jez. They're ex-teachers and live five minutes away. If you want to avoid going in search of restaurants in nearby Gouarec, you may book a vegetarian meal with them. This is a terrific place for a couple – though not if you're at all creaky. Listen to the church bells and enjoy the lavender in the garden. *Sawday B&B also. Meals on request.*

Price	£175-£275 per week; €60 per day.
Sleeps	2.
Rooms	1 double; 1 bathroom.
Closed	Never.

Julie & Jez Rooke
Laniscat, Côtes-d'Armor
Tel   +33 (0)2 96 36 98 34
Email   jezrooke@hotmail.com
Web   www.phoneinsick.co.uk

Brittany

Le Manoir du Neveit - Hydrangea Cottage

It was love at first sight when Carolyn and Steve discovered the 16th-century manor house, slumbering virtually unseen in the green heart of the Côtes d'Armor, a marvellously bucolic spot. The gîte is attached to the house, with a private gravelled area outside and views that spread over open countryside to forested hills. Inside is an open-plan space of terracotta floors and painted wood or limed walls, two squishy sofas, a new pine dining table and six rush-seated chairs. No designer pretensions here: the decoration is simple but cheerful, the country kitchen has ochre and white tiles, the china is bright, the saucepans gleam. The shower room is downstairs, the cottagey bedrooms are under the eaves; spotless in their pastel garb, they present lace coverlets and southerly views. Posies of flowers are a thoughtful touch – these generous English hosts have embraced their new life and love to look after their guests. Roam the untamed gardens (there's plenty of planting still to do), pluck the pears from the trees, listen to the birds, soak up the peace. Callac is a three-mile drive. *B&B also.*

Price	€375-€695 per week.
Sleeps	6.
Rooms	3: 2 doubles, 1 bunk room; 1 shower room, separate wc.
Closed	Never.

Steve & Carolyn Sheppard
Duault, Côtes-d'Armor
Tel +33 (0)2 96 21 56 75
Fax +33 (0)2 96 21 56 75
Email stephen.sheppard@wanadoo.fr
Web www.lemanoir-duneveit.com

Entry 90 Map 2

Manoir Le Cosquer

A lake with its own small island, a rose garden, lawns, a copse… the seven-acre grounds of this majestic stone manor are full of enticements. The house, some of it 15th century, is reached via a tree-lined avenue; the baker's is a stroll. The two guest wings divide easily for a big family or two groups of friends: two entrances, two staircases, one of them Louis XIV. Some bedrooms are in the oldest part of the house, others are more modern, furniture is a good mix of both. The big top-floor Hirondelle suite looks out over the garden to the fields beyond and children love the space in the other attic bedrooms. A glorious Breton fireplace dominates one end of the vast sitting room; then there's a reading area, a good-shaped dining room with another open fireplace and garden views, and a farmhouse kitchen with modern appliances, a range cooker and… an open fireplace. Oak and chestnut beams give character, the landscaped park calls you to sunset drinks, the active will find a fitness room, badminton, table tennis, games galore. *B&B when not rented. Catering, cleaning and babysitting available.*

Price	£2,625-£3,590 per week.
Sleeps	12-18.
Rooms	6: 2 doubles, 1 twin, 1 room with 2 singles & bunks, 1 family room for 3, 1 family room for 5; 2 baths, 4 showers.
Closed	Never.

Alison Sinclair & Mauro Leccacorvi
Pommerit le Vicomte, Côtes-d'Armor

Tel	+33 (0)2 96 21 74 12
Fax	+33 (0)2 96 21 74 12
Email	lecosquer@tiscali.fr
Web	www.lecosquer.com

Brittany

Ti-Koad

The charming Coquendeaus built this high-tech little house five years ago on the far side of their pretty, sloping, shrub-filled garden with views to the sea. Walls, steps, decking: it is all warmly woody, as is the summer house for fishing nets and bikes. The ground floor is coolly tiled, white-beamed and open plan, there's a fresh, modern feel and the attention to detail is impressive – from the welcome pack with Breton cider to the electric blinds. Up an open-tread spiral staircase are two shipshape bedrooms with a nautical air; open the windows and you can sniff the sea. Nicely painted floors, high rafters, excellent beds and a small dressing room between the rooms; *tout simple*. Downstairs is the bathroom, gorgeous with twin zinc basins, matching driftwood mirrors and big shower, and there's a laundry in the basement. The house is beautifully planned, has a wood-burner for cosy winter nights and is perfect for a civilised holiday by the sea. Visit the gannets on Les Sept Îles, hire a boat from the yacht club and enjoy the seafood – your helpful hosts have all the info. *B&B also.*

Price	€595–€895. €476 for 2 (low season only). Prices per week.
Sleeps	4 + cot.
Rooms	2: 1 double, 1 twin; 1 shower room.
Closed	Never.

Monsieur & Madame Coquendeau
Perros-Guirec, Côtes-d'Armor

Tel	+33 (0)2 96 91 15 61
Fax	+33 (0)2 96 23 08 90
Email	coquendeaucy@wanadoo.fr
Web	perso.orange.fr/yvonnick.coquendeau

À la Corniche

The ever-changing light of the great bay shimmers in through your big windows. Sit in your armchair and gaze as the boats go by, or walk to the beautiful sands and waters of Trestriguel beach – it's ten minutes away. The village is close too. Marie-Clo does B&B in the big house; attentive and generous, she has decorated your teensy white cottage in soft blues and lemons, enlivened with her own patchwork and embroideries, provided DVD and games for rainy days. On one floor you have the open-plan sitting/dining room, a diminutive well-provided kitchen behind, and more radiant views from the little bedroom. Furniture is fresh and new and in keeping with the house; the bed is pine, the dining chairs blue with painted birds. Outside, you have your own patch of garden with small terrace, barbecue and lawn. Set out for walks along the pink granite coast, make the most of the seafood restaurants and Breton crêperies and be sure not to miss the Sept Îles archipelago – the most magnificent seabird colony in France. *Cot & highchair available. Use of owner's washing machine. Easy parking behind. Sawday B&B.*

Price	€600 per week.
Sleeps	2-4 + cot.
Rooms	1 double, 1 sofabed in sitting room; 1 shower room, separate wc.
Closed	Never.

Marie-Clotilde Biarnès
Perros Guirec, Côtes-d'Armor
Tel   +33 (0)2 96 23 28 08
Mobile   +33 (0)6 81 23 15 49
Email   marieclo.biarnes@wanadoo.fr
Web   perso.wanadoo.fr/corniche/

Villa Germiny - Gîtes I & II

On a small side road that winds its way along the coastline, surrounded by tall pines and cypresses, the villa faces west overlooking the lovely Sables Blancs beach: the sunsets will glow through you. The garden is more English than French, the climate is warm – roses, lilies and lavender grow in profusion. On the lower ground floor, the gîtes have French windows to private terraces and views over garden and coastline. Breton landscapes hang on freshly-painted walls, the brown leather sofas are comfortable, the tiled floors are great for sand-filled feet back from an afternoon at the beach. Bedrooms, too, are simple, with pale-painted panelling, no shortage of storage space, firmly comfortable mattresses, lace curtains for privacy. Bathrooms are white, good new kitchens have cheerful china, and modern comforts include central heating and WiFi. In the villa above live the owners, friendly, warm and well-travelled, happy to prepare a light meal for your arrival – just ask. Locquirec, a charming seaside village, rejoices in an excellent brasserie as well as several restaurants and crêperies.

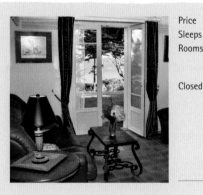

Price	€430-€750 per week.
Sleeps	Gîte I: 4-5. Gîte II: 2-3.
Rooms	Gîte I: 1 double, 1 twin; 1 bathroom, sofabed.
	Gîte II: 1 double; 1 bathroom, sofabed.
Closed	Mid-May to mid-September.

Comte & Comtesse Hubert de Germiny
Locquirec, Finistère
Tel	+33 (0)2 98 67 47 11
Fax	+33 (0)2 98 67 47 11
Email	villagerminy@hotmail.com
Web	www.villagerminy.com

L'Écurie - Manoir de Coat Amour

Surrounded by 12 lush acres of ancient oak, lime trees, sequoia, Japanese maple and orchard, you could be on a country estate. But no, Morlaix, its bustling port and medieval streets, are a five-minute drive; the only clue is distant traffic hum. The converted stables of a 19th-century manor house, all one level and wheelchair friendly, are your introduction to country-style living; the soft, sober colours, the space and the light lend a low-key luxury. In the beamed, open-plan living area are oriental rugs on tiled floors, cream leather sofas, antique pine, a polished dining table and a winter fire. A bar separates the new and well-equipped kitchen. Airy, sunny bedrooms have good-quality curtains and bedspreads; big windows overlook the grounds; one room has French windows onto a terrace. Bathrooms are traditional, one designed for disabled guests. Explore the fishing ports, the beaches, the nature reserves, and Brest. Return to a shady spot to read, a dip in the pool and an evening stroll in a green paradise. *Shared pool. Sawday B&B.*

Price	€650-€1,400 per week.
Sleeps	7.
Rooms	3: 1 double, 1 twin, 1 room with bunks & single bed; 1 shower room, 1 bathroom, separate wc.
Closed	Rarely.

Stafford & Jenny Taylor
Morlaix, Finistère

Tel	+33 (0)2 98 88 57 02
Fax	+33 (0)2 98 88 57 02
Email	stafford.taylor@wanadoo.fr
Web	www.gites-morlaix.com

La Maison du Jardinier

The old gardener's cottage was used as a guard post during World War II; aircraft drawings still fly in the bedroom. Your newly renovated, upside-down gîte (salon upstairs, luxurious bedroom down) comes with a modern glass extension and views over 12 acres filled with rare trees. It's a successful blend of old and new – a 'boutique gîte', a doll's house for two, a bit of a gem. Up the steps, enter a small elegant living room with soft green walls and gardener-green checks, a wood-burner for a winter stay, an antique table and a dresser in walnut, a sleek grey-green kitchen with every modern thing. It would be a delight to cook here but there's also table d'hôtes in the main house – the owners are charming – and even a local company to deliver fresh meals to the door. You have your own secluded terrace with barbecue, and landscaped grounds and summer pool to share. There's croquet on the lawn, a decorated chapel for reflection, restaurants, shops and market in beautiful Morlaix (within strolling distance) and beaches and oyster farms a short drive away. *Shared pool Sawday B&B. Meals on request.*

Price	€410-€750 per week.
Sleeps	2-4.
Rooms	1 double; 1 shower, sofabed.
Closed	Rarely.

Stafford & Jenny Taylor
Morlaix, Finistère

Tel	+33 (0)2 98 88 57 02
Fax	+33 (0)2 98 88 57 02
Email	stafford.taylor@wanadoo.fr
Web	www.gites-morlaix.com

  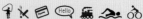

Le Manoir de Prévasy

You enter through tall oak doors onto flagstones and gaze up the wonderful old staircase, timeworn and creaky. This stunningly renovated 16th-century manor is clearly a house of character, not too grand or precious, with huge fireplaces and curtains that show off the stone. The new kitchen/dining room is a revelation, light streams in from three tall windows and the feeling of space, the potential for convivial evenings around the enormous Morbihan chopping block, make you want to linger. Sam has repainted and started refurbishing the good old bedrooms, the slightly dated bathrooms are to be revamped in 2008. It feels like a large country house – antiques, gilt, silks, old polished floors, coffee-table books – with touches of glamour such as the huge fawn modern sofas round the fire and the balled glass lamps. A rural idyll laden with history: wherever you look are remains of old terraces and fortified walls – what a story these stones could tell. The chapel is in ruins, badminton is played in the old graveyard, a secret passage is rumoured. Fascinating, fun, and perfect for large groups.

Price	£600–£1,700 per week.
Sleeps	House 8-12. Cottage 2.
Rooms	House: 2 doubles, 2 twins, 1 family room for 6; 4 bathrooms, 1 shower room, separate wc. Cottage: 1 twin; 1 shower room.
Closed	Never.

	Sam Sudderth
	Carhaix Plouguer, Finistère
Tel	+1 305 915 9025
Mobile	+1 305 915 9025
Email	samsudds@gmail.com
Web	www.prevasy.com

Brittany

Guillec Vihan

In a wooded valley deep in the Breton countryside is a cluster of farm buildings, a lazy river winding through the fields below. It's all part of Robbie and Fiona's 50-hectare arable farm: a lively, sociable place to bring the family! Their own children and grandchildren are often around, plus seven cats, one dog and an assortment of horses. Close by is another gîte and the Rainbirds' own house – there's always something going on. The cottage, recently restored, has traditional stone doorways and oak window frames. Fiona has an eye for a dramatic effect, coupled with an interest in the past. In the kitchen/dining room, rush-seated chairs pull up around an oil-clothed table; upstairs, the dormer-windowed bedrooms are star-spangled. The ground-floor double, ideal for the less mobile, has a huge canopied bed, an old armoire and a hand-painted mural. On one side of the cottage is a gravelled terrace, on the other a big lawn; everywhere, climbing roses and clematis – Fiona loves her garden. One of Robbie's passions is tractors (you'll hear the odd rumble), another is restoring old cars.

Price	€325-€665 per week.
Sleeps	6.
Rooms	3: 1 double, 2 twins; 2 bathrooms.
Closed	Never.

Robbie & Fiona Rainbird
Collorec, Finistère

Tel	+33 (0)2 98 73 93 60
Fax	+33 (0)2 98 73 93 60
Email	info@rainbird-gites.com
Web	www.rainbird-gites.com

Ty Bois - Rosnoen

Leaving tiny hamlets behind, you're on the track leading down to the river; then a very steep climb up, through a lovely garden lined with agapanthus flowers. The wooden chalet at the summit, modestly fringed by forest trees that conceal a tennis court, sits on the last remaining river plot in the Parc Régional d'Armorique. No wonder the window in the main bedroom is huge! Minimalist bedrooms are decorated with panache: deep purple blushes against neutral tones, piles of large linen pillows on French brocante beds, glimpses of baroque fabric. Big bathrooms downstairs exude a luxurious simplicity. The sociable ground floor also embraces kitchen, dining area and salon in alpine fashion, with splashes of funkiness in artwork and pouffes. The compact, perfectly equipped kitchen has grey-painted cupboards and trim zinc surfaces. Claire and Andrew provide a welcome pack as exceptional as the rest, live nearby and are on hand whenever you need them. The Crozon peninsula is worth exploring; leave the car behind and take the boat or kayak out instead. Fabulous.

Price	£495-£1,250 per week.
Sleeps	6.
Rooms	3: 2 doubles, 1 twin/double; 1 bath, 1 shower.
Closed	Never.

Claire Bernard
Rosnoen, Finistère

Tel	+33 (0)2 98 55 29 26
Mobile	+33 (0)6 87 01 56 15
Email	info@frenchberry.fr
Web	www.frenchberry.fr

Brittany

Ty Traez

Even within the masterly seclusion of high stone garden walls, at 300 paces you can smell the sea. Trust Claire to find this family *maison de maître*, tucked into a Breton hamlet with open views of sea-fields; the inside is equally impressive. Slip into the languid ease of long draping linen and voile curtains brushing against neutral walls and natural matting. Venerable beds – one with re-formed shutters for a headboard – are too good to resist. Local artisans made blush-red shelves for the zinc and wood kitchen, and brought similar genius to bathrooms. Modern sofas dance with antique bergère armchairs on quarry-tiled floors, to the amusement of stately armoires; seashells are piled high in glass vases and there's a lovely log fire for the winter. Send fidgeting children to the converted attic with table tennis and huge cushions. And as the nightly ocean breeze tickles candles in their mounts, old sea prints jostle with younger pictures – do they know Pointe du Raz is the most westerly point on the European mainland? All this, and delicious seafood in a pretty Audierne restaurant.

Price	£495–£1,450 per week.
Sleeps	8.
Rooms	5: 3 doubles, 2 singles; 3 bathrooms.
Arrival	Friday.
Closed	Rarely.

Claire Bernard
Primelin, Finistère

Tel	+33 (0)2 98 55 29 26
Mobile	+33 (0)6 87 01 56 15
Email	info@frenchberry.fr
Web	www.frenchberry.fr

Entry 100 Map 2

The Gatehouse

The art of good living is no book title, it's this charming stone cottage gatehouse in the heart of Brittany. Built in the 19th century to serve the fairytale château of Kistinic, the cottage's young interior belies its history. A luxurious minimalism is on display here, with a good dose of joie de vivre thrown in. Emerging from indulgent bedding and stepping onto polished wooden floors is a fine way to start the day, as is discovering a spacious bathroom with natural stone flooring. Claire and Andrew love it when families stay – and this cottage is made for easy living, with its uncluttered, glass-chandeliered sitting and dining area and its smartly equipped kitchen. Wonder, too, at the setting... No surprise to learn that Claire once researched locations for television productions. Run reckless through the rhododendrons – as the azaleas and camellias do – growing among enough woodland and lawns to cause delusions of grandeur from your bedroom window. Swim in the infinity pool, explore historic Quimper, follow the winding trails through the woods. C'est magique! *Whole château available (sleeps 12).*

Price	£350-£825 per week.
Sleeps	5.
Rooms	3: 2 doubles, 1 twin; 2 bathrooms.
Closed	Rarely.

Claire Bernard
Quimper, Finistère

Tel	+33 (0)2 98 55 29 26
Mobile	+33 (0)6 87 01 56 15
Email	info@frenchberry.fr
Web	www.frenchberry.fr

Brittany

Cap Coz

How clean, small and timid you look among your neighbours, Cap Coz... All the better to reveal myself slowly, as more pretty rooms open under your exploring eye. Beyond the white façade is a light and refreshingly simple up-to-date interior with a mixture of antique and modern furniture and some bright abstract paintings. Cap Coz is a most welcoming, child-friendly place set in a grassy embrace, fenced and safe and rejoicing in pines, palms and mature shrubs, a well maintained lawn and a stone terrace. Here you find good wooden furniture, the barbecue and a spare table for children to paint or beat their plasticine on. The front gives onto the small road to the beach and the downstairs bedroom is double-glazed. The cheerful décor is soft-coloured striped seaside style; collections of shells, Moya's father's model boats and her sister's paintings make it deeply personal. Add plenty of storage, unpretentious family bathrooms, a super new kitchen, the coastal path and sailing school just down the road and you have a great-value family seaside house. The owners leave you a fine Breton welcome.

Price	£330-£925 per week.
Sleeps	8-9.
Rooms	5: 2 doubles, 1 twin, 1 single, 1 room with bunks; 1 bathroom, 1 shower room.
Arrival	Flexible.
Closed	Never.

Moya Connell
Fouesnant, Finistère

Tel	+44 (0)1428 642 535
Email	moya@house-hire.com
Web	www.house-hire.com

Château du Quengo - Le Petit Quengo

This may not be luxurious living but the place oozes authenticity and charm. Four centuries old, overlooking a pigeonnier that has been beautifully restored, the gîte at Quengo takes up two floors of the old coach house and feeds into the stables – now a games room – complete with original wood panelling and wrought-iron hayracks. The upstairs was used for drying hemp… you can still see the holes for the hanging poles in the trusses. Step into a sprawling, open-plan living space with fantastic beams above and sofas and easy chairs below, an old trunk for a coffee table, horse prints on the walls, small lamps for atmosphere, a cupboard on the landing for books and games. Nothing looks shabby or out of place. Up the stairs are patterned duvets on comfy beds and wooden floors warmed by big rugs, masses of storage, big bathrooms and two sloping ceilings. Families will adore the outdoor space and the swings, the friendly Leonberg mountain dog, the organic potager, the restaurant you can walk to and the owners who greet you like long lost friends. A deeply eco-friendly place. *Sawday B&B. Unfenced water.*

Price	€410-€750 per week. Heating extra.
Sleeps	11.
Rooms	4: 2 doubles, 1 triple, 1 quadruple; 2 bathrooms.
Closed	Never

	Anne & Alfred du Crest de Lorgerie
	Irodouër, Ille-et-Vilaine
Tel	+33 (0)2 99 39 81 47
Email	lequengo@hotmail.com
Web	www.chateauduquengo.com

Entry 103 Map 4

Le Bois Coudrais - Bakery, Granary, Mills One & Two

Claire and Philippe manage the impossible: their little hamlet feels miles from anywhere yet there's masses going on. A campsite, pool, play areas, bicycles, café/bar, animals to feed – among private patios and shady trees. Beyond lie woodland walks and countryside. The four gîtes – converted farm outbuildings, three linked, one detached – are prettily grouped near the pool, close enough for the children to make friends but distant enough for privacy. Cosy, characterful and homely, with beams, exposed stonework and granite fireplaces, the open-plan living areas have simple furniture, earthy coloured rugs on tiled floors, companionable wood-burning stoves, and compact kitchens suitable for holiday meals. Whitewashed walls, laminate floors and pretty fabrics make the most of the small, slopey-ceiling bedrooms. The Yberts are energetic, enterprising people and will steer you towards the many nearby historic towns, castles, zoos, aquariums, markets and, of course, Emerald Coast beaches. This place is about having fun, making friends and relaxing out of doors. *Shared pool.*

Price	€205-€684 (£140-£475) per week.
Sleeps	Bakery, Mill Two & Granary 4. Mill One 4-5.
Rooms	Bakery, Mill Two & Granary: each 1 double, 1 twin; 1 shower. Mill One: 1 double, 1 triple; 1 shower.
Arrival	Saturday, but flexible.
Closed	Never.

Claire & Philippe Ybert
Cuguen, Ille-et-Vilaine
Tel   +33 (0)2 99 73 27 45
Email   cpybert@wanadoo.fr
Web   www.vacancebretagne.com

Les Chouettes, Les Alouettes & Les Hirondelles

To stay or to go? So much to do here, and so much to discover beyond! In rolling fields-and-woodland countryside, these cottages are perfectly placed for families. Breton beaches, adventure park, zoo, aquarium and Mont Saint Michel are all within driving distance; and there are free bikes and walks from the door. In two acres of lawned gardens, with trampoline, swings and slides, football and boules *and* fabulous heated pool, this sprawling row of farm buildings goes right back to the 17th century. Inside you have the best of country cottage living: thick walls, exposed beams, steep wooden stairs (in very old Les Hirondelles), cosy rugs on tiled floors. Bedrooms (upstairs and down) have fresh colours and simple wooden furniture; bathrooms are practical and spacious. A joy are the open-plan living areas where everyone can do their thing – cook, read, play. It's home-from-home comfy with kitchens that are functional and well equipped. Chouettes has a wood-burner; Alouettes an open fire; rustic Hirondelles is the most compact. Susan loves children and is endlessly helpful. Come for a weekend – or longer.

Price	£210–£1,800 per week.
Sleeps	Chouettes 12. Alouettes 6-8. Hirondelles 4.
Rooms	Chouettes: 3 doubles, 1 bunk room, 2 twins; 1 bath, 1 shower. Alouettes: 2 doubles, 1 quadruple; 1 shower, 2 separate wcs. Hirondelles: 1 double, 1 bunk room; 1 shower.

Susan Hazelwood
Tremblay, Ille-et-Vilaine

Tel	+33 (0)2 99 97 74 20
Email	susan.hazelwood@wanadoo.fr
Web	www.brittany-cottages.co.uk

Brittany

Le Gohic

Chocolate-box pretty, this private hamlet is too good to be true. A cluster of deep-roofed stone cottages, wrapped around with plants and flowering shrubs, it will be found down a lane in the lush Blavet valley. Secluded and generous, it would be brilliant for family get-togethers with its heated pool, playground and teenage den full of games, as well as bicycles and grassy woodland for pottering around in. Or you'll come to make friends with strangers in this cosy set-up: the five cottages sleep a total of 30 and l'Écurie's huge sitting/dining room even seats 30 for dinner. Open-plan living areas are cottage-pretty with oak beams, deep fireplaces, plaster and stone walls, welcoming sofas and rustic Breton pieces. Nothing fussy, nothing precious, parents can rest easy. Kitchens and bathrooms are neat and functional while bedrooms are simple and quaint. Some cottages have French windows, all have terraces and small gardens. Shops are a five-minute drive and Robin and Sheila are brimming with ideas for walks, markets, beaches. Why not explore the coast in their skippered boat?

Price	Cidre: £255-£725. Puits £295-£795. Principale & Écurie: £360-£1,075. Mairie: £465-£1,445. Whole hamlet £1,740-£5,075.
Sleeps	Cidre 4. Puits, Principale & Écurie 6. Mairie 8.
Rooms	Cidre; 1 double, 1 twin, 1 bathroom. Puits, Écurie, Principale: each 1 double, 2 twins; 1 bathroom, separate wc. Mairie: 2 doubles, 2 twins; 2 bathrooms.

Robin Berwick
Quistinic, Morbihan

Tel	+33 (0)2 97 39 76 28
Email	robin.berwick@wanadoo.fr
Web	www.cottagesofbrittany.com

Le Rhun - Four Gîtes

Your children will tumble out of the car and head for the sandpit, swings and small pool, or volleyball, basketball and boules. For grown-ups, there are shady hammocks and a sauna. Family-friendly, easy-going, this lovely German couple have done a high-class renovation job on their cluster of Breton outbuildings – and with two B&B rooms as well as four gîtes, the farmstead becomes a lively place in the holidays. Rooms are simply furnished, colours light and fresh, kitchens modern and well-equipped and everyone gets a terrace and a garden. The ground floors are open-plan; the cooking areas are tucked into a corner or quite separate. You have tiled floors, white walls and beamed ceilings, perhaps an old armoire, a stone table or a drawing by Jurgen's cousin to add an individual touch. Bedrooms feel Scandinavian – pale, uncluttered spaces with shots of colour from curtain or headboard; bathrooms are clean and functional. Cows graze next door, the little lake attracts birds and there are five acres to explore. Beyond: beaches, the castle at Pontivy and canoeing on the river Blavet. *Sawday B&B.*

Price	€242–€553 per week. Linen not included.
Sleeps	4 gîtes: 1 for 2; 2 for 4; 1 for 6.
Rooms	Gîtes One & Two: 2 doubles; 1 shower room. Gîte Three: 1 double; 1 shower room. Gîte Four: 3 doubles; 1 bathroom, 1 shower room.
Closed	October-April.

Eva & Jürgen Lincke
Pluméliau, Morbihan

Tel   +33 (0)2 97 51 83 48
Fax   +33 (0)2 97 51 83 48
Email   eva.lincke@web.de
Web   www.lerhun.de

Western Loire • Loire Valley

Le Relais de la Rinière

You're surrounded by vines: this is Muscadet country and the clay soils of the area produce some particularly ambitious wines. Indulge in some private tastings in the owners' garden – a cocktail of wisteria, lawns and colourful surprises (and great play equipment for children). Or pop off to one of the nearby *caves*. You'll like your delightful hosts who do B&B in the imposing coaching inn next door; Louis was a baker, Françoise is a keen jam-maker, and they've moved here from Normandy. Your two-storey cottage is a converted outbuilding with its own little garden. In a spacious and sunny living area with a well-equipped kitchen, a fine armoire guards pretty crockery, there's an oak table for family gatherings and a sofa with a bright throw. Up steep wooden stairs is a loft room decorated in white and blue – perfect for children. The downstairs double, its beams painted blue, has the original bread oven. Discover historic Nantes, with its splendid 18th-century houses and its château, or visit the slick wine museum at Le Pallet. There's great cycling, too. *Sawday B&B.*

Price	€220–€450 per week.
Sleeps	4-5.
Rooms	2: 1 double, 1 twin (double beds) with sofabed; 1 shower room; extra futon.
Closed	Never.

Françoise & Louis Lebarillier
Le Landreau, Loire-Atlantique

Tel	+33 (0)2 40 06 41 44
Fax	+33 (0)2 51 13 10 52
Email	riniere@netcourrier.com
Web	www.riniere.com

Entry 108 Map 3

La Besnardière

Scuttling chickens, fresh eggs for breakfast, ducks on the pond, a few goats, a donkey: a wholesome feeling of being 'down on the farm'. It's close to Baugé yet acres of woodland – a carpet of flowers in the spring – poplar trees and fields are all you can see. Delightful Joyce has turned the farmhouse into a B&B and the stabling into a super gîte – a bright, sunny space of exposed beams, timbers and terracotta. Roof windows flood the upper rooms with light, bedrooms are jolly affairs with colourful covers and rugs, simple wooden furniture and modern lamps; shower rooms are neat and spotless. Relax in the sitting room or discover the sunny spot on the landing with its little seats. There's a holiday mood in the kitchen, a quirky room of mismatched china, scrubbed wooden table and the original hayrack; not state-of-the-art but all you need to rustle up a meal. Or let Joyce cook you a vegetarian meal – organic produce from her garden – and eat under the stars. Loire châteaux, local markets, swimming in the lake at La Flèche; a super place for families. *Aromatherapy treatments available. Sawday B&B. Meals on request.*

Price	€450-€500 per week.
Sleeps	4-7 + cot.
Rooms	2: 1 double, 1 quadruple; 3 shower rooms, sofabed.
Closed	January-February.

Joyce Rimell
Fougeré, Maine-et-Loire

Tel	+33 (0)2 41 90 15 20
Fax	+33 (0)2 41 90 15 20
Email	rimell.joyce@wanadoo.fr
Web	www.holidays-loire.com

Logis de la Roche Corbin

On the 'old-town' side of the Loire at Angers, a secret, special place. The couple behind this hugely sympathetic restoration of a 16th-century house are Michael, an American painter, and Pascale from Paris, who move out for two months every summer, entrusting guests with their charming home. The house is on the corner of a medieval street whose high wall opens to a courtyard garden with a cobbled path, a climbing rose, a sweet box hedge and a bunch of lettuces to keep the tortoise happy. From the first-floor living room – reached via a magnificent old rough-hewn oak staircase – the view sweeps down the hill and over to the younger side of town. It is a big light room with a polished terracotta floor, an open fire, an eclectic mix of old and new furniture, a coffee table made from recycled boards on a wrought-iron base. Be charmed by bedrooms with fine ceiling beams, some sloping, ultra-contemporary bathrooms, a big kitchen with good oak cupboards, a walled garden with a round blue table. A splendid house in a small but dynamic town; borrow the bikes and explore. *Shared pool. Sawday B&B.*

Price	£820 per week.
Sleeps	6.
Rooms	4: 2 doubles, 2 twins; 3 bathrooms.
Closed	Available for rental July & August only.

Michael & Pascale Rogosin
Angers, Maine-et-Loire

Tel	+33 (0)2 41 86 93 70
Fax	+33 (0)2 41 86 93 70
Email	logisdelaroche@wanadoo.fr
Web	www.logisdelaroche.com

Western Loire

Les Bouchets

The best of both worlds: deep in the countryside – a gentle Loire landscape of copses and fields, orchards and vines – yet two miles from town. Baugé has shops, restaurants, a twice-weekly market, tennis and a pool. Madame is proud of her house and her rooms, welcomes you with a drink and a full basket of goodies and recommends you join her table d'hôtes at least once. It would be a pity not to: she and her husband had a restaurant in Angers and now hold cookery courses on certain weekends. Your farmhouse (once their own holiday home) is next to theirs and your garden is safe for the children to play in; at the end of a no-through road, the rolling countryside spreads in every direction. Inside it feels generous, roomy, tidy and in tip-top condition; the house's history is most evident in the kitchen's large open *four à pain*. Gleaming reproduction furniture mixes with the odd antique, the 'cons' are 'mod' but the feel is traditional and bedrooms sit cosily under the roof. The bathroom is newly furbished and, like all the rest, it is spacious and spotless. *Sawday B&B. Meals on request.*

Price	€370-€430 per week. Linen, heating not included
Sleeps	6-7 + cot.
Rooms	3: 1 double, 1 twin, 1 family room for 3; 1 bathroom.
Closed	Never.

Michel & Géraldine Bignon
Le Vieil Baugé, Maine-et-Loire

Tel	+33 (0)2 41 82 34 48
Mobile	+33 (0)6 71 60 66 05
Email	bignonm@wanadoo.fr
Web	www.lesbouchets.com

Le Studio

A tiny stone cabin in a big leafy garden, one cleverly arranged space for two with all the bits you could need – sitting, sleeping, cooking, eating, washing – in perfect, pretty order. The beams are really old, the kitchen is brand new, as are all the fittings and furniture, two intriguingly shaped original windows look out onto the lily pond – whose frogs eat all the bugs – and the front door opens to views of the meadow where the Clarkes' two horses graze (their owners are keen carriage drivers). It's as bucolic and secluded as you could wish. Behind your little den is a deck and a patch of private garden with table, chairs and barbecue while the solar-heated pool, shared with the owners and their B&B guests, is beyond the hedge. There's a hot tub, too. Should you need entertainment in your own space, there are board games, a CD player, even satellite television. Or borrow a couple of bikes and explore the lush countryside, dash to the village bakery for treats, push on to Baugé market for proper shopping. *Shared pool. B&B also.*

Price	£180–£350 per week.	
Sleeps	2-4.	
Rooms	1 double; 1 shower room, separate wc, sofabed.	
Arrival	Saturday July & August. Flexible other months.	
Closed	Rarely.	

Joan & Peter Clarke
Auverse, Maine-et-Loire
Tel   +33 (0)2 41 82 11 84
Fax   +33 (0)2 41 82 11 84
Email   joan@theloireaffair.co.uk
Web   www.theloireaffair.co.uk

La Chouannière - La Cabane

Your gîte is an observation studio from Russia! Twenty square metres of wooden sturdiness, furnished with a sitting area and a kitchenette, a ship's bed behind curtains, a small power shower, a balcony for al fresco meals, and views for the wildlife: birds, boar, game, deer. Lamb's wool insulates the walls, hemp the floors, the bed wears bright colours to match the curtains that Madame has made, an espadrille dangles above, guarding a torch, and there's an antique portmanteau trunk so you may hang up your frocks. These smiley, generous hosts, Gilles and Patricia, do table d'hôtes in the old stables; stay for delicious dinner, then take a stroll round the woodland garden, complete with old pigeonnier and new bakery — Gilles makes croissants, pastries, brioche and bread. Pâtés, rillettes, aperitifs and jams are homemade too, and there's a summer kitchen for you to share. Walking and biking tours start from the door; trails run through the forests and past the wildlife ponds into the Anjou. And the bubbles of the jacuzzi will entice you home. *Sawday B&B. Meals on request.*

Price	€525 per week. €70 per night in low season (minimum 4 days).
Sleeps	2.
Rooms	1 double; 1 shower.
Arrival	Flexible in low season.
Closed	January.

Patricia & Gilles Patrice
Brion, Maine-et-Loire
Tel   +33 (0)2 41 80 21 74
Fax   +33 (0)2 41 80 21 74
Email   chouanniere@loire-passion.com
Web   www.loire-passion.com

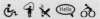

Manoir des Rosiers

Rosemary and Richard are new to running chambres d'hôte and gîte – they do it well! Rosemary is a passionate cook, makes her own jams, once sold antiques and has an eye for classic pieces; both love their guests. Your solid stone house – possibly the original stables – sits in the manoir's garden. Step into a large and luminous living space with white beams above and rosy tomettes below, stunning stone fireplace and cream stone walls, early 19th-century fauteuils and elegant antique mirrors. The neatly contemporary white and wood kitchen is tucked into one end of the dining room where dove-grey ladderback chairs encircle the dining table, topped by a chandelier. The country-fresh minimalism reaches upstairs, to snowy linen under characterful old beams, whitewashed floors, muslin drapes and baths incorporated into bedrooms. Outside is your own little knot garden, sweet, safe, secluded and furnished with twirly French chairs. Such tranquillity – and if you seek company, wander off to the pool. Or the orchard where Rosemary's hens range. *B&B also.*

Price	€490–€1,120 per week.
Sleeps	4-6.
Rooms	2: 1 four-poster, 1 twin, 1 sofabed; 2 bathrooms, 1 shower.
Arrival	Flexible.
Closed	Rarely.

Rosemary Conquest
Noyant la Plaine, Maine-et-Loire
Tel +33 (0)2 41 51 38 14
Mobile +33 (0)6 65 70 87 50
Email rosemary@manoirdesrosiers.com
Web www.manoirdesrosiers.com

Western Loire

Manoir du Buisson Perron

A crunchy drive sweeps through gates to a perfectly proportioned, creamy façade. Despite its elegance, this 18th-century manor does not intimidate; it's the Tarrades' family home. (They move between house and cottage according to the let.) Rooms are big, friendly and lightly furnished with antiques: Arnauld is an antiques dealer. Step through the door and you're swept into the kitchen/dining room: beams, polished tile floor, big dressers, a range in the fireplace and a candelabra over the table. There are plenty of places to relax: a light-filled salon of comfortable chairs and paintings, a magnificently beamed billiard room, a snug study. No-one will feel outdone in the bedroom stakes; choose a Venetian bed, a four-poster or a Louis XVI-style room with exposed stone walls. Children will love their sunny room with its toys, books and funny pictures. Modern bathrooms are slipped into beautifully timbered rooms. With utility rooms, twice-weekly cleaning, pool, patio, huge garden and helpful, cultured hosts nearby, this is a terrific place for family or friends' gatherings. *Shared pool.*

Price	€2,400-€3,800 per week, including cleaning.
Sleeps	10.
Rooms	5: 3 doubles, 1 twin, 1 suite; 4 bathrooms, 1 shower room.
Closed	Never.

Arnauld & Annick Tarrade
Saumur, Maine-et-Loire

Tel	+33 (0)2 41 51 00 52
Mobile	+33 (0)6 08 77 49 34
Email	arnauld-tarrade@wanadoo.fr
Web	www.saumurfrance.com

Manoir du Buisson Perron - La Petite Maison

A cosy retreat in the bountiful grounds of the manor where you can choose privacy or company. Spread over the ground floor of an 18th-century stone cottage, your rooms overlook gardens or rich farmland and combine a simple elegance with traditional charm. The beamed sitting room, with a sofabed for a child or an extra couple, opens into a sunny dining room lightly furnished with 20th-century antiques. A well-equipped open kitchen is tucked into the corner while French windows leading out onto a pretty patio. The small bedroom is stylishly arranged in olive and burgundy with painted furniture and soft lighting while the good-sized bathroom has pretty touches of flowers and scent bottles, although sofabed sleepers must cross the bedroom to reach it. Wander where you will; behind the gracious manor is a pool and large garden with bosky corners for snoozing. The owners, an artistic, interesting and helpful couple, are happy to chat over a drink or respect your privacy. You are wonderfully placed for Loire Valley vineyards and castles, and restaurants in Saumur – rejoice! *Shared pool.*

Price	€450-€600 per week.
Sleeps	2-4.
Rooms	1 double; 1 bathroom; 1 separate wc, sofabed.
Closed	Never.

Arnauld & Annick Tarrade
Saumur, Maine-et-Loire

Tel	+33 (0)2 41 51 00 52
Mobile	+33 (0)6 08 77 49 34
Email	arnauld-tarrade@wanadoo.fr
Web	www.saumurfrance.com

Entry 116 Map 4

La Maison Aubelle - Tour, Gaudrez & Jardin

A 16th-century nobleman's house in an old country town, Aubelle stands in secluded gardens flanked by high stone walls, renovated by craftsmen and thoughtfully equipped by Peter and Sally. The original apartments are Tour, Jardin and Gaudrez. Tour – in the tower, as you'd expect – is one flight up a spiralling stone stair; it has a beamed living room/kitchen below with trim red sofas and wraparound views. The garden apartment, with terrace, is as neat as a new pin. White-walled Gaudrez has a 16th-century window, discovered during restoration. The feel is airy, relaxing, comfortable; crisp linen, central heating and daily cleaning are included and the quality is superb. There's a terrace and games room for all and an appropriately large pool. If you can't face cooking, let the Smiths do it for you: they whisk up delicious meals five times a week, cheerfully served in the dining room in winter, on the terrace in summer. Peter and Sally are also on hand to advise, translate or leave you in peace. And they run French courses. *Children over 12 welcome. Shared pool & laundry. Meals on request.*

Price	Tour & Gaudrez €945-€1,200 each. Jardin €840-€945. Prices per week, including cleaning. Apartments may be rented together. Minimum 3 days.
Sleeps	Tour & Gaudrez 4. Jardin 2.
Rooms	Tour: 2 doubles; 2 shower rooms. Gaudrez: 2 doubles; 2 shower rooms. Jardin: 1 double; 1 bathroom, separate wc.
Closed	Rarely.

Peter & Sally Smith
Montreuil Bellay, Maine-et-Loire

Tel	+33 (0)2 41 52 36 39
Fax	+33 (0)2 41 50 94 83
Email	maison.aubelle@aubelle.com
Web	www.aubelle.com

La Maison Aubelle - Coach House & Stable

No sooner had the Smiths finished one renovation than they turned their hands to the old stable and coach house. And with aplomb – the exterior and interior are impeccable. Walls are whitewashed or exposed stone, some ceilings slant, there are lovely old beams and attractive new windows. In the old stable the original hayrack graces the sitting room. You'll find the odd country chest, good sofas, heating beneath terracotta floors (winter warmth is guaranteed). In summer, play chess in the lovely, garden, dine on the terrace, meet fellow guests round the pool. There's daily cleaning, fitted kitchens are packed with all mod cons and linen is provided; all you need do is turn up. Venture beyond the walls to discover the last remaining walled town in the region; the three-minute stroll to the château is rewarded by gorgeous watery views of the Thouet. Stretch out a little further and explore Fontevraud Abbey: Eleanor of Aquitaine and Richard the Lion Heart are buried here. *Properties interconnect for same-party bookings. Children over 12 welcome. Shared pool & laundry. Meals on request.*

Price	Coach house €1,050-€1,200. Stable €945-€1,100. Prices per week, including cleaning. Minimum 3 days.
Sleeps	Coach House 4. Stable 2.
Rooms	Coach House: 2 doubles; 2 shower rooms. Stable: 1 double; 1 bathroom, 1 separate wc.
Closed	Rarely.

	Peter & Sally Smith
	Montreuil Bellay, Maine-et-Loire
Tel	+33 (0)2 41 52 36 39
Fax	+33 (0)2 41 50 94 83
Email	maison.aubelle@aubelle.com
Web	www.aubelle.com

Entry 118 Map 4

Château de Salvert - La Brosse & Le Pressoir

Quel château! It's a neo-Gothic masterpiece and these little houses lie deep within its parkland. Handsome, comfortable and a delight to spend time in, both were restored by the indefatigable owners, with deft combinations of old and new. La Brosse is a 14th-century farmhouse, modest but dignified, all stone walls and great oak beams upstairs and down. Old the bedsteads may be, on floors of wood or tomettes, but the mattresses are new, the mats are seagrass and the mood is unexpectedly luxurious. Bathrooms are very 21st-century, some tiled imaginatively with old terracotta, all with old beams and tiny windows, kitchens are big, authentic and well-equipped, furniture is classically French. The swimming pool is a four-minute stroll through the grounds and each house has a private, enclosed garden but you can join forces with your neighbours should you wish. Monsieur is jovial and welcoming, his wife equally friendly and impressively energetic. This is a fine address in an area which is impossibly rich in culture, starting with France's largest Romanesque church in nearby Cunault. *Shared pool. Sawday hotel.*

Price	Brosse €1,500. Pressoir €1,600. Prices per week.
Sleeps	Brosse 6. Pressoir 8.
Rooms	Brosse: 1 double, 2 twins; 1 bathroom, 1 shower room. Pressoir: 1 double, 1 twin, 1 single, 1 triple; 1 bathroom, 1 shower room.
Closed	Never.

Monica Le Pelletier de Glatigny
Neuillé, Maine-et-Loire

Tel	+33 (0)2 41 52 55 89
Fax	+33 (0)2 41 52 55 89
Email	info@salvert.com
Web	www.chateau-de-salvert.fr

Entry 119 Map 4

Le Four de Villeprouvé

Oodles of history and a cranny-filled cottage full of stories and character. It used to be the grain store for the monks in the 15th-century priory nearby, now it's a farm and B&B run by the delightful Christophe and Christine. As well as raising cattle and children and caring for guests, they've miraculously found time to lavish care and attention on this spick-and-span stone house: she sewed the colourful hangings for the antique four-poster, he fashioned a new stair within an old frame. Original features have been kept: stone walls, roof timbers, bread oven; and aged artefacts added: a travelling chest, an old loft ladder, a Corsican settle in which the hens used to lay their eggs. The sitting room and kitchen are cosy with a medieval feel and thoroughly up-to-date equipment; the bathrooms are small. Enjoy a barbecue in the small fenced garden as the children swing, or book in for Christine's wholesome table d'hôtes if the B&B is not full. Ducks paddle in the wildlife pond, cows graze the grass, apples become cider and your hosts are generous and charming. *Sawday B&B. Meals on request.*

Price	€315–€361 per week.
	Linen not included.
Sleeps	4-8.
Rooms	3: 1 double, 1 double on mezzanine,
	1 family room for 4; 2 bathrooms,
	2 separate wcs.
Arrival	Flexible in low season.
Closed	Never.

Christophe & Christine Davenel
Ruille Froid Fonds, Mayenne

Tel	+33 (0)2 43 07 71 62
Fax	+33 (0)2 43 07 71 62
Email	christ.davenel@wanadoo.fr
Web	perso.orange.fr/villeprouve/gite

Les Basses Touches

The Sarthe is one of France's best-kept secrets. Among picture-book meadows, by lilting little rivers, wizened villages wave roses in your eyes and chime their runcible stones in your ears. Les Basses Touches is a plain, solid, totally French family holiday house with all you need for a family with youngsters: space to play and run around in (there's a Wendy house in the big grassy garden), a super attic dormitory, a big kitchen and dining area with a table for meals and a table for games, and an open fireplace for cosy moments in French chairs at the end of the day. You will find good beds, one or two nice pieces of furniture, chenille bedcovers and bathrooms with all the essentials. The house is an ideal base for exploring this gentle country. Nearby Le Mans has twisty old streets and fascinating medieval stained glass. 100km away for easy outings are Angers of the extraordinary tapestries, Saumur with castle and crack cavalry, Chartres, Tours and the Normandy coast. You will come across long-forgotten pastoral scenes, unexpected châteaux and endless lovely picnic spots. *Shops 4km.*

Price	€335-€365 per week. Linen not included.
Sleeps	7.
Rooms	3: 2 doubles, 1 triple; 1 bathroom, 1 shower room, separate wc.
Closed	Never.

Odile & Daniel Ricordeau
Moitron sur Sarthe, Sarthe
Tel +33 (0)2 43 34 43 89
Fax +33 (0)2 43 34 43 89
Email contact@lesquatresaisons.fr
Web www.lesquatresaisons.fr

Château de Saint Paterne

Could there be anywhere more special for that holiday or house-party of a lifetime? It's a 21st-century fairy tale: the 500-year-old château was abandoned by its owners for 30 years, then rediscovered by the heir who left sunny yellow Provence for cool green pastures to resurrect the old shell. He and his wife have redecorated with refreshing taste, respecting the style and history of the building, adding a zest of southern colour to panelled, antique-filled rooms, pretty country furniture before ancient fireplaces and hand-rendered, rough and 'imperfect' finishes — nothing stiff or fixed. Sitting, dining and first-floor bedrooms are in château-style; the Henri IV room (he had a mistress here, of course) has thrillingly painted beams; ancestors and *objets* adorn but don't clutter. The attic floor is fantasy among the rafters: nooks, corners and split levels, a striking green and red bathroom, another bath sunk below the floor. Set off for a day in Chartres, Deauville or pretty old Le Mans and return to perfect service and seriously good food. An attractive mixture of past and present values. *Sawday hotel. Meals on request.*

Price	€12,000–€15,000 per week. Fully catered.
Sleeps	20-22.
Rooms	10: 5 doubles, 1 twin, 1 triple, 3 suites; 10 bathrooms, 2 separate wcs.
Arrival	Flexible.
Closed	January-March.

Charles-Henry & Segolène de Valbray
Saint Paterne, Sarthe

Tel	+33 (0)2 33 27 54 71
Fax	+33 (0)2 33 29 16 71
Email	chateaudesaintpaterne@wanadoo.fr
Web	www.chateau-saintpaterne.com

Entry 122 Map 4

Écrin de Vendée

No wonder they call it a jewel case (*écrin*): the farmhouse sits like a gem among lush green fields and a tracery of trees. Two pretty, single-storey outbuildings have been renovated in the traditional manner and painted, like the house, bright white with blue shutters. Inside, they are sparklingly modern: pale walls, white-painted rafters, good prints, comfortable furniture. Les Toucandines, close to the main house, has an open-plan living area, an L-shaped, light-filled bedroom and a small second bedroom that squeezes in bunks and a single bed. Les Florentines, tucked away at the bottom of the garden, has a little double bedroom and a sofabed in the living room. Kitchens are small – in Les Toucandines you'll need to breathe in to pass the narrow door! – but fully equipped. Private decking and lawn make good places to sit and watch the horses graze – on the other side of the electric fences; the pool is planted with lavender and olives and in the orchard are swings, slide and a climbing frame. This is marsh land with navigable water channels, so why not try punting in a yole?

Price	Toucandines €410–€950. Florentines €300–€720. Prices per week.
Sleeps	Toucandines 5. Florentines 2-4.
Rooms	Toucandines: 1 double, 1 triple with bunk & single; 1 bath. Florentines: 1 double; 1 shower; sofabed.
Closed	Rarely.

Frédérique & Frédéric Stoll
Sallertaine, Vendée

Tel	+33 (0)2 51 35 30 73
Email	contact@ecrin-vendee.com
Web	www.ecrin-vendee.com

La Fraternité

The lovely, lively Pikes, brimming with optimism and pleasure, have reared game birds here for twenty years and delight in their adopted country. Up the outside stairs, in the former apple and grain loft of their 1900s family farmhouse, the beamy, old-fashioned, simply renovated apartment has two cheerful, comfortable rooms for restful seclusion: a double bedroom with a good big bed and a sitting room with an extra-wide sofabed and some pleasing country antiques. All details are cared for, there's a little galley kitchen, and a private piece of garden with its own barbecue. Pure air and clean land are your quiet companions while ever-helpful Ian and welcoming Janty, ready to point you towards the multifarious activities and hidden treasures of the area they have come to love, finish the picture of peace. The Atlantic beaches are wide and wonderful, the island of Noirmoutier has a low-key fascination and the spectacular Puy du Fou son-et-lumière is a must (book well in advance, it is hugely popular). *Sawday B&B. Two gîtes for 4-6, one with pool, 3km away (not seen by us).*

Price	£150–£275 (€240–€400) per week. Heating extra in low season.	
Sleeps	2-4.	
Rooms	2: 1 twin/double, 1 sofabed; 1 bathroom, 1 shower room.	
Arrival	Saturday, flexible out of season.	
Closed	Never.	

Janty & Ian Pike
Aizenay, Vendée
Tel +33 (0)2 51 55 42 58
Email janet.pike@wanadoo.fr
Web perso.orange.fr/lafraternite/

Château de la Flocellière - The Keep & The Pavilion

The Vicomtesse has exacting standards and she oversees every detail of her vast dominion, from the topiary to the maids' attire. All is opulence and beauty and wafting beeswax. There are superb hotel rooms in the château and two historic buildings for rent in the grounds – a medieval Keep and a Louis XIII Pavilion. Impossible to choose between them, the one sturdy 11th century, the other classically graceful 17th century. Both are architectural gems, both have all you might need, both feel exceedingly grand. The Renaissance fireplace in the Keep's salon is monumental and roars with logs in winter beneath the splendidly painted and domed ceiling. Equally refined, the Pavilion has a gracious, immaculate feel and a brand new kitchen. This is living at its most sedate, children are welcome providing they behave impeccably, snacks are no-go in the pool area: "a terrace, not a beach." You also have your own secluded garden with barbecue. Weddings and receptions are not limited to weekends; the setting is sensational. Historic, magnificent, hospitable. *Dinners by arrangement. Sawday hotel. Shared pool.*

Price	Keep €1,950. Pavilion €1,950. Prices per week.
Sleeps	Medieval Keep 8-10. Louis XIII Pavilion 10-14.
Rooms	Keep: 2 doubles, 3 twins/doubles; 2 bathrooms, 1 shower room, sep. wc. Pavilion: 2 doubles, 1 twin/double, 1 quadruple, 1 single; 1 bathroom, 2 shower rooms, 2 sep. wcs.
Arrival	Saturday, flexible out of season.
Closed	Never.

Vicomte & Vicomtesse Patrice Vignial
La Flocellière, Vendée

Tel	+33 (0)2 51 57 22 03
Fax	+33 (0)2 51 57 75 21
Email	flocelliere.chateau@wanadoo.fr
Web	www.flocellierecastle.com

La Coquetière

Christophe has cleverly restored this farm building next to the family's 16th-century manor using rescued stones and beams to create an historically authentic house: the staircase of old railway sleepers is a joy. The airy, open-plan living area, with grand fireplace for chillier nights, is traditionally beamed and terracotta-tiled, furnished with country antiques and Claudine's paintings (she's a talented amateur). A small but well-equipped kitchen is to one side plus a useful utility room. No tantrums over choosing the bedrooms: all are equally stylish. One has a lofty cathedral-timbered ceiling, two have high antique box beds behind beautiful curtains, and there's a pretty children's room; all overlook the Vienne valley or the garden. There are three acres of deer-filled woodland, water, and scented and medieval gardens to explore and you also have your own private terrace and pool. The owners are delightful, happy to tell you about walks, bike trails, rides (stables nearby), weekly markets and the summer cheese festival. And it's a lovely walk through the woods to the village restaurant.

Price	€400–€1,500 per week.
Sleeps	8-10.
Rooms	4: 3 doubles, 1 quadruple; 1 bathroom, 2 shower rooms, 2 separate wcs.
Closed	Never.

Christophe Leroux & Claudine Leprince
Ports sur Vienne, Indre-et-Loire
Tel   +33 (0)2 47 65 15 88
Email leprince2leroux@aol.com
Web   www.lacoquetiere.com

The Cottage

Set back from the little road, its pretty old stone walls tucked around with swathes of wisteria, its shutters a Provençal blue, this was the owners' home while they restored the farmhouse across the courtyard. And the views are stunning. Step straight into a sitting room as cosy as can be, with a beamed ceiling, a tiled floor, comfortable leather chairs and a wood-burning stove. The yellow-and-blue kitchen is a cosy place for a meal, but on summer nights you'll be eating outside among the herbs and the lavender. Neat bedrooms have cream or exposed stone walls and seagrass floors; there are pretty marble-topped bedside tables in one, bright striped duvets in another. It's not swish but it's inviting, and most of the time you'll be soaking up the sunshine in the walled and flower-trellised garden – or popping across the lane for the sports! Here are a saltwater pool, croquet, boules, table tennis and, soon, tennis on grass. Friendly and fun, Antony knows the best walks, bike rides, châteaux and wine caves. A quiet, simple place for families, with activities on tap. *B&B also.*

Price	£300-£800 per week.
Sleeps	4.
Rooms	2: 1 double, 1 twin; 1 shower.
Closed	Never.

Antony Paget and Irene Ermelli
Barrou, Indre-et-Loire
Tel +33 (0)2 47 94 90 75
Email antonpaget@hotmail.com

La Silonnière – The Studio

A professional artist and a delightful presence, Lyn holds classes in modelling and sculpture. She moves into the farmhouse when guests book into the studio. Kit is a traveller and photographer; he too holds classes. You, of course, are free to do nothing. Let the peace wash over you and the setting enchant you – the cornfield and meadow views are unbroken. Drift from your suntrap patio to the lovely sunken garden, pluck the figs, pick the fruits, cool off in the above-ground pool. Your little studio is atmospheric and alluring and the walls are lined to the rafters with Lyn's work: figurative plaques, ethereal pictures. There's a sofa, a rug, a wood-burning stove, a sink in the corner. A simple staircase leads to the galleried mezzanine with a little two-burner hob, a small oven, a single bed, a table and chairs, two antique chests of drawers. The bedroom proper is deeply restful with its seagrass floor and chalky white walls, its window over the garden and the luxury of old French linen. Ancient Loches is a ten-minute drive. And the sunsets can be absolutely wonderful. *Shared pool.*

Price	£250-£400 per week. Electricity extra.
Sleeps	2-3 + cot.
Rooms	1 double; 1 bathroom; extra single bed.
Arrival	Flexible.
Closed	Never.

Kit and Lyn Constable Maxwell
Ciran, Indre-et-Loire

Tel	+33 (0)2 47 59 98 57
Email	lyn@lynmax.com
Web	www.kitmax.com/loire-valley

Loire Valley

La Basse Lande

A lovely old farmstead in gentle Touraine, where you can walk and cycle for miles. The house sleeps ten, with an extra room in an attractive building outside. And there are plenty of corners in the garden in which to find solitude and shade. Downstairs are two double bedrooms furnished in neat country style, with good French wardrobes and peaceful views, and a light and tranquil living room that opens to the garden. Floors are fine old terracotta, subtle lighting reveals the beauty of the 200-year-old beams and the fireplace guards a wood-burner – logs provided. Upstairs are three big bedrooms that lead one into the other (plus a small snooker table) – fun for children. The partly open garden has fruit trees and grass and a big level space that's just asking for a good old English game of rounders. The pretty village, a short drive, sits in the valley of the Indrois, with a 12th-century church and one baker... not to be confused with medieval Loches, famous for its culture, its citadel and its squares that burst into life when the cheese makers, wine producers and market gardeners come to town.

Price	€630–€1,120 per week.
Sleeps	10.
Rooms	5 doubles; 2 shower rooms.
Arrival	Saturday, but flexible.
Closed	Never.

Sally Markowski
Loché sur Indrois, Indre-et-Loire
Tel   +44 (0)20 8998 6851
Fax   +44 (0)20 8998 6851
Email   stm@latymer-upper.org
Web   www.holiday-gite-france.co.uk

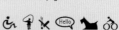

La Maison Rose

With its gorgeous pink roses and creeper-clad stone walls, the private courtyard garden in which this 18th-century farm cottage stands is magical. Take breakfast out to the lavender bushes and absorb the peace of the pretty village on the poplar-lined banks of the Indrois. Inside, it is no less charming, the bohemian furnishings and old oak beams exuding homeliness and relaxed well-being. The English owner teaches art and design and the walls are hung with his colourful paintings. For the cooler months you have books, games and a wood-burner (logs provided). Bedrooms are traditional with arty touches; the twin, on the landing, leads into one double; the shower is upstairs, the bathroom is down. Artists will celebrate the limpid Touraine light, foodies will love the bakery just over the river (the *pains aux raisins* (raisin buns) are legendary) and everyone will love Loches, its medieval citadel and blue slate roofs, its cobbled streets and its market. Buy a locally reared poussin or a piece of gleaming fish, then bring it back and turn it on the barbecue, discreetly hidden behind an old stone wall.

Price	£399-£599 (€590-€890) per week.
Sleeps	6.
Rooms	3: 2 doubles, 1 twin; 1 bathroom, 1 shower room.
Arrival	Saturday, but flexible.
Closed	Never.

Flora & James Cockburn
Loché sur Indrois, Indre-et-Loire
Tel +44 (0)20 8872 8203
Email mrsfscockburn@aol.com
Web www.lamaisonrose.com

La Challerie - La Dépendance

Floor-to-ceiling windows in the main bedroom and a full Touraine view: the restoration is excellent, the setting a balm. In two grassed acres with orchards, close to unrestored farm buildings full of charm, the 15th-century *Dépendance* has an irresistible appeal for those who love 'la belle France'. Its spacious two storeys have been charmingly furnished with country antiques and the best of brand new: warm red sofas in the salon, beechwood table and chairs in the dining room, a fine oak bed upstairs. The walls are pale exposed stone or fresh white plaster with natural wood beams, the kitchen is delightful and there's new oak for the stairs. L-shaped bedrooms, a wood-burner (logs provided) and original floor tiles add character. You have a terrace for barbecues under the stars, the orchard's peaches, plums and pears to pluck, honey, goat's and ewe's cheeses produced down the road. Stroll into 11th-century Montrésor for delectable bread and pâtisseries, visit Loches for its twice-weekly market. There's a lake at Chemillé, a pool here and concerts, châteaux and wines to discover.

Price	£350–£700 per week.
Sleeps	4–6.
Rooms	2: 1 double, 1 triple, 1 sofabed on mezzanine; 1 shower room, 1 separate wc.
Closed	Never.

Henry & Sue Dixon
Montrésor, Indre-et-Loire

Tel	+44 (0)1824 790 254
Fax	+44 (0)1824 790 030
Email	sue@allthedixons.com

Château du Breuil

A leafy drive, a quiet river, lush lawns and dense forests — enter another age. This elegant stone château, handsome with turrets, tall windows and extravagant chimneys, wraps you in its history. Roxanna is an architect and passionate about the building, preserving the original lovelies then furnishing with a light touch. The gîte, in the 15th-century east wing, is spaciously and graciously self-contained and full of little corridors, polished oak floors and solid doors. The oak-panelled sitting room, all squashy sofas and hunting trophies, has French windows to a terrace for sun-drenched mornings and shady evenings. A homely dining room, pretty with old baskets and ancient china, has a kitchenette, traditional and simple. For the swathe of fireplaces there is a cellar stocked with logs. Bedrooms are in country-house style with a light mix of French and English antiques, bathrooms have grand roll tops, one with original fittings. Visit historic Loches, walk the old hunting ground of kings — there are wild flowers in spring, mushrooms in autumn — and return to restful gardens and utter privacy.

Price	€1,000–€1,480 per week.
Sleeps	8–10.
Rooms	3: 1 double, 1 double with child's single, 1 quadruple; 3 bathrooms, 1 separate wc. Extra bed available.
Closed	Never.

Roxanna McDonald
Chédigny, Indre-et-Loire

Tel	+33 (0)2 47 92 55 88
Fax	+33 (0)2 47 92 55 88
Email	chateau-du-breuil-chedigny@orange.fr

Loire Valley

Moulin de la Follaine

A tranquil place that feels as old as the hills. The mill workers who worked opposite lived in this house; ask Danie to show you the old Azay flour sacks. Your charming young hosts run a B&B in the medieval mill house but gîte guests have their own patio, barbecue and cottage garden (colourful flowers, immaculate lawn) so there's privacy and peace. The dining/sitting room is pleasingly decorated with a mix of modern and antique country pieces, the stone fireplace is stacked with logs for low-season stays. Bedrooms are similarly uncluttered, white walls sport friezes and the kitchen has every mod con. All is spotless, everything matches – Danie is a stickler for detail – and baguettes are delivered for breakfast. There's masses to do right here, from cycling to ping-pong to fishing (tackle supplied) and gardens to enjoy, their trickling waterways and the lake dotted with ornamental ducks. Don't miss the weekly markets in Azay and Loches and, when you've had enough of cooking, there's a choice of auberges and traditional restaurants nearby. *Unsuitable for young children: unfenced water. Sawday B&B.*

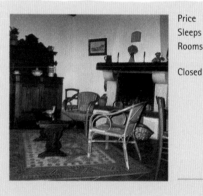

Price	€380-€600 per week.
Sleeps	4-6.
Rooms	2 family rooms for 3; 1 bathroom, 1 separate wc.
Closed	Rarely.

Madame Danie Lignelet
Azay sur Indre, Indre-et-Loire

Tel	+33 (0)2 47 92 57 91
Fax	+33 (0)2 47 92 57 91
Email	moulindelafollaine@wanadoo.fr
Web	www.moulindefollaine.com

Domaine de Beauséjour

Dug into the hillside with the forest behind and a panorama of vines in front, this wine-grower's manor successfully pretends it was built in the 1800s. In fact, it is 20 years old; Gérard was an architect before he inherited the winery. The gîte is on the lower ground floor, its living room reached directly from the garden. You may be below stairs but the sunlight streams in through your French windows and you have long views of vineyards and valley. The big living room, with exposed stone walls and large patterned rugs, has its dining area at one end, its kitchenette in the corner (sink, double hob, small oven), and its sitting space beyond, round a corner. Divan style beds, ideal for children, are sprinkled with florals; an uncle's pictures grace the walls. The main bedroom is generous; a vast gilt mirror hides the fireplace, bedcovers match curtains and there are great bowls of artificial flowers. The patio is yours, terraces hold the pool, there's wine to taste and buy and exuberant Marie-Claude looks after everyone beautifully. A stunning spot, and the walks are wonderful. *Sawday B&B. Shared pool.*

Price	€534–€600 per week.
Sleeps	2-4.
Rooms	1 twin/double, 2 divan beds; 1 bathroom, 1 shower.
Closed	Rarely.

Marie-Claude Chauveau
Panzoult, Indre-et-Loire

Tel	+33 (0)2 47 58 64 64
Fax	+33 (0)2 47 95 27 13
Email	info@domainedebeausejour.com
Web	www.domainedebeausejour.com

Entry 134 Map 4

Loire Valley

Le Pigeonnier

No artificial pool here but a safe, rock-ringed lagoon – swim where fish jump, coypu nest, and kingfishers, terns and herons fish. There are three gîtes on site of which Le Pigeonnier is one, plus an annexe for each. Reached through lush water meadows, Le Pigeonnier is attached to the main house, with views up and downstream. Only the frogs disturb the peace of the grassy garden whence a path leads down to the magical riverside with seating and barbecues for each gîte. Le Pigeonnier is an inviting little two-storey house for five. The pretty main bedroom, up chunky open-tread stairs, is in the pigeon loft, complete with nesting holes; across the landing, the second bedroom has a garden view; the bathroom is small, its bath tucked behind a beam. The ground floor is open plan, with a step up from the kitchen/dining area to the cosy sitting room with an open fire. An excellent spot for châteaux lovers, cyclists, gourmets, twitchers and those wishing to mess about in boats – a punt, rowing boat and small sailing boat are all available. And you can swim in the river itself – just watch the sandbanks. *Shared laundry.*

Price	€452-€882. Annexe €148. Prices per week.
Sleeps	4-5. Annexe 2.
Rooms	2: 1 double, 1 twin, 1 sofabed; 1 bathroom. Annexe: 1double; 1 bathroom.
Closed	End October to March.

Gordon Baker
Chinon, Indre-et-Loire

Tel	+44 (0)1440 702 627
Fax	+44 (0)1440 708 790
Email	bookings@pigeonnier.co.uk
Web	www.pigeonnier.co.uk

Entry 135 Map 4

5 rue des Averries

Michel, an interior designer and erstwhile antiques dealer, has a wonderful eye and has brought an uncluttered grace to the interior of this elegant sweep of 19th-century stone. It started life as a *longère* (a long, low outhouse) and the dormer window in one bedroom was the entrance to the hayloft. In the sitting room, gleaming stone walls are adorned with the odd oil painting, the tiles are warmed by a bright rug, there are pretty fabrics at windows and an open log fire for winter. Low, slopey-ceilinged bedrooms are under the eaves, a delightfully French mix of contemporary and traditional. You'll find antique bedside tables, good prints on the walls, fine linen. The bathroom is up, the shower room is down, and the largest bedroom, dressed in delicious lilacs and limes, has a door to an outside stone stair that sweeps you down to a big, beautiful garden – roses, shade-giving trees and unobtrusive pool. Doors from the immaculate kitchen open onto a terrace furnished with wrought-iron tables and chairs. Michel lives next door; shops, restaurants and market are a 15-minute walk. One of the finest.

Price	€900–€1,400 per week.
Sleeps	6.
Rooms	3: 2 doubles, 1 twin; 1 bathroom, 1 shower room, 2 separate wcs.
Closed	Never.

Michel Rondeau
Bourgueil, Indre-et-Loire
Tel   +33 (0)2 47 97 60 83
Fax   +33 (0)2 41 51 74 86
Email   m.rondeau@wanadoo.fr

Loire Valley

Le Clos Saint André

After years of doing B&B, the lively Pinçons have converted their fine old wine-grower's house into a self-catering home – great for a large party. On arrival, a welcoming drink will be thrust into your hands by your hosts, delighted to tell you, in fluent English, all about the region and how time is measured here in vintages not hours. Enter a big, sunny, blue-painted dining room furnished with a new kitchen. The comfy salon has wicker armchairs and glass-topped tables, books, games and a good open fire. Up the fine old oak staircase to three bedrooms, the master room the biggest and best, with dove-grey panelled walls and antiques. Up again, opening directly off the stairs and under some ravishing rafters, are the children's rooms – air conditioned for hot summer nights. Bath and shower rooms are smallish and en suite, there's a grocery box on arrival and Michèle's homemade meals on request. Best of all is the secluded garden, big enough for children to roam or swing in and leading to a fenced-in pool, yours for much of the day. There's tennis in the village and you are surrounded by vines.

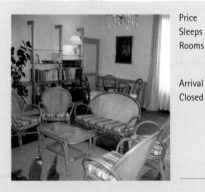

Price	€900-€1,800 per week.
Sleeps	15 + cots.
Rooms	5: 2 doubles, 1 family room, 1 triple, 1 quadruple with 1 extra bed; 5 bathrooms/shower rooms.
Arrival	Saturday, but flexible.
Closed	Never.

Michèle & Michel Pinçon
Ingrandes de Touraine, Indre-et-Loire
Tel   +33 (0)2 47 96 90 81
Email   mmpincon@club-internet.fr
Web   www.clos-saint-andre.fr

La Petite Giraudière

An exceptional and luxurious retreat. Béatrice, who lives next door, still keeps a few goats – and pigs, hens, cockerel, rabbits and pony. Children love it! Until 1790 the fine stone building was inhabited by nuns, then it became a tithe farm to the magnificent Château de Villandry next door. The old farm buildings, with their terracotta roofs and local stone walls, have been beautifully restored; the newest have become a farm shop and a delightful restaurant. A weeping willow dips its branches in the duck pond, your own entirely private roof terrace catches the sun. Indoors… dreamland. There are hand-painted cupboards, big beds, beams and rafters and subtle toile de Jouy. The new bathroom has a stunning spa bath; the triple room in the eaves is reached via the double on the gallery, up a spiral stair; there are antique carvings, stone walls, seagrass floors. The whole place swims in light and you share a big peaceful garden full of roses. Delightful Béatrice speaks fluent English and Spanish; her way is to provide the best of everything, and she adores this place – and her guests. *Restaurant on site.*

Price	€965-€1,110 per week.
Sleeps	4-6.
Rooms	3: 2 doubles, 1 triple; 2 bathrooms, separate wc.
Closed	Never.

Béatrice de Montferrier
Villandry, Indre-et-Loire

Tel	+33 (0)2 47 50 08 60
Fax	+33 (0)2 47 50 06 60
Email	beatrice.de-montferrier@wanadoo.fr
Web	www.letapegourmande.com

Loire Valley

Domaine de l'Hérissaudière

The château was Diane de Poitiers' hunting lodge. Your pleasant quarters are in the long, low *longère*, once the tack room for the horses. It's a one-storey building, one-room deep, light and appealing. You have the bedrooms on your right and the living area on your left: a blue sofabed before a small open fire (and central heating on chilly days), blue curtains, a tablecloth on a round table. Walls are white, beams dark and low; a rug adds warmth to tiles, country furniture adds personality. The kitchen, separated by a breakfast bar, is new and well-designed with matching blue and white crockery. The double bedroom is a good size, crisp and cool, with a large painted wardrobe (again blue!); the twin is a lot smaller. Outside, the best of both worlds: the privacy of your own walled and tree'd garden, with barbecue, swing and slide, and the lovely grounds to share, with tennis court to hire. The pool is for B&B guests only but there's a good public pool 10km away. A peaceful place for a family to stay – and an excellent restaurant five minutes away, recommended by hospitable Madame. *Sawday hotel.*

Price	€500–€800 per week.
Sleeps	4–6 + 1 child.
Rooms	2: 1 double + child bed, 1 twin, 1 sofabed in sitting room; 2 shower rooms, separate wc. Cot available.
Closed	Never.

Madame Claudine Detilleux
Pernay, Indre-et-Loire

Tel	+33 (0)2 47 55 95 28
Email	info@herissaudiere.com
Web	www.herissaudiere.com

La Cornillière

A lovely place with delightful owners. Monsieur, an antique dealer with artistic inklings, studied art in Tours 40 years ago, met Madame – and here they are in their elegant house. Beside it, the dear little 18th-century vine-workers' cottage has been decorated with restraint in charming traditional style. Inside, it is as warm and relaxing as your hosts. The furniture is country antique, the walls are plain, the old tiles gleam. From the mantel above the sitting room fire, great-great grandparents look down on cosy armchairs and pretty rugs; bedrooms are two up, one down. There's antique crockery in the kitchen/dining room, antique garden furniture and deckchairs in the garden. Madame is lucky, her husband is also a passionate gardener and happily digs and delves, bringing peace to the outside as well; his mini-Villandry is a marvel; the woods hold box trees once harvested for regimental buttons. Beyond the stone walls of the grounds is the Loire valley with its vineyards and châteaux and the classy city of Tours with shops, opera and great restaurants (simpler auberges lie nearby). *Meals on request.*

Price	€550-€770 per week.
Sleeps	5.
Rooms	3: 1 double, 1 twin, 1 single; 2 shower rooms, 2 separate wcs.
Closed	Never.

	Catherine Espinassou
	Mettray, Tours, Indre-et-Loire
Tel	+33 (0)2 47 51 12 69
Mobile	+33 (0)6 03 13 66 12
Email	catherine@lacornilliere.com.fr
Web	www.lacornilliere.com.fr

Entry 140 Map 4

Loire Valley

Château du Plessis - The Cottage

Some cottage! It's huge. Step into its big old-fashioned kitchen full of mod cons and central heating for winter. Next door, a quintessentially French dining room, its walls yellow and red striped, its furniture dark wooden, its floor parquet. There's a big homely sitting room with a tiled floor and seating that includes a comfortable leather sofa. Then up to the bedrooms and yet more space: a bedknobs-and-broomsticks brass bed, a Henri II wardrobe dressed up in Louis XVI style, traditionally carpeted floors, a big, light, lovely bathroom in cream and blue. Outside are a private garden full of flowers and 12 acres for the children to explore. There's a well-defined play area with wooden climbing frame shared with the owners' young sons, and other areas designed for more violent sports such as football. For the grown-ups: a 1930s grass tennis court (expect the odd strange bounce) and a delicious pool with teak loungers. Loire châteaux, riding and boating are nearby; two good restaurants are a 10-minute drive. A fun, friendly place. *Shared pool. Sawday B&B.*

Price	€750-€1,275 (£500-£850) per week.
Sleeps	6.
Rooms	3: 2 doubles, 1 twin; 1 bathroom, 1 separate wc.
Closed	Never.

Elizabeth & Gil Barrios
Saint Antoine du Rocher, Indre-et-Loire

Tel	+33 (0)2 47 56 50 69
Mobile	+33 (0)6 70 04 57 59
Email	elizabeth@chateauduplessis.com
Web	www.chateauduplessis.com

Château du Plessis - The Lodge

Sweep through parkland, step out of the car, fall in love with the setting. The Lodge is next to one end of the turreted 1750 château, once home to the playwright Eugene O'Neill. A later, less romantic use of the château was as a horticultural boarding school; such is the size of the place. Now it is all being revived by Elizabeth and Gil (she from Kent, he from Paris) who live with their children in their own well-defined quarters but are very much there for you if you need them. You enter directly into a large living room with cool tiled floors, big solid windows and wood-burner in the fireplace (backed up by electric radiators for winter). An old-fashioned red leather sofa and chairs for comfort, a dresser equipped with all the crockery, a big sober table and chairs, a practical kitchen next door. Two of the bedrooms are on this floor: patterned carpets, an Empire wardrobe, a dressing table, a sparkling new bathroom; then up to a twin, a large, low, beamy double and a corner bath big enough to fit a few toddlers. Outside is a lovely private garden – and all the park to share. *Sawday B&B.*

Price	€900–€1,650 (£600–£1,100) per week.
Sleeps	6 + 2 children.
Rooms	4: 2 doubles, 1 twin, 1 children's twin; 3 bathrooms.
Closed	Never.

Elizabeth & Gil Barrios
Saint Antoine du Rocher, Indre-et-Loire
Tel   +33 (0)2 47 56 50 69
Mobile   +33 (0)6 70 04 57 59
Email   elizabeth@chateauduplessis.com
Web   www.chateauduplessis.com

Entry 142 Map 4

Loire Valley

Château du Guerinet

There is an overriding sense of space and light here; surely they inspired that Prussian prince to build this proud abode for his humble bride, a woodman's daughter. With its terrace and hunting scenes across its walls, the downstairs bedroom is snugly majestic. Stepping lightly up the broad staircase brings you to a four-poster room, an effortless mix of rich dark wood and panelling; in a smaller double, the blue-purples of curtains, canopy and Chinese rug mix stylishly; elegant suites trumpet William Morris designs. Waltz in the Greco-Roman bathrooms/chambers of mirrors, some with claw-foot tubs. The more modest top-floor rooms – three sharing a bathroom – have soaring ceilings and are perfect for youngsters and the semi-professional kitchen, although not huge, is up to any feast you care to imagine – and cook. Superlatively grand reception rooms, yet it's a splendid place for families and outdoor pursuits. There's a barbecue, garden seating for 16 or more, phenomenal hide-and-seek, wildlife-spotting – and super young Australian owners. *Infrared sauna; pool in 2008. B&B option. Meals on request.*

Price	€5,500-€7,500 per week. Short breaks available except July & August.
Sleeps	15-23.
Rooms	9: 7 twins/doubles, 1 family room for 3, 1 suite for 4; 7 bathrooms, 5 separate wcs.
Arrival	Flexible in low season.
Closed	Rarely.

Clemence Family
Orchaise, Loir-et-Cher

Tel	+33 (0)2 54 70 10 13
Fax	+44 (0)20 7691 7575
Email	corina@loirechateau.com
Web	www.loirechateau.com

L'Ermitière & La Lissière

Six sporty families could take these two gîtes together – they sleep 24 in comfort and would be super in summer. You share a smart tennis court, a circular pool and 150 hectares of woods and wildlife. The Dehen family owns the château; Philippe and his wife own the two mid-19th-century buildings facing each other across the immaculately kept courtyard: the wisteria-draped stables with tack room (La Lissière) and the charming cart shed (L'Ermitière). Step in to a neat décor with a French bourgeois feel: pristine floor tiles, polished mantels, stippled walls, formal Louis XVI furniture and the odd comfy sofa. Smart kitchens are equipped for expert cooks, bathrooms shine, there's a Greek-style wall frieze here, a teddy bear frieze there (in the crisp children's twin) and prettiness rules upstairs in canopied beds and matching toile de Jouy. Teak outdoor furniture and a barbecue are housed in L'Ermitière's bandstand-like gazebo, La Lissière's garden is private, separated from the owners' by a hedge. Royal French history surrounds you (Blois, Chambord, Cheverny), restaurants are two miles.

Price	Ermitière €1,140-€1,800. Lissière €840-€1,350.
Sleeps	Ermitiere 12. Lissière 8-12.
Rooms	Ermitière: 1 doubles, 3 twins, 1 twin/double; 2 bathrooms, 1 shower, separate wc. Lissière: 2 doubles, 4 twins; 2 bathrooms, separate wc.
Closed	November-April.

Philippe & Pascale Dehen
Mer, Loir-et-Cher

Tel	+33 (0)2 54 81 11 64
Fax	+33 (0)2 54 81 11 64
Email	philippedehen@yahoo.fr
Web	www.gite-de-beaumont.com

Les Gîtes de la Gaucherie

Aurélia, who's French, once ran a restaurant and studied art in New York. She and her English husband Cyril love light and simplicity: their colours are beige and écru, furniture wooden, cupboard doors roughly planed. The larger gîte, a generous converted stable block beside the main house, has a rustic sitting room with wood-burning stove and red sofas; floors are terracotta or seagrass; pebbled or mosaic'd bathrooms are separated from uncluttered bedrooms by half walls, one with a whirlpool bath and a decadently tempting chaise-longue. More modest in size and style, more intimate and inward-looking, Le Marronnier is comfortable in its garb of wood and natural colours and the sofa and chairs invite you to flop at the end of the day; then the well-equipped good-sized kitchen has all you need. Each gîte has its own garden area with chairs and table. If required, the two gîtes can communicate. Old and young will love the ponies, the little boat on the lake, the heated pool, and the home-produced organic eggs and lamb. The whole place has a fresh, young and welcoming charm. *Sawday B&B. Meals on request.*

Price	Marronnier: £138-£360.
	Noisetier: £600-£1,850.
Sleeps	Marronnier 2-4. Noisetier 8.
Rooms	Marronnier: 1 double, 1 sofabed;
	1 shower, 1 wc.
	Noisetier: 4 doubles; 1 bathrooms,
	3 shower rooms, 4 separate wcs.
Closed	Mid-January to mid-February.

Aurélia Curnin
Langon, Loir-et-Cher
Tel   +33 (0)2 54 96 42 23
Email   lagaucherie@wanadoo.fr
Web   www.lagaucherie.com

La Taille Rouge

One misty morning you may catch a glimpse of a doe and her fawn deep in the woods. La Taille Rouge's 120 tranquil acres are heaven to explore and the house, with its steep tiled roof and silver-brown beams, is lovely, too. A long, pretty living room, full of books and country antiques, takes up much of the ground floor. Big comfortable sofas and chairs are grouped around the stone fireplace at one end; at the other, a fine old table with wrought-iron chairs… and there's a new sheltered area for ping-pong. On both sides are windows looking out to the woods or the heated pool. The ultra-well-equipped kitchen has a veranda – a pleasant place to breakfast – and a laundry room. Upstairs are four charmingly individual bedrooms, each with an old carved door and a gorgeous bathroom. They're furnished with a few choice antiques and extra-wide double beds which can also be twins. Out in the summer house are many bicycles – early risers can be dispatched two miles to the village bakery for fresh breakfast rolls. Everyone loves this place. *Booking reserved nine months in advance.*

Price	€1,100–€1,800 per week.
Sleeps	8-9.
Rooms	4: 2 doubles, 2 twins/doubles, 1 single bed on landing; 2 bathrooms, 2 shower rooms.
Closed	Never.

Thierry & Nicole Hiltzer
Viglain, Loiret

Tel	+33 (0)6 12 81 49 25
Mobile	+33 (0)6 12 81 49 25
Email	taille.rouge@laposte.net
Web	www.la-taille-rouge.fr

Entry 146 Map 5

Loire Valley

La Brosse

The white stone cottage was the next-door monastery's bread oven. Now it's a remarkable gîte, restored single-handedly by a remarkable owner. Generous Isabelle has a zest for living; when she moved into her medieval cloisters twelve years ago, she barely knew the tumbledown, bramble-smothered cottage existed. Now it is an unpretentious bolthole for two, ingeniously re-designed to maximise the space. The ceiling is white, the rafters exposed, the mezzanine window is triangular and a loft ladder unites the two floors. The cheerfully carpeted bedroom has a low, pattern-sprigged bed, the bathroom and kitchen are a decent size. It's a bucolic setting overlooking a large pond – mercifully free of mosquitoes – surrounded by trees with farmland beyond, and you have your own little terrace with a pergola. There's an amazing wildlife park two miles from the house – listen for wolves! – a good, cheap restaurant in the village and glorious old Loches with its market is a 20-minute drive. At the end of a long lane, seclusion and peace – a simple writer's retreat or hideaway for two.

Price	€400 per week.
Sleeps	2-3.
Rooms	1 double, 1 sofabed in living room; 1 bathroom.
Closed	Never.

Isabelle de Billy
Cléré du Bois, Indre

Tel	+33 (0)2 54 38 79 28
Fax	+33 (0)2 54 38 79 28
Email	idebilly@hotmail.com

Entry 147 Map 9

La Chemolière

Tomatoes, peppers, peas, strawberries, melons are yours for the asking, from the family's vegetable plot. Organic, too. Your warm and friendly hosts have done a fine restoration on these old farm buildings just outside the little village (one shop, one café-bar). Relax in the shade of an ancient pear tree, repair for a barbecue to your vine-clad pergola warmed by a wood-burner on cool nights. Inside, the huge stone-floored living room is a timbered delight, its thick walls keeping you warm in winter, cool in summer, its aged character married with modern comforts: a floral three-piece suite, a wood-burning stove, books, games and videos aplenty. The kitchen, with limed units, country tiles and olive trim, has every conceivable appliance to tempt one to cook, the dining area is rustically stone-walled. Up the old oak staircase to two bedrooms and their bathrooms under the eaves; roof windows open to the sky and there's space for a coffee table and a French sofa. Soak in the raised plunge pool, take to the lawns for outside games or potter in the 25 peaceful acres of pasture and wood.

Price	£195–£550 per week.
Sleeps	4.
Rooms	2: 1 double, 1 twin/double; 1 bathroom, 2 shower rooms.
Closed	Never.

Nick & Bev Bull
Cléré du Bois, Indre
Tel   +33 (0)2 54 38 86 32
Mobile +33 (0)6 24 53 66 96
Email   la_chemoliere@yahoo.co.uk
Web   lachemoliere.com

Le Grand Ajoux - Lavande

One family comes here every year to watch the dragonflies hatch on the estate's two lakes. On the edge of the Brenne National Park – famous for its thousand lakes – and in 53 hectares of private parkland, the place is a paradise for birdwatchers and nature lovers. Lavande is one of two stables (see opposite) which have been converted in a country-rustic style by the owner – sometimes absent – who lives in the old manor house next door. At opposite ends of a heated and lavender-fringed pool each cottage has a secluded patio pretty with Mediterranean plants. Inside, cheerful blue chairs and soft furnishings contrast boldly with the old-gold stone walls, ceiling beams and lovely terracotta floors, with old and new pieces of furniture sitting happily side by side. The galley kitchen is well equipped; the bedroom's French windows open to the main courtyard and views of the paddocks where horses and donkeys graze. There are plenty of walks from the door – the countryside is truly magnificent – and George Sand fans can drive to the Vallée Noire, where she lived, and visit the museum at La Châtre. *Shared pool.*

Price	€550–€1,100 per week.
Sleeps	6.
Rooms	3 doubles; 1 shower room, 1 bathroom.
Closed	Never.

Aude de la Jonquière-Aymé
Chalais, Indre

Tel	+33 (0)2 54 37 72 92
Mobile	+33 (0)6 80 30 92 74
Email	audeayme@wanadoo.fr
Web	grandajoux.tripod.com

Le Grand Ajoux - Amande

Great swathes of park and woodland are yours to roam – if you're lucky, you'll spot a couple of deer or a wild boar. Alternatively, fish in the private lake (bring your own rod), or simply unwind by the heated rose- and lavender-bordered pool – it's a short walk from your pretty blue bedroom door. Charmingly cosy, this tiny 300-year-old converted stable has been imaginatively restored while keeping original stone walls and tiled floors. The beamed bedroom – green checked bedspread, big old wardrobe – sits cosily next to the small rustic sitting room with its two armchairs, check curtains and small stone fireplace. Outside, your secluded west-facing patio overlooks fields of horses, donkeys and a tree-lined pond: bucolic is the word. There's the Abbey of Saint Savin with its 13th-century frescoes of the hermit Saint Savinus to visit, the Loire châteaux are a 90-minute drive, there are wines to taste, if you're an *aficionado*: try Vouvray and Chinon from Touraine... At the end of the day you'll want to rush back to blissful seclusion and let the owls hoot you to sleep. *Shared pool.*

Price	€250-€550 per week.
Sleeps	2.
Rooms	2 doubles; 1 shower room, 1 separate wc.
Closed	Never.

Aude de la Jonquière-Aymé
Chalais, Indre

Tel	+33 (0)2 54 37 72 92
Mobile	+33 (0)6 80 30 92 74
Email	audeayme@wanadoo.fr
Web	grandajoux.tripod.com

Entry 150 Map 9

Poitou – Charentes • Limousin • Auvergne

La Boulinière - Châtaignier, Maison de Chasse, Noyers

Play the grand life and take on this 30-acre estate – or enjoy a slice of it with your own garden and terrace. Set in rolling French countryside – hedgerows, copses, cattle – three gîtes surround the elegant *maison de maître*. Ex-farmer Tim and ex-nurse Maggie ensure it's a family-friendly place: a games barn for teenagers, sandpit and slides for little ones, gardens and woodland trails. Interiors are Anglo-French elegant yet rustic in atmosphere. Châtaignier, a long, stone cottage sprinkled with creepers, overlooks the old farmyard. Step into a sunny beamed living room with sofas round the fire and a long wooden dining table. Like Châtaignier, La Maison de Chasse is great for three-generation families: plenty of bathrooms, a jolly children's room and a ground-floor bedroom with doors to the garden. In Les Noyers, children have a super bunk bedroom. Take the path to one of the pools or your piece of garden and bask in the birdsong for which this area, near the Brenne National Park, is famed. The GR48 passes the front door. *B&B also. Two pools.*

Price	£375-£1,750 per week. Winter lets for 2-4 at reduced rates.
Sleeps	Châtaignier 10. Chasse 12. Noyers 5-6.
Rooms	Châtaignier: 3 doubles, 2 twins; 3 bathrooms. Chasse: 3 doubles, 1 triple, 1 family room for 3; 3 bathrooms. Noyers: 1 double, 1 twin, 1 room with bunks; 2 shower rooms.
Arrival	Flexible.
Closed	Never.

Tim & Maggie Willcocks
La Trimouille, Vienne

Tel	+33 (0)5 49 91 75 47
Mobile	+33 (0)6 25 14 03 94
Email	maggieandtim.willcocks@club-internet.fr
Web	www.bouliniere-french-holidays.com

La Grande Métairie - The Cottage

The stuff of dreams! Rose was bewitched by La Grande Métairie which she thought looked like an Arthur Rackham illustration. Fourteen years on, this ancient farm cottage with views over the Creuse valley has kept its enchantment. The stone farm buildings with their unusually angled roofs surround a courtyard shaded by fruit trees; under one stands a life-size effigy of your opera-singer host Richard. This fun and cultured couple do B&B next door and are often around to help if needed. The inside of the cottage will cast its spell over you too: friendly old armchairs round a wood-burner in the cool kitchen/living room, wonderful gnarled beams. Upstairs there are ancient iron bedsteads (with modern mattresses) and thoroughly beamed ceilings. Have a game of tennis on the private court, dine out on your terrace in the large dreamy garden, slip into the shared, enclosed pool, landscaped with shrubs and 200 rose bushes beyond. The well-named Rose runs rose-pruning days in season and makes splendid jams. *Can be let with adjoining studio. Babysitting available. Shared pool. B&B also.*

Price	€570–€975 (£380–£650) per week.
Sleeps	4-5.
Rooms	3: 1 double, 1 twin, 1 single on landing; 1 bathroom.
Closed	Never.

Richard & Rose Angas
Leugny, Vienne

Tel	+44 (0)20 8743 1745
Mobile	+44 (0)7966 041 744
Email	angas@freeuk.com
Web	www.lagrande-metairie.com

La Grande Métairie - The Studio

There's wood everywhere in this jewel-among-the-rafters in the old farm stables. Stripped age-worn beams bear the sloping ceilings and there are hefty old boards on the floor. A large iron-framed double bed is screened from the living area and kitchen corner by pretty Indian-print curtains; similar fabrics cover the sofabed. You look onto the grassy courtyard on one side and onto the Creuse valley on the other – glorious. A tennis court and a lovely, enclosed pool are shared with the owners and the occasional B&B guest but you get your own space too: stone steps lead up to your front door and down to a private terrace and patch of garden. Come to enjoy the company – out of season – of your interesting hosts, Rose and Richard, and to discover this unspoiled area of France. Once you've explored the farmstead's three acres of gardens and woodland there are châteaux to visit, restaurants and wines to sample and pleasant walks and cycle rides. A baker delivers daily and you can walk to the local farm to buy fresh eggs and honey. *Can be let with adjoining cottage. Babysitting available. Shared pool. B&B also.*

Price	€390–€645 (£260-£430) per week.
Sleeps	2-3.
Rooms	1 double, 1 single sofabed; 1 shower room.
Closed	Never.

Richard & Rose Angas
Leugny, Vienne

Tel	+44 (0)20 8743 1745
Mobile	+44 (0)7966 041 744
Email	angas@freeuk.com
Web	www.lagrande-metairie.com

Château de la Motte

Stark against the skyline is a pearly grey, turreted, medieval castle, dominating the village as if plucked from a fairytale. And there, sheltering in the lee of its walls, is your farmhouse home. Its views stretch serenely over Usseau and down a long, soft valley – stunning. Wisely, the interior does not try to compete, it just has that rustic elegance of simple but attractive furniture set against polished parquet, dark-red, beautifully worn quarry tiles and exposed stone walls. There are two good-sized bedrooms in fresh colours – more views – and a cosy room under the eaves that peeps over the garden. The Bardins' paintings are everywhere and there's a butterfly stencil in the shining bathroom. The light-filled living room has doors to the garden – you may barbecue from the old bread oven – and a brand-new kitchen. This is easy living: close to the Loire, restaurants in Châtellerault, a pool shared with the castle's B&B guests. The Bardins are full of energy – creating a monastic garden, running art courses, intelligently filling you in about the area. Great hospitality. *Shared pool. Sawday B&B.*

Price	€450–€600 per week.
Sleeps	6-7.
Rooms	3: 2 doubles, 1 triple; 1 bathroom, 1 shower room, 1 separate wc.
Arrival	Saturday, but flexible.
Closed	Rarely.

Jean-Marie & Marie-Andrée Bardin
Usseau, Vienne

Tel	+33 (0)5 49 85 88 25
Fax	+33 (0)5 49 85 88 25
Email	chateau.delamotte@wanadoo.fr
Web	www.chateau-de-la-motte.net

Château de la Gatinalière - La Maison du Jardin

A tree-lined avenue leads to a sophora tree and a lake of shimmering lavender. To the side of the château your cottage peeps out between well-ordered lime trees and surveys the gorgeous scene. Hidden behind, a private, informal garden bursts with colour and fruit (pick and pluck as you will), perfectly positioned for the evening sun. Stylish but simple, the Maison's rooms are large, liveable spaces. The sitting/dining room, with windows on three sides, has plenty of sofas, a polished oak table and a large fireplace; to one side, the well-equipped kitchen overlooks the garden. Bedrooms spoil for choice. Downstairs is elegant with seagrass flooring, whitewashed walls, deep claw-foot bath and French windows to the courtyard. Up the steepish stairs is a cathedral-beamed loft with masses of windows, a curtained-off bedroom and a little salon in which to pen a first novel. There are two other gîtes and B&B in the château but, with all that parkland, there's space for everyone. Come for stylish country living close to the Loire châteaux and Romanesque Poitou, and good walking and cycling. *B&B also.*

Price	€800 per week. €2,000 per month.
Sleeps	4–5.
Rooms	2 doubles, sofabed in sitting room; 1 bathroom, 1 shower room.
Closed	Never.

Bernard & Christine de la Touche
Antran, Vienne

Tel	+33 (0)5 49 21 15 02
Mobile	+33 (0)6 72 17 65 07
Email	gatinaliere@orange.fr
Web	www.chateauxcountry.com/chateaux/gatinaliere

Poitou – Charentes

La Roseraie

Freshly baked croissants for breakfast? It's a two-minute walk to the bakery in town but you could be in deepest Poitou. These vast and child-friendly grounds embrace a big orchard, a vegetable garden, vines and a heated, salt-treated pool. Behind the 19th-century house – where B&B guests are elegantly housed in one wing – one end of a stone outhouse has been converted into two gîtes overlooking a courtyard. They have quiet style and comfort with a double and a triple bedroom apiece. Each has its own diminutive patio with barbecue, table and chairs; everyone shares the run of the grounds. (Just as well there are four acres: in high summer, there could be up to 20 guests here at a time.) The Lavenders, delightful people with a brace of lively Jack Russell terriers in tow, are English, though Heather was brought up in Zimbabwe. You can watch walnut oil being made down the road and the town has a big weekly market. Hire bikes and spread your wings further: the flat landscape makes for easy cycling and there's masses to visit within an easy drive. A super spot for two families. *B&B also. Shared pool.*

Price	£445-£795 per week.
Sleeps	Marguerite 5. Atelier 5.
Rooms	Marguerite: 1 double, 1 triple; 1 shower room, 1 bathroom, separate wc. Atelier: 1 double, 1 triple; 2 shower rooms, 2 separate wcs.
Closed	November or January.

Michael & Heather Lavender
Neuville de Poitou, Vienne

Tel	+33 (0)5 49 54 16 72
Fax	+33 (0)5 49 51 69 04
Email	info@laroseraiefrance.fr
Web	www.laroseraiefrance.fr

Château de Saint Loup sur Thouet - The Keep

Come play Puss in Boots: this exquisite château and the glamorous Marquess of Carabas inspired the author of that immortal tale. Yours is the medieval keep where the Black Prince held the King of France in 1356. Your host fell in love with Saint Loup at first sight in 1990 – and is still renovating. Passionate about its history, he gives his all to share it with guests and the public (it's open to visitors in summer): his latest creation is a huge, medieval bedroom at the top of the keep, so authentic it has no electricity (but myriad candles) or running water (on the landing only). It's ancient, romantic, peerless. What matter the odd mote? Bedrooms, some with four-posters, are big, period furnished in brocade and character. The Black Prince room has two vast fireplaces and thick red-stained beams. Reception rooms are lofty and grand: it's a dream place for your special gathering, with astoundingly beautiful gardens, the whole estate bounded by a great moat. Charles-Henri's exhilaration at the scale and power of the ship he steers is infectious – in impeccable English. *Château dinner available. Sawday hotel.*

Price	€3,900 for 6 days.
	Enquire about shorter stays.
Sleeps	16.
Rooms	7: 4 doubles, 2 twins, 1 suite for 4;
	6 bathrooms, separate wc.
Arrival	Sunday, but flexible.
Closed	Rarely.

Comte Charles-Henri de Bartillat
Saint Loup Lamairé, Deux Sèvres

Tel	+33 (0)5 49 64 81 73
Fax	+33 (0)5 49 64 82 06
Email	st-loup@wanadoo.fr
Web	www.chateaudesaint-loup.com

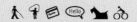

Entry 157 Map 9

Château de Puy Chenin

Wake up to the dancing reflection of water on the ceiling. Below your room is a moat, shimmering with fish, frogs, ducks and water lilies. Impossible to believe you have this remarkable, square-towered castle to yourselves. Medieval, its appearance was softened in the 17th century when big windows were let into thick walls... the sense of history remains. Stately, stylish bedrooms, each named after a previous owner, have exquisitely canopied beds and whitewashed beams. One is on the ground floor; the rest are reached by stone spiral staircases (one without a handrail...). The kitchen, vast and lovely, has an immense fireplace and sun-streamed windows. Come evening, settle into the luminous great salon, or plump for the sofas of the television room. This exceptionally lovely castle stands in 30 acres between two rivers – leave your cares behind. The heated pool is as lovely as the rest and the owners reserve the right to use it for an hour each day. Wander through the various fine gardens or follow the long, winding trail through the woods; the tranquillity is extraordinary. *Unfenced moat & pond.*

Price	€3,100–€3,950 per week.
Sleeps	14.
Rooms	6: 2 doubles, 2 twins, 2 triples; 6 bathrooms.
Arrival	Friday.
Closed	Never.

Christiane & Henry Lewis
Xaintray, Deux Sèvres
Tel   +33 (0)5 49 77 28 28
Email   puychenin@wanadoo.fr
Web   www.puychenin.com

Bois Bourdet - Farmhouse, La Bergerie, La Petite Maison

The couple who own Bois Bourdet are warm, charming and gregarious, and have a little girl; they discovered the tumbledown old place before she was born. What you find now, at the end of the long, bumpy, winding lane, is a beautiful 18th-century farmhouse with barns around, fringed by a horse chestnut and a lime tree from which a swing hangs. It's as pretty as a picture and as stylish as can be. There are flowers on window ledges, box trees in pots and chickens strutting pure 'France profonde'. The Farmhouse is in a private wing of the main building, the Bergerie is a lofty, one-storey barn and the Petite Maison, with the old bread oven, is a hideaway for two. All have been sympathetically restored to reveal original rafters, beams and creamy stone walls; the Nicholsons then added chunky terracotta floors, charming kitchens, white bathrooms and fresh furnishings. Sheer relaxing delight – plus heated pool, potager, patios, playhouse and treasure hunts. Not forgetting warm eggs from those hens and freshest veg straight from the garden. *Aga cookery courses Sept-May. B&B also. Meals on request. Shared pool.*

Price	Farmhouse £250–£850. Bergerie £250–£775. Petite Maison £200–£375 per week.
Sleeps	Farmhouse 2-7. Bergerie 2-5. Petite Maison 2 + cot.
Rooms	Farmhouse: 1 double, 1 twin; 2 baths. Extra family room for 3 & cots on request. Bergerie: 1 double, 1 twin & single bed on mezzanine; 1 bath, separate wc. Petite Maison: 1 double; 1 shower.
Arrival	Saturday, but flexible.
Closed	Never.

Les & Louise Nicholson
Souvigné, Deux Sèvres

Tel	+33 (0)5 49 76 35 39
Email	info@boisbourdet.com
Web	www.boisbourdet.com

Entry 159 Map 9

Rue de la Cour - Le Four du Boulanger

With its sunflower fields, honey stone walls and carthorses, the tiny village of Mandegault is a reminder of how rural France used to be. Life slows to a tranquil trot, a pace which English owners Alison and Francis have been delighted to adopt at their 18th-century farmstead. Hens and ducks potter in the courtyard (children may collect the eggs at feeding time), a family of black sheep grazes their garden and wisteria strews the pergola of yours (which is private and charming). The couple have been equally respectful of local styles. Here, in the bakery, the original vaulted stone bread oven and authentic diamond-shaped *œil de bœuf* windows have been kept, while beautiful natural fabrics, oak beams and creamy stone walls create a mood of soothing elegance. There's pretty red stencilling on the floorboards in the main bedroom, and a dash of colour to curtains and cover on the splendid carved bed. The bathroom is downstairs. The owners are lovely and keep guests supplied with home-grown veg and fresh eggs; and there's a shared games area with a small raised pool. Great for families.

Price	€365-€645 per week. Linen not included.
Sleeps	4-6.
Rooms	2: 1 double, 1 twin, 1 sofabed in living room; 1 bathroom.
Closed	Never.

Francis & Alison Hudson
Mandegault, Deux Sèvres
Tel   +33 (0)5 49 29 65 31
Email   mandegault@aol.com
Web   www.ruralretreats.org

Rue de la Cour - Les Écuries

Enjoy a glass of chilled pineau des Charentes, that wickedly delicious aperitif, under the wisteria-clad pergola of these sweet stone stables. Alison and Francis, the delightful, artistic owners, have put their combined talents to excellent use in this rustic, charming, ground-floor cottage. As in the old bakery next door (see entry...), natural colours and fabrics predominate and rooms keep their honey-coloured open-stone walls and oak beams. Spotless bedrooms are small and simple yet elegant, with scrubbed wooden floorboards and iron or polished wooden beds. Pick herbs from your garden and sprinkle them over the fresh organic vegetables the Hudsons supply. Your garden is secluded and pretty, with fig trees, lawn and teak loungers, and interconnects with the one next door if two families rent the cottages together. Wander off to discover those sheep, ducks and hens. There's a large paddling pool for children to share and bikes to hire. Chef Boutonne, the nearest town, has a fairytale château, fascinating old washhouses and a Saturday market: don't miss the Charentais melons.

Price	€320–€550 per week. Linen not included.
Sleeps	4.
Rooms	2: 1 double, 1 twin; 1 shower room.
Closed	Never.

Francis & Alison Hudson
Mandegault, Deux Sèvres
Tel   +33 (0)5 49 29 65 31
Email   mandegault@aol.com
Web   www.ruralretreats.org

Entry 161 Map 9

Le Ruisseau Perdu

The name means 'the lost stream' and the wells are here still, in the 'untamed' ('sauvage') village. The stone house was roofless when these English owners took it on. Two centuries old, standing in three acres of meadows, your sweet gîte was once half cattle stall, half cottage. It has been most sympathetically reconstructed then redecorated with quiet flair. At the front is a gravelled area, at the back is the lane. Step into a charming interior of exposed stone walls and white painted beams, underfloor heating and wood-burning stove, original lavabo and *œil de bœuf* window. Downstairs are the living areas and a 'writer's retreat' – with antique desk; upstairs are the bedrooms – with antique beds. All feels fresh, rustic, spotless; an old armoire here, a chic basin there, painted floorboards, country checks, art by Alison and Francis. Stray beyond these gentle delights and you come to the sands at La Rochelle and the Futuroscope at Poitiers. Future plans include a secret garden and a pool. The owners' house is a short drive and there's a restaurant 5km away.

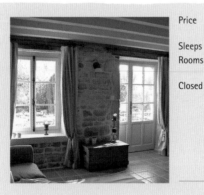

Price	£400–£900 per week. Long winter lets £250 per week all inclusive.
Sleeps	7-9.
Rooms	3: 2 doubles, 1 triple; 2 bathrooms, 1 separate wc, sofabed.
Closed	Rarely.

Francis & Alison Hudson
Lorigné, Deux Sèvres

Tel	+33 (0)5 49 29 65 31
Email	mandegault@aol.com
Web	www.ruralretreats.org

Le Logis de la Broue – Le Maître de Chai & Le Vigneron

The town may not delight you but the house is beautifully secluded. Open the front gates to 12 hectares of rolling fields, the whinny of a horse (Madame breeds them) and the hum of a tractor. The 15th-century Logis is built round a big cobbled courtyard bursting with hydrangeas and topiary: a hint of what is to come. Enter your cottage, a converted winery outbuilding, luxurious in the extreme. Flamboyant fabric walls with curtains to match will at first astonish you, then seduce you, floor tiles are stamped with œnopoetic images, perfect china lines custom-made cupboards. Beds are large and comfortable with antique white linen, tiny kitchens are logically planned and all is immaculately French, including Madame, who invites guests to pineau tastings in a vaulted cave and gives you a luscious pool with a bar for cool drinks and outdoor showers. Vigneron has a large secluded garden that leads to the orchard and pool, Maître de Chai simply has a gravelled eating area at the front. *Shared laundry & pool. Sawday B&B.*

Price	Chai €600–€900.
	Vigneron €300–€600.
	Prices per week.
Sleeps	Maître de Chai 4. Vigneron 2.
Rooms	Maître de Chai: 1 double, 1 twin;
	1 bathroom, separate wc.
	Vigneron: 1 double; 1 bathroom.
Closed	Never.

Sylviane & Vincent Casper
Saint Claud, Charente

Tel	+33 (0)5 45 71 43 96
Mobile	+33 (0)6 72 14 68 94
Email	sylviane.casper@wanadoo.fr
Web	www.logisdelabroue.com

Entry 163 Map 9

Poitou – Charentes

Blacksmith's Cottage

What a pretty stone cottage, this former village blacksmith's house. His forge is next door and Elspeth and Graham have breathed new life into reclaimed timbers and old stones. The dapper exterior hides a snug indoors and the full architectural works: beamed ceilings, stone walls, fine wooden floors. The style is artistic, rustic and easy on the eye. The downstairs bedroom has French windows that open to a pretty terrace and private garden where a walnut tree looms. The kitchen/living room, its flagged floors drenched in golden morning light, has an unusual wooden staircase made by monks that spirals up to the other rooms, one of which has a Goldilocks feel – fun for little ones. The kitchen holds all you need. The charming walled garden comes with a lawn, parasols, barbecue and shade-giving trees, and there's a wild vegetable and fruit garden from where you may harvest whatever is in season; the nearest shops are at Néré, three miles away. The pool is beautifully private in its walled and gated garden between the cottage and the owners' house. *Extra room for two nearby. Shared pool.*

Price	£325–£450 per week. Linen not included.
Sleeps	4 + 2 children.
Rooms	3: 1 twin, 1 double, 1 children's room; 1 bathroom, separate wc.
Closed	Rarely.

Graham D'Albert & Elspeth Charlton
Romazières, Charente-Maritime
Tel   +33 (0)5 46 33 60 88
Fax   +33 (0)5 46 33 60 88
Email   elspeth.charlton@wanadoo.fr

Entry 164 Map 9

Manoir Souhait - Le Verger

The dining room still has the stone oven where the former inhabitants cooked their pigeons. The birds, a delicacy reserved for the gentry, were reared in the pigeonnier just outside the gates. The house stands in the grounds of the 19th-century manoir where British owners Liz and Will live and do B&B. Camaraderie comes easily to them so you can get to know each other by the fenced and heated pool – a boon for families with its section for children – the sauna or the jacuzzi, and you can arrange to join them at a tempting table d'hôtes dinner in the dining room of the Manoir or on the garden terrace. There's snooker, badminton and table tennis, too. Le Verger used to house farmworkers who made cognac. Inside, it is light and clean and the furniture mostly modern pine, with ancient roof beams to add character. In the pretty town of Cognac, a 20-minute drive, you can tour the distilleries of Rémy Martin, Hennessy and Courvoisier. Try the area's other tipple too, pineau des Charentes, a sweet aperitif. Bikes can be hired locally and there are lovely rides and walks. *B&B also. Meals on request.*

Price	£415–£790 per week.
Sleeps	4-5.
Rooms	2: 1 twin, 1 family room for 3; 1 bathroom.
Closed	Rarely.

Will & Liz Weeks
Gourvillette, Charente-Maritime

Tel	+33 (0)5 46 26 18 41
Email	weeks@manoirsouhait.com
Web	www.manoirsouhait.com

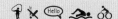

Entry 165 Map 9

Fisherman's Cottage

Leave the summer throng behind you, wind through the creamy, cobbled backstreets of Saint Martin and discover your peaceful fisherman's cottage. Step from the street straight into the beamy sitting room snug with open fire, comfy sofas and the owner's collection of ceramics. The sitting room blends into the peppermint kitchen and then into a small but perfectly formed garden. It may be teensy but everything is here: walls for privacy, tumbling plants… dine on the terrace, sprawl on the rug-sized lawn, gaze on the buttresses of the medieval abbey that rise majestically above. The twin upstairs comes with portholes that look on to the stairwell; the double has a brass bed, a sloping pine ceiling and a picture window overlooking the garden, the terracotta roofs and the abbey, illuminated at night. If you don't feel like cooking, stroll down into fashionable Saint Martin, pick a harbourside restaurant and watch the bobbing boats. Ré is ideal for family holidays: its lovely white sand beaches are a short walk or bike ride away. *Bike hire close by.*

Price	£375–£495 per week. Linen not included.
Sleeps	4 + cot.
Rooms	2: 1 double, 1 twin; 1 bathroom.
Closed	Rarely.

Graham D'Albert & Elspeth Charlton
Saint Martin de Ré, Charente-Maritime

Tel +33 (0)5 46 33 60 88
Fax +33 (0)5 46 33 60 88
Email elspeth.charlton@wanadoo.fr

Maison Cothonneau

Swap four wheels for two on peaceful Île de Ré. The island is criss-crossed with cycle paths and wrapped in 30km of white beaches. In a quiet back street, your cottage is stunningly stylish, beautifully relaxed, full of personal attentions. Eat out in the sunny, flagged, high-walled courtyard dotted with potted palms and an outdoor shower for sluicing sandy children. Downstairs is one large and lovely living space: chunky beams, terracotta, a gentle palette of whites and greys. The smart kitchen can be screened off, a cupboard hides the telly, a Louis XVI fireplace keeps you cosy. Up the 17th-century staircase are three bedrooms pretty with pistachio paintwork, seagrass flooring and flowery throws; the third room is suitably shipshape with a lantern for bedtime reading, cabin-style cupboard doors and a top bunk with a sliding ladder; the bathroom has sparkling new tiles, a 1920s basin, a vintage showerhead. Pop down the road for local oysters and newly landed fish from the bustling harbourside. Welcome gestures include a choice of coffees and leaf teas, fresh flowers, daily croissants… exceptional.

Price	€990–€2,050 per week.
Sleeps	5-6.
Rooms	3: 1 double, 1 twin/double, 1 room with bunks; 1 bathroom, separate wc.
Closed	Never.

Saint Martin de Ré, Île de Ré,
Charente-Maritime

Tel	+33 (0)6 10 28 09 14
Email	infos@maison-cothonneau.com
Web	www.maison-cothonneau.com

Poitou – Charentes

Les Grands Vents - Le Cottage

The friendly old Pyrenean mountain dog stands guard like a great big ball of fluff. The owners are equally friendly, caring for their B&B guests and delighted to help in any way they can. Set back from the main road within walled and gated grounds are the old pineau merchant's house with outbuildings. Your one-storey cottage, once the stables, is close by. The big oval pool, surrounded by sun loungers and palms, is irresistible on a warm day; for privacy you have your own large and impeccably mown lawn, with swings and a terrace for barbecues. Inside, all is light, bright and spotless. A red sofa and white leather chairs sit stylishly on a delightful wood and tile floor, walls are pattern-papered or exposed stone, there's an open fire for winter and white metal furniture for summer. In the kitchen, little green curtains hide pots and pans, the shower room's shelves are packed with crisp towels, and beds and bedding are excellent. It's very private, very peaceful and if you want action there's Surgères, four miles away, home of the most delicious butter in France. *Sawday B&B. Shared pool.*

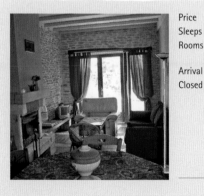

Price	€560–€760 per week.
Sleeps	6.
Rooms	3: 2 doubles, 1 twin; 1 bathroom, 1 shower room, separate wc.
Arrival	Sunday.
Closed	November-February

Valérie & Nicolas Godebout
Chervettes, Charente-Maritime
Tel +33 (0)5 46 35 92 21
Fax +33 (0)5 46 35 92 21
Email godebout@club-internet.fr
Web www.les-grands-vents.com

Entry 168 Map 8

Le Donjon du Château de Crazannes

Old stones, old bones: the Black Prince stayed here in 1362. The *donjon*, or keep, one of the oldest remaining parts of the castle and a listed monument, has twisting stone staircases, crennellations and magical views over the moat and the 16-acre estate. Absorb the fascinating history among surroundings that are utterly peaceful and unashamedly luxurious: furniture is antique, maids will clean daily, you share a heated swimming pool with the château B&B guests and you can even hire a chef. Eat out on the terrace or in the large stone-walled dining room with its grand fireplace, soft sofas and beautiful waxed terracotta floors; gilt mirror and chandelier give a sense of wealth and warmth. Wind your way up to the elegantly simple bedrooms, one a four-poster with a gorgeous blue butterfly sofa, the perfect spot to unwind and soak up the dreamy view; then on to a splendidly contrasted monastic room and a smart navy blue one; yet further, a study and a great terrace up in the clouds. The kitchen is, of course, way below stairs, the garden is superb. *Cook on request. Sawday B&B. Shared pool.*

Price	€1,500-€2,500 per week. Reductions for small groups.
Sleeps	6.
Rooms	3 doubles; 3 bathrooms.

	Monsieur Fougerit Crazannes, Charente-Maritime
Tel	+33 (0)6 80 65 40 96
Fax	+33 (0)5 46 91 34 46
Email	crazannes@worldonline.fr
Web	www.crazannes.com

Château Mouillepied - La Maison du Vivier

Big French windows overlook the lily-strewn fishpond which gives the house its name. A graceful, 18th-century cottage, it was once the château's summer house and stands at the edge of the gardens. Inside, all is open-plan airy with unobtrusive, modern furniture and a plain understated look. The whole of the first floor is one big family room, white beds lined up along the long white wall, where exposed beams and a new pine floor give an effect of fresh simplicity. The single bed hides behind heavy linen curtains. The big sunny living room has an open fireplace and a decent kitchen area. You have your own, unfenced garden *and* the beautiful grounds, which hold a fine dovecote and various intriguing outhouses, including one with huge decorated *lessiveuses*, the 18th-century precursor of the washing machine. More for the adventurous than luxury-seekers, all in pretty countryside close to the Charente; stroll the banks, pick up a fishing licence from the local bakery, dangle a hook. Martine and Pierre are lovely and will, on request, deliver croissants to your door. *Sawday hotel.*

Price	€280–€550 per week.
Sleeps	2-3.
Rooms	1 family room for 3; 1 bathroom, 1 separate wc.
Closed	Never.

Pierre & Martine Clément
Port d'Envaux, Charente-Maritime
Tel   +33 (0)5 46 90 49 88
Fax   +33 (0)5 46 90 36 91
Email   info@chateaumouillepied.com
Web   www.chateaumouillepied.com

Le Logis de Fondouce

The countryside is softly undulating with sunflowers and vines, the hamlet slumbers and the old home of the Lords of Massac is timelessly beautiful. Step into the secret walled garden that surrounds the manor house; fall under the spell of this special mellow place. With its own little garden to the front, the old barn has become a charming, stylish hideaway for seven; the delightful Slees (David a genealogist, Brit a garden designer) have decorated in Norwegian style. All is beauty and light, from the pointed stone walls with their whitewashed render to the pretty checked curtains and painted cream dresser. Bedrooms upstairs – one on the living room mezzanine – have lovely old floorboards and fat duvets; the big bathroom is chic with a mosaic shower and an ancient ladder for towels; beams are plain chestnut or Gustavian grey; the bread oven is in perfect working order. Families adore it here, the pool, all yours, looks luscious and David is more than up for a table tennis challenge or a kick around with a ball while parents slumber in the hammock. The nearest auberge is a mile away. *Children over 5 welcome.*

Price	£600-£850 per week.
Sleeps	7.
Rooms	3: 2 doubles, 1 triple; 2 shower rooms.
Closed	November-February.

	David Slee & Brit Solheim
	Massac, Charente-Maritime
Tel	+33 (0)5 46 33 35 50
Email	solheimslee@wanadoo.fr
Web	www.cognac-gites.com

Maison Brives

A grand 19th-century presbytery in a small Charentais village. It has long pastoral views and is owned by Elisabeth, sculptor, gardener and entrepreneur. Inside, all is elegantly traditional: ochre walls and polished antiques, a downstairs loo with a big antique sink, French windows opening to a 40-foot terrace. The kitchen comes with all mod cons; the charming marble-tiled bathroom has a six-foot Victorian bath; for nights in, there's satellite telly. An elm staircase winds up through shafts of light to bedrooms that exude a gentle stylishness: powder-blue and dusty-pink walls, beautiful fabrics, big comfortable beds. The grounds, impeccably kept and summer-scented, are entirely enclosed and full of shady corners, with a splendid summer saltwater pool. Nearby Saintes exults in an amphitheatre for musical events, a market most days and a *foire* on the first Monday of the month: feast your eyes on Atlantic seafood, artisan cheeses and vegetables still muddy from the earth. And vans deliver croissants, bread and essentials to the village. *Unfenced but alarmed pool. Over eights welcome.*

Price	£900-£1,600 per week.
Sleeps	6.
Rooms	3: 2 doubles, 1 twin; 3 shower rooms.
Arrival	Friday/Saturday – by arrangement.
Closed	October-December & March-April.

	Elisabeth Whittaker
	Brives sur Charente, Charente-Maritime
Tel	+44 (0)20 8995 9255
Email	info@maison-brives.eu
Web	www.maison-brives.eu

Les Deux Marronniers - House & Barn

In the soft light of the Charente, far from the summer crowds, one magnificent chestnut tree (*marronnier*) greets you at the entrance, a second shades the peaceful courtyard. The solid stone farmhouse and outbuildings, typically Charentais, are now the owners' family house, which stands on one side of the yard, and the guests' garden and two gîtes on the other. Inside, they are elegantly cool: smart modern sofas on old wooden floors, wrought-iron tables, country chairs, shades of off-white: comfortable, easy living. Both gîtes have open fires and central heating, each has its own small terrace. Pale beamy bedrooms have pretty toile de Jouy or crisp checks and muslin: shades of their former English owners; views roll greenly past. Crunch across the yard through a stone archway to the lovely pool hidden behind high walls, with canvas parasols and a terracotta-roofed lean-to for shade. The essential visits include Romanesque churches, cognac cellars and summer festivals while a spring-fed lake with pedalos and restaurant is a 20-minute drive and the Atlantic just an hour's scenic outing.

Price	Barn €450-£900. House £250-£700. Prices per week.
Sleeps	Barn 6. House 4.
Rooms	Barn: 1 double, 2 twins; 1 shower room, 1 bathroom. House: 1 double, 1 twin; 1 bathroom. Two extra rooms available in main house (1 double, 1 twin; 1 bathroom, 1 wc).
Closed	Never.

Christophe & Valérie Vuitton
Saint Palais du Né, Charente

Tel	+33 (0)5 45 78 47 25
Mobile	+33 (0)6 22 45 25 60
Email	christophe.vuitton@wanadoo.fr
Web	www.charente-gites.net

Moreau - The Farmhouse

Understated elegance and homeliness are skilfully combined in this 18th-century farmhouse; its mood of tranquillity and sophistication beguiles and soothes. Plain yet luxurious, it is decorated throughout with antiques; no surprise to learn that the English owner Marian is an antiques dealer. The house used to be a wealthy farm where the aperitif pineau was made; the chestnut beamed ceilings and stone fireplace have been superbly preserved. The spectacular kitchen – the old distillery – has a huge vaulted ceiling, a wood-burning range and dazzling white walls and floors to set off a sensational display of navy and white china. Enjoy the dreamy views over the fields from the big carpeted bedroom with fabulous antique bed and huge beams. Outside, a private garden with a raised pool. Stock up in Cercoux, or shop at the twice-weekly market at pretty Coutras, a 20-minute drive. Nearby medieval Montguyon holds a folklore festival in July and August; there's also a lake for swimming and a beach area with a little café. Marian is delightful, available yet unobtrusive. Readers are full of praise.

Price	£300-£550 per week.
Sleeps	6-7.
Rooms	2: 2 family rooms for 3, 1 daybed in sitting room; 1 bathroom, 1 shower room.
Closed	November-March. Winter lets by arrangement.

Marian Sanders
Cercoux, Charente-Maritime
Tel   +33 (0)5 46 04 01 66
Fax   +33 (0)5 46 04 01 66
Email marianatmoreau@hotmail.com
Web   www.holidayatmoreau.com

Moreau - Le Pressoir

Like the house next door, this fine 18th-century Charentais house is a treasure chest of fascinating antiques and artefacts, all chosen and carefully composed by Marian. The front doors were once French windows from a local château, there's a pitch-pine armoire from a priest's house in Bordeaux and, in the kitchen/dining room, brass chandeliers from Nantes. Marian's great skill, however, is that she's kept furnishings as simple as possible so as to let this lovely stone building speak for itself. Rooms are large, airy and stylish, with pure white walls and original terracotta tiled floors. French windows lead from the kitchen to a big walled terrace, perfect for sunny breakfasts, and a big, private garden with a raised pool beyond. The cool and spacious downstairs double bedrooms are in the old pressoir where grapes were pressed to make pineau de Charentes, the aperitif for which the area is famous. Colours are muted beiges and pinks, beds are handsome brass and views are of the garden. Worth every penny. *Owners organise trips to antique markets in low season.*

Price	£400–£650 per week.
Sleeps	7.
Rooms	3: 2 doubles, 1 triple; 1 bathroom, 2 shower rooms.
Closed	November-March. Winter lets by arrangement.

	Marian Sanders
	Cercoux, Charente-Maritime
Tel	+33 (0)5 46 04 01 66
Fax	+33 (0)5 46 04 01 66
Email	marianatmoreau@hotmail.com
Web	www.holidayatmoreau.com

Entry 175 Map 9

Limousin

Fleuret - Main House

The setting of this solid stone 17th-century farmhouse is breathtaking: views of hills and woodland fill every window. This is a sensitive restoration by the architect owner, who lives with wife Gilly and their family in the other half of the building. Walls are thick and space plentiful. The kitchen/dining room is immense with warm wooden flooring, a wood-burner in the ancient hearth, an antique table for family feasts; the sitting room has colourwashed walls, some exposed stone, comfortable sofas — wholly delightful. One double room is downstairs, the other four are in the attic with gabled ceilings, white walls, no clutter. There are books, games, a video library and Tim's photographs on the walls (ask about his courses on landscape photography). On the same site are a separate barn and a cottage — all share farmyard, games room and pool. So, plenty of comings and goings, but peace and privacy too. Medieval, hilltop Curemonte, waving to you across the valley, has a market that opens in summer, and there are masses of castles and caves to discover. *Shared pool. Cook on request. Further house for 4 with pool, 8km from Beaulieu.*

Price	€1,190–€1,950 per week.
Sleeps	10–11 + cots.
Rooms	5: 2 doubles, 2 triples, 1 single; 1 bathroom, 2 shower rooms.
Arrival	Mid-week in low season.
Closed	Never.

Tim & Gilly Mannakee
Curemonte, Corrèze

Tel	+33 (0)5 55 84 06 47
Fax	+33 (0)5 55 84 05 73
Email	info@fleuretholidays.com
Web	www.fleuretholidays.com

Limousin

Fleuret - The Cottage

The old bread oven adds a rustic note to the big characterful kitchen, its brick surround charred by the ages. It was discovered and restored by Tim and Gilly, who have revived the red sandstone farm cottage with imagination and sensitivity. Stonework and ancient beams have been properly preserved and terracotta floors and pine cupboards added; cookery books, strings of garlic and board games add a personal touch. The sitting room is charming with cherry-pink sofas and stove; attic bedrooms are simple and cosily carpeted, with small dormer windows to pretty views. French windows let you out of the kitchen into an outdoor barbecue area where you can dine and gaze on fields, woods and never-ending hills. Outside you find a big, walled-off pool, shared with your delightful British hosts next door, and an amazing barn with a vast oak floor that you may use whenever you like: table tennis, billiards, dancing, grand piano; it can also be hired for weddings. A wonderful home for a family in search of peace and space. *Shared pool. Cook available on request. With Main House sleeps 14.*

Price	€520-€990 per week.
Sleeps	4.
Rooms	2: 1 double, 1 twin; 1 bathroom.
Arrival	Mid-week in low season.
Closed	Never.

Tim & Gilly Mannakee
Curemonte, Corrèze
Tel +33 (0)5 55 84 06 47
Fax +33 (0)5 55 84 05 73
Email info@fleuretholidays.com
Web www.fleuretholidays.com

Entry 177 Map 9

Limousin

La Treil

In this dazzling and original place, traditional meets futuristic, steep stone tiles hang beside a living eco-roof and swathes of plate glass. The architect owners hewed out the rock behind the old pigeonnier to build an iron-pillared glass-fronted wing with stupendous views over the hills and down the secret valleys, a steeply terraced garden of structural, architectural plants and a remarkable living space. Minimalist and eclectic in style, the vast room has good sofas, a wooden table designed and made by the owner, 1960s chairs and polished cement floors. You cook, inspiredly without a doubt, in a concrete and plaster-white space beyond: ceramic worktops, stainless steel drawers. The two bathrooms, free-formed from polished concrete, have bright white basins. Bi-coloured bedrooms in the pigeonnier, two with that view, are smartly simple in their modern steel and glass light fittings and plain furniture. More than a place to stay, La Treil is a work of art. If you can tear yourself away, lovely Beaulieu is nearby, the turrets of medieval Curemonte peep into distant view, Dordogne riches lie all around.

Price	€900–€1,800 per week.
Sleeps	8.
Rooms	4: 2 doubles, 2 twins; 1 bathroom, 1 shower room, 3 separate wcs.
Closed	Never.

Tim & Gilly Mannakee
Altillac, Corrèze
Tel +33 (0)5 55 84 06 47
Fax +33 (0)5 55 84 05 73
Email info@fleuretholidays.com
Web www.fleuretholidays.com

La Farge

As ideal a hideaway today as it was for refugees during the war, this large Correzian barn overlooks the pastures of the plateau above the Dordogne. English owners Helen and Keith do B&B across the lane, have a wealth of local knowledge and give guests a big welcome; their charming neighbours may stop for a chat, too. Hens potter about the lane, the beautiful Limousin cows occasionally pass by. Inside, there's a fresh feel to the big, terracotta-floored living room, amply furnished with chunky chairs in flowery covers and usefully stocked with books, games and CDs. The kitchen is just as well-fitted. There's a large white bathroom and a cool, blue bedroom with new pine beds, blue-painted furniture and round blue rug. Big blue pots of geraniums surround the barn in summer and 'Le Parc', as it is known by the locals – a large, enclosed area of lawns and trees, with good garden furniture and a barbecue – is all yours. Enjoy the Archibalds' attentive welcome at all times and their sheltered pool in summer. Perfect for those seeking quintessential rural France. *Sawday B&B. Meals on request.*

Price	£210–£315 per week + £40 with pool.
Sleeps	2.
Rooms	1 twin; 1 bathroom.
Closed	Never.

Keith & Helen Archibald
Monceaux sur Dordogne, Corrèze
Tel +33 (0)5 55 28 54 52
Email archi-at-lafarge@wanadoo.fr
Web www.chezarchi.com

Entry 179 Map 10

L'Abbaye du Palais - Moines

Another graceful restoration by Dutch owners in rural France. In five hectares of forest, meadow and orchard stand a Cistercian abbey, chapel, outbuildings and ruins. Your delightful hosts, with three children and a background in hotel management, have poured hearts and talents into this special place. They live in the 12th-century abbey, do popular B&B and have converted the old monks' bakery into a gîte for six. A tangle of greenery envelops this generous, two-storey cottage, with its terracotta floors, stone walls, cream drapes, antiques and open fire. The bread oven – still intact – is medieval, the kitchen new. A U-shaped bar separates it from the dining area, there are French windows to a west-facing patio with wooden loungers and barbecue, serenity and light. This has to be child heaven: hollow trees to hide in, woods to build dens in, a dressing-up box to raid; bikes, ping-pong, trampoline, pool and games; rabbits, cats, dog and pony – and jolly trailer tractor rides. On Saturdays, great big barbecues are held in the courtyard for (mostly Dutch) guests and friends. *Sawday B&B. Cookery courses.*

Price	€600-€1,250 per week.
Sleeps	6-8.
Rooms	4: 1 double, 3 twins; 2 bathrooms.
Closed	Never.

Martijn & Saskia Zandvliet-Breteler
Bourganeuf, Creuse

Tel	+33 (0)5 55 64 02 64
Fax	+33 (0)5 55 64 02 63
Email	abbayedupalais@wanadoo.fr
Web	www.abbayedupalais.com

Raymond

Walk out of this traditional Auvergnat house into stupendous countryside. You can hear a gurgling stream from your bed and all around are breathtaking views of the cone-shaped *puys*. The 200-year-old house was once two cottages. One half retains the living room where once the family lived, ate and slept: it still has the original wooden beams, long table and inglenook fireplace where you can toast your toes and wind down after a day in the mountains. The other half, a ruin when the Haines found it, feels more modern, extra windows add airiness and light. Bedrooms vary too: ancient, crannied and characterful or light and modern. View the volcanoes from the terrace, visit local cheesemakers to sample Cantal, shower under the waterfall in the river, trawl the market in Aurillac. You can buy fresh milk, yogurt and goat's cheese from the farmer next door and a travelling shop comes three times a week – listen for his horn. There are guided mountain walks, some with donkeys, and adventure sports all summer, mushroom-picking in the autumn, cross-country skiing 1km away in winter. Marvellous.

Price	€350–€500 per week. Linen not included.
Sleeps	6.
Rooms	3: 2 doubles, 1 twin/double; 2 shower rooms, separate wc.
Closed	December-Easter.

Ann & Stephen Haine
Aurillac, Cantal

Tel	+44 (0)20 7267 8936
Mobile	+44 (0)7977 307 554
Email	annhaine@blueyonder.co.uk
Web	www.auvergne-cottage.com

Auvergne

La Roche

Clinging to a hillside where woods and birds abound and water gushes in the valley below, La Roche stands at the end of the lane in glorious isolation and a blaze of flowers. The delightful, knowledgeable English owners live in the old farmhouse, you are in the remarkably converted barn at the front end of the building. Through the high arched doors a splendid split-level living space ascends to old oak beams. The main floor, lit by that glazed barn door and high windows onto your private patch of wild garden, is where you will cook and eat and gather in unexpectedly urbane 1980s bucket chairs by the wood-burner. The mezzanine has two bottle-green futons, a table and chairs for board games and super photographs of life in old Auvergne. Beyond, two snug bedrooms share a clever little grey-green bathroom where the bath is countersunk to floor level so that you shan't bang you head when showering. The other shower and laundry are in the basement. Nature is queen here and summons you forth whatever the weather; or explore those unspoilt villages and towns. *Book via Gîtes de France: www.gite-laroche.com.*

Price	€300–€450 per week.
Sleeps	4-8.
Rooms	2: 1 double, 1 twin; 1 bathroom, 1 shower room, 2 separate wcs, 2 futons.
Arrival	Flexible.
Closed	Rarely.

Catherine & Michael Slater
Oradour, Cantal

Tel	+33 (0)4 71 23 37 92
Fax	+44 (0)117 973 8393
Email	catherine@slater-laroche.com
Web	www.gite-laroche.com

Auvergne

Château de Coisse - Gîte & Studio

After years in tourism and adventure sports, this dynamic couple met a greater challenge: to transform a muster of rambling ruins (dated 1100s to 1700s: carvings, towers, remnants of former rustic grandeur) where the local lord reigned. The river Dore (for picnics) and 'toy' railway run at the bottom, long fields stretch to distant hills, birds flock, cats and dogs thrive. With their own high barn door and fine great hallway, the two gîtes are independent in blue, white and pine with superior fittings, kitchen equipment and bedding. The big first-floor flat is fully child-friendly (stair gates, cots, high chair). A vast plateau of a living room, pine-floored, beamed and light, leads out to a private patio-terrace and up to three bedrooms, one blue, one green, one peach, under the sloping roof: simple and pretty, with practical hanging racks and sock baskets. Within immensely thick walls, the small ground-floor flat is cosy and just as well done. Fiona leaves a super welcome quiche. She and Graham are fascinating about their project-of-a-lifetime but you can be as close or distant as you please.

Price	€400-€600. Studio €200-€300. Prices per week.
Sleeps	Gîte 6-8 + 2 cots. Studio 2-4 + cot.
Rooms	Gîte: 1 double, 2 twins, 1 sofabed in living room; 1 shower room, 1 separate wc. Studio: 1 twin/double, 1 sofabed in living room; 1 bathroom.
Closed	Never.

Fiona & Graham Sheldon
Arlanc, Puy-de-Dôme

Tel	+33 (0)4 73 95 00 45
Email	fiandgra@chateaudecoisse.com
Web	www.chateaudecoisse.com

Aquitaine

Pey au Bruc

Despite the elegance and the antiques, this is the warmest, most child-friendly of places. An 18th-century stone farmhouse, it has the unmistakable air of a house that is lived in and enjoyed. Jane describes it as 'shabby-chic' but there's not an awful lot shabby! Everywhere has been subtly and thoughtfully restored without in any way being precious. The big, delightful bedrooms have comfortable antique French beds – Napoleonic *lits d'enfants* for the little ones – and the nursery room is packed with toys, games and dressing-up costumes. Children will also love the Pey au Bruc bunnies running free in the garden and discovering the house's secret places, reached by unexpected ladders and low doors. They have their own sitting room, too, just off the (fabulous) kitchen, so adults can keep a watchful eye. The main sitting room is gracefully proportioned, with warm stone walls and an open log fire. Out in the big garden, set in woods and very private, is a lovely stone-edged swimming pool; if you prefer the sea, you are six kilometres from the beach.

Price	£2,000-£3,000 per week.
	Linen not included.
Sleeps	15-16 + cots.
Rooms	6: 3 doubles, 1 double with child's bed,
	1 family room for 3, 1 children's room
	for 4; 5 bathrooms.
Closed	Rarely.

Jane Butler
Vendays Montalivet, Gironde

Tel	+33 (0)5 56 41 73 44
Fax	+33 (0)5 56 41 73 44
Email	jane.butler@wanadoo.fr
Web	www.medoc-holidays.com

Aquitaine

The Beachhouse

It matters not a jot if the children trail sand into the house or bounce beach balls in the bedroom. This pretty 1930s wooden seaside house, five minutes from the beach, is just perfect for families. It's painted green and white and is wholly simple yet very inviting. Jane has bleached the floorboards and painted the smallish bedrooms attractive shades of blue and green. The furniture is 1930s – including the beds, with their firm new mattresses and dazzling white covers – and there are two small galley kitchens. The sitting room isn't huge either; no matter, you'll be spending every spare moment in the cane rocker on the gorgeous covered veranda. This stretches the length of the house and is decorated with floats from old fishing nets; a great place for lunch. The house has its own little garden and is in the centre of town, so expect some noise. There are miles of Atlantic beaches, no shortage of bars and restaurants and a huge daily market in Montalivet. And the fabulous wines of Médoc are just a short drive away. Charming. *B&B when house is not let.*

Price	£1,200-£1,800 (£400 for 4, £800 for 8). Prices per week. Linen not included.
Sleeps	16–17. Can be divided into 2 apartments for 4 & 8.
Rooms	6: 4 doubles, 1 family room for 3, 2 children's rooms for 3; 3 bathrooms.
Closed	Mid–November to mid–March.

	Jane Butler
	Vendays Montalivet, Gironde
Tel	+33 (0)5 56 41 73 44
Fax	+33 (0)5 56 41 73 44
Email	jane.butler@wanadoo.fr
Web	www.medoc-holidays.com

Château Coulon Laurensac - Pomerol, Margaux & Sauternes

If you have a passion for wines and want to know more about them, your time here, above the Garonne overlooking Bordeaux, will be delightfully spent. Ronald, knowledgeable and enthusiastic, organises very special tours taking small groups to see the most famous cellars of Médoc or Saint Émilion from the inside – not forgetting a delicious lunch along the way. He and Margaret came to this pretty, compact, 18th-century château with their two young sons and a Jack Russell – aptly named Bouchon – a few years ago. They have converted the outbuildings into luxurious guest accommodation: 'Pomerol' was once the cellar master's house; 'Margaux' and 'Sauternes' are in the *chai à barriques*, where wine was aged in gigantic wooden barrels. Pomerol is an exquisite little house spread over two stories, all chunky stone walls, polished tiles, white ceiling beams, black leather sofas. The apartments too have a roomy elegance, and a French style. Kitchens are superbly kitted out, bathrooms are sumptuous, the swimming pool has Roman steps and breakfasts are gourmet. The wines are superb, naturally. *Sawday hotel.*

Price	€750–€1,250 per week.
Sleeps	Pomerol 4. Margaux & Sauternes 2.
Rooms	Pomerol: 1 double, 1 twin; 1 bathroom. Margaux: 1 double; 1 bathroom. Sauternes: 1 family room for 3; 1 bathroom.
Closed	Never.

	Ronald & Margaret Rens Latresne (Bordeaux), Gironde
Tel	+33 (0)5 56 20 64 12
Fax	+33 (0)5 56 21 79 44
Email	coulonlaurensac@wanadoo.fr
Web	www.CLBX.com

L'Arbousier

The house, just south of Saint Émilion, may be deep in the countryside but pretty villages spring up frequently as one bowls along; your house is in one: perfect for those seeking peace but not isolation. The garden rolls out from the terrace of this fine, green-shuttered building, a medieval pigeonnier and formal parterre to the left, a wild spot made for dens to the side, roses and lavender, an orchard and a pergola – gorgeous. The ground-floor sitting room has exposed stone walls and beams, a big fireplace and a leather sofa. Otherwise, furniture and fabrics are French antique with a country feel. In the kitchen/dining area a mix of stone and stainless steel, Belfast sink and candle chandelier give a cool, contemporary feel. There are more walls of dressed stone in the big, calm bedrooms upstairs, and stylish touches of femininity in toile de Jouy and mosquito nets. Floors are limed wood, there's an iron cot for babies, a glass chandelier and big bright bath towels. This is a fabulous area for visits and gastronomics: enjoy the châteaux, the cycling and the wines.

Price	£500-£950 per week.
Sleeps	6 + cot.
Rooms	4: 2 doubles, 2 singles; 1 bathroom, 1 shower room, separate wc.
Arrival	Saturday, flexible low season.
Closed	Rarely.

Gundi Royle
Romagne, Gironde
Tel +44 (0)20 7033 0142
Email gundiroyle@btinternet.com
Web www.arbousiergite.com

Le Chalard

It is rare indeed to visit an empty house in midwinter and instantly feel a warmth that brings the whole place to life: your cosmopolitan French/Australian hosts have the gift of hospitality tenfold, would welcome you to any family party in the wonderful old barn and want to share their passion for producing organic wine. Jean-Michel's wine knowledge is vast, unpretentious, riveting; Jacqueline can arrange for cookery courses or meals to be prepared on the spot; together they will make your stay unforgettable. Your space is the 400-year-old sunny-ochre pigeon house and pigsties. A glazed door takes you into the stylish yet cosy vaulted and beamed living room with a very effective patterned tile floor, minimal high-quality furniture and original stone walls – a super conversion. The pale bedroom feels fresh and light with all its windows and drapes, the single beds are on the mezzanine. Every summer Castillon gives a re-enactment of the last battle of the 100 Years War; Saint Émilion is nearby, the beaches of Arcachon or the classy boulevards of Bordeaux a little further afield. *Pool occasionally shared.*

Price	€500–€800 per week.
Sleeps	4–5.
Rooms	1 double, 2 single beds in mezzanine room; 1 shower, separate wc.
Closed	Never.

Jacqui & Jean-Michel de Robillard
Flaujagues, Gironde

Tel	+33 (0)5 57 40 15 66
Mobile	+33 (0)6 13 38 26 85
Email	houstonderob@wanadoo.fr
Web	frenchperspectives.com

Les Collines Iduki - Apartments

An attractive holiday complex — 22 gîtes in all, some with one storey, others with two — overlooking one of the prettiest bastide villages of France. A dreamy river sweeps round below, 100-year-old oak trees and fields surround you. Hillside Iduki was designed in Basque style by the architect who built Les Halles in Bayonne and it fits its landscape perfectly. Whitewashed apartments have private terraces with teak furniture and parasols, brightly painted shutters and well-dressed interiors. Small bedrooms have coordinated fabrics, checks and stripes, bathrooms are white, kitchens well-equipped and broadband is throughout. Sitting rooms have stencilled walls, tiled floors, wooden furniture nicely painted. All is comfortable and gently stylish. There are a pool, a play area and organised activities in summer — a treat for sporty couples and active families. The Haramboures run the restaurant by the river and meet you on arrival; the village is a four-minute walk. Come in the last week of July for the fête and three days of carousing in the old village square. *Shared laundry & pool.*

Price	Type A €250-€1,075. Type B €450-€1,450. Type C €535-€1,950. Prices per week. Half-board €22-€28 p.p.
Sleeps	36 apartments. Type A 2-4. Type B 4-6. Type C 6-8.
Rooms	Type A: 1 double, sofabed; 1 bath. Type B: 1 double, 1 twin, sofabed; 1 shower, 1 bath. Apartment C: 1 double, 2 twins, 1 sofabed; 1 bath, 2 showers.
Arrival	Flexible in low season.
Closed	Never.

Marie-Joelle Haramboure
La Bastide Clairence, Pyrénées-Atlantiques

Tel	+33 (0)5 59 70 20 81
Fax	+33 (0)5 59 70 20 25
Email	iduki@iduki.net
Web	www.iduki.net

La Conciergerie

In parkland that includes a majestic blue cedar, the River Saison gurgling by just a two-minute woodland walk away, this pretty little Béarnais building stands under the wing of the bigger, younger château, like a doll's house in its own garden. The new English owners are nurturing roses, oleanders and shrubs: flowering things love it here. Inside, untouched original details include some beautifully variegated terracotta tile work. Two tall windows give an uplifting sense of light streaming into the ground floor from all sides. Sitting and dining rooms are painted in easy-blend colours and are simply furnished in wood and wicker, while colourful Basque fabrics add personality. A charming little narrow staircase takes you up to two smallish bedrooms where more light bounces off their original chestnut floorboards and yellow or red-and-white colour schemes. There are birds, butterflies, even otters down at the lovely wild riverside, horse breeding next door and a country road passing by. There's fabulous walking in the Pyrenean foothills, skiing higher up in winter, surfing in Biarritz. A great welcome, too.

Price	€350–€450 per week.
Sleeps	4.
Rooms	2 doubles; 1 shower room.
Arrival	Saturday, but flexible.
Closed	Rarely.

Ian & Liz Granville-Miller
Osserain Rivareyte,
Pyrénées-Atlantiques
Tel +33 (0)5 59 38 51 89
Email elisabeth.granville-miller@orange.fr

Aquitaine

The Farmhouse

Families are in clover. The list of child facilities is inspiring, from babysitters (mature English ladies) and baby welcome packs (order ahead) to bicycle seats, balls and sterilisers, toys, buckets and spades. But you get more than comfort and practicalities – there's charm too. The delightful old farmhouse has all the beams, local stonework and 18th-century rusticity you could imagine, and has been studiously, stylishly restored. Floors are of new pale oak or rosy terracotta, bed linens are natural, paint colours harmonious, the kitchen splashback is multi-coloured, the oven range hand-built La Cornue. Sheer pleasure to stay! Well set back from the village road, with contained garden to front and side and fields and Pyrenees beyond, the setting is inviting and the views are spectacular. The owners leave masses of information on what to do and chose the site for its proximity to sand and snow. Biarritz is one hour away, winter sports half an hour, there's white water rafting at Navarrenx and riding and swimming up the road, in unspoilt, idyllic little Gurs. Fabulous all round, and good value.

Price	£595-£995 per week.
Sleeps	6-8 + 2 cots.
Rooms	3: 2 doubles, 1 twin; 1 bathroom, 1 shower room, separate wcs. Extra beds on separate mezzanine area.
Closed	Never.

Samantha Adams
Gurs, Pyrénées-Atlantiques
Tel   +44 (0)1622 747 840
Mobile   +44 (0)7905 795784
Email   sam@mountains-2-coast.co.uk
Web   www.mountains-2-coast.co.uk

La Bergerie

Perfect peace in the middle of the largest forest in Europe. You stay in a lovely old shepherd's house rich with timbers, tucked in total privacy a few yards behind the home of the delightful owner; there's space for all. Step straight into the homely main living area with its big open fireplace, comfy sofas and country furniture; radiating off here are the timber-framed bedrooms with their latched doors, terracotta floors, limed furniture, hand-decorated headboards in wood and wrought iron, pretty linens and French country charm. Only one bathroom, but there's a second loo outside on the terrace that overlooks your own large pool and the beautifully cared-for garden (trees, shrubs, hammock and swing). The galley kitchen is white and duck-egg blue, functional and well-stocked; good restaurants are a short drive. Danièle, who teaches French, is a mine of information about the local area and even knows of sandy beaches that don't get crowded in summer. Great for families, with forest hiking and biking from the door, and aquatic parks not much further. *French courses available.*

Price	£425–£1,525 per week.
Sleeps	8–10.
Rooms	4: 3 doubles, 1 twin; 1 bathroom, separate wc.
Closed	Never.

Tessa Cook
Sabres, Landes

Tel	+44 (0)1727 811 414
Mobile	+44 (0)7810 501 591
Email	tessa@frenchcountryvillas.com
Web	www.frenchcountryvillas.com

Aquitaine

Les Combes

In rare contrast to the self-conscious chic of so many places, this old bakery has been beautifully and authentically restored. Plaster walls are plain white, floors are of dark glossy wood or old mellow tiles, and, at its heart – which draws you whenever you are indoors – is the irresistible kitchen. Imagine two big farmhouse tables, shelves of interesting china and numerous recesses and unexpected corners. Best of all, the old bread oven is still there and still usable, though you have an Aga and a gas oven as well. Passages wander intriguingly to other rooms, aglow with old country furniture and pieces made by Quentin; the vivid paintings on the beamed walls are by his partner and friends. An open wooden staircase leads you up to delightful bedrooms softly lit by small windows. The lovely old quilt-covered beds are smallish doubles – expect cosy nights! You are surrounded by fields and trees and it's utterly peaceful – just the occasional chug-chug from the tractor next door. No pool but a terrace smothered in vines, and bikes – marginally less old than the house – are on tap. Truly charming.

Price	€700–€800 per week. Linen not included.
Sleeps	5-7.
Rooms	3: 2 doubles, 1 family room for 3; 2 bathrooms.
Closed	Rarely.

Quentin Lowe
Lot et Garonne, Lot-et-Garonne
Tel +34 926 564176
Email qlowe@wanadoo.es
Web quentin.lowe.googlepages.com

Château de Rodié - L'Appartement

More fortress than château, Rodié comes complete with canon holes, long-drops and tower… wander at will. The story of how Pippa and Paul breathed new life into old stones is inspiring: Paul had a serious accident, they bought the 13th-century ruin and its 135 acres (now their organic farm and a nature reserve) and began the triumphant restoration. In contrast to the tough medieval architecture, they have furnished this excellent big apartment, at a right angle to unshakeable gallery arches, with Empire-period antiques and super metal and wood beds, finishing the rooms with gentle fabrics and rugs that let the old glories glow. Walls are white or pointed stone; atticky windows onto the courtyard and the managed-but-wild nature reserve are small and low with deep sills through the mighty walls. And as it's just been finished, kitchen and bathroom are fully fitted and spanking new. Paul and Pippa farm sheep and run a B&B; Pippa cooks her guests sumptuous organic dinners using much of their own produce: you may arrange to join them. A super-friendly, atmospheric hideaway. *Sawday B&B. Meals on request.*

Price	€250–€400 per week. Shorter periods available.
Sleeps	3.
Rooms	2: 1 double, 1 single; bathroom.
Closed	Rarely.

Paul & Pippa Hecquet
Courbiac de Tournon, Lot-et-Garonne

Tel	+33 (0)5 53 40 89 24
Fax	+33 (0)5 53 40 89 25
Email	chateau.rodie@wanadoo.fr
Web	www.chateauderodie.com

Aquitaine

Château Cardou

Children adore Cardou because they have their little rooms upstairs – tucked far away from the parents. Grown-ups like it because it's a beautiful, elegant place. Built of golden stone, the 'new' castle (just 220 years old) dominates its own secluded valley and has views that swoop ten miles to hilltop Monflanquin. Enter a long wide hall dotted with tapestries and art, and a baby grand at the far end framed by large windows. Off here: a peaceful drawing room with rose-pink sofas; an airy dining room with an open fireplace and a fine long table; a big farmhouse kitchen with a door to the terrace; and light-filled bedrooms gorgeously furnished. Upstairs is the biggest surprise: an open-plan space that reaches from one end of the château to the other, opening to the rafters. Little bedrooms and bathrooms are ingeniously positioned in corners, leaving the central area wide open for sofas and play. There's swimming and tennis in the grounds, maid service three mornings a week and Joanna, who's been letting out her châteaux for years, lives close by. The sunsets are unmissable. *Chef on request.*

Price	£860–£4,900 per week.
Sleeps	18–20 + cots.
Rooms	9: 6 doubles, 3 twins; 7 bath/shower rooms. Extra beds.
Closed	Rarely.

William & Joanna Stuart-Bruges
Tournon d'Agenais, Lot-et-Garonne

Tel	+44 (0)1635 291 942
Mobile	+44 (0)7787 550 413
Email	joanna.sb@free.fr
Web	www.chateau-rentals.com

Château du Trichot

Huge thick walls keep you cool in summer, logs from the estate warm you in winter and the peacefulness soothes you all year round. The history, too, is enticing. It was the magnificent wide stone staircase that the owners fell in love with first, its shallow steps designed with horses in mind; those valuable beasts were stabled upstairs in more turbulent times. The patina on the stonework is superb, the terracotta tiles are charming, the ceilings are lofty or vaulted. Under a 12th-century arch, enter a lovely enclosed courtyard off which lie an atmospheric sitting room, a vaulted dining room and a vast, darkish, well-equipped kitchen. Upstairs: a fascinating mix of sleeping quarters, from a simple triple in the old stables to a high room dominated by a red-draped four-poster bed, carved with the Stuart-Bruges coat of arms. One room has a mezzanine, another, reached via a spiral stone stair, is next to a space for guests under the eaves – complete with its own nesting owl. The delightful owner lives nearby, the vineyard is next door and you can drink the chateau's wines. *Chef on request.*

Price	£780–£4,500.
Sleeps	12–14.
Rooms	6: 3 doubles (1 with bed on mezzanine), 2 triples, 1 single; 5 bath/shower rooms.
Closed	Never.

William & Joanna Stuart-Bruges
Tournon d'Agenais, Lot-et-Garonne
Tel	+44 (0)1635 291 942
Mobile	+44 (0)7787 550 413
Email	joanna.sb@free.fr
Web	www.chateau-rentals.com

Aquitaine

Manoir Serenita

In a huge clearing in a wood, at the end of a drive planted with young poplars and willows, smartly floodlit at night, one of the indefatigable Taylors' fine restoration. Up the steps and into a huge sitting room, its tiled floor and open fireplace standing in immaculate contrast to its aged oak beams. Antique stained-glass doors lead off one side to a TV room, off another to a dining room that seats 18 with no trouble at all. The kitchen is oak-fitted, the French windows open to the pool, the gardens stretch beyond and the vast games room trumpets darts, exercise machines and snooker; everything is on a grand and generous scale. Upstairs are old armoires and period beds, tapestry-style curtains with matching cushions, pictures and plates on ochre walls, sisal-wool carpets and fine rugs, brand new mattresses and top-of-the-range linen. Bathrooms have blue or green tiles, gleaming fittings and old oak doors. The ten acres of gardens and field are fenced to keep out the deer so children may roam to their hearts' content while you lounge on the long, deep patio with a barbecue for star-lit nights.

Price	£2,500-£3,995 per week.
Sleeps	18.
Rooms	9: 5 doubles, 4 twins; 2 bathrooms, 8 shower rooms.
Closed	Rarely.

Christopher & Louisa Taylor
Fargues sur Ourbise, Lot-et-Garonne
Tel   +33 (0)5 53 20 88 03
Fax   +33 (0)5 53 83 61 79
Email   louisa.taylor@wanadoo.fr
Web   www.frenchmanoirs.net

La Brugère

A treasure trove of surprises lies behind the sober facade of this 19th-century house, once a hunting lodge. Tapestries and curtains glow in the dining room off a wood-panelled hall, the drawing room, elegant in cream and draped gold, has a stone fireplace, sofas and antiques. Vast French windows open onto two sides of the terrace. There's a panelled library with telly and a fabulous kitchen: two fridges, a large oven, silver cutlery for the dining room, stainless steel for the terrace. Two of the double rooms have four-posters with luscious curtains, chandeliers and polished wooden floors; the master bedroom is reached by its own staircase and the trompe l'œil in its bathroom is fantastic. The twin room has antique sleigh beds. The lavish, even breathtaking, decoration and comfort holds all the way to the parasols round the pool and the delicious towels. Yet the house feels like a home and children will love it; there's badminton and table tennis, three acres of parkland to explore and swimming and fishing in the river Isle. The owners' daughter lives nearby, full of friendly advice. A magnificent place.

Price	£1,500–£2,800 per week.
Sleeps	12.
Rooms	6: 5 doubles, 1 twin; 5 bathrooms.
Closed	Never.

Lisa Grist
Nantheuil de Thiviers, Dordogne

Tel	+44 (0)1438 831 239
Fax	+44 (0)1993 630 038
Email	pgrist@tractionseabert.com
Web	www.labrugere.com

Entry 198 Map 9

Aquitaine

Les Taloches - La Grange

Another big, comfortable place to stay in the same grounds as its neighbour La Châtaigne. The airy living space, reaching up to the rafters, has great glass doors across the entrances at either end — a legacy from its past as a drive-through barn. Today a courtyard lies to one side and a large private pool to the other. In the main room is a magnificent fireplace, a long monastery table that could seat two dozen; down a few steps is the kitchen. Also on the ground floor, hidden behind the fireplace, is a large bedroom with its own wisteria-clad patio and a rather grand four-poster. A second sitting area on the mezzanine, filled with a lustrous light, houses the television, DVD and a tempting library of books. Upstairs, beds and walls are patterned or floral, there are two small and dramatically beamed twins and a discreet double, with a private entrance and a balcony terrace. Peaceful, tranquil, secluded, Les Taloches is a lazy walk from the pretty riverside village of Tourtoirac — take a drink in the café/bar, pick up your croissants. The Château of Hautefort and its gardens are near, too. *Occasional dinner in summer kitchen.*

Price	£650-£1,500 per week.
Sleeps	8.
Rooms	4: 2 doubles, 2 twins; 3 bathrooms, separate wc.
Closed	Never.

Jo & John Sturges
Tourtoirac, Dordogne
Tel   +33 (0)5 53 50 20 26
Mobile   +33 (0)6 30 84 29 05
Email   jsturges@wanadoo.fr
Web   www.les-taloches.com

Entry 199 Map 9

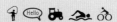

Les Taloches - La Châtaigne

You're faced with a dilemma here, in 18 lovely hectares of woodland and meadows: which house to choose? Set either side of a courtyard, one is the old farmhouse, the other its barn. Both are spacious and extremely comfortable, both have their own private gardens and fenced pools. La Châtaigne is beautifully proportioned and full of character with creaky old staircases, twisted beams and bright white walls. The attractive sitting/dining room has a warm stone fireplace at either end and russet floor tiles; the kitchen is super, modern and well-equipped, with a breakfast area overlooking the pool. A double bedroom on the ground floor opens on to the terrace; two more (a double with a small, bunk-bedded room off) are on the first floor while up in the attic is a vast and delightful family suite – but mind your head in the bathroom! Set well away from both houses are a communal play area and a covered barn with table tennis. There's also an outdoor summer kitchen – a brilliant touch – where Jo will cook meals for guests from time to time.
Occasional dinner in summer kitchen.

Price	£750–£1,700 per week.
Sleeps	12.
Rooms	5: 2 doubles, 1 twin, 1 room with bunks, 1 family suite for 4; 4 bathrooms, separate wc.
Closed	Never.

Jo & John Sturges
Tourtoirac, Dordogne
Tel +33 (0)5 53 50 20 26
Mobile +33 (0)6 30 84 29 05
Email jsturges@wanadoo.fr
Web www.les-taloches.com

Aquitaine

Forge Basse - The Barn & The Cottage

The Forge Master's House, 1480: how real does that ring on your 21st-century anvil? One of the most atmospheric places possible, the forge once had some 55 iron-sweated workers producing cauldrons for the West Indies, cooled by the river that still rushes past the door. Each gîte occupies half a fine stone barn with an extra room in the middle for one or the other. The well-named Barn is all height, beams and open plan. Huge granite blocks from the forge rise again in the door surrounds. The Cottage is cosy with its wood burner in the old fireplace. Both have a talented mix of old furniture and modern style, good quality and simplicity: simple carpeted bedrooms with good lighting and beds, bright bathrooms, open, well-fitted kitchens and lots of light. Each has its own wisteria-clad patio for privacy and barbecues but you all share the super garden, its heated pool, rowing boat and fishing. Nontron's knife factory and art galleries must be seen, lovely Brantôme is a bit further. And your charming knowledgeable hosts hold open house for aperitifs on Mondays. *Shared laundry & pool. Unfenced water.*

Price	£490-£1,180 per week.
Sleeps	Barn for 8. Cottage for 6.
Rooms	Barn: 2 doubles, 2 twins; 2 bathrooms, 2 separate wcs.
	Cottage: 2 doubles, 1 twin; 2 bathrooms; 2 separate wcs.
Closed	November - Easter.

Robin Fenton
Nontron, Dordogne
Tel +33 (0)5 53 56 99 71
Email robin@forgebasse.com
Web www.forgebasse.com

Jovelle - La Chartreuse

White walls, pale oak floors, a rolling loft space, peace – city chic in the country. The 19th-century house, on the site of a monastery, has been rigorously renovated by the owners, who live across the courtyard in the main house, to create a modern space alongside original features. The open-plan living area sweeps across the ground floor; quarry tiles, a grand fireplace, antique furnishings, underfloor heating. The shiny-smart kitchen – convivially at one end – is a cook's delight. Bedrooms are bright, uncluttered spaces of oak boards and sandblasted beams. Bring well-behaved friends and you also get the use of the vast attic apartment in the main house: two bedrooms, sloping beamed ceilings, antique furniture and claw-foot baths, and a soaring loft space scattered with rugs and comfy sofas. There's a smallish garden, a terrace for alfresco meals, a saltwater pool with a shower, and you are well-placed for exploring the Dordogne, the vineyards of Saint Émilion and pretty riverside Brantôme. Too tired to rustle up a meal? A Leith-trained cook is to hand – just say when. *Saltwater pool. Meals on request.*

Price	£700-£950 or €900-€1,500 per week. Extra charge for rooms in main house.
Sleeps	4 (8 with main house).
Rooms	2: 1 twin, 1 double; 2 bathrooms (2 doubles, 2 bathrooms available in main house).
Closed	Christmas.

John & Sally Ridley-Day
Leguillac de Cercles, Dordogne

Tel	+33 (0)5 53 56 51 19
Fax	+33 (0)5 53 56 52 53
Email	sallyridleyday@hotmail.com
Web	www.lachartreusedordogne.com

La Geyrie - Gîte Maison

La Maison is attached to the Dunns' house, across the yard is Le Pigeonnier. The goats are reared organically, solar panels provide the hot water and Louise has allowed dry stone walling students to practise on her walls – many are tumbledown. This is a working farm: sheepdogs roam, cats doze, there are hens in the yard and a clutch of Jack Russells. Farmstead and countryside have a marvellously ancient feel, Peter and Louise are busy and committed and everyone may happily muck in. Inside are the classic limewash walls and terracotta floors, chairs are straight-backed, the sofa is small and a 1930s dresser houses the crockery – plain but genuine. Bedrooms and bathroom upstairs feed into each other with a fine-sized bedroom at the front dominated by an old fireplace and a bedroom at the back that is big enough for a double bed, two singles and bunks. Mattresses are new, cotton sheets are coloured, the bathroom is for everyone and the small kitchen even has a dishwasher! This is an outdoorsy place where free-range families will be happy. *Service wash available.*

The Dunns' goat farm has been eco-certified since 2000 so their goat products, fruit and nuts are pure organic. Concealed in the woods, the new goat barn-cum-milking parlour is the epitome of eco-friendship: rainwater collector, reed beds to process the effluent, solar panels to heat water for cleaning the milking machines. The old goat barn is to become a car park to hide guests' 4x4's. They think their greening through intelligently and hope to guide guests as well as other farmers towards taking more care. Peter is also enthusiastically germinating seed for vegetable garden and flowers.

Price	£240–£390 per week.
	Linen not included.
Sleeps	4–8.
Rooms	2: 1 double, 1 quadruple + bunks;
	1 bathroom.
Closed	Never

Louise & Peter Dunn
Verteillac, Dordogne

Tel	+33 (0)5 53 91 15 15
Fax	+33 (0)5 53 90 37 19
Email	peter.dunn@wanadoo.fr
Web	www.lageyrie.com

SPECIAL
GREEN ENTRY
see page 18

Aquitaine

La Geyrie - Le Pigeonnier

A pair of nesting owls sometimes takes up residence in the tower of this 15th-century pigeonnier… you might spot roe deer in the woods, too. Your charming little pigeonnier is pleasantly cool, with tiled floors downstairs, floorboards up and everywhere, heavenly old rafters. Furnishings are basic and well-used – an upright pale green sofa, a set of pine shelves with yellow crockery, a corner kitchen with a new gas cooker. There are rugs scattered on floorboards, 1940s furniture, a fine armoire, pastoral views; the almost-as-big shower room reveals its pigeon holes and a rustically paved floor. You may not be steeped in *le grande luxe*, but the simple pleasures of a farm and a small tribe of animals (there's a brand-new goat barn hidden in the woods) should more than compensate. Borrow the bikes or bring your own: the nearest shops, market and restaurant are a mile away in La Tour Blanche. Down the road, the wonderful Limousin-Périgord National Park; in the Limodore reserve nearby, rare orchids. Louise knows the area and has all the guides. *Service wash available.*

Price	£205–£320 per week. Linen not included.
Sleeps	2 + 2 children.
Rooms	1 double, 2 extra single beds; 1 shower room.
Closed	Never.

Louise & Peter Dunn
Verteillac, Dordogne

Tel	+33 (0)5 53 91 15 15
Fax	+33 (0)5 53 90 37 19
Email	peter.dunn@wanadoo.fr
Web	www.lageyrie.com

La Meynardie - Kabarole

'Kabarole' is a Ugandan invitation to 'come and see' what this dramatic old barn is about. Discover sweeping terracotta tiles, a striking terrace that runs the length of the building, a pool and barbecue hewn into the hillside. Raids on the vegetable patch begin and end here, dining al fresco on your green-gotten gains. Sheep graze beyond the meadows, in full view of the family's château-manoir home (filled with stone staircases, monumental rooms and, some say, a secret passage to perfect Siorac and its medieval church). All this is rivalled by Kabarole's own offerings. Twin beds are tucked into the attic; downstairs bedrooms reach up to lofty chestnut and oak-beamed ceilings; there are lime-rendered walls and mushroom-pink terracotta floors. With enough room for a celebratory dance around Ugandan chairs, nothing stands in your way to the generous, wood-columned bathroom. The living area arranges itself round a limestone chimneypiece, a relaxed dining area set behind, and a modern white-on-white kitchen to the side. Wonderful spaces, timbers, fittings – and great for families. *Shared pool.*

Price	€725–€1,560 per week.
Sleeps	8-9.
Rooms	4: 2 doubles, 2 twins; 2 bathrooms. Extra sofabed.
Closed	Never.

Judith & Nigel Nicholson
Siorac de Ribérac, Dordogne
Tel   +33 (0)5 53 91 84 60
Email   meynardie.siorac@wanadoo.fr
Web   www.meynardie.com

Entry 205 Map 9

Domaine de Foncaudière - Gros Dondon & Ange Gardien

Hard to believe you're minutes from Bergerac town. A winding driveway takes you through woodland and suddenly, in a clearing, voilà! – the manoir, built 250 years ago on the foundations of a medieval castle. Beyond: the tiny estate hamlet – a scattering of extraordinarily pretty cottages which Marcel and his partner have restored with tender care. Each honey-coloured building has oak beams, stone and timbered walls, wood or terracotta floors. Each is charmingly furnished – antiques and new sofas, perfect kitchens and bathrooms. One-storey Gros Dondon (above) was the baker's house (the great stone ovens are still in place); Ange Gardien (below) the caretaker's. Both have their own gardens with lawns, fruit trees (figs, walnuts, cherries), barbecues, rustic furniture. Age-old paths criss-cross the meadows; the pool is down a sloping hill; views are wonderful. The estate covers 100 acres and takes its name from a hot spring. Farmers used to bring their animals to drink here when everywhere else was frozen. The sense of peace and history is profound. *Shared laundry. Private chef available May-Oct. Sawday B&B.*

Price	€1,100-€2,100 per week.
Sleeps	Gros Dondon 3-4. Ange Gardien 6.
Rooms	Gros Dondon: 1 double, 1 room with bunks; 1 bathroom. Ange Gardien: 1 double, 2 twins; 1 bathroom.
Closed	Rarely.

Marcel Wils
Maurens, Dordogne

Tel	+33 (0)5 53 61 13 90
Fax	+33 (0)5 53 61 03 24
Email	info@foncaudiere.com
Web	www.foncaudiere.com

Domaine de Foncaudière - Fraise Soûle & Parfum de Rose

Two more oh-so-pretty cottages on the domaine; they share one roof but are otherwise independent. Fraise Soûle, with its large kitchen/dining room and separate sitting room, has three fine bedrooms; Parfum de Rose has two and is next to ancient stalls which once housed the estate's farm animals. (Is there an irony in the name?). Both cottages have been restored, then furnished with care. The jolly kitchens are a pleasure to cook in, the shower rooms gorgeous, the beds well-sprung. Apart from the pool there's a barn full of games to gladden children's hearts, a period library in the château, bikes for hire so you can pedal beyond. You could spend a whole week just exploring these 40 hectares; Marcel gives you a map – seek out La Cave, where a medieval priest went into hiding during the Wars of Religion. There's a pond, too, inhabited by a 100-year-old carp, and a beech walk, even a medieval potager. You can buy organically grown herbs and vegetables from the estate and your lovely hosts are happy to advise on markets, wine tastings and regional specialities. Magical. *Shared laundry. Chef available May-Oct. Sawday B&B.*

Price	€800–€2,100 per week.
Sleeps	Fraise Soûle 6. Parfum de Rose 4.
Rooms	Fraise Soûle: 2 doubles, 1 twin; 1 shower room. Parfum de Rose: 1 double, 1 twin; 1 shower room.
Closed	Rarely.

	Marcel Wils
	Maurens, Dordogne
Tel	+33 (0)5 53 61 13 90
Fax	+33 (0)5 53 61 03 24
Email	info@foncaudiere.com
Web	www.foncaudiere.com

Le Moulin de Jarrige

The road from here goes blissfully nowhere. Woodland and fields stretch as far as the eye can see; within minutes you'll be packing a picnic and out of the farmhouse door. There are bikes to borrow, a children's den in the barn, badminton and boules; the more slothful may prefer gazing over the countryside from the pool. This 200-year-old farmhouse is about simple pleasures. Colours are mellow, rooms uncluttered and old features retained – exposed stone walls, beamed ceilings, open fireplaces. The large kitchen, with its Shaker-style fittings and big farmhouse table, is a cook's joy; it opens into a comfy sitting room invitingly strewn with cushions and throws. There's also a light-filled study where you can curl up with a book. Bedrooms spread over the ground floor on gently split levels – creamy-cool spaces of simple painted furniture, wooden floors and brightly checked bedcovers. Plenty of bathrooms, too, all white, bright and super-duper. Although remote, you're not isolated; local shops are two miles, tennis, canoeing and riding are nearby and you're surrounded by vineyards. *B&B also.*

Price	£800–£1,800 per week.
Sleeps	8.
Rooms	4: 2 doubles, 2 twins; 2 shower rooms, 2 bathrooms.
Closed	Never.

Keith & Maureen Fenton
Saint Méard de Gurçon, Dordogne
Tel   +33 (0)5 53 82 27 40
Email keithfenton25@hotmail.com
Web   www.jarrige.co.uk

Les Marais

Set quite alone on an old flood plain, the unfussy clean lines of this former cattle barn find echo in the regimented vines that march in perspective away from the garden, the wooded ridge rising towards Saussignac giving relief. Made of local materials, the house has a modern contemporary feel. Walls are stone, the roof terracotta, the wide-open ground floor done in big black slates – a magnificent living space. A floor-to-ceiling window in the centre of the house brings light pouring in, a rafter-hung contemporary chandelier hovers over the solid wood table, the super-comfy sitting area will soon have an open log fire and the generous kitchen is fine oak and stainless steel. Ian and Annabel, the young owners who live nearby, are justly proud of their new renovation (the garden comes next). A staircase takes you up to a gangway that feeds the properly simple plaster and pine bedrooms with soft-toned plain-coloured bed linen, white blinds and a pristine white bathroom each. A great place to do your own thing, taste wines, discover old villages, swing through the trees, crash out – and excellent value.

Price	£250–£550 per week.
Sleeps	4–6.
Rooms	2: 1 double, 1 twin, 1 sofabed; 2 bathrooms, separate wc.
Arrival	Flexible.
Closed	Rarely.

Ian & Annabel Hull
Saussignac, Dordogne
Tel   +44 (0)87 1218 2886
Fax   +44 (0)87 1218 2886
Email enquires@lesmarais.co.uk
Web   www.lesmarais.co.uk

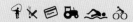

Le Roudier - Le Chai, La Garenne, La Ferme, Le Nid

The gites at Le Roudier lie in a pretty rolling countryside of sunflowers and corn, with 15 acres of bird-rich woodland in which to roam. Converted from old farm buildings with letting in mind they are clean, comfortable and perfect for families. There's even satellite TV... not that you'll be spending many days indoors. What makes this place special is the vast terraced pool that drops away to the meadows. In the old bakehouse is a summer kitchen and games room with table tennis, plus a paddling pool, slides, swings and mountain bikes. The smaller gîtes have patios on which you may barbecue; the larger have shady, vine-strewn terraces that face the pool but are fenced and secure. Inside, the usual terracotta floors and open-plan kitchen/diners, spotless and excellently equipped. In La Garenne and La Ferme, steepish staircases lead to extra bedrooms sky-lit under the eaves. The whole enterprise is run by the Smiths, an English/Irish couple with a young child who do all they can to make you happy. Rabbits in the meadows, three golf courses within striking distance, canoes at Eymet, vineyards all around. *B&B also.*

Price	Garenne & Ferme €780–€1,770 each. Chai €550–€1,200. Nid €405–€795. Prices per week.
Sleeps	Garenne 7-8. Ferme 8. Chai 4. Nid 2.
Rooms	Garenne: 1 double, 1 twin, 1 triple, 1 single on landing; 1 bathroom, 1 shower room. Ferme: 1 double, 3 twins; 1 bathroom, 1 shower room. Chai: 1 double, 1 twin; 1 bathroom. Nid: 1 double; 1 shower room.
Arrival	Friday.
Closed	Never.

Paul & Dearbhla Smith
Razac d'Eymet, Dordogne

Tel	+33 (0)5 53 24 54 96
Email	leroudier@wanadoo.fr
Web	www.leroudier.com

La Martigne

This glorious stone *chartreuse* is utterly, incontrovertibly French – it could be nowhere else. It is a pleasing mix of simple yet luxurious, unadorned yet ornate. Splendidly isolated, with magnificent views of the Périgord Noir, the house has been beautifully restored by its French owners who have lived here for generations. Members of the family occasionally use the grounds but otherwise the cascading terraced lawns, the private park and the pool are all yours. Dark antiques and pretty fabrics harmonise with simple bare stone, soft painted walls and aqua-blue doors with their china handles. Polished wooden floors gleam in the two living rooms, comfy sofas and elegant blue and white upholstered Regency chairs invite you; next door is a formal dining room with rich red wallpaper and attractive rugs. There are several open fireplaces, one of them the focus of one of the bedrooms which, huge and light, all open onto the south-facing terrace and the loveliest views. The kitchen is as well fitted out as you would expect and the bathrooms are super. *Security deposit of £400 payable on booking. Meals on request.*

Price	€1,500-€2,500 per week.
Sleeps	8-9.
Rooms	4: 1 double, 2 twins, 1 family room for 3; 1 bathroom, 2 shower rooms, 2 separate wcs.
Closed	Never.

Jane Hanslip
Lamonzie Montastruc, Dordogne

Tel	+44 (0)7768 747 610
Mobile	+33 (0)6 32 62 43 15
Email	jhanslip@aol.com
Web	www.dordognerental.com

Entry 211 Map 9

Le Bourdil Blanc

All this could be yours: a fine 18th-century manor with a long, tree-lined avenue, views down to the lake and a super big pool. When you've finished lazing in the huge grounds or being sporty around tennis or croquet balls, retreat to the sitting room, with its lovely old wooden floors, open fire, comfortable sofas. The dining room, magnificent with William-Morris-type fabrics, mirrored fireplace and polished floors, seats 14 on upholstered chairs. Upstairs, a long, light passage leads to the roomy bedrooms and bathrooms; then, in the loft, three bedrooms with brand new shower rooms. The sunny kitchen and the bathrooms are more functional than fabulous, and there's central heating so you're as warm as toast in winter. The Wing is less grand than the main house but has an open fire, tiled floors, warm kilim rugs, some good antiques and a fitted kitchen; the Pigeonnier is charming, with fine furnishings, stunning stone fireplace and private walled garden. So much space indoors and out, and stacks to do in the area. *Cooking & babysitting. Riding & wine-tasting. Rent House & Wing together in July & August. Meals on request.*

Price	House €1,400-€2,900. Wing & Pigeonnier €800 each. July-August: House & Wing (must be taken together) €6,000 (with Pigeonnier €6,800). Prices per week.
Sleeps	House 14-16. Wing 2. Pigeonnier 4.
Rooms	House: 3 doubles, 3 twins, 1 double, 1 single, 1 single in passage, 2 sofabeds; 8 bathrooms. Wing: 1 double, 2 sofabeds; 1 bathroom. Pigeonnier: 2 doubles; 1 bathroom.
Closed	Never.

Jane Hanslip
Saint Sauveur de Bergerac, Dordogne

Tel	+44 (0)7768 747 610
Mobile	+33 (0)6 32 62 43 15
Email	jhanslip@aol.com
Web	www.dordognerental.com

Les Bigayres

You won't forget the bedrooms of this elegant converted dovecote: one has gnarled beams that grow like trees through the tall pointed ceiling, another has an amazing *Princess and the Pea* bed with the highest mattress ever. Teenagers will go for the third, a sunny bunk bedroom with its own poolside entrance. In 30 acres of grounds belonging to a lovely 17th-century manor, and with its own private drive and terrace, this beautifully furnished cottage is quite a find. You share the pool with the French owners but they use it infrequently so you'll often have it all to yourself. The open-plan kitchen and living area is pure, light and roomy, with white or exposed stone walls, grey-green beams supported by unusual stone columns and prettily patterned red and green curtains. Fine, hexagonally-laid tiles run through the ground floor, there are wooden boards upstairs. Wallow in luxurious sofas by the stone fireplace, stroll out of the French windows to the lawn with its long wooded views. You have everything you need, from dishwasher to barbecue, and charming Bergerac is no distance at all. *Shared pool.*

Price	€700–€1,500 per week.
Sleeps	6-8.
Rooms	4: 2 doubles, 1 room with bunks, 1 sofabed; 1 bathroom, separate wc.
Closed	November-February.

	Jane Hanslip
	Liorac sur Louyre, Dordogne
Tel	+44 (0)7768 747 610
Mobile	+33 (0)6 32 62 43 15
Email	jhanslip@aol.com
Web	www.dordognerental.com

Aquitaine

Domaine des Blanches Colombes - Monet & Renoir

The doves are still here; only their cooing ruffles the calm, and the distant hum of the tractor. The Domaine is a 17th-century manor in a hilltop hamlet, built of golden stone, encircled by high walls. It belongs to Clare and Steven, a friendly and enthusiastic couple. Steven organises rock concerts, Clare looks after their two boys and runs the gîtes. Two of their cottages stand side by side in the west wing but still manage to feel private. Renoir is creeper-covered, Monet has an array of hanging baskets. They are engaging, comfortable, homely: wooden or tiled floors, open-plan living rooms, blue and white crockery, gay gingham. The furnishings are a mix of old-fashioned and funky modern and the kitchens are brilliantly equipped. Give them notice and Clare and Steven will rustle up a meal – perhaps bœuf bourguignon, fresh fruit pavlova – deliver it to your table, then clear up afterwards. They can arrange for bread and croissants to be delivered each morning, too. With a shared games room, garden and pool, a super place for families. *Shared pool. Babysitting available. Meals on request.*

Price	Monet €395–€1,200. Renoir €595–€1,400. Prices per week.
Sleeps	Monet: 4. Renoir: 6.
Rooms	Monet: 1 double, 1 twin; 2 bathrooms. Renoir: 1 double, 2 twins; 1 bathroom, 1 shower room.
Arrival	Flexible in low season.
Closed	Never.

Clare Todd
Grand Castang, Dordogne
Tel +33 (0)5 53 57 30 38
Email clare.todd@quality-gites.co.uk
Web www.quality-gites.com

Entry 214 Map 9

Domaine des Blanches Colombes - Degas & Matisse

Just over the road are Clare and Steven's other two gîtes, converted from an old village house. They're relaxing, friendly, comfortable places to stay, each with its own terrace and brand new kitchen. Degas (above) is diminutive and cosy with a painted double bed, views over rooftops to the rolling hills and a little purple and green bathroom downstairs. Matisse is larger and full of character, with a wooden staircase that winds up to two attractive big bedrooms (below). Both cottages share the delights of the Domaine. A fabulous L-shaped pool shelters in the angle of two barns and is surrounded by trees and shrubs, another barn has been converted into a games room. If the ball pit, pool table, darts and table tennis don't keep the young happy, every cottage has a DVD player (you can hire titles from Steven's vast collection) and there are board games – just ask. Six miles off is Lalinde, a pretty village with a spectacular Thursday market. Bergerac is close by, and there are the caves of Lascaux. *Babysitting available. Two apartments for two next to river in Mauzac also available.*

Price	Degas €300-€475.	
	Matisse €395-€1,100. Prices per week.	
Sleeps	Degas 2. Matisse 4.	
Rooms	Degas: 1 double; 1 bathroom.	
	Matisse: 1 double, 1 twin;	
	1 bathroom.	
Arrival	Flexible in low season.	
Closed	Never.	

	Clare Todd
	Grand Castang, Dordogne
Tel	+33 (0)5 53 57 30 38
Email	clare.todd@quality-gites.co.uk
Web	www.quality-gites.com

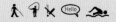

Aquitaine

Le Gers

The views from this hilltop farmhouse, over lovely Limeuil where two rivers meet, are mesmerising. Peaceful, too, yet you are a ten-minute stroll to the shops, craft studios and restaurants of the old walled town. Restored in bold fashion by a previous artist owner, the farmhouse has touches of quirkiness and heaps of space. The soaring living room – exposed stones, high beams, brick walls – is overlooked by a mezzanine sitting area with books, music and TV. Light and brightly furnished, it's a wonderful space to eat, relax, chat. The separate kitchen has a more rustic feel: a working fireplace and all the pans you need. Then up the open staircase to two floors of bedrooms, uncluttered, inviting and stylishly simple. Cream stone walls, wooden floors, colourful rugs, soft lamps: such a friendly feel. Unexpected touches include an innovatively tiled bathroom and a stained glass window. Treat the children to La Bugue, with its aquarium and working farms; return to the pool (it's a walk down from the house) and the views, badminton in the barn and the sunsets over the valley. *Heating extra.*

Price	€770-€1,900 (£525-£1,500) per week. Heating extra.
Sleeps	6 + cot.
Rooms	3: 2 doubles, 1 twin; 2 bathrooms, separate wc.
Arrival	Flexible in low season.
Closed	Rarely.

Louise Bonafoux
Alles sur Dordogne, Dordogne
Tel   +44 (0)23 8055 5486
Email   lbonafoux@hotmail.com
Web   www.le-gers.com

Domaine de Leygue - Four Cottages

This is a pretty pocket of France, peaceful and pleasing on the eye: five acres of grounds insulate you from all but wildlife. And here are four tidy little cottages: two near the courtyard and the owners' house, two (more modern) beyond a pretty grove of walnut trees. All are utterly private and aimed at couples. There are even two pools and, as the sunbeds stay by the cottages, you'll have plenty of private swims. And more: an excellent tennis court, boules, even bikes for those who wish to pedal round paradise... Peter and Geraldine have thought of everything. Domaine de Leygue was once a small farm and two of the gîtes are conversions, two newly built; all have stone walls and a neatly furnished terrace. All bedrooms are on the ground floor bar those in the Tower cottage, where views stretch over farmland and woods. All is spotless, light, immaculate – checked sofas in one, new cherrywood in another, chestnut beams, Villeroy & Boch china. There's central heating for cool days, fans for warm nights and no TV or children to disturb the peace. Perfection in the heart of the Dordogne.

Price	£520–£730 each per week.
Sleeps	4 cottages for 2.
Rooms	Each cottage: 1 double; 1 bath or shower room.
Closed	October–May.

Peter & Geraldine Jones
Bourniquel, Dordogne
Tel   +33 (0)5 53 73 83 12
Fax   +33 (0)5 53 73 83 20
Email   GeraldineJones@shieling.biz
Web   www.shieling.biz/leygue

Entry 217 Map 9

Aquitaine

Château de Cazenac

This is the lap of luxury, an adjective-defying 17th-century *petit château* that conceals a dazzling classic/contemporary interior. There are black and white marble floors, stone staircases and a *grand salon* in which multiple French windows flood the room with light and open to a terrace. A terrifically grand place yet not a daunting one; easy to imagine yourself kicking off your shoes. Bedrooms astonish, be it the double with the vaulting timber-framed ceiling, the twin with its view-filled balcony, or the master suite with its big round-tower bathroom. The dining room can seat 20, the kitchen has murals and a cavernous fireplace. Elsewhere: African masks, a grand piano, statues here and there. Step outside and roam through 25 hectares of private grounds. Long, dreamy views stretch over the Dordogne river and there's a secluded swimming pool with a private terrace. The château sleeps up to 24 so its price is not quite as steep as you might think. If you want to splash out on a once-in-a-lifetime treat, you won't be disappointed: a fabulous place for a wedding. And lovely people.

Price	€4,500–€7,500 per week.
Sleeps	14-24.
Rooms	7: 3 doubles, 3 twins, 1 triple, 1 dormitory for 8; 7 bathrooms.
Closed	Never.

Famille Constant
Le Coux et Bigaroque, Dordogne

Tel	+33 (0)5 53 31 69 31
Mobile	+33 (0)6 74 37 73 72
Email	info@cazenac.fr
Web	www.cazenac.fr

Château de Cazenac - La Maison & La Ferme

The Maison stands high on a steep hill whence dreamy views over the river... there's a simple shop a mile away but you feel beyond the call of the outside world. The interior of this 16th-century Périgord farmhouse is a charming mélange of old antique furniture, lime-rendered walls and ancient terracotta. Windows frame sublime views of valley and forest while rooms combine a studied rusticity with a kaleidoscope of colour. Vast bedrooms have vaulted ceilings and exposed beams, bathrooms a Moroccan touch, the open-plan living room's sliding glass doors open to a terrace, then a pool, and the kitchen reveals two pretty dressers. There's a vine-shaded terrace for barbecues and a delightful garden in which to fall asleep to the sounds of the valley. The newly-renovated Ferme sits just outside the château walls in its own private garden with an above-ground pool abutting an old barn wall. Inside: more style, more charm. Chestnut floors are scattered with rugs, beams are exposed, paintings hang on rendered walls. A delectable place, run with great enthusiasm by a new generation of Constants. *Winter truffle breaks are planned.*

Price	€1,000–€2,200 per week.
Sleeps	Maison 6-7 + cots. Ferme 7-8.
Rooms	Maison: 2 doubles, 1 twin; 3 shower rooms, 3 separate wcs, 1 extra bed. Ferme: 1 double, 1 twin, 1 triple; 3 bathrooms, 3 separate wcs, extra bed.
Closed	Never.

Famille Constant
Le Coux et Bigaroque, Dordogne
Tel +33 (0)5 53 31 69 31
Email info@cazenac.fr
Web www.cazenac.fr

Aquitaine

Beaux Rêves

Only the honey-coloured stone walls and one window are original but you'd never guess it: this 18th-century barn has been so perfectly restored. Four years ago it was in ruins; now it stands, complete with pigeonnier, under a demure grey roof. Opposite is the main house where Eric and Helen live. She's English, he's French and they juggle B&B with running a five-hectare estate and bringing up two young children. They've given enormous thought, care and money to this new project. The ground floor is one vast room, with tawny floor, stone walls and a wood-burning stove at its very centre. A few steps lead up to the kitchen, arresting in its faultless simplicity and superbly equipped. Lounging on a white leather sofa in the sitting area, enjoy the dazzling view of St Anne's church, spectacularly floodlit at night. Upstairs are three big, white bedrooms, each with vivid rugs, interesting pictures, a fine antique. Bathrooms are big, bright and excellent. You have the gardens to explore, your own private fenced pool, a Michelin-starred restaurant and a small pub a stroll away. *B&B also.*

Price	€1,050–€2,250 per week.
Sleeps	6–8.
Rooms	3: 2 doubles, 1 family room for 4; 2 shower rooms, 1 bathroom.
Closed	Rarely.

Eric & Helen Edgar
Saint Crépin Carlucet, Dordogne
Tel   +33 (0)5 53 31 22 60
Email   lescharmes@carlucet.com
Web   www.carlucet.com

La Treille Haute

The setting smacks of a fairy tale and five of the Périgord's most spectacular châteaux, clinging to the craggy cliffs of the Dordogne, are a short drive from this converted stone barn. You can even see the floodlit Château de Beynac, awesome and grand, from the comfort of the bed. English owner Felicity lives in the adjoining house: metre-thick walls between the two buildings ensure total privacy and you have your own sweet garden with amazing views. Old exposed stone walls with the vaulted beamed bedroom may have sheltered pilgrims: one stone bears a Templar cross. The modestly furnished open-plan ground-floor living area includes the kitchenette – with a hob, a microwave/oven and a glazed door to the terrace – and also leads to the bathroom. The historic village has a shop with fresh produce and an excellent boucherie/charcuterie. Treat yourself to some of the local specialities and picnic in the wooded hills, or explore the steep, fascinating, stone villages of this understandably popular area. *B&B also. Babies & children over four welcome: garden unsuitable for toddlers.*

Price	€310–€590 per week. Extra twin €50 per day. Linen not included.
Sleeps	2-5 + cot.
Rooms	1 double, 1 sofabed; 1 bathroom. Extra twin room with separate entrance.
Arrival	Saturday, flexible in winter.
Closed	Never.

Felicity Martindale
Castelnaud La Chapelle, Dordogne

Tel +33 (0)5 53 29 95 65
Fax +33 (0)5 53 29 95 65
Email martindale@free.fr
Web martindale.free.fr

Lavande

Brigitte and Christophe spotted this 18th-century farmhouse and its wooded acres while on holiday. It was love at first sight; several busy years on they run an enchanting B&B and have converted the stone stables into two self-catering cottages. Lavande, with its serene views over wooded hills, is the larger and, although near the other buildings, is peaceful and private. The inside has been thoroughly restored and has a newish feel within old beams and exposed stones. In the living room: sumptuous black leather armchairs and a sofa on an immaculately polished wooden floor; in the dining room: an antique trestle table and chairs. The pièce de résistance, however, is the beamed white and blue bedroom which looks like a piece of Delft china. Gourmets will make a beeline for the restaurant L'Esplanade in Domme – you can glimpse the splendid hilltop town from here. You share the delightful park – and saltwater pool – with other guests; if you like good home cooking, you may share meals, too. Do buy Brigitte's delicious homemade pâtés for your picnic baguettes. *Shared pool. Sawday B&B. Meals on request.*

Price	€620–€1,260 per week. Linen not included.
Sleeps	6-8.
Rooms	3: 1 double, 1 twin/double, 1 mezzanine twin; 1 bathroom, 1 shower room, separate wc; 1 sofabed.
Closed	November-March.

Brigitte & Christophe Demassougne
Cénac et Saint Julien, Dordogne

Tel   +33 (0)5 53 29 91 97
Fax   +33 (0)5 53 29 91 97
Email   contact@la-gueriniere-dordogne.com
Web   www.la-gueriniere-dordogne.com

Les Milandes - Manoir, Ancienne Mairie, Maison du Gardien, Arc en Ciel

The view from here must be one of the most ravishing in Europe. Part of the good-looking village that clusters round the château walls and hangs out over the banks of the Dordogne, these houses rejoice in a lord's position above the sweeping river. Their pretty terraced gardens are full of interest. Be your choice the aristocratic manor or one of the former workers' cottages, you will find a well-planned living area with polished wooden floors and good rugs, smart comfortable furnishings – soft-painted beds, ornate bedcovers, floral or Chinese or pastel walls – and, of course, quite a lot of beams, sometimes painted white to give a lighter feel. You may have a fireplace, always a restrained elegance, lots of good crocks in well-fitted kitchens, fine modern shower rooms. Milandes' most famous name is Josephine Baker, the black cabaret artiste who took Paris by storm in the 1920s, adopted France, Milandes and lots of children, and brought them together in the château here. A great jump-off place for all those Dordogne explorations. *Manoir & Mairie have a pool each; Gardien & Arc en Ciel share pool.*

Price	Manoir £2,000-£3,000. Mairie £800-£1,700. Gardien & Arc en Ciel each £600-£975. Prices per week.
Sleeps	10; 6; 4; 4.
Rooms	Manoir: 2 doubles, 2 twins, 1 single, 1 child's room; 4 baths. Mairie: 1 double, 2 twins; 2 baths, separate wc. Gardien: 1 double, 1 twin; 2 baths. Arc en Ciel: 2 twins; 2 baths.
Arrival	Flexible.
Closed	Never.

Christopher & Sarah Chapman
Castelnaud La Chapelle, Dordogne

Tel	+44 (0)1458 223 192
Fax	+44 (0)1458 223 192
Email	info@lesmilandes.com
Web	www.lesmilandes.com

Midi – Pyrénées

Photo: istock.com

La Marguerite

Even if you try, you can't suppress the frisson of excitement that comes with knowing that pilgrims en route to Santiago de Compostela have for 1000 years climbed the leafy lane that passes this old épicerie, the best seat in honey-coloured Carennac. Begin on the small terrace by tucking into a welcome basket tailored to your arrival, tracing with your eye the pretty streets that rush down to the banks of the Dordogne. From here, plan all your forays to shops, markets, cafés, village crêperie and throbbing Rocamadour. Step inside, past the shop window, to enter a bright, well-furnished space, where the snug assortment now on offer includes a wood-burning stove, striped armchairs, red sofa, framed posters and petite dining table. Blue and yellow crockery on the dresser marks the border between hall and neatly packed kitchen, while pale floor tiles continue upstairs to a shining new bathroom and discreet and simply furnished bedrooms. British owners Kathy and Paul have the house next door and will make sure you return home as irrepressible Francophiles. *Dinner occasionally on request.*

Price	£150–£375 per week. £25–£60 per day. Linen not included.
Sleeps	2-4.
Rooms	2: 1 double, 1 twin; 1 bathroom.
Arrival	Friday.
Closed	Rarely.

Paul & Kathy Godfrey
Carennac, Lot

Tel	+44 (0)1628 523 755
Mobile	+44 (0)7710 290 759
Email	kathy@pgassocs.wanadoo.co.uk

Entry 224 Map 9

Le Couvent

Marie-Claude uses the interiors of her beautiful home to express her wonder for faraway places. The result is an imaginative, extravagant and surreal tour de force. Adults will sense the enchantment; children's imaginations will gallop away. Madame has her own apartment but the whole is her home; she is welcoming, interesting, loves children… her concern guarantees an unforgettable stay. On the first floor are a kitchen (compact, cluttered, well-equipped), a small salon (subdued, risqué), and a living room (large, light, airy; big table, tan sofa, Cantou fireplace, carved dresser). Upstairs, more magic, more surprises. In restful bedrooms, a large bare branch is hung with white lanterns, a wind-up mobile drifts across a ceiling, a Mexican rug brightens a carpeted floor, silk cushions join photographs of turn-of-the-century Paris. One bathroom has double rose-edged basins, a street light and small park bench, the other is mauve with 40 immaculate towels. A large terrace overlooks pool and tennis court, some trees are older than the convent itself and beyond you glimpse the village below. *Formidable!*

Price	€2,800–€3,300 per week.
Sleeps	6-7.
Rooms	4: 2 doubles, 2 singles; 2 bathrooms, 1 shower room, 2 separate wcs.
Arrival	Saturday, but flexible out of season.
Closed	Rarely.

Marie-Claude Maignal
Saint Sozy, Lot

Tel	+33 (0)5 65 32 23 48
Mobile	+33 (0)6 80 23 02 57
Email	mcmaignal@free.fr

Domaine de Roubignol

Roubignol is an 18th-century winemaster's house. The title impresses, the house even more so. Breathtaking in its scale and architectural peculiarities, it has ancient stone floors, creaking floorboards, hidden alcoves and a beam to duck; three eating places inside, four terraces and, cut into the steep cliffside, an infinity pool, underwater-lit at night. There's even an old bell to summon people to lunch from pool frolics or barn table tennis. The house has five bedrooms, from the tiny single in the pigeonnier to the large Romeo and Juliet room with canopied bed and balcony, of course. The Tower has a twin room, central heating and a sofabed in its top-floor sitting room. Furniture is a happy mix of French antique and modern, the L-shaped sitting room is big enough to waltz in, the antique-dealing owners have an eye for the odd quirk (the semolina cave painting in the loo is by a member of the RA...). You are five minutes from Luzech's shops and market (25 on foot down the valley path) and spoilt for wine-tastings and gastronomic choice. The views sweep and soar... a heavenly place. *Cook on request.*

Price	Main house €930–€2,150. Tower €300–€430 only available July–August with main house. Prices per week. Linen not included.	
Sleeps	House 9. Tower 2-4.	
Rooms	House: 3 doubles, 1 twin, 1 single; 2 bathrooms, 1 shower room. Tower: 1 double, 1 sofabed in sitting room; 1 bathroom.	
Closed	Main house: November–March. Tower: Never.	

	Roger & Jill Bichard Luzech, Lot
Tel	+44 (0)1225 862 789
Email	info@moxhams-antiques.demon.co.uk
Web	www.moxhams-antiques.demon.co.uk

Le Couvent

This elegant village retreat started life as a convent school for girls: today's sunlit rooms were classrooms and dormitories. Rosalie and Malcolm have renovated in abundant style: original wooden floors, painted furniture, fluttering muslin at shuttered windows, charming antique finds. (One wonderful bed left France for Cairo in 1850, took a detour to Sussex and is now back home.) There's a dreamy sense of country life: old floral linen cushions on a bedroom sofa, light bouncing off colour-washed walls, a chandelier rescued from a barn gracing the salon. The old well stands in the gorgeous three-level garden that leads you up to the woods, so you can chase the sun or retreat to the shade (and the hammock). The dining room table is made from a neighbour's oak wine vat and there's a hungry wood-burner in the beautifully fitted country kitchen. The medieval village is listed: a lovely collage of tiled roofs and mellow stone houses, it rests peacefully in a lush valley encircled by the river Vers. Rosalie's warmth and artistry is reflected in every corner. Really special. *Enquire about children when booking.*

Price	£450–£600 per week.
Sleeps	6.
Rooms	3: 2 doubles, 1 twin; 2 bathrooms.
Closed	November–April.

Rosalie Vicars-Harris
Lauzès, Lot

Tel	+44 (0)20 7483 2140 / +33 (0)5 65 31 28 91
Mobile	+44 (0)7966 799 916
Email	rosalievh@yahoo.co.uk
Web	www.lecouvent.pwp.blueyonder.co.uk

Cubertou

For a family week, a tribal gathering, a workshop or a wedding party, Cubertou is ideal: its capacity is elastic, you just occupy more or fewer rooms. As a whole, it sleeps up to 23 but rent the main house alone and you still have the place to yourself. Vines cascade, crickets hum, buzzards wheel, there are acres of meadow and woodland to escape to. Round a grassy courtyard, the farmhouse and barns were previously a summer art school run by a painter and his ballerina wife. Their love of colour still shows, particularly in the striking, peacock-blue salon with its Provençal cushions. Bedrooms – two in the pigeon tower – and bathrooms are simple, views are to the valley. Cooking for large numbers is no problem in the brilliantly designed kitchen or on the terrace barbecue. The huge open barn is a great place for candlelit suppers. Generous owners, friendly locals, a housekeeper and babysitter on request, and various lively village markets selling melons, strawberries, goat's cheese, foie gras… Perfect for big parties, exceptionally quiet. *Run your own courses: music, yoga, art. Catering on request.*

Price	€640-€2,300 per week.
Sleeps	8-23.
Rooms	13: 1 double, 6 twins, 5 singles, 1 family room; 1 bathroom, 4 shower rooms, 5 separate wcs.
Closed	November-March, except Christmas & New Year.

Claire & John Norton
Saint Martin le Redon, Lot

Tel	+33 (0)5 63 95 82 34
Fax	+33 (0)5 63 95 82 42
Email	claire@cubertou.com
Web	www.cubertou.com

Entry 228 Map 9

Château de Couanac - Forge, Métairie, Fournil

Near the ancient château – a lovely weatherbeaten 13th-century pile, buried deep in the Lot, now with a wonderful restaurant – and set outside the quadrangle walls but still under the seigneurial eye, the three gîtes were once barns or estate workers' cottages. Each has its own garden area, Fournil has a delightful inner courtyard, all are near the very generous pool, there's an indoor games area for children – and masses of space in the château grounds. Inside, find plaster and rough stone walls, original beams, steep stairs, small windows for atmosphere, stone floors to keep you wonderfully cool. The mix of country antiques and new is in sympathy with the architecture and there are some striking touches – huge copper bowls, a spinning wheel, modest chandeliers. For those who hanker after château splendours, one of its great rooms is the restaurant, serving the freshest estate-grown food, with a fireplace big enough to roast one of Monsieur d'Armagnac's 500 sheep. Madame la Comtesse runs the show and is an absolute poppet. *Shared pool 12mx8m. Restaurant on site.*

Price	€525–€1,365 for 8. €475–€1,015 for 6. €425–€725 for 4. Prices per week. Linen not included.
Sleeps	Forge 8. Métairie 6–7. Fournil 4.
Rooms	10: Forge: 3 doubles, 1 twin, 1 bathroom, 1 shower room, 2 sep wcs. Métairie: 2 doubles, 2 singles, 1 shower room, sep wc. Fournil: 1 double, 1 twin, 1 shower room, sep wc.
Closed	November–April.

Jayne Millard
Limogne en Quercy, Lot
Tel   +33 (0)6 12 74 32 39
Email jaynemillard@wanadoo.fr
Web   www.frenchcountryhouses.com

Domaine Lapèze - Cottage & Terrasses

Once a resting place for pilgrims on their way to Santiago de Compostela, this is a place to linger. Those who come find much to recharge city-drained batteries: pool, vineyards, plum orchards, peace. The starkly beautiful collection of old stone buildings is wrapped in 12 acres of blissful rolling country and you can gaze across to an 11th-century tower in Montcuq (charmingly French, with two markets, three bars, four restaurants, shops with all you need). Terracotta tiles keep you cool, white walls soak up the sun and there are warm colours inside. In the Cottage, expect an open-plan living area with a large lemon sofa and armchairs and a lovely big fire for winter. The bedrooms are reached from separate doors on the upper terrace. The Terrasses apartment, nice and private for two or four, has marvellous views from… its terrace. There's a gorgeous pool (floodlit at night) which you share with B&B guests, lakes to swim in, wine to taste and Romanesque churches to visit. Knud is on hand to help during the week, Caroline appears at weekends, both are delightful. *B&B also. Shared pool.*

Price	Cottage: €600–€900.
	Terrasses: €500–€800. Prices per week.
Sleeps	Cottage 4. Terrasses 4.
Rooms	Cottage: 1 double, 1 twin;
	1 bathroom, 1 separate wc.
	Terrasses: 1 double, 1 twin; 2 bathrooms.
	Flexible rental period out of season.
Closed	Rarely.

Caroline & Knud Kristoffersen
Montcuq, Lot

Tel	+33 (0)5 65 24 91 97
Fax	+33 (0)5 65 24 91 98
Email	lapeze@fastmail.net
Web	www.domainelapeze.com

Entry 230 Map 14

Le Bourg

A round tower, shining grey slates, curving eaves and a backdrop of huge cedars give this barn an almost fairytale appearance. It stands in Bridget and Peter's garden surrounded by greenery, and they have converted part of it (though not the tower, where barn owls roost) to create living space on three floors. Such a sense of space and light! On the ground floor is a well-equipped blue and white kitchen and an open-plan living room with French windows opening to the terrace and a private part of the garden. An attractive modern iron and glass staircase climbs to the big galleried landing, two colourwashed bedrooms, a charming bathroom complete with antique claw-foot bath, and a shower. Upstairs again is a huge, low-beamed, twin-bedded loft (hot in high summer!) and a small, separate sitting area – the perfect hideaway for a quiet read. The saltwater pool in the garden is shared with the Lewises; you'll find Bridget charming, helpful and discreet. Touffailles is a pretty village with its own épicerie and bakery – a short stroll. Great value. *November-March.*

Price	£250–£750 per week.
	Short stays available.
Sleeps	6.
Rooms	3: 1 double, 2 twins; 1 bathroom,
	1 shower room, 2 separate wcs.
Arrival	Flexible in low season.
Closed	Never.

Bridget and Peter Lewis
Touffailles, Tarn-et-Garonne
Tel   +33 (0)5 63 94 30 91
Email   bridget@lewis.eu.com
Web   www.lewis.eu.com

Le Moulin de Salazar

Kingfishers, herons, the occasional otter and a couple of terrapins… This magnificent old watermill proved irresistible to Paulette and Bernard when they abandoned the rat race in 2000. The river flows below and the machinery and sluices still work; Bernard knows how to operate them. In the mill room is the original grindstone – a fascinating communal space where guests can meet over drinks – or dine. On the first and second floors, Paulette has created four bright, welcoming apartments. They have glorious views and are superbly equipped, each with its own colour scheme, open-plan living area, sofabed, WiFi. Outside, take your pick of many different and delightful areas in the five acres of grounds. Laze in the vast garden, take a portable barbecue to a secret shingle beach, fish in the well-stocked pool, set off in a small motor boat. There's a swimming pool, too, and bikes, boules and table tennis – Paulette and Bernard have thought of everything and simply couldn't be nicer. Utterly stress-free and relaxing, but leave small children at home – there's that river!

Unfenced water. Lunch & supper on request.

Price	€840 each per week. €120 per day.
Sleeps	4 apartments for 2-4.
Rooms	Each apartment: 1 double, 1 sofabed; 1 bathroom.
Arrival	Flexible.
Closed	Rarely.

Paulette Palmer
Lauzerte, Tarn-et-Garonne

Tel	+33 (0)5 63 94 68 01
Fax	+33 (0)5 63 94 18 66
Email	paulette@salazarholidays.com
Web	www.salazarholidays.com

Entry 232 Map 14

Caussé

Nothing is too much trouble for Sue and Robert, eager that your stay be perfect. The pretty little studio apartment just below their own 300-year old cottage has been thoughtfully and generously fitted out – small indoors, enormous outside. Traditionally restored, it has a cool tiled floor, exposed stone and yellow plaster walls, very comfortable beds – a double plus bunks – and excellent linen. There's a small corner kitchen with some charming crockery and French windows that open to a private terrace overlooking the 17-acre garden, resplendent with fruit trees and potager (you're welcome to help yourself) and enticing spots, sunny or shady, in which to settle with a drink and a book. It's a great-value place to stay and Robert and Sue are infinitely kind – and flexible about arrangements. They'll provide breakfast at a small extra charge, or a picnic lunch; they'll even, on occasion, babysit or cook dinner. Robert's pâté is excellent, especially if he has been listening to Verdi! (Mozart, apparently, provides a less inspiring background for paté production.) *Shared pool. B&B also. Meals on request.*

Price	€350–€476 per week. Shorter stays welcome: enquire about rates (minimum 3 days).
Sleeps	2-4.
Rooms	Studio apartment:1 double & adult-size bunks; 1 shower room.
Arrival	Flexible.
Closed	Rarely.

Sue & Robert Watkins
Saint Paul d'Espis, Tarn-et-Garonne

Tel	+33 (0)5 63 29 14 22
Fax	+33 (0)5 63 29 14 22
Email	causse.stpaul@orange.fr

La Petite Grange & La Petite Maison

In a delicious setting, these two diminutive gîtes stand at different levels with their backs to the hillside in the Nortons' seven-acre grounds, just outside the hamlet of Tréjouls. Thick stone walls keep you cool and rooms are pleasantly furnished with splashes of colour from cushion and poster. Up a flight of steps, Petite Grange is a stables conversion, its several doors opening onto the lawn: a comfortable, one-storey house with an L-shaped living room/kitchen. Lavender and morning glory edge the patio. The other,open-sided, end of the stables barn provides shade for hot-weather meals near the pretty pool. Petite Maison is smaller, with a long, south-facing terrace. Its bedsitting room has spectacular views; shower and loo have a separate entrance from the terrace. John and Claire are a thoughtful and delightful couple with two student children – and two friendly cats who love to visit. In winter, bask in the greater comfort of La Petite Grange, with its household appliances and central heating. Great value. *Shared pool. An NGO to reduce environmental damage and improve life for the poorest is based here.*

Price	Grange €280–€425.
	Maison €210–€325. Prices per week.
Sleeps	Grange 2. Maison 2.
Rooms	Grange: 1 double; 1 bathroom.
	Maison: 1 double; 1 shower room.
Closed	Grange: Never.
	Maison: November–March.

	Claire & John Norton
	Tréjouls, Tarn-et-Garonne
Tel	+33 (0)5 63 95 82 34
Fax	+33 (0)5 63 95 82 42
Email	claire@cubertou.com
Web	www.cubertou.com/petite

Las Bourdolles - Le Puits

In the fruit garden of France, where orchards are laden with peaches and pears, is this ground-floor gîte for two. The old bread oven – all Quercy limestone and ancient timbers – has been simply, dreamily revived, one step and a curtain dividing bedroom from living and kitchen area. Imagine 20 square metres of warm maple, walls of soft pale stone, a bed dressed in white linen and a chair of vintage wicker. The living space has a wood-burning stove, an L-shaped timber kitchen, a farmhouse table with church pew and almost every mod con. A sliding glass wall leads to the stone terrace; take a glass of something local (Loupiac, maybe) to the teak table and relax in the shade of the chestnut tree. Erica and Linda are happy for you to share the organic vegetables and eggs, the saltwater pool fringed by banks of lavender; and the valley views – stunning whatever the weather. Book in for a meal and you may feast on seared salmon with fresh sorrel sauce. Cazes-Mondenard has a Romanesque church and provisions, Montcuq a Sunday market and a 12th-century dungeon. *Sawday B&B. Meals on request.*

Price	€500–€700 per week.
Sleeps	2.
Rooms	1 double; 1 shower room.
Arrival	Saturday, flexible out of season.
Closed	Never.

Linda Hilton & Erica Lewis
Tréjouls, Tarn-et-Garonne
Tel +33 (0)5 63 95 80 83
Email lewiserica@mac.com
Web www.lasbourdolles.com

Las Bourdolles - Le Pigeonnier

Deep in rural France, a square stone tower topped by a pointed roof. Its deep-set windows look out over 20 acres of woods and fields belonging to the 17th-century farmhouse owned and run by hospitable Erica and Linda. Having restored the main house and established a B&B, they have now turned the little pigeon house into a delightful gîte. Ladder-like stairs link each rough-walled room to the one above. At ground level are a small, newly fitted kitchen, dining area and shower room; on the first floor, a simple, attractive bedroom with painted screens and a handmade oak bed. (A roll top bath stands in front of the window, so you may gaze at the countryside as you soak.) Up another stair to the comfortable sitting room with a sofabed and a gloriously beamed ceiling. You have your own tiny courtyard, and terraces to chase sun or shade. Wander at will in the lovely grounds, enjoy the pool. There's central heating and an open fire to keep you snug in winter, and if you tire of self-catering you can dine at the farmhouse: Linda and Erica are fabulous cooks. *Shared pool. Sawday B&B. Meals on request.*

Price	€450–€650 per week.
Sleeps	2.
Rooms	1 double; 1 bathroom, 1 shower room.
Arrival	Saturday, flexible low season.
Closed	Never.

Linda Hilton & Erica Lewis
Tréjouls, Tarn-et-Garonne
Tel +33 (0)5 63 95 80 83
Email lewiserica@mac.com
Web www.lasbourdolles.com

Catusse-Haut - La Fermette & La Grange

What a place to celebrate a special birthday! Jo delights in cooking for occasions and will make the dinner table look magical; even if it's not a special day, she's happy to cook for you twice a week. She and Robert, a friendly, considerate couple, have taken the best bits from all the places they've stayed in over the years and introduced them to their own barn conversions. The immaculate Fermette is given a smart-rustic makeover thanks to deep sofas, pretty beams, books and watercolours painted by the family – and there's a farmhouse-style kitchen in which to linger over meals. All the bedrooms are pleasing but you need to climb some rather steep stairs to reach the crowning glory – a gorgeous, white, loft suite with a sitting area at one end and a fabulous shower room. La Grange is smaller but charming and full of light: its big, living/kitchen area is open plan, walls are exposed stone and the décor includes pieces picked up by Jo in Thailand. Each house has its own private terrace, partly covered for shade, with wide views over rolling farmland. The lovely pool beckons. *Meals on request.*

Price	La Fermette €485-€1,325.
	La Grange €395-€940.
	Prices per week.
Sleeps	La Fermette 8. La Grange 4.
Rooms	La Fermette: 2 doubles, 2 twins;
	2 shower rooms.
	La Grange: 1 double, 1 twin;
	1 shower room.
Closed	Rarely.

Jo & Robert Everett
Montalzat, Tarn-et-Garonne
Tel   +33 (0)5 63 03 17 93
Email   relax@catusse.co.uk
Web   www.catusse.co.uk

La Barrière

On the edge of the hamlet, a house of delights. Artist Catherine and builder-designer Des rescued the stunning 17th-century farmhouse and gave it back its character. Beams, terracotta floors, stained glass and nooks and crannies are complemented by Catherine's stencils, paint washes and exotic finds. Relax in the open-plan living area with its deep sofas, rugs, wood-burning stove and kitchen units fashioned from wine barrels. Bedrooms are wonderfully individual: one open to the rafters, another bright in sunburst colours, another cool in blue... and the cosy single is every child's dream. Bathrooms, anything but bland, are dotted with flowers, shells and bowls. Eat on the wisteria-covered balcony, by the pool or on a shaded terrace. There's also a walled garden full of secret sitting places and organic fruit and veg for you to pick. This is the couple's home; they move into an adjoining studio. Calm and smiley people, they will help you with advice or leave you alone. After a day of discovery (medieval villages, markets, the lovely Bonnette valley) it is lovely to return to such peace.

Price	£550–£1,150.
Sleeps	7.
Rooms	4: 2 doubles, 1 twin, 1 single; 3 bathrooms.
Closed	November–March.

Catherine Smedley & Des Dornan
Lacapelle Livron, Tarn-et-Garonne
Tel   +33 (0)5 63 24 00 05
Email   catherine.smedley@wanadoo.fr
Web   www.labarriere.iowners.net

Barrau

Bliss for those who wish to leave creature comforts behind and lose themselves in the hills. The main house, where Jennifer lives, is 30 yards away. Secluded on a 15-acre hillside estate with two private sitting-out areas, one filled with lavender and figs, Barrau is perfect for a couple or a solo traveller. And trees, long views and wildlife. Deer and badgers live on the land, 42 species of butterflies have been identified, nightingales sing, the odd salamander scampers by and beehives dot the landscape. Your retreat, a former house for the pigs and hens that goes back to 1890, has been renovated simply. It's rather like camping but without the tent and with a bathroom. You have a pine-floored room with rugs and a plain table, a cupboard, a radio/cassette player, two beds and two easy chairs, a tiny painted-brick shower room and a corridor kitchen. Charming Jennifer lives simply and happily, is passionate about her "wildlife guests" and an expert on the local churches and brocante fairs too. Beneath pollution-free night skies, the tree frogs will sing you to sleep.

Three hectares of indigenous oak survive on these hillsides, inaccessible to big machinery. Ecosystems include unimproved meadow (early purple orchids) and damp meadow with marsh grasses and willow. Buildings are gutterless so water runoff maintains the same vegetation as always. There is no concrete and the soft ground holds lots of earthy shelters: a mouse digs a hole, a toad moves in later. Wild blackberry gives nectar for bees and cover for birds nests. There are hoopoes, golden orioles, treecreepers: the whole farm is burgeoning with wildlife, a testament to careful knowledgeable management.

Price	€190-€330 per week. Heating extra.
Sleeps	2.
Rooms	1 twin; 1 shower room.
Arrival	Saturday, but flexible out of season.
Closed	Rarely.

Jennifer Boncey
Esparsac, Tarn-et-Garonne

Tel   +33 (0)5 63 26 12 72
Email   boncey@wanadoo.fr
Web   www.haumont.com

SPECIAL
GREEN ENTRY
see page 18

Daramousque

You are surrounded by 14 hectares of mature gardens, rolling hills and stunning views. Sarah and Michael fell in love with this 19th-century farmstead three years ago, already beautifully renovated and restored. It also came with a big open space perfect for children and a saltwater pool. Theirs is the farmhouse, yours is the villa, and its vast open-plan living area is lofty and light. Three French windows lead to a long veranda on whose stylish sofas you will idly sprawl before rising for a lazy dip in the secure shared pool. The furnishings are a pleasing mix of French modern and French antique enhanced by soft golds, ochres and creams, the open-plan kitchen is unquestionably lavish and the two ground-floor bedrooms are spacious and cool, one overlooking a courtyard, the other the garden; the third, a fabulous suite, is upstairs. You are minutes from the shops, restaurants and weekly market of pretty Monclar de Quercy. For the cooler months: log fires and warm-as-toast tiles; these gentle, generous owners want nothing more than for you to be happy. *Shared pool. Cottage for four also available.*

Price	€700–€1,500 (based on four sharing).
Sleeps	4–6.
Rooms	2 twin/doubles; 1 bathroom, 1 separate wc. Extra double room on request.
Closed	November–March.

Michael & Sarah Rule
Monclar de Quercy, Tarn-et-Garonne

Tel	+33 (0)5 63 28 26 17
Email	michael.rule@wanadoo.fr
Web	www.daramousque.com

Gîte de Figarol - Lower & Upper Gîtes

Jean and Neil lost their hearts to this farmhouse the moment they saw it. Fields and wooded hills roll to the distant Pyrenees; buzzards and kites swirl above; the garden glows, shady spots invite you to linger. One is irresistibly drawn to the terraces of these two gîtes – the ground and first floors of a converted barn – to drink in the scenery. Inside, all is simplicity and charm. The living area of the lower gîte is a cottagey mix of beamed ceiling, tiled floors and well-loved furniture; the kitchens of both are sturdy affairs with generous helpings of crockery and pans. In the gîte upstairs, no sitting room – but who cares when a covered terrace stretches the width of the place? You'll do all your living outdside here, a patio heater ensuring warmth on cooler nights. Bedrooms are simple, modern and colourful. This is outdoors country – walking, birdwatching, fishing; there are markets at spa town Salies du Salat, Pau has its castle and Toulouse is 45 minutes. Too tired to rustle up supper? Jean loves cooking and Neil is an expert on local wines. Unpretentious, friendly hosts, and great value. *Sawday B&B. Meals on request.*

Price	€280–€480 each per week.
Sleeps	Lower gîte 4. Upper gîte 4.
Rooms	Lower gîte: 2: 1 double, 1 twin; 1 bathroom. Upper gîte 2: 1 double, 1 twin; 1 shower room.
Closed	Lower gîte: Never. Upper gîte: November-March.

	Jean & Neil Adamson
	Figarol, Haute-Garonne
Tel	+33 (0)5 61 98 25 54
Fax	+33 (0)5 61 98 25 54
Email	info@figarolgites.com
Web	www.figarolgites.com

Midi – Pyrénées

La Guiraude - La Toscane

The name suggest the colours of Tuscany: ochres, siennas and terracottas prevail. Your friendly hosts, who live next door (see opposite), have poured energy into their second conversion: the attention to detail is superb and summer staff keep it tickety-boo. Lovely Toscane, in spite of its size, has an intimate feel. At both ends of the sitting/dining area, French windows lead to terraces, one with a teak table for ten; there are big lamps, good sofas, an open fire for the cooler months. Bedrooms have colourwashed walls and original beams, the furnishings are immaculate and there are towels for bathrooms *and* pool. New appliances in the kitchen, swish crockery and glassware, every bedroom en suite – this is better than home! Each house has its own fragrant walled garden; pathways are illuminated by night and views stretch across landscaped trees to far fields. The pool is tucked discreetly to one side with a stylish pool house; there are secret spots, an arbour with a pond and a playground with swings. Cathar trails, châteaux and vineyards beckon – should you want to leave. *Shared pool. Sawday hotel.*

Price	€1,200-€2,500 per week.
Sleeps	8-10.
Rooms	4: 2 doubles, 1 twin, 1 family room for 4; 4 bathrooms.
Closed	Rarely.

Janine & Alistair Smith
Beauteville, Haute-Garonne
Tel +33 (0)5 34 66 39 20
Fax +33 (0)5 61 81 42 05
Email guiraude@wanadoo.fr
Web www.guiraude.com

La Guiraude - La Grande Maison

On its own at the end of a country road, the 1843 farmhouse has a stylish Spanish hacienda feel. You have here three homes in one (including your hosts'): a large, light, cool complex of indoor spaces and outdoor terraces, secluded gardens and heated pool. A huge hall leads to an even huger sitting room with lofty ceilings and the original fireplace. Art decorates eggshell walls, Chinese rugs soften pale tiles and there's a light-filled gallery brimming with leather sofas, books, music and French and English TV. From the dining room, French windows lead to a big terrace with shade and panoramic views. The modern, well-equipped kitchen has a refrigerator of which Americans would be proud, the games room sports table tennis, exercise bike and step machine, bedrooms have big beds and cheerful colours, bathrooms have walk-in showers and are as immaculate as the rest. But, however tempting the kitchen, you don't have to chop and stir if you don't wish; Alistair, an excellent cook, is unfazed at the prospect of catering for 20 when a retreat group or wedding party takes on the whole fabulous place. *Sawday hotel. Meals on request.*

Price	€1,700–€3,300 per week.
Sleeps	10.
Rooms	5: 3 doubles, 2 twins; 5 bathrooms.
Arrival	Saturday in high season.
Closed	Rarely.

Janine & Alistair Smith
Beauteville, Haute-Garonne

Tel	+33 (0)5 34 66 39 20
Fax	+33 (0)5 61 81 42 05
Email	guiraude@wanadoo.fr
Web	www.guiraude.com

Entry 243 Map 14

La Ferme Plate

With their long low hilltop profiles rising from seas of waving golden grain and islands of green woods these 19th-century buildings always look sunny and welcoming. The "flat farm" faces the distant Pyrenees in a pretty marriage, old to new, of river stone, Toulouse brick, original balconies and wisteria. Let the children loose in his 14-acre heaven of lawns, woods, space, even a secret pond. The cosy old farmhouse has a beautifully fitted open oak kitchen, a multitude of beams, a wood-burner that warms the soft-couched sitting area, three attractive bedrooms and a huge bathroom upstairs. If you want more space, throw open the door to the converted stables next door and take over the huge salon with its massive open fireplace, pool table and more sofas (plus a post-swimming shower). Up above, a superb set of timbers supports the roof over a very big, airy, sun-filled bedroom. The décor is warm and friendly but Mark is ever ready to listen to guests' tips on making it even cosier. A wonderful perk: you may harvest as many spuds, beans and tomatoes from the potager as you can eat.

Price	€630–€1,330 per week.
Sleeps	4–10.
Rooms	3: 2 doubles, 1 family room with bunks; 1 bathroom, 1 shower room. Extra double en suite can connect.
Arrival	Flexible.
Closed	Never.

Mark Taylor
La Bastide de Besplas, Ariège
Tel +33 (0)5 61 69 26 40
Mobile +33 (0)6 86 60 03 93
Email mtaylor@orange.fr
Web www.ariege.com/lafermeplate

Les Rosiers

Breathe in the fresh mountain air as you step out of this old farmer's cottage, drink in the High Pyrenean panorama from the controlled-wild garden. As the coffee warms on the stove and you plan your day's pilgrimage, get out the walking boots or prepare for a shopping trip to Saint Girons to stock up the larder. Les Rosiers stands wonderfully secluded on the edge of Cescau, an ancient village embedded in a steep hill facing those breathtaking mountains. Its owners, Teresa and Bernard, are artists with a lifelong love of peace and natural beauty that will inspire the creative flow. They care deeply about the environment and community culture, organising concerts and exhibitions. The décor is unpretentious country style, its wooden floors and beams give a nice old rustic feel, it's all friendly and definitely not posh. Children will enjoy the amazing wooden spiral stair – tread carefully! – up to the twin bedroom under the rafters with skylights for moon gazing, while you will rest easy in your huge bed downstairs after a hearty meal cooked over the old stone barbecue. *Sawday B&B.*

Price	€350–€450 per week.
Sleeps	4 + cot.
Rooms	2: 1 double, 1 twin; 1 bathroom.
Closed	Never.

Teresa & Bernard Richard
Cescau, Ariège

Tel	+33 (0)5 61 96 74 24
Fax	+33 (0)5 61 04 98 24
Email	tizirichard@caramail.com
Web	www.ariege.com/les-rosiers

Le Poulsieu - Paris & Amsterdam

Hairpin bends and a single-track road lead you up to a world of hillside villages. High in the foothills of the Pyrenees, this place has a haunting but beautiful remoteness. The air is clean, the views sharp, the peace tangible. Although Andorra, medieval Mirepoix and the castle at Foix are within driving distance, this is an outdoorsy place; 5,000 kilometres of trails criss-cross the area. Hans, an experienced walker, will advise or arrange riding, rafting and fishing. Or you could loll by the pool, shared with B&B guests, and breathe in the views. The two gîtes, in farmhouse outbuildings, are well separated, each with a terrace for al fresco meals. Wooden floors, beams, whitewashed walls and a wood-burning stove create a rustic comfort, and furniture is simple – all you need after an exhilarating day outside. 'Amsterdam', with its well-equipped dining kitchen and fun, four-bedded room, suits families. 'Paris' is perfect for a couple, perhaps with one child. Dutch-born but English-speaking, Hans and Mieke are relaxed hosts and offer good-value suppers. *Meals by arrangement. Sawday B&B.*

Price	Paris €295–€595. Amsterdam €395–€725. Prices per week.
Sleeps	Paris 2-4. Amsterdam 4-6 + cot.
Rooms	Paris: 1 double, sofabed in living room; 1 bathroom. Amsterdam: 1 double, 1 quadruple; 1 bathroom, separate wc.
Closed	Never.

Mieke van Eeuwijk & Hans Kiepe
Serres sur Arget, Ariège

Tel	+33 (0)5 61 02 77 72
Fax	+33 (0)5 61 02 77 72
Email	le.poulsieu@wanadoo.fr
Web	www.ariege.com/le-poulsieu

Belrepayre Airstream & Retro Trailer Park

Groovy, those Airstream trailers, time-warp their interiors: 30 to 50 years old, with original radios and vinyl, even period magazines. Once the rolling hills of Belpayre's 23 hectares, the untouched forests, the vast skies, have expanded your senses – step into your aluminium pod and a sensational contrast: space is cosy-cosy, beds and showers for less-than-giants. Summits of intimacy can be achieved in here, enveloped in nostalgia. Another life happens outside. Belpayre is not only a totally eco-friendly estate – meat, milk, ice cream from their organic sheep here and in Spain, plates made of leaves, home-made jams, local produce if they don't grow it, solar-heated water – Perry and Coline are also genuine sharers. A retired clown (yes indeed), Perry now runs the tapas bar from an Airstream that once sold cold drinks under the Eiffel Tower, and creates an inspired atmosphere all round the 'camp' while his son gives magician courses. Lovely Coline makes the organic tapas, has a little shop for 'campers' and watches over the cedarwood hot tub. Not camping, a wraparound experience. *Spa & organic tapas bar on site.*

Price	€400–€500 each per week. Linen not included.
Sleeps	7 trailers for 2 or 4. Pitches have full hook-up.
Rooms	Each trailer: 1 double or 1 double & 2 single beds; shower & wc. Communal shower & wc block.
Arrival	Flexible.
Closed	October–April.

	Perry & Coline
	Manses, Ariège
Tel	+33 (0)5 61 68 11 99
Web	www.belrepayre.com

La Petite Écurie

Cross the courtyard from the Furnesses' grand 18th-century townhouse and there is La Petite Écurie, '1758' inscribed over its door. John and Lee-anne have done much of this stables conversion themselves – and made a great job of it. The overall effect is assured, pleasing and comfortable. In the bedrooms you have chestnut wood floors and exposed stone walls to show off the tapestries that hang richly behind the beds; the beamed living room is restful and elegant; the kitchen has every appliance you can think of. This is a quiet corner of town and the garden, with its hammock and pool, is pleasant and secluded. John and Lee-anne came to live here in 1999: they're Australians, enthusiastic and very likeable. Lee-anne is an accomplished chef and you can book a meal with them in their fine big house where they do B&B. They love living here and know all about the area and its scattering of Cathar castles. Take a picnic hamper (Lee-anne will provide – very well) and go exploring, or spend the day basking on the sunny shores of Lac Montbel. *Sawday B&B. Meals on request.*

Price	€370–€620 per week.
Sleeps	4.
Rooms	2: 1 double, 1 twin; 1 bathroom, 1 shower room.
Closed	Rarely.

John & Lee-anne Furness
Leran, Ariège
Tel +33 (0)5 61 01 50 02
Mobile +33 (0)6 88 19 49 22
Email john.furness@wanadoo.fr
Web www.chezfurness.com

Au Chicot

Stargaze from the terrace. Au Chicot stands on a hilltop, a sunny, mellow, 18th-century fermette reached by a road winding up through vineyards. All around are fields of sunflowers and corn, dotted with oak woods. The feeling of space and the views are invigorating. To one side of the L-shaped stone house is a dappled orchard; across the lawn, close to the pool, an ancient open barn – a lovely place for boules or table tennis out of the sun. Beyond the garden, a rough field is being transformed into a wildflower meadow. As for the house, it's been beautifully architect-restored, its stones and beams exposed, its fireplaces opened, to create a superbly light and practical family home. White walls, golden wood in ceiling and floor, a touch of gingham, an old rocking chair… there's a New World flavour. Bathrooms are white and sparkling, bedrooms (two on the ground floor) airy and inviting with quilts, bookcases, writing tables, while the sitting room, furnished with big ivory-pale sofas, is gorgeous. Hard to pull yourself away from all this and discover the Gers, but do: it's a sumptuous corner of France.

Price	£900–£1,650 per week.
Sleeps	8 + cot.
Rooms	4: 2 doubles, 2 twins; 4 bathrooms.
Arrival	Thursday.
Closed	November–April.

	Jane Bennett
	Mouchan, Gers
Tel	+44 (0)1799 540 813
Email	ronaldbennett@mac.com
Web	www.gasconymagic.com

Castelnau des Fieumarcon

Traffic-free, full of secret places: heaven for kids, fascination for all. Leave your car, your laptop, your phone outside the walls, step through the gateway and wrap yourself in history. This fortified village on a rocky spur overlooking the Ouchy valley has been reclaimed with the lightest of touches by owner Frédéric Coustols and his parents. Built in the 13th century by local feudal lords – for a time during the Hundred Years War they pledged allegiance to the English crown – the stronghold had been left to crumble until, a couple of decades ago, the Coustols family restored the ramparts, renovated the houses, created gardens for each one and left much of the creeper-clad old stone untouched. There is nothing mock or tricksy here: the golden Gers stone and the old terracotta floors glow, gardens have ancient trees and the pool is outside the walls with valley views. Getting in is almost an initiation: pass through a large Renaissance portal and spot a music stand and a welcome sign; then ring the gong – if all you hear is a bird calling, you are in the right place. *Sawday hotel. Meals on request. Shared pool.*

Price	€700-€2,200 per house per week. €150-€350 per day.
Sleeps	Up to 52.
Rooms	10 houses sleeping 2-8.
Arrival	Flexible.
Closed	Never.

Frédéric Coustols
Lagarde Fieumarcon, Gers

Tel   +33 (0)5 62 68 99 30
Email   office@lagarde.org
Web   www.lagarde.org

Castelnau des Fieumarcon

Rooms in even the smallest house feel luminous and generous, with the grandeur that comes from original gems – a gracious spiralling stone stair, a great 11th-century beam, a chunk of 13th-century wall. The houses are not 'interior decorated' but simple, with understated touches of sophistication: framed dried herbs on the painted walls; mosquito-net canopies; a massive Louis XV armoire; antique Gascon treasures. Beds are individually designed, some with those canopies, all with white linen and masses of pillows; bathrooms are large, comfy and cool with mosaic showers. Kitchens are less high-class – small ovens, half fridges – but fine for holiday cooking; bread is delivered every morning. Castelnau is on high ground so the views from every window are astounding, giving off a timeless hazy glow from the low-lying hills and surrounding fields. Stendhal called it the French Tuscany. He would be at home here: no cars, no tellies, no telephones. Instead, vineyards, fairs, brocante, foie gras and Toulouse a little further. Not cheap but priceless as a rare pearl. *Sawday hotel. Meals on request. Shared pool.*

Price	€700–€2,200 per house per week. €150–€350 per day.
Sleeps	Up to 52.
Rooms	10 houses sleeping 2-8.
Arrival	Flexible.
Closed	Never.

Frédéric Coustols
Lagarde Fieumarcon, Gers
Tel   +33 (0)5 62 68 99 30
Email   office@lagarde.org
Web   www.lagarde.org

Le Vieux Presbytère

This is armagnac country and Richard is happy to organise informal wine tastings. (A wine merchant, he's something of an expert!) He and Jackie have converted a 50-year-old barn in the grounds of their beautiful old timber-frame house into two dormer-windowed gîtes. The rooms may not be huge but they are full of light. Furnished in a mix of French country and English cottage style, all feels crisp, fresh and inviting. Up on a beamed mezzanine with pale walls and gleaming wooden floors, bedrooms in soft green and ivory open onto balconies. L'Hérisson has a sitting area upstairs too; La Mouette, a bathroom up and a second bedroom down, and each has a ground-floor shower room, an open-plan sitting/dining area with sofabed, a small kitchen and a barbecue patio. If you want to be thoroughly spoiled one evening, Jackie will prepare dinner and bring it to you. Eat out on the terrace, surrounded by garden, woods and vine-covered hills, with distant views of the Pyrenees. Next door is a church, its spire visible above the trees, its bell plaintively tolling the hours. *B&B also. Meals on request.*

Price	La Mouette £375–£675.
	L'Hérisson £250–£475. Prices per week.
Sleeps	La Mouette 4–6. L'Hérisson 2–4.
Rooms	Mouette: 1 double, 1 twin; 1 bath,
	1 shower; sofabed & futon.
	L'Hérisson: 1 double; 1 shower; sofabed.
Closed	Never.

Jackie & Richard Wallace-Jones
Noulens, Gers

Tel	+33 (0)5 62 06 48 62
Email	wallacejones@escapetogascony.com
Web	www.escapetogascony.com

Place de l'Église - Two Apartments

A village address in the gently rolling Gers. The village is a jewel, predating even the lovely bastide towns of the region; the Place de l'Église is a medieval colonnade opposite the church and beside the village green. The old bakery – divided into one apartment for the owners and two for the guests – is at the end of the colonnade. It's a sensitive restoration that reveals the original colombage, the Toulouse-style brickwork and the lovely tomettes. Each home has two floors – downstairs light, lofty and open plan, upstairs cosy. Shower rooms are compact, the twin bedrooms are small but ideal for kids, and furnishings are plainly traditional: white walls, floral curtains, new sofas, brocante finds. At the back is a little courtyard in which you may barbecue a brochette in summer, then take a table into the colonnade and enjoy it. The helpful couple who live opposite welcome you with an aperitif and before you know it you're immersed in village life. Tillac has a bar/restaurant, a friendly shop (try the yeast-free *campaillou*) and a flower festival in spring.

Price	£230-£350 each per week.
Sleeps	2 apartments for 4 + cot.
Rooms	Each apartment: 1 double, 1 twin; 1 shower room; sofabed.
Arrival	Saturday preferred.
Closed	Never.

	Ann & Geoff Coombs
	Tillac, Gers
Tel	+44 (0)1275 474 451
Fax	+44 (0)1275 472 554
Email	tillac@btinternet.com
Web	www.holidaysintillac.com

Setzères - Le Grenier

In the same setting of fine old buildings, green garden and stunning views, the smaller Setzères cottage is in the old grain loft and a rustic outside staircase leads to its typically gabled front door and yet another clever conversion. There's a lovely warm feel (boosted by central heating in winter), with four characterful old armchairs on an oriental carpet, a round table with Windsor chairs and a lens-like window homing in on a slice of green topped by snowy peaks – seen when you stand up. In a roomy, one-storied space for two large or four snug people, the sky-lit kitchen rises to medieval joists in a mix of natural wood and blue tiles at one end while the compact bedrooms open off either side. The pink double is small and has its own basin; the pink-tinged twin room is larger; both are well lit, have good storage and furnishings and share the pink bathroom. A terrace area and a good patch of garden are for you and yours alone but you can also share the wonderful grounds and pool with other residents. White-water rafting is a two-hour drive. *Sawday B&B. Meals on request.*

Price	€375–€895 (£260-£620) per week. Long winter lets: £400 per month.
Sleeps	4.
Rooms	2: 1 double, 1 twin; 1 bathroom.
Closed	Never.

Christine Furney
Marciac, Gers

Tel	+33 (0)5 62 08 21 45
Fax	+33 (0)5 62 08 21 45
Email	setzeres32@aol.com
Web	www.setzeres.com

Setzères - Petit Setzères

The house is the converted stables of a fine manor set on soft slopes in this unspoilt part of rural France. Petit Setzères has a big, well-furnished, ground-floor living area where you can snuggle down in front of a log fire in winter (there's oil central heating, too). In summer, take lunch into the lush garden and picnic on the terrace under a high old barn roof; the Pyrenees look down on you in the distance with a different face every day. Above the living room are three pretty bedrooms with good beds, functional storage, lots of books and glorious views. One bathroom upstairs, a shower room downstairs and a fully-fitted kitchen complete the picture. You feel perfectly secluded and have your own garden space by the lily pond, yet are free to share the pool and main garden with other guests and the attentive, civilised owner. It is a quiet and beautiful spot with badminton, table-tennis and croquet to keep you busy. You could even set off for a day's skiing in the Pyrenees: leave at 8am and you'll be there by ten; the coast is three hours. *Sawday B&B. Shared pool. Meals on request.*

Price	€518–€1,630 (£360–£1,130) per week. Long winter lets: £600 per month.
Sleeps	6–7.
Rooms	4: 1 double, 1 twin, 1 room with bunks, 1 tiny single; 1 bathroom, 1 shower room.
Closed	Never.

Christine Furney
Marciac, Gers

Tel	+33 (0)5 62 08 21 45
Fax	+33 (0)5 62 08 21 45
Email	setzeres32@aol.com
Web	www.setzeres.com

Domaine à Marmande - Apartment

The warmth of the colours is matched by the welcome: you are beautifully cared for here. The owners are Californian and Dutch and have two daughters between them. Charles teaches acupuncture, shiatsu and tai chi, and they run 'pamper yourself' weeks out of season. The old Gascon house, surrounded by fields of sunflowers and maize, exudes a sense of peace; no surprise that the domaine was a sanctuary centuries ago. Now it has been sympathetically revived, the terracotta floor tiles and timber frame restored, the walls washed with Mediterranean colours. Your apartment is privately housed in the end wing. You get a wooden-floored kitchen/dining room with white free-standing units and chunky modern table, a comfy sofabed and easy chairs, and bedrooms spacious and simple. Bathrooms are fun – one with blue and green tiles at a jaunty angle, the other with a Moroccan basin. There are lakes for boating and fishing, bikes to borrow and a farmers' market and restaurants in Mirande, just two miles away. Return to a sweet decked pool and a garden full of serenity and scrambling roses. *B&B also. Meals on request.*

Price	€325-€700 per week.
Sleeps	4-6.
Rooms	2 twins/doubles, 1 sofabed; 1 bath, 1 shower.
Closed	Never.

Caroline van Berkel
Berdoues, Gers
Tel   +33 (0)5 62 65 74 88
Email carolinevan.berkel@gmail.com
Web   www.domaineamarmande.com

Coutène

It's a privilege to be able to share the owners' love of this house. Its face is smothered in wisteria and climbing roses, its pretty timber frame has been restored and its 18th-century tomettes are polished to perfection. The charming English Coates come here as often as they can; in their absence, Coutène is entrusted to you. Almost every luminous room preserves its original wide floorboards and strong dark beams, and each is decorated in modest English good taste, a touch of chintz here, an elegant rug there. The smaller of the sitting rooms is particularly charming, with its softly painted faux panelling and original 16-pane windows; the larger has a big open fire. The kitchen holds all the eager chef needs, the dining room is formal and flourishes two beautiful antique sideboards, the polished oak staircase sweeps you up to restful bedrooms, one with wool mattresses made in the Gers. You have a swimming pool and a ping-pong barn, tennis, golf and bicycle hire are close by, there's sailing and fishing on several lakes, and the medieval village of Simorre is a six-minute drive. Special.

Price	€985–€1,500 per week.
Sleeps	8.
Rooms	4: 2 doubles, 2 twins; 1 bathroom, 2 shower rooms.
Closed	November–March.

Simon & Kate Coates
Simorre, Gers
Tel   +44 (0)1398 361 271
Email coutene@gmail.com

Domaine de Peyloubère - Fermier

Look out for hoopoes by the waterfall; it's fed by the river Gers that flows through the estate of the 17th-century manor. With 35 acres of lawns, Italian gardens, woodland and wonderful trees, there's space to roam. You'll scarcely be aware of the guests in the adjoining cottages, or of the delightful English owners. Peyloubère used to be a working farm and Fermier was the farmer's cottage: its original beamed inglenook fireplace still warms the living room. Today it is super-cosy with central heating and furnishings crisp and new: light beech furniture, deep-blue sofas, full-length curtains. The state-of-the-art kitchen is painted grey-green and sunflower-yellow, with a Saint Hubert dresser and steps to a sunny downstairs double bedroom. French windows take you out to the patio, the large heated pool shared with the other gîtes, and the garden beyond. Gaze over the fields, listen to the birds, identify wild flowers, fish in lake and river – and don't forget the armagnac after supper, the dry golden brandy for which the area is famous. *Health spa with sauna for guests. Shared pool. Sawday B&B.*

The Martins are surely setting the standards of eco-friendly estate restoration and care. Their wildlife sanctuary, agreed with local shooting groups, protects animals, birds and plants on these life-nurturing streams and lakes, woods, pastures and mature trees. Grey water is used for the garden, leaves are composted each year for mulch to reduce weeding and watering, the organic potager flourishes; heat pumps heat the pools; the septic tank and filter beds treat sewage biologically; their first composting loo is a total success. And they naturally encourage guests to use their systems, here and back at home.

Price	€800–€1,600 per week.
Sleeps	8.
Rooms	4: 2 doubles, 2 twins; 1 bathroom, 1 shower room, 2 separate wcs.
Closed	Never.

Theresa & Ian Martin
Pavie, Gers

Tel	+33 (0)5 62 05 74 97
Fax	+33 (0)5 62 05 75 39
Email	martin@peyloubere.com
Web	www.peyloubere.com

SPECIAL GREEN ENTRY
see page 18

Domaine de Peyloubère - Les Rosiers

Peyloubère is a dreamlike grouping of 300-year-old buildings in acres of gorgeous parkland. There are a river, a lake, a rose garden and langorous walks across the fields. The owners do B&B in the manor house once inhabited by the 20th-century Italian artist Mario Cavaglieri. Les Rosiers, on the ground floor of this fine house, feels nicely private, and the Martins' sensitive refurbishment makes the most of its one piece of "genuine Cavaglieri": a vibrant, hand-painted ceiling. No longer the dining room, this room now has an extremely comfortable brass bed. The living room is large and airy with white-painted beams, walls are chalk-washed and an inglenook fireplace stands ready to swallow you in comfort. For inclement days there are books, games, videos, music and central heating. Beyond tall French windows lies a private shady garden with the original well house – in working order but safely secured – and children will love the woods and the magical waterfall. Even better – a heated swimming pool, table tennis, badminton and a spa in the former pig shed. *Shared pool. Sawday B&B.*

Price	€600–€1,250 per week.
Sleeps	4.
Rooms	2: 1 double, 1 room with bunks; 1 shower room.
Closed	Never.

Theresa & Ian Martin
Pavie, Gers

Tel	+33 (0)5 62 05 74 97
Fax	+33 (0)5 62 05 75 39
Email	martin@peyloubere.com
Web	www.peyloubere.com

Ferme de Técouère

The night skies are aglow with stars and peace, here in the gentle wooded countryside of southern France. You'll get a lovely welcome from this young, humorous, generous French family living The Good Life at the foot of the Pyrenees. They have renovated their 1930s farmhouse, turned the connecting barn into a gîte, decorated with natural paints, installed geothermal heating for warm floors and added solar panels for hot water. With a plant nursery and a potager this is a foodie's delight; special for children too, thanks to a tribe of flop-eared rabbits, hens and geese, and the fine pool with views. The gîte has new terracotta tiles, pale-gold stone walls and a feastful of beams, squashy sofas round the fire, an armoire of games, a kitchen with mod cons. Rustic bedrooms lie at the top of some fairly steep stairs (stair gate in place), their pretty antique beds inviting with new mattresses and white laundered linen. Book in for table d'hôtes if you can: you may be treated to duck cooked over an open fire, and a glass of bitter-sweet armagnac before bed. *B&B also. Meals on request.*

Price	€400-€950 per week.
Sleeps	5 + cot.
Rooms	2: 1 double, 1 triple; 3 shower rooms.
Closed	Never.

	Françoise & Patrice Pawlak
	Sauveterre,
	Hautes-Pyrénées
Tel	+33 (0)5 62 96 32 62
Email	tecouere.pawlak@wanadoo.fr
Web	www.gites-de-france-65.com/fermedetecouere

La Poujoulie

This restoration of a rustic old farm building combines meticulous attention to detail with oodles of history and charm. It is quietly luxurious – a rare treat. The English owner was an interior decorator and her feeling for colour and texture – wood, stone, textiles, tiles – shines through. The whole gorgeous place wraps itself round a big, gravelled, sheltered courtyard furnished with a fragrant, plant-strewn pergola and solid teak dining table and chairs. Come too for the delectable solar-heated pool, the spectacular views over the Tarn, the magnificent games room and, to the side, the two-storey cottage for grandparents or teenagers. But don't dream only of visiting in summer. There's a fireplace with a wood-burner that would be a joy to come home to, a kitchen range worthy of the classiest chef, a bath you could wallow for hours in. It's a 15-minute drive to cafés, shops and bistros; for farm-pressed cassis juice and Toulouse sausages, you can't do better than the market at Villefranche; for history and culture, don't miss Albi, Cordes or Najac.

Price	£700–£1,500 per week; see owners' website for details. Heating & logs extra.
Sleeps	House 6. Cottage 4. (Cottage not available on its own.)
Rooms	House: 2 doubles, 1 twin; 1 bathroom, 1 shower room, separate wc. Cottage: 1 double, 1 twin; 1 shower room, separate wc.
Closed	Rarely.

Tim & Chrissie Davidson
Montirat, Tarn

Tel	+44 (0)1256 389 578
Email	timdavidson@metronet.co.uk
Web	www.relaxintarn.com

La Croix de Fer

The 18th-century barn has it all – stone walls, beamed ceilings, rolling views, ancient peace – but it is the way in which Jacqui and Francis have decorated that makes it shine. Step into a big, light living and kitchen area, with cream tiles, soft green sofa and chairs, a vase of dried flowers. On one side, the palest exposed-stone wall, on the other, white rough plaster; the space spills with light. The twin bedroom is soft lilac and lemon; Jacqui fell in love with the bed throws and linen, then designed the room around them. The double comes in cream and rose, with sofa, beams, wrought-iron bed and windows on two walls that pull in the views. The house stands in ten acres of grass and woodland, the silence broken only by birdsong. There are deckchairs, shady trees and a delicious terrace by the stunning fenced pool. Jacqui has thought of just about everything: fluffy towels in excellent bathrooms, music, books and a wooden kitchen beautifully equipped. Hire bikes in the village, go riding nearby or walk your socks off in the valley of the Aveyron. *Candlelit dinners for special occasions.*

Price	£350–£750 per week.
Sleeps	4.
Rooms	2: 1 double, 1 twin; 1 bathroom, 1 shower room.
Arrival	Saturday, flexible out of season.
Closed	November–April.

Jacqui & Francis Suckling
Saint Martin Laguépie, Tarn
Tel   +33 (0)5 63 56 25 20
Fax   +33 (0)5 63 56 25 20
Email suckling@wanadoo.fr

Les Rochers

A magnificent place, it stands on high ground whence stunning views over three very different landscapes. The big stone house has the fabulous internal courtyard and outside staircase so typical of the region: beautifully cool in summer and a lovely place to eat. A generous terrace runs round the two living-room sides of the house, leading to the flowers, birds and views of the stress-lifting garden. Done with modern furnishings and no knick-knacks, the interior has a terrific feeling of space, light and comfort: a good fireplace and stone or plaster walls in the red and blue living room, a long pine table in the bright and friendly yellow kitchen, French windows onto the shimmering terrace and garden. Bedrooms, bright and sunny on their pine floors, are done with cream tones, wicker chairs and cheerful bed linen. Bathrooms are, of course, excellent and… the first floor also contains a second sitting room where masses of books and modern prints invite you to a quiet read. A light, vibrant house, just five minutes' drive from Laguépie with its shops and good-value restaurant, this is a hard place to leave.

Price	£750-£1,350 per week. Available longer periods out of season.
Sleeps	8-14.
Rooms	4: 2 doubles, 2 twins; 1 bathroom, 2 shower rooms, separate wc. Additional rooms available.
Arrival	Saturday, but flexible.
Closed	Rarely.

	Nicki & Duncan Evans Saint Martin Laguépie, Tarn
Tel	+33 (0)5 63 56 01 74
Email	nicki@farmhousesandvillas.com
Web	www.farmhousesandvillas.com

Maraval

There's a feeling of remoteness here, although Cordes is no distance at all; only birdsong and the stream flowing beneath the house tickle the peace. Maraval, an ancient mill house in 100 magical acres of woodland, cliffs and pasture, stands at the end of a long, secret country lane. Behind, at the head of the valley, trees cluster steeply round the lawned garden and the lovely pool. The house itself is full of original features – massive beams, uneven floors, a creaky, eccentric staircase – and has white-painted walls and stunning views. Books, pictures, corner sofas and rugs make the split-level sitting room particularly inviting. The kitchen, too, is a delight, with a vast open fireplace (and logs for cool evenings), an ancient farmhouse table, blue and white tiles and an armoire stuffed with crocks and glassware. Outside is a wonderful covered dining terrace. The large, pretty bedrooms are carpeted and furnished with rural antiques and comfortable beds; one bedroom suite is on the ground floor with French windows onto the terrace; the other two are upstairs with the second bathroom.

Price	£700–£1,100 per week.
Sleeps	6.
Rooms	3: 2 doubles, 1 twin; 2 bathrooms.
Arrival	Sunday.
Closed	October–June.

Nicki & Duncan Evans
Cordes sur Ciel, Tarn
Tel   +33 (0)5 63 56 01 74
Email   nicki@farmhousesandvillas.com
Web   www.farmhousesandvillas.com

Entry 264 Map 15

La Bourthoumarié

Gaze from the fountain at the mesmerising views, doze by the pool or take your book and a glass of something to the shady breakfast terrace. So much space, so many rolling views of vineyards (the best wine in the Gaillac area); you could lose the rest of your party and only meet at mealtimes. This handsome, prettily shuttered *maison de maître* is full of light and cool with space. Rooms are uncluttered yet comfortable, antique-shop finds mixing with contemporary lighting and sofas to show off the richness of the original features – wide spiral staircase, beams, timber and terracotta floors. Bedrooms are restful with pale walls, traditional rugs on polished floors, dressing rooms, antique washstands and mirrors in the bathrooms. Children will love the quirkily beamed attic rooms. Visit historic Cordes or Saint Antonin, go wine tasting or spend the day at home, playing games on the sweeping lawns. Cooking dinner is fun in the big, farmhouse-style kitchen. More fun is eating it in the huge, three arched, open barn. Lunches will be long, suppers may drift into dawn.

Price	£825–£1,500 per week.
Sleeps	8.
Rooms	4: 2 doubles, 2 twins; 3 bathrooms, separate wc.
Arrival	Friday.
Closed	Never.

Nicki & Duncan Evans
Vieux, Tarn

Tel	+33 (0)5 63 56 01 74
Email	nicki@farmhousesandvillas.com
Web	www.farmhousesandvillas.com

Le Presbytère

Who never dreamed of growing up in a rambling old rectory with space and corners for everyone to hide in? The dream comes true in Vieux. In the quiet square, the ancient church sets the scene, bells ring the Angelus, you turn the iron handle, push the hefty old door and enter the thick walls of your family refuge. The house has beams and a wide creaky staircase, a salvaged confessional door decorates one wall, the big comfortable living room is furnished with seriously heavy pieces that are entirely fitting and, with its wood-burner for cooler weather, it is a supremely relaxing space for the whole family. Two generous master bedrooms with super bathrooms, great rooms for the younger generation on the top floor, modern, bright, inviting décor and sunlight pouring in – the perfect solid family house. One of the bedrooms has its own balcony. The good big kitchen has all the equipment and space for a team of cooks. Beyond is an attractive terrace, a help-yourself herb bed and the walled cottage garden, a sheer delight of scent, colour, form – and thornless roses, ideal beside the fenced pool.

Price	£775–£1,395 per week.
Sleeps	8.
Rooms	4: 2 doubles, 2 twins; 2 bathrooms, 2 shower rooms, 2 separate wcs.
Arrival	Saturday, flexible out of season.
Closed	Rarely.

Nicki & Duncan Evans
Vieux, Tarn

Tel	+33 (0)5 63 56 01 74
Email	nicki@farmhousesandvillas.com
Web	www.farmhousesandvillas.com

Château La Roussillé - Apartment

Nicki and Duncan have restored this grand 18th-century hunting lodge to its former glory with superb attention to detail, some adorable Shetland ponies, and other furry friends. The apartment occupies the first floor of the west wing, above the original wine cellars and press. Enter through a gated, shingled courtyard that is totally private and blessed with fine country views. The rustic front door leads to an open living area filled with light from both sides, the huge wood-burner making it ideally cosy in cooler seasons. Colours are mainly blue and white, light and cool against ancient beams and creaky floorboards. Nicki, who loves cooking, has equipped the kitchen with all a keen cook could want plus stacks of crocks. Bedrooms are just as light and comfortable, one has a four-poster; excellent bathrooms combine mosaics, good mirrors, space and storage. Altogether an intriguing mix of old bones and contemporary comforts – and Duncan has carved out some great paths through the paddocks. They are remarkable hosts if you need them. *Shared pool. Meals on request. Restaurants in Cordes, 5 mins.*

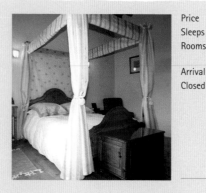

Price	£650-£1,150 per week.
Sleeps	4-6.
Rooms	2: 2 doubles; 1 bathroom, 1 shower room. Extra double en suite if required.
Arrival	Friday, but flexible.
Closed	Rarely.

Nicki & Duncan Evans
Vindrac-Alayrac, Tarn
Tel +33 (0)5 63 56 01 74
Email nicki@farmhousesandvillas.com
Web www.farmhousesandvillas.com

Domaine de Villeneuve

A *maison de maître*, a sublime house set in private parkland, with ravishing views across meadows to an ancient church steeple; if you're lucky, bells will chime. The pool is flanked by rampant greenery with a rose pergola to one side, the terrace is sail-shaded with long views across open country. Inside, a sweeping wooden staircase, an enormous stone fireplace, oak and beamed ceilings and a *fleur-de-lys* tiled floor; the whole house swims in light. The owner, a collector, has a good eye. Acquisitions include an antique pram, a restored water trough, church pews and antique baskets. Large airy bedrooms have cotton curtains and timber floors; one upstairs has a marble fireplace, another a canopied wooden bed; the one on the ground floor has floor-to-ceiling windows opening to the garden. Expect unremitting comfort: deep sofas, period furniture and old rugs… a place to hole up in for a week in blissful isolation at any time of year. French windows lead from the well-equipped kitchen to a terrace that runs along two sides. The medieval towns of Albi and Cordes are close by.

Price	£1,050–£1,850 per week.
Sleeps	12.
Rooms	6: 4 doubles, 2 twins; 4 bathrooms.
Arrival	Sunday.
Closed	Never.

Nicki & Duncan Evans
Villeneuve sur Vère, Tarn
Tel +33 (0)5 63 56 01 74
Email nicki@farmhousesandvillas.com
Web www.farmhousesandvillas.com

Entry 268 Map 15

Château de Fourès

Swap stress for bliss at this gem of a cottage in the grounds of a 19th-century château. Come for a beautiful renovation, a tranquil setting in the foothills of Cordes and a secluded tennis court and superb pool which you have almost entirely to yourselves. The charming and hospitable owners live here – Madeleine from Paris and Swiss husband Peter – but are discreet. The also speak excellent English. Inside, the cottage is steeped in charm: furnishings are good quality, furniture is country antique or new pine, there are pictures on open stone walls, vintage lamps suspended from beamed ceilings, cheerful checks and fresh flowers. You eat at a round table in the bright, light corner kitchen that is beautifully equipped, or outside in your own delightful courtyard garden. And the grounds and flowering gardens are yours to share. Relax by the lily ponds, set off for lively Cordes, a mile away, or soak up the peace and the woodland views from your own roof terrace. Unbeatable value and perfect for two or a family with children.

Price	€600-€900 per week.
Sleeps	2-4.
Rooms	1 double, 2 pull-out beds in sitting room; 1 shower room.
Closed	November-April.

Madeleine Camenzind-Acory
Campes/Cordes, Tarn

Tel	+33 (0)5 63 56 13 55
Fax	+33 (0)5 63 56 13 55
Email	camenzind@wanadoo.fr

Domaine du Buc - Apartment

Brigitte's lovely domaine and château, built in the 1890s, appears in our B&B guide; now you may stay in your own apartment on the second floor. It's a good puff up a wooden staircase (originally the servants', of course) to reach it but, once there, you have glorious parkland views. A prime spot from which to view them – and perhaps dash off the odd postcard home – is Grandmother's pretty little writing desk at the window of the main bedroom. Another bedroom is named after Toulouse-Lautrec (there's a family link). The apartment is traditionally furnished with family antiques, formal rugs on polished wooden floors, comfortable beds. There's a modest kitchen with a sloped ceiling but if you don't feel like cooking, dinner can be provided. Outside: a huge pigeonnier with a revolving ladder in the tower, a patch of garden just for you, a shared pool. Brigitte's family has lived here for 100 years and she is passionate about the place. She is a truly engaging person, and involved with the tourist office in Albi too, so a great source of local information. *Shared pool. Sawday B&B. Meals on request.*

Price	€650–€850 per week.
	Shorter periods possible low season.
Sleeps	6-7.
Rooms	3: 2 twins/doubles, 1 twin;
	2 bathrooms.
Closed	Rarely.

Brigitte Lesage
Marssac sur Tarn, Tarn
Tel   +33 (0)5 63 55 40 06
Fax   +33 (0)5 63 55 40 06
Email   contact@domainedubuc.com
Web   www.domainedubuc.com

Château de Mayragues

Superlatives cannot describe this remarkable cottage in its château grounds. It has everything: history, vineyards, atmosphere. The château is 14th century and, with its overhanging balcony circling the upper storey, is an outstanding example of the region's fortified architecture. Its authentic 20-year restoration won charming Laurence and her husband Alan a national prize. Your home is, improbably, the château's old bakery; it is the prettiest place imaginable and has a south-facing terrace on which to relax with a glass of organic estate wine. It's cosy, light and simply but charmingly furnished – a mix of old and new. There's a living room with a wonderful contemporary kitchen at one end and an open stair to a tiny mezzanine with a single bed. The cool, roomy double has a blue and white theme with pretty checked curtains and new sisal on the floor; the shower room is excellent. Look out onto the 17th-century pigeonnier 'on legs'. Should you tire of being here, there's walking country all around and the medieval hilltop village of Castelnau de Montmiral is well worth a visit. *Sawday B&B.*

Price	€400-€500 per week.
Sleeps	2-3.
Rooms	2: 1 double, 1 mezzanine with single bed; 1 bathroom.
Closed	Never.

Laurence & Alan Geddes
Castelnau de Montmiral, Tarn
Tel   +33 (0)5 63 33 94 08
Fax   +33 (0)5 63 33 98 10
Email   geddes@chateau-de-mayragues.com
Web   www.chateau-de-mayragues.com

La Chênaie

On the edge of the owners' land, but not overlooked, this is a creative renovation of a farmworker's house and wine press with colourwashed shutters. Martin has done a great job. Step in: the sunny character of the rooms reflects Irish Nuala's personality and the overall impression is one of comfort, generosity and space. There is reclaimed wood for floors and rafters, split levels to add interest, no stairs; best of all, French windows that open to a lovely, two-level, sun-protected terrace. The kitchen is for cooks, full of country crocks and a multitude of shining pots and pans; the furniture – some old country pieces, some modern – is country style; the bed linen is pretty, and there are prints and pictures on the walls. View are far-reaching, of forests and fields, and there's space to rampage outside: the fenced garden is child-friendly, the games room is covered, the pool area is safe. It's a brisk walk to Salvagnac (20 minutes at the most) and there's a produce-laden, people-watching market in Gaillac on Friday mornings. Friendly, heart-warming – and spotless.

Price	€700–€2,000 (£485–£1,400) per week. Long rentals on request.
Sleeps	6.
Rooms	3: 2 doubles, 1 twin; 1 bathroom, 2 shower rooms, separate wc.
Arrival	Flexible out of season.
Closed	Long winter lets possible.

	Nuala O'Neill
	Salvagnac, Tarn
Tel	+33 (0)5 63 40 50 05
Email	m.scott@wanadoo.fr
Web	www.holidayfarmhouseinfrance.com

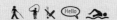

Midi – Pyrénées

Maison Puech Malou - The Cottage

In its own little garden, the prettiest gîte. You step into a very delightful open-plan interior with wood-burning stove, cheerful red sofa, books and easy chairs. The galley kitchen has sun-yellow tiles, dishwasher, hob and oven. The bedroom is cosy and cool – white walls, antique pine, bed linen with towels to match, and shower room en suite. You get your lovely private terrace and garden, with barbecue, at the back and, off the courtyard, reached via an outside stair, an extra bedroom you can rent – ideal for grandparents, older children or anyone wanting independence. Monique is charming, bakes her own bread (which she's happy to sell), keeps her own hens. There's nothing she likes better than to prepare dinner for a big friendly crowd: enjoy table d'hôtes in the big, terraced garden. You're high on a sunny hill (*puech* means 'hilltop' in the regional dialect, *malou* is a type of apple), in a garden lush with lavender, hibiscus and shady corners. Teillet for simple shops is a five-minute drive, Albi and Toulouse are under an hour. *Pool may be available by arrangement. Sawday B&B. Meals on request.*

Price	€450-€650. With extra room €700-€1,000. Prices per week. Enquire about renting whole property.
Sleeps	2-4 (12-14 with Farmhouse).
Rooms	1 double; 1 shower room. Extra double & shower available with outside entrance.
Closed	Never.

Monique Moors
Teillet, Tarn

Tel	+33 (0)5 63 55 79 04
Fax	+33 (0)5 63 55 79 88
Email	info@maisonpuechmalou.com
Web	www.maisonpuechmalou.com

Maison Puech Malou - The Farmhouse

Here is a restoration that is both beautiful and rustic. You arrive at the creeper-clad 19th-century farmhouse by a very pretty back road through wooded country. Inside, a friendly, calming home full of antiques swims in crisp light. Walls are exposed stone or white, the floors are terracotta, the ceilings are beamed in heavy oak: sense the weight of age. The master bedroom has a good big bed and a romantic feel, a couple of bedrooms come with stripped pine boards, another, super-private, is entered by a staircase that rises from the covered courtyard where pots grow colour. You will find two huge open fireplaces in the sitting room, a big rustic dining table beneath more great beams, a generous and delightfully-designed kitchen. Good teak furniture stands on the terrace and the lawn runs down to the pool; there's a vegetable garden you are welcome to plunder and a marked trail that leads from the truly gorgeous garden into the hills. Dutch Monique is friendly, hands-on, bakes her bread daily and is a great cook. Wonderful. *Cooking holidays available. Sawday B&B. Meals on request.*

Price	€1,350-€2,400.
	With cottage, €1,800-€3,050.
	Prices per week.
	Enquire about renting whole property.
Sleeps	10 (12-14 with Cottage).
Rooms	5: 2 doubles, 3 twins; 1 bathroom,
	2 shower rooms, separate wc.
Closed	Never.

Monique Moors
Teillet, Tarn

Tel	+33 (0)5 63 55 79 04
Fax	+33 (0)5 63 55 79 88
Email	info@maisonpuechmalou.com
Web	www.maisonpuechmalou.com

Les Buis de Saint Martin

A heavenly place for a couple. The 19th-century manor, in its park on the banks of the Tarn, has been Jacqueline's home for 30 years; the gîte is in its own wing. How delightful to wander down to the water's edge in this peaceful, special place, where a private pedalo waits to carry you downriver. Inside, a charming minimalism prevails. The ground floor is terracotta, the first floor polished wood; muslin blinds hang at deep-set windows, walls and beams are whiter-than-white. Its contemporary look suits the light and lofty space: wood and wicker, a clean-cut sofa, a big lemon-yellow bed, a few pictures, a simple rug. The galley-style kitchen is beautifully equipped, the walk-in shower is white and chic, and Jacqueline, who does B&B in the manor, is a dear. Outside, too, is lovely: your own secluded garden by the river, with heated plunge pool and teak loungers. Little Marssac has the basic shops, Albi and hilltop Cordes are close by, the area is filled with good restaurants and the wines of Gaillac, less well-known than the Bordeaux, are one of France's best-kept secrets. Brilliant. *Sawday B&B.*

Price	€400-€650 per week.
Sleeps	2-4.
Rooms	1 double, 1 sofabed in living room; 1 shower room, separate wc.
Arrival	Saturday, but flexible out of season.
Closed	Never.

Jacqueline Romanet
Marssac sur Tarn, Tarn

Tel	+33 (0)5 63 55 41 23
Mobile	+33 (0)6 27 86 29 48
Email	jean.romanet@wanadoo.fr
Web	perso.wanadoo.fr/les-buis-de-saint-martin/

Les Secrets du Bonheur

A triumphant conversion, the 200-year-old barn stands like a medieval lookout on a ridge above the lush Brommes valley and its kaleidoscope skies, a perfect foil in scale and natural solidity for this wild and wonderful region. The architect's renovation is as dramatic as that view: you will revel in the sweep of the split-level living space down to the vast windows, the suspended central hearth, the phalanx of leather sofas, Tony's hefty timber furniture (his hobby, or so he says), a brilliant kitchen area, a brightly clothed futon – all held in by those venerable working stones, all done with much calm taste and very little colour. Up the beautiful new staircase, the best bedroom is more of the same: space and lovely materials, luxurious minimalism and a private balcony over the valley. Below the living floor are the two twin bedrooms with the same excellent bedding and doors onto a little terrace each, the garden – and the view. Superb bathrooms, as you would expect, and generous, enthusiastic owners in the old farmhouse next door who always go the extra mile. *B&B also. Dinner on arrival by arrangement.*

Price	€650–€950 per week.
Sleeps	6-8.
Rooms	3: 1 double, 2 twins; 4 bathrooms, 1 futon.
Arrival	Flexible.
Closed	Never.

Tony & Hanneke Herbert
Mur de Barrez, Aveyron

Tel	+33 (0)5 65 48 88 31
Email	lessecretsdubonheur@wanadoo.fr
Web	www.lessecretsdubonheur.com

La Salesse

A heavenly surprise lurks behind this house, a secret garden of shrubs and shingled paths leading to the pool area, its tall trees, and heart-relaxing views over the meadows of a walker's paradise. Once past the untidy farm where lively geese and angora goats hold sway, you will delight in a property whose superb restoration reveals a sunny personality and a well-loved home: solidly held between low beams and steep stairs, it hums with light and mementoes from eastern travels. In the open-plan first-floor living area, comfortable easy chairs by the wood-burner, baskets of maps and dried lavender greet you. The pastel bedrooms are restful and well furnished in pine with Indian wall hangings, the second twin room being the TV and video mezzanine. The sense of trusting welcome is an essential ingredient: use anything from the well-stocked cupboard, try the wines in the open rack – simply replace them for the next guests. Buy your fresh produce on Sunday at the bustling street market in unspoilt medieval Najac or on Thursday in Villefranche. Charming Rod will give you all the help and advice you need.

Price	£550–£1,000 per week.
Sleeps	6.
Rooms	2: 1 double, 1 twin; 2 shower rooms, 2 wcs, 2 beds on mezzanine.
Arrival	Flexible out of season.
Closed	November–April.

Rod Millard
Najac, Aveyron

Tel	+33 (0)6 21 13 64 70
Email	enquiries@letsstayinfrance.com
Web	www.letsstayinfrance.com

La Montarnie

People love this little cottage and its postcard-pretty setting: cattle graze, birds sing, there are orchids in the meadows in spring. Relax on the wooden swing-seat in the shade of the walnut tree, spot the wagtails nesting in the barn wall, or dine into the early hours. The stone house, dated 1860, was once a barn and stands engulfed by a sea of greenery and wild flowers. It's a rustic little farming hamlet and the cottage, the owners' second home, is furnished in a wonderfully warm contemporary style. Bedrooms are light and delightful, cool in summer and with good views onto the walled garden. Downstairs: wicker dining chairs, a comfortable cream sofa, CDs, books, and an open fire for winter (central heating, too). Baskets hang from beams and you eat at a long pine table with wooden church pews resting against stone walls. Rent bikes in nearby Najac, one of the loveliest old towns in the northern Cathar country. Fish, canoe, swim in the river, trawl the Thursday market in Villefranche, don't miss Rodez and Albi. Simple, rural France refreshingly free of tourists, especially out of season.

Price	£350-£500 per week.
Sleeps	4-6.
Rooms	3: 2 doubles, 1 room with bunks; 1 bathroom, 1 shower room, 2 separate wcs.
Arrival	Sunday.
Closed	Winter.

Charles & Sarah Drury
Lescure Jaoul, Aveyron

Tel	+44 (0)1981 550 235
Mobile	+44 (0)7970 510 110
Email	sarah@lamontarnie.com
Web	www.lamontarnie.com

Midi – Pyrénées

The School House

An undiscovered corner of paradise, six kilometres from the village of Brusque. David from London, Carlos from Brazil, interested in travel, history and people, toured the world before falling under this hilltop hamlet's spell. Abandoned since the 1960s, Blanc has been brought to life thanks to their passionate restoration and the locals have welcomed them with open arms. The Schoolhouse sits high, in one of the finest positions, with magical views across the wooded valley to the church and 9th-century château. Solid, inviting, the interior is a calm, contemporary space: white plaster, fresh terracotta, pale pine, cream linen. Balinese wall hangings, trinkets and books add warmth, there's a wood-burner for winter and the logs are on the house. The kitchen is big and friendly, its doors opening to a terrace; sit out here with birdsong and river sound for company. One bedroom is downstairs, the other under the eaves. Carlos and David know about the Templar cities, the markets, the walks (many start from the village)… they organise village events in the barn and can even cook you dinner. *Meals on request.*

Price	€250–€600 per week.
Sleeps	4.
Rooms	2: 1 double, 1 twin/double; 1 bathroom, separate wc.
Closed	Rarely.

David Morris-Johnson & Carlos Barbosa
Peux et Couffouleux, Aveyron
Tel   +33 (0)5 65 49 31 58
Email   blanc@blancsursanctus.fr
Web   www.blancsursanctus.fr

Languedoc – Roussillon

Can Llouquette - The Gîte

Birdsong, the rush of water, the rustle of leaves... half-way up Mount Canigou, in the Mediterranean Pyrenees, this lovely old fruit farm in 11 verdant acres has dreamy views of green-cloaked mountains. Immensely restful, it makes the bumpy journey worth it. Your sturdy little gîte, a former sheepfold, is all soft-coloured stone and eau-de-nil shutters, full of light and simplicity. An open-plan living area – new terracotta, recycled wood – makes the most of the space with modern furnishings: pale elm table, oak chairs, black leather sofa, colourful prints. There's a crisp white kitchen with panoramic windows and doors to a terrace with breathtaking views. Bedrooms are comfortably unfussy in restful neutrals, their bathrooms have walk-in showers, there are no curtains at windows so you could be sleeping under the stars. Simon and Ashley, warm and friendly, live in the farmhouse and know the best walks, cycle routes, the closest restaurant, market and bars (a 15-minute walk). The coast and Perpignan are under an hour; return for a swim and those heavenly views. *Shared pool.*

It's not easy being green but this young couple are determined. They say their house is already two-thirds sustainable with washing water pumped from the river, drinking water from the spring, heating from a wood-fired boiler fed with their own timber, electricity from their hydro-turbine and the sewerage dealt with by two septic tanks and micro-filtration. Less mechanical, the grass is mown by horses and calves. Once the land is ready, they will plant an orchard. It all seems right, natural and good. Their ultimate aim is to convert all their systems in order to use only sustainable energy suppliers.

Price	£576–£822 per week.
	Linen not included.
Sleeps	4.
Rooms	2: 1 double, 1 twin; 2 bathrooms.
Closed	Rarely.

Simon Williams & Ashley Barrington
Montferrer, Pyrénées-Orientales
Tel	+33 (0)4 68 8916 64
Email	sa@can-llouquette.com
Web	www.can-llouquette.com

SPECIAL
GREEN ENTRY
see page 18

El Pinyol d'Oliva

In March the valley is a sea of blossom: the little walled town is the peach capital of France. Views sweep from your roof terrace to the streets below and the snowy peaks of the Canigou beyond. The old house sits in a small square, a stone's throw from the church, and its large, luminous rooms glow with good taste. Whitewashed walls rub shoulders with bare Catalan stonework, beams are high, floors terracotta and the entrance has a hand-set pebble floor. Cushions and curtains give bright bursts of colour, there's art on the walls and one of the shower rooms is triangular – the whole house vibrates with light and originality. On the ground floor is a studio that can be let individually; slip out early for croissants from your private door. Up a winding stair to a rustic-chic kitchen and a farmhouse table that seats 12; original walnut doors lead to a bedroom at either end. Then up to a sitting room with sofas and books and a bedroom with sloping rafters. Perpignan is a 15-minute drive, the airport 20, and you are in Spain within half an hour. *Cookery courses & walking tours. B&B option available.*

Price	€1,400-€2,100 per week.
Sleeps	8-10.
Rooms	4: 1 double, 3 twins/doubles; 2 bathrooms, 2 shower rooms.
Closed	Never.

Anne Guthrie
Île sur Têt, Pyrénées-Orientales
Tel   +33 (0)4 68 84 04 17
Email web-enquiry@elpinyoldoliva.com
Web   www.elpinyoldoliva.com

Le Château

A captivating kitchen – cookery books, dappled sunlight, wide shelves of china – sets the tone. This is a huge, friendly, family house, the village's 19th-century manor, and it's brimful of original features. In the light-washed hall: diamond floor tiles, marble fireplaces and a commemorative oar on the wall (George rowed for Cambridge). The drawing room has a chic but lived-in feel: antique tiles, throw-draped sofas, an entertaining display of straw hats, brocante finds. Bedrooms are big, bright and comfortable and the house spreads over three floors; the top level can be closed off or included. The house faces south on the edge of a small, charming village and the views are a joy. At the back is a saltwater pool in a tranquil walled garden – figs, palms, roses – overlooking trees and terracotta roofs. George and Sally, a remarkable pair, live nearby and may be prevailed upon to cook on occasion. Take up their offer of a wine tour and you'll be driven to the vineyard in a 1951 Riley; or tour the Cathar castles with George – 'His Lordship' knows the history.

Price	€1,000-€1,250. Whole house €2,500.
Sleeps	6-12.
Rooms	3: 2 doubles, 1 twin; 1 bathroom, 1 shower room, separate wc. Top floor available by arrangement: 1 double, 2 twins; 1 shower room.
Closed	November-March. Open Christmas & New Year on request.

George & Sally Crocker
Lasserre de Prouilhe, Aude
Tel +33 (0)4 68 69 28 04
Email sally@chateaulasserre.com
Web www.chateaulasserre.com

La Maison d'Oc

The 'Occitan' house is a perfectly restored gamekeeper's cottage with its own walled courtyard complete with flowers, teak chairs, stone barbecue and splash pool. Relax here with a glass of fruity Minervois after a day discovering new-old medieval Carcassonne or the Canal du Midi – or take a dip in the beautiful pool under the spreading cedar, shared with your delightful hosts and their B&B guests. A stable door leads directly into the kitchen/living room, generously big for two, cosily snug for four, beautifully done in white and blue with a neat corner kitchen: a sparkling hob with a small dishwasher below, a washing machine and dryer, a traditional stone sink. Upstairs is a fabulous new marble-tiled shower room and a charming red-spread, mahogany-furnished double room with its useful divan sofa for that extra person. On the second floor, the main bedroom is an atmospherically romantic space where warm orange-ochre fabrics combine with teak, coconut matting and bamboo. There's plenty of storage space, sweeping vineyard views – and Carcassonne is a five-minute drive. Gorgeous. *Sawday B&B. Shared pool.*

Price	€650–€1,100 per week.
Sleeps	4–5.
Rooms	2 doubles, 1 single sofabed; 1 shower room.
Closed	Rarely.

Christophe & Catherine Pariset
Villemoustaussou, Aude

Tel	+33 (0)4 68 77 00 68
Fax	+33 (0)4 68 77 01 68
Email	cpariset@trapel.com
Web	www.trapel.com

Le Relais Occitan - Lo Barralier

This fabulous old winery, with its giant oak vats – one now a library! – antique tools and buildings that go back 300 years, has been turned into four holiday cottages by Anita and Jean Louis. It's been a labour of love, but labours of love are nothing unusual for this interesting Franco-Italian couple. Both writers and journalists – their passions history and poetry – they are as likely to discuss troubadour verse as 19th-century winemaking techniques over your welcoming aperitif. Surrounded by sunflowers and vines, all the cottages here – once the homes of the families working on the vineyard – have been refurbished with a rustic simplicity. Lo Barralier, once inhabited by the barrel-maker, is the oldest and smallest. Within its simple living room is a tiny kitchen with a Fifties feel; a Catalan staircase leads up to a beamed bedroom for three, a second sitting room and a small roof terrace with shimmering views. A huge covered barbecue area with a wood-burning oven for homemade pizza is yours to share; on Sundays there are pizza and wine parties, hugely popular with guests. *B&B also.*

Price	€310–€460 per week.
Sleeps	2-4.
Rooms	1 family room for 3; 1 shower room; 1 sofabed.
Closed	Never.

Jean Louis Cousin & Anita Canonica
Marseillette, Aude

Tel	+33 (0)4 68 79 12 67
Fax	+33 (0)4 68 79 12 67
Email	j-l.Cousin@wanadoo.fr
Web	perso.wanadoo.fr/relais.occitan/

11 rue des Deux Ponts - Riverside, Balcony, Market Place

Once upon a time, many centuries ago, there were two houses divided by a cobbled lane. Several centuries later, the cobbled lane was replaced by a steep winding stairwell and a vast sky-lit hallway. Today, this hallway separates three charming apartments. It feels a privilege to stay here, in the medieval ramparts of one of the most historic villages of France, home to a distinguished abbey, a celebrated market square and a major literary festival in summer. And it's wonderful for young children: the small garden at the back of Balcony, shared by first-floor Riverside and Market Place, borders the limpid river so you can paddle in the waters of the pebble beach or wander down to the 11th-century bridge. The apartments are light-filled and lovely, with lofty beamed ceilings and sweeping terracotta floors, pretty bathrooms and modern kitchens, colourful throws on comfy old sofas, quirky brocante finds and good family pieces. The owners, a charming young couple, are passionate about the Corbières and hugely helpful with guests.

Price	Riverside €390–€990.
	Balcony €450–€1,250.
	Market Place: €350–€700.
Sleeps	3 gites for 4–5.
Rooms	Riverside: 1 double, 1 triple;
	1 bathroom.
	Balcony: 1 double, 1 triple;
	1 bathroom, 1 shower room.
	Market Place: 1 double, 1 twin;
	1 bathroom.
Closed	Rarely.

	Kate & Roger Sampson
	Lagrasse, Aude
Tel	+33 (0)4 68 43 19 35
Mobile	+33 (0)6 78 88 27 22
Email	holidays.lagrasse@gmail.com
Web	www.holidays-lagrasse.com

The Courtyard Gîte

Tucked into a sweet courtyard garden, here is a charming bolthole for two. You're in a village yet no-one would know you were here, your little house is so snugly private – that's half the attraction. Step into an open-plan living area with stone and lime-plaster walls, comfy blue sofa, mosaic-topped table and a galley kitchen decked out in yellow and blue. It's spotlessly clean and you have all you need: coffee maker, decent crockery, CD player, good reading lamps. Then it's up the open staircase to the bedroom under the beams. Handsome, high-quality bedding is set off by a simple pine floor, white walls and prettily exposed stone. A 'Juliet' balcony overlooks the garden; the bathroom, with walk-in shower, dazzles in white and blue. Best of all is the courtyard with its flowered tubs and climbing shrubs, attractive table and chairs and quirky collection of tools and rustic keys. Delightful Alan and Sandra live opposite, on hand to help but respecting your privacy. They'll tell you all about the markets and restaurants, the lake for swimming and the stunning walks. *B&B formula if preferred.*

Price	£220–£350 per week.	
Sleeps	2-4.	
Rooms	1 twin/double, 1 sofabed in sitting room; 1 bathroom.	
Arrival	Flexible.	
Closed	Rarely.	

Sandra Dalgleish & Alan Buckley
Arques, Aude
Tel   +33 (0)4 68 20 63 69
Email   alanbuckleyindia@hotmail.com

Entry 286 Map 15

Gîte Bio - Eco-Cottage

Far from all things urban, in a tiny hamlet, up the cobbled street, past the cascading wisteria, Jeanine (ex-acupuncturist) has restored the little old chestnut dryer behind her 1850s country house with all her passion for preserving nature and the planet: nothing but natural materials and the absolute minimum use of fossil-fuel energy. It is perfect for slender young lovers (and others!): cosy intimacy, a table for two, a sofabed for two, storage for two and the futon bed up a ladder, half way to the sky. Neat behind its curtain under the mezzanine (no space for a door...), the snug shower space, basin and night-pee loo are just enough. There's a full kitchenette and the old bread oven for barbecues; ethnic touches and a wood-burner (logs extra) but you'll want to sit on the terrace, surrounded by greenery, butterflies, birds and all the peace in the world. You can walk (with donkeys, too) and bicycle through these lovely hills, go to music festivals, hear poetry in Lodève, visit the Tibetan Buddhist temple, the Orthodox monastery, or the non-violent Arche community. Amazing greener-than-green value.

The restoration was done using hemp and cork, wood and stone and the natural surroundings: no pollution here, just woods, springs and mountains. Water is solar heated, the futon mattress is pure cotton, grey water is recycled, the dry composting loo uses ashes and wood shavings: just below the gîte, it is great, very secret and safe with a wonderful view. Jeanine is carefully protecting the wildlife on her piece of the planet – butterflies, wild flowers, woodland creatures; she grows organic fruit and veg, makes her own jams and will prepare you a simple, delicious meal if you ask.

Price	€83–€180 per week. Linen not included.
Sleeps	2 & child.
Rooms	1 double sofabed, 1 futon bed on mezzanine; shower room, extra compost wc outside overlooking fish pond.
Arrival	Flexible.
Closed	Never.

	Jeanine Vancoppenolle
	Avène les Bains, Hérault
Tel	+33 (0)4 67 23 00 36
Email	vancoj2004@yahoo.fr
Web	www.gite-bio.com

SPECIAL
GREEN ENTRY
see page 18

Le Château – Le Pêcheur, Le Peintre & L'Écrivain

There's proper fishing here: the Orb and the Jaur pass 700 metres from the château, and Sébastien, a fishing guide, is on hand to advise. Hence the name, Le Pêcheur. This gîte is fresh with whitewashed walls and sandblasted beams, super-comfortable with CD systems and satellite TV. Le Peintre is so-named because of the painting courses that your friendly hosts organise several times a year, along with music evenings in the newly converted vaulted cellars, while the newest gîte, L'Écrivain, is in the 14th-century tower, a chic retreat for six and truly delightful. The whole area is a national park, the walking is some of the best in France, whatever the season, and you can stride out from the château and follow paths into the hills that rise behind. In autumn there are mushrooms to pick, in spring, wild flowers bring a patchwork of colour, in summer, the scent of rosemary hangs in the air. Try riding, cycling, kayaking, swimming in the river... or just rustle up a picnic in the summer kitchen by the pool. Sunday aperitifs for all, organised by your lovely hosts, are the cherry on the cake.

Price	Le Pêcheur & Le Peintre €575–€1,375 each. L'Écrivain €400–€1,650. Prices per week.
Sleeps	Le Pêcheur 5. Le Peintre 5. L'Écrivain 6.
Rooms	Le Pêcheur: 2 doubles, 1 single; 1 bathroom. Le Peintre: 2 doubles, 1 single; 1 bathroom. L'Écrivain: 3 doubles, 3 bathrooms.
Closed	Never.

Thérèse Salavin & Chris Elliott
Colombières sur Orb, Hérault

Tel	+33 (0)4 67 95 63 62
Fax	+33 (0)4 67 23 25 58
Email	christopher.elliott@club-internet.fr
Web	www.gitesdecharme.biz

Le Château – Le Randonneur & Le Musicien

A rural wonderland, lazy Languedoc at its best. Blow with the wind and you will chance upon hilltop villages, mountain streams, ancient vineyards, the Canal du Midi. And where better to stay than in an immaculately turned-out gîte on a château estate that's been in the family for 200 years? You are welcomed where the olives were once pressed, by Thérèse, who has poured heart and soul into restoring the fine old cellars, wine press and outbuildings. Across the courtyard, four dwellings, each with its own private (though not secluded) terrace. Inside: brand new sofas on parquet or terracotta, perfectly equipped kitchens, double basins in most bathrooms, fresh bedrooms with charming fabrics and the odd antique. Thick walls keep you cool in summer and warm in winter, along with log fires and heating; one-storey Le Musicien, generously beamed, is brilliantly geared up for wheelchairs. The delightful owners are involved in the Slow Food movement and will happily organise a paella dinner. As for the village, it's tiny: just one *épicerie* and a summer snack bar in the Gorges.

Price	Le Randonneur €650–€1,475.
	Le Musicien €575–€1,300.
	Prices per week.
Sleeps	Le Randonneur 6. Le Musicien 4-5.
Rooms	Le Randonneur: 1 double, 2 twins;
	1 bathroom.
	Le Musicien: 2 twins; 1 bathroom.
	Extra bed for living room.
Closed	Never.

Thérèse Salavin & Chris Elliott
Colombières sur Orb, Hérault

Tel	+33 (0)4 67 95 63 62
Fax	+33 (0)4 67 23 25 58
Email	christopher.elliott@club-internet.fr
Web	www.gitesdecharme.biz

Les Palmiers

The town is one of the oldest in the Languedoc, peaceful but alive with locals – and a sprinkling of tourists in summer. And, right on the market square, a stroll from the river (beach, rock pools, swimming), is this sunny, charming *maîson de maitre*. Sweep into an elegant salon with tall windows and sober chandelier, linen-dressed sofas and white wicker chair, grand marble (working) fireplace and kilim rug on pale floor. The cool downstairs bedroom is restful in soft pink; the kitchen contains everything in cupboards that climb to the ceiling; French windows open to a south-facing, palm-studded garden with a Moroccan mosaic table, shielded from the street by iron railings and high wall. Back inside, stairs curl up to a wide landing and the large luminous bedrooms: white curtains, white mirrors, tall windows, old tomettes, patterned tiles. The Dutch owners live conveniently nearby, while shops, market, cafés and restaurants (just two) are a lazy step away. The Mediterranean is at its best out of season; tempting to book a long stay. *Private garage.*

Price	€345–€690 per week. Linen not included.
Sleeps	6.
Rooms	3: 2 doubles, 1 twin; 1 bathroom, 1 shower.
Closed	Never.

Monique & Reinoud
Weggelaar-Degenaar
Cessenon sur Orb, Hérault

Tel	+33 (0)4 67 95 63 40
Fax	+33 (0)4 67 89 63 40
Email	monique@midimaison.com

La Roque

The garden slopes down, via several grassed terraces, to the lovely rushing river and the private beach. For lunch, your picnic table is in the dappled shade of old trees... the owners provide a rucksack containing plates, glasses and cutlery. Children can play in the shallows, swimmers can float with the current to the bridge, idlers can rest in the hammocks and watch the canoeists pass by. Back at La Roque, two period café doors replace the originals – the entrance to the old wine cellar and stables of the century-old wine grower's house. (The owners, when they come, live upstairs, but all you hear are birdsong and river.) In your very private space you have an open-plan living area with shiny terracotta floors, a wooden kitchen with white crockery and views of old Vieussan clinging to the hills above, a stylish iron sofa painted white with big blue cushions, a round table, a corner for ping-pong. Bedrooms have white walls, new beds, ethnic rugs, mosquito blinds; the open shower is huge. This is a place for lovers of quiet and of walks in the hills – and there's a great restaurant/bar in the village.

Price	€430–€1,160 (£300–£800) per week.
Sleeps	6.
Rooms	3: 1 double, 2 twins/doubles; 1 shower, separate wc.
Closed	November–February.

Annabel & Martin Shaw
Vieussan, Hérault

Tel	+33 (0)4 67 97 51 69
	+44 (0)1273 328 604
Email	vieussan@gmail.com
Web	www.vieussan.net

Languedoc – Roussillon

Hameau de Cazo - La Vigne

Simple and quietly elegant, this little pink village house will delight all who eschew fuss and clutter. And the views of the vineyards and the red-earthed hills of the Minervois will enchant you. In a small working hamlet, these three storeys have been beautifully restored by Dutch owners Monique and Reinoud, who live in a village nearby. Box trees flank the front door and the garden promises summer shade. Inside, original patterned floor tiles are enhanced by clean white walls and simple furniture. Dine round the farmhouse table or among the almond trees and lavender in the small walled garden. Upstairs are colourful bedspreads and curtains, russet-red tomettes and, in the double, an open fire. It's a charming little house, and a well-equipped one: central heating and two open fires, TV, CDs, DVDs, coffee-maker, dishwasher, washing machine. Walk in the vine-braided hills and the Mont Caroux, swim in peaceful rivers, drink in simple village life – along with a glass of Saint Chinian – while you watch sheep and goats lazily graze. Perfect, too, for a winter stay. *House for 4-5 available next door.*

Price	€325–€670 per week.
Sleeps	4 + 1 child.
Rooms	2: 1 double, 1 twin & child's bed; 1 bathroom.
Closed	Never.

Monique & Reinoud Weggelaar–Degenaar
Saint Chinian, Hérault

Tel	+33 (0)4 67 95 63 40
Fax	+33 (0)4 67 89 63 40
Email	monique@midimaison.com
Web	www.midimaison.com

12 rue de la Croix Rousse

On the edge of delightful Poilhes ('poy'), surrounded by a great expanse of lawn, guarded by luxuriant mimosa, palm trees and rose bushes, traffic-free and not overlooked, this modern house has, at the bottom of that lovely garden, near-private access to the Canal du Midi which runs along the edge of the lawn carrying its cohort of superb old plane trees. The public path is on the opposite bank, the cruise barges stop in the village to shop. The house has two kitchens and two living rooms and can be taken for six or ten: a brilliant solution for two families or groups of friends wanting to holiday together. Furnishing is simple, modern and good in cotton and wood, white leather and marble with comfortable sofas and Moroccan lights, a wood-burning stove and geo-thermic underfloor heating, a big flat telly and all the hi-fi. Bathrooms in lovely unpolished marble tiling are thoroughly up to date and the kitchens impeccable. You can take your own barge trip to medieval Minerve, go canoeing on the Orb or explore endless bits of history and architecture. *Unfenced water.*

Price	£1,200–£1,900 per week.
Sleeps	6-12.
Rooms	3: 2 doubles, 1 room with bunks; 1 bathroom, 1 shower room. In extension: 2 doubles en suite.
Closed	Never.

Drs Khalid & Grainne Hussain
Poilhes, Hérault

Tel	+33 (0)4 67 11 94 06
Mobile	+44 (0)7950 233 649
Email	khalid.hussain@orange.fr

Entry 293 Map 15

Paradix - Apartment One

The handsome gateway is 19th century but the interiors are resolutely modern: old and new coexist effortlessly in this collection of four apartments (see next entry). This was once a prosperous wine merchant's house and vines sweep in every direction. The stables and outbuildings have been imaginatively transformed by architect Colin and his Swiss wife, Susanna; they once ran an inn in Tuscany, now they live here. Apartments have two storeys and a small patio garden; the rest – lawns, shady spots, chlorine-free pool – are to share. Inside: a minimalist look with the occasional cushion or Matisse print in colourful contrast to perfect white walls and pale terracotta floors; there's light, space, clean lines. Apartment One, the biggest, sleeping four, has an immaculate kitchen with every mod con, a large sitting/dining room with space in which to sit and read, and views to the lovely jasmine- and oleander-tumbled gardens that keep each apartment private. A yellow spiral staircase leads to luxurious but stylishly simple bedrooms, with beds dressed in fine white linen. *Shared laundry.*

Price	€900-€1,120 per week. Full board available.
Sleeps	4.
Rooms	2 twins/doubles; 1 shower room.
Closed	Never.

Susanna, Colin & Yvonne Glennie
Nissan lès Ensérune, Hérault

Tel	+33 (0)4 67 37 63 28
Fax	+33 (0)4 67 37 63 72
Email	glennieauparadix@wanadoo.fr
Web	www.glennieauparadix.com

Paradix - Apartments Two, Three, Four

You can tell from the beautiful blue and white kitchens that Colin Glennie was once a professional chef: they're so well equipped that the most reluctant cook will be inspired. All is perfection in these apartments, the interiors a serene symphony of light woods and natural fabrics. Study, read or relax in the large, light sitting/dining rooms; the lighting is excellent and central heating keeps you cosy in winter. In summer, swim in the delicious pool, read under the plane trees, or stroll among the roses and oleander in the communal garden. Or set off for Béziers (don't miss the riotous four-day *feria* in August), the Oppidum d'Ensérune (the nearby site of a 1,600-year-old Gallo-Roman settlement) and the Canal du Midi with its colourful barges. If you want a cheaper option, there's a first-floor studio for two, where striking blues and reds are offset by white walls. Come to Paradix if you're seeking a week of minimalist perfection in discreet and beautiful surroundings and a village you can walk to: Nissan is a lively little place with both market and shops. *Shared laundry.*

Price	€620–€890 each per week.
Sleeps	3 apartments for 2.
Rooms	Each apartment: 1 twin/double; 1 shower room.
Closed	Never.

Susanna, Colin & Yvonne Glennie
Nissan lès Ensérune, Hérault

Tel	+33 (0)4 67 37 63 28
Fax	+33 (0)4 67 37 63 72
Email	glennieauparadix@wanadoo.fr
Web	www.glennieauparadix.com

Languedoc – Roussillon

Maison Hirondelles

Wine and tennis, a winning combination. Antiques dealer Simon knows about the former, Meg is the local tennis champ and will whirl you around the courts. Fun and interesting, they moved to the pretty, wine village of Cazedarnes a few years ago, turning the 19th-century stone house into a two-bedroom B&B with a gîte on the top floor. With your own entrance you can be as private or as sociable as you like: you may share the pool and verdant garden or retreat to your secluded courtyard with its shady chestnut and Japanese maple. High sloping ceilings, plenty of windows and cool white walls give rooms space and light. The open-plan living area, comfortably but unfussily furnished, has French windows to a veranda with views of vineyards and hills. The kitchen is crisp, modern and in excellent order; the bedrooms have antiques, pretty bedcovers, super bath and shower rooms and lovely views. With maps and bikes to borrow you can explore vineyards, hike in the Canal du Midi, browse markets and visit Carcassonne or the coast (a 40-minute drive). No wonder readers love this place. *Shared pool. B&B also.*

Price	€330–€1,100 per week.
Sleeps	6.
Rooms	3: 1 double, 2 twins/doubles; 1 bathroom, 2 shower rooms.
Closed	Rarely.

Meg & Simon Charles
Cazedarnes, Hérault
Tel   +33 (0)4 67 38 21 68
Email megsimon@wanadoo.fr
Web   www.maison-hirondelles.com

Entry 296 Map 15

Couvent des Ursulines - 4 Apartments

Step from the street into a high-walled garden and catch your breath. Opening before you is a serene view of plane trees, palm trees, hammocks and green – in the heart of old Pézenas. Jean-François (French) and Nikki (English) spent two years transforming the graceful 19th-century convent into four strikingly contemporary apartments. Arched French windows lead from terraces into open-plan salons: light airy spaces that combine minimum furnishings with maximum comfort. Sweeping tiled floors and stippled or washed walls make the most of each room's lofty proportions while leather sofas, polished dining tables and hand-crafted chandeliers add a bold edge. Each delicate metalwork spiral stair leads to a snug mezzanine sitting room; neat kitchens are tucked into corners. Light-filled bedrooms, warm in peach and pink, have a sprinkling of choice antiques. Take a dip in the pool, pick the garden herbs, visit the coast. Jean-François and Nikki are passionate about this place; they and the convent will charm you. They also run a lively café in town. *Shared pool. Massage, French lessons & guided excursions.*

Price	€850–€1,500 each per week.
Sleeps	4-8; 4-6; 4-6; 4-6.
Rooms	Apartment One: 2 doubles; 3 bathrooms; 2 sofabeds (one on mezzanine). Apartments Two, Three & Four: 2 doubles; 2 bathrooms, separate wc; sofabed on mezzanine.
Arrival	Saturday July & August, flexible other months.
Closed	Rarely.

	Jean-François & Nikki Marques-Quist Pézenas, Hérault
Tel	+33 (0)4 67 90 64 77
Fax	+33 (0)4 67 09 49 51
Email	info@pezenas-ursulines.com
Web	www.pezenas-ursulines.com

Château de Grézan - Les Meneaux

Enter the battlemented gateway in the 'medieval' castle walls (those turrets are 19th-century follies), cross the cobbled yard and ascend the old stone stairs. Les Meneaux feels big and somehow modern – yards of lovely, wide, original floorboards, high rafters, immaculate white walls and a kitchen that is resolutely 21st-century. The flat is big, light and uncluttered, its paintwork picked out in blue, its sideboard filled with well-chosen china. It has country furnishings, a pretty blue double bedroom, a smaller, spring-flowered twin and two beds up on the mezzanine beneath the roof window. Outside the castle walls is the swimming pool, beautifully protected by palm trees and bamboo, where you can relax and eat; beyond, a sea of vines shimmers beneath the great Languedoc sky. The garden, a superb mixture of wild and formal, has some fascinating native species and you can buy estate Faugères wine. Delightful Madame has a restaurant within the walls and a gîte in the tower, so others share the pool and the grounds. A lovely relaxed place with masses of space. *Sawday B&B*.

Price	€515–€1,200 per week. Linen not included.
Sleeps	4-6.
Rooms	3: 2 twins/doubles, 2 singles on mezzanine; 1 bathroom.
Arrival	Saturday, but flexible out of season.
Closed	Never.

Marie-France Lanson
Laurens, Hérault

Tel	+33 (0)4 67 90 28 03
Fax	+33 (0)4 67 90 05 03
Email	chateau-grezan.lanson@wanadoo.fr
Web	www.grezan.com

Château de Grézan - La Tour

La Tour is inside the castle gate, by the lovely pool, and its kitchen and bathroom fit within a circular tower – amazing. The antique-style oval windows and the 'arrow-slits' allow limited light from the outside world but with great beams, old stones and fresh paintwork this is more atmospheric than gloomy, and blessedly cool in high summer. A sofa and a couple of deep chairs still leave space on the tiled ground floor for a good country table and a great armoire full of crockery. To one side is the double bedroom with a soft-curtained bed and window opening onto the vines. The twin room, behind a curtain on the beamed mezzanine, gets air and light from the entrance hall and faces the old-fashioned bathroom in the tower at the other end of the gallery. The kitchen, off the living area below, is diminutive but fine for holiday cooking. A wildly romantic castle setting, a pool beneath the palms, sloping lawns and massive trees, a little restaurant in the ramparts, and holistic massage to tempt you. Madame Lanson, who is charming, has organised a fascinating wine trail for English speakers. *Sawday B&B.*

Price	€400-€940 per week. Linen not included.
Sleeps	2-4.
Rooms	2: 1 double, 1 twin on mezzanine; 1 bathroom.
Arrival	Saturday, but flexible out of season.
Closed	Never.

	Marie-France Lanson
	Laurens, Hérault
Tel	+33 (0)4 67 90 28 03
Fax	+33 (0)4 67 90 05 03
Email	chateau-grezan.lanson@wanadoo.fr
Web	www.grezan.com

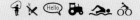

Domaine du Cayrat - Alicante, Ramonet, Sellerie

It must seem like heaven to the Barys who retired here after stressful careers in Paris. The domaine has been in the family for generations and Jacques and Monique have energetically and carefully transformed their trio of barns into well-equipped gîtes. Each one is fresh, simple and immaculate, with space, finely thought-out detail and views over the surrounding vineyards. The furniture is a good mix of old and new: Monique has obviously enjoyed seeking out the right pieces – a mirror wreathed in vine leaves, the perfect bedside lamp… French windows open from big white living rooms onto private terraces fringed with infant oleanders, each with its own teak furniture and barbecue. Beyond is the grassy shade of the courtyard, dominated by a magnificent, century-old fig tree. Beyond again, hidden behind the courtyard wall, is the pool. This is a great place for families – the Barys' own grandchildren put in an appearance from time to time – and there's masses to do in the area. If you're a Molière fan, elegant Pézenas, one of his favourite towns, is nearby. Fancy having your wedding party here? You can. *B&B also.*

Price	€650–€1,700 each per week.
Sleeps	Alicante 6. Ramonet 6. Sellerie 6.
Rooms	Alicante: 1 double, 2 twins; 1 bath, 2 showers.
	Ramonet: 1 double, 2 twins; 3 showers.
	Sellerie: 1 double, 2 twins; 1 bath, 2 showers.
	Two extra en suite doubles available.
Arrival	Flexible low season.
Closed	Never.

Monique de Bary
Cazouls d'Hérault, Hérault

Tel	+33 (0)4 67 25 15 44
Fax	+33 (0)4 67 25 15 44
Email	info@lecayrat.com
Web	www.lecayrat.com

Domaine de Rives Près

Fling open the French windows and scent fills the air: lavender, thyme, rosemary, pine. The ground-floor rooms of this generously restored farmhouse open directly to the perfumed garden. Beyond, the Languedoc vineyards roll into the hazy distance. This is an indoors/outdoors place with cool tiled rooms drifting into terraces, balconies, trees for shade and a secluded swimming pool. Inside, all is space, light and white: stone or plaster walls, beams, vast windows, a series of archways linking the downstairs rooms. Furnishings are uncluttered – white linen sofas, modern paintings, fine bronze sculptures and well-loved family antiques. Plus smart bathrooms, fresh bedrooms with glorious views and a smallish but well-equipped kitchen (and another on the second floor). Toss a coin for the master suite with its balcony and window'd veranda, or the garden bedroom with terrace, ideal for grandparents. Canoeing and sailing nearby, beaches an hour away, shops, restaurants and weekly market walkable – a place of taste that is perfect for large families who love peace, luxury and style.

Price	£750–£1,750 per week.
Sleeps	9–10.
Rooms	5: 2 doubles, 2 twins, 1 single + 1 folding bed; 4 bathrooms, 1 separate wc.
Closed	Never .

	Brenda Kemp
	Saint André de Sangonis, Hérault
Tel	+33 (0)4 67 96 61 25
Fax	+33 (0)4 67 96 61 25
Email	bookings@rivespres.net
Web	www.rivespres.net

Mas de Villetelle

A simple, rustic hideaway – a joy for those who want to unwind. You are in glorious countryside yet a 15-minute bike ride from Gignac with its restaurants and Saturday market. You stay in a charming converted farm building (the rest are still in ruins) in total privacy with your own shaded patio, hammock, deckchairs and barbecue. Step into an open-plan living space of terracotta floors, white walls, a wood-burner, two comfortable sofas, books. There are basket drawers for pots and pans, no modern gadgets and a basic four-ring gas hob, but you can walk to a lovely auberge down the road. Bedrooms are up a steep pine ladder staircase (not for tots!) and are plain and pretty with touches of brocante, good mattresses, white cotton sheets. Views are stunning, over vineyards and umbrella pines. A shower room with hand-made tiles sits between the two bedrooms; hot water for washing, and electricity for lights, fridge and music are solar powered. The owners live nearby and leave a bottle of wine and fresh wild flowers for when you arrive. *No washing machine. Use of owners' pool by arrangement.*

Price	€350 per week.
Sleeps	4.
Rooms	2 doubles; 1 shower room.
Closed	End September to Easter.

Terri Andon
Gignac, Hérault

Tel	+33 (0)4 67 86 16 03
Fax	+33 (0)4 67 57 48 24
Email	terri@louma.fr

Gîte du Pic Saint Loup

A gentle place to stay beneath the wind-singing umbrella pines, your little holiday home is the ground floor of the owners' house yet you can be as private as you wish with your own pretty terrace and garden, even your own drive for the car. The Mortiers have done a beautiful, simple conversion using soft ochre-limed walls, lamps, tables and rugs from Morocco (they lived there for 30 years), wooden furniture and an excellent big shower room. It is all high quality, there's plenty of storage and no clutter. Cooks will love the battery of equipment in the green and yellow kitchen, the third person's sofabed in the living room hides behind a curtain at bedtime, simple white crockery decks the old farmhouse table and the terrace is perfect for morning shade and sunset vigils. Walk or bicycle out into the quiet countryside where grapes and olives grow, take the children to the nearby 'Ecology' centre or leave the car in Jacou and catch the tram to young and lively Montpellier for a shot of culture or shopping. A perfect marriage of city and country living. *Restaurants 3-10km.*

Price	€450-€650 per week.
Sleeps	2.
Rooms	1 double/ twin; 1 shower room.
Closed	Never.

Yvonne & Patrick Mortier
Prades le Lez, Hérault

Tel	+33 (0)4 67 59 56 37
Email	patrick@mortier.nom.fr
Web	giterural-herault.com

Languedoc – Roussillon

La Maison des Pierres

Wrapped in apple orchards, this sturdy old farmhouse gives no clue as to the boldness within. A 19th-century family mas, the building has been artfully decluttered to reveal huge, open spaces. Vast, single-pane windows let light flood in to rooms of honey-coloured stone and beamed ceilings. Furnishings are ultra-simple, softly coloured, minimal but not bare; walls, if not stone, are ivory. The open-plan living space, with its pale grey floor tiles and coffee sofas, opens to a terrace, a garden and a pool. To one side is a plain white kitchen, sleek and modern with fun-coloured, rush-seated chairs. Bedrooms (one on a mezzanine overlooking the living area) are cool and restful with rich wooden floors, wicker or bamboo beds, funky lights, modern curtains. The owners, gentle and welcoming, live across the courtyard but do not intrude. Although deep in the country, you are eight kilometres from the Petite Camargue, 15 from the beaches. Or slip off your shoes and relax by the pool, glass in hand, gazing over orchards, rooftops and church. Peace, perfection, simplicity. *Owner has Sawday hotel in Montpellier.*

Price	€980–€2,080 per week.
Sleeps	4–6.
Rooms	3: 1 twin/double, 1 double, 1 twin/double on mezzanine; 1 bathroom, separate wc.
Closed	Never.

Alain de Bordas
Mudaison, Hérault

Tel	+33 (0)4 67 70 39 69
Mobile	+33 (0)6 07 47 41 23
Email	mascom@wanadoo.fr
Web	www.masdumoulin34.com

Domaine du Luc

Way up in the wildness of the Larzac plateau among high old oaks and open pastures, there is something magical about this old hunting lodge. Definitely a family home, its bones and sinews, wildlife and wild orchids, have been treasured by generations. With tower and chapel, dark panelling and big dining room, well-kept and spotless in rich colours and family-grown comfort, it is a house of generosity and candlelit dinners. You will feel welcomed in the deep red armchairs before the open fire, happy to cook in the friendly, slightly old-fashioned kitchen and eat off the mountain of good china, ready to sleep under a stitched cotton quilt in an antique-furnished bedroom. One of the butterflies here is found nowhere else, vultures, even the occasional eagle, wheel lazily, owls hoot under the vast spread of stars, deer come to nibble, and there is no pollution: wonderful exploring for children in the woods. The walled Templar city of La Couvertoirade is a must and so is the devastatingly beautiful hyper-modern Millau viaduct. A place of rest and renewal for body and spirit. *Auberge-restaurant with pool 100m.*

Price	€1,200 per week. Minimum stay 1 week. Linen not included.
Sleeps	8-10.
Rooms	3: 2 family rooms for 3, 1 twin; 2 bathrooms, 1 shower room.
Closed	November-March.

Françoise & Marie-Emmanuelle du Luc
Campestre et Luc, Gard
Tel +33 (0)4 67 81 07 60
Fax +33 (0)4 67 81 07 60
Email francoiseduluc@aol.com
Web www.causses-leluc.com

Bastide d'Esparon

Two great old houses converted for gentle family living, linked by a terrace outside, doors inside: ideal for one large or two small families. The untouched hamlet is genuine rural France, the eagle's-eye views are amazing, the ancient houses have vaulted ceilings, two of which cover a pair of dark, enfolding bedrooms lifted by pretty stitched bedcovers. Upstairs is lighter, everywhere are lovely kilim rugs and pieces brought back from the owners' travels – fine old wooden chests, antique wardrobes, paintings, books. A well-restored place, much loved by the creative, colour-conscious family who have owned it for 50 years, it has two of everything: sitting rooms with fireplaces, kitchens (one outside), one terrace for privacy and peace, another for joyous gatherings. Inside, history speaks through several levels and thick old walls (some say it was the local Merovingian castle). A most atmospheric, æsthetic retreat from the busy world, cooled by mountain breezes in the blistering summer, with superb walks, rivers for swimming or canoeing down in the valley, unusual excursions galore – and just 9km from all shopping.

Price	Upper house for 5-7: €500-€2,000. Whole house for 10-11: €1,050-€2,500. Whole house with annexe for 14-15: €1,450-€3,000. Prices per week.
Sleeps	10-15.
Rooms	Main house:1 suite, 3 twins, 2 singles; 1 bathroom, 2 shower rooms. Annexe: 1 double, 1 family, 1 shower room.
Arrival	Flexible.
Closed	Rarely.

Martine Fougeron de Monès
Le Vigan, Gard

Tel	+1 212 929 8755
Mobile	+1 917 622 8755
Email	info@martinefougeron.com
Web	www.bastide-esparon.com

La Rouvière

Not for party animals! This secluded place is reached via a long and winding drive and just when you think you've arrived, there's further to go… but the beauty of the place suffuses your soul. The word *rouvière* comes from the patois for 'oak' and the hillsides are full of them; chestnut trees too. No hint of civilisation to be seen: just the slate roofs of an old farmhouse in the valley below. Come in May and June for the wild flowers, in autumn for the trees, in summer for buzzing bees, cicadas and birds. This is almost a *hameau*, with the lovely old house, the barns and the terraces on many levels. Dining room, sitting room and kitchen drift into a terrace, there are two sofas, a fireplace that works, a round dining table, a polished old floor; easy to make this one's home. Grey-painted cupboards hide white plates in the well set-up kitchen and bedrooms have pine bedsteads and beams (a secret double room lies beyond the terrace). Outside are a pool with spa jets and a hammock under a fig tree: gaze on vast views and dream. The owners live next door and can cook for you if you wish. *Meals on request.*

Price	€500–€900 per week.
Sleeps	5.
Rooms	3: 2 doubles, 1 single; 1 bathroom, 2 separate wcs.
Closed	November–March.

Claude & Annette Jost
Bonnevaux, Gard

Tel	+33 (0)4 66 61 18 17
Mobile	+33 (0)6 84 09 06 11
Email	claudejost@free.fr
Web	claudejost.free.fr

Mas de la Bousquette - Le Grenier

Before you, meadows of silky, waving grass – a place for children to romp with the Forsters' affable dogs. This lovely mas was once a sheep and cattle farm: ancient stone buildings cluster round an entrancing courtyard, a cypress tree pushes through a gap in a hotchpotch of slanting roofs, goldfish glitter in a pool. The garden is big and open, with a willow tree beside a pond, hammocks and lazy chairs, plenty of shade. There's an old orchard too – peg out your washing among the rare-breed chickens (their organic eggs are so good), a couple of peacocks pecking round your feet. The two gîtes, separated by a long covered veranda, are equally fetching. In the old grain store – two storeys in the south-west tower – you sit and eat in a lovely big split-level space: rafters, creamy stone walls, fresh modern décor. Bedrooms have large and comfortable beds, French windows open to a private terrace, there are ceiling fans for summer. The kitchen is perfectly equipped, there are bikes to borrow, and the gardens have a heated pool and a barbecue spot just for you. *Extra B&B room for two on request. Shared pool.*

Price	€750–€1,550 per week.
Sleeps	4–6.
Rooms	2: 1 double, 1 twin & sofabed on mezzanine; 2 bathrooms.
Closed	Never.

Tim & Pippa Forster
Lussan, Gard

Tel	+33 (0)4 66 72 71 60
Mobile	+33 (0)6 89 72 11 56
Email	mas-bousquette@wanadoo.fr
Web	www.mas-bousquette.com

Mas de la Bousquette - Le Mûrier

The ancient, rose-roofed mas rests at the foot of high-perched, castle-topped Huguenot Lussan. The countryside rolls out before you, the air is pure and the sun is golden – even in winter. In the north-west tower where silkworms were once reared is a charming little gîte, its balcony-terrace tucked beneath a glorious roof. Fresh and clean with inspired touches, it makes a romantic nest for two. Living room and kitchen are beautifully equipped and the bedroom has a delightful simplicity: white walls, terracotta floor, antique iron and brass bed, muslin curtains. Pippa and Tim are warm, generous people and offer you everything: books, games, bicycles, binoculars, fresh fruit, lavender, fresh bread at your door, towels for the heated pool. Pippa loves cooking, gives guests' kids healthy cooking lessons and you a free dinner on arrival, and runs a little shop selling delectable homemade jams and organic eggs. This is southern France at its most peaceful. Within walking distance of an excellent restaurant, near lovely Uzès, not far from Avignon and Nîmes. *Extra B&B room for two on request. Shared pool.*

Price	€550–€1,200 per week.
Sleeps	2-4.
Rooms	1 double; 1 bathroom, sofabed.
Closed	Never.

Tim & Pippa Forster
Lussan, Gard

Tel	+33 (0)4 66 72 71 60
Mobile	+33 (0)6 89 72 11 56
Email	mas-bousquette@wanadoo.fr
Web	www.mas-bousquette.com

L'Auzonnet

A magical place. One minute you're in an ordinary village street, the next you enter a cool dark stone tunnel and emerge into a sunlit, secret courtyard. Hydrangeas splash the walls with colour, a stone stairway leads up to the little gîte: it's totally enchanting. The kitchen/living area has painted panelling, pine furniture and brightly coloured crockery. Up on the mezzanine is a Wedgwood-blue and white bedroom – light, pretty and open-plan – and a mosaic shower room. The private terrace overlooks the Auzonnet river but you're also welcome to make the most of the wonderful garden. Cross the courtyard, go through another arch and you find yourself at the top of lovely green terraces dropping down to a small pool and the tranquil river (you may fish). Sit and watch and wait and you may glimpse a heron or the blue flash of a kingfisher – and there will be mimosa in spring. This is the edge of the Cévennes National Park and the village is secluded and peaceful. Lucy and Duncan are on site, happy to give advice on what to see and where to go. *Shared pool. Unsuitable for young children or the infirm.*

Price	€500–€700 (£350–£500) per week.
Sleeps	2-3.
Rooms	1 double, sofabed; 1 shower room.
Closed	Never.

Lucy & Duncan Marshall
Les Mages, Gard

Tel	+33 (0)4 66 25 39 98
Email	lucy@auzonnet.com
Web	www.auzonnet.com

La Maison de Marie

The village clings to the hillside under the ruins of the château, the house stands just above, looking across to Mont Lozère. You park in the square below, then ascend – it's not far. And you arrive… to music, books and a south-west-facing terrace with views that stretch all the way to the Cévennes. It is a seductive, deeply peaceful place. This is also a house that feels it belongs; Marie comes here to meditate and write when there's no-one else around. Starting from the bottom up: the cellar, housing washing machine and bikes, then the kitchen/dining room with terrace. Up a circular wooden stair to a sitting room filled with sunshine and a shower room to the side; and the bedroom on a mezzanine under white-painted eaves. A country mood fills the kitchen, with its fresh walls, new terracotta floors, pleasant blue paintwork and gaily checked table; the most reluctant cook would happily put a meal together here. Marie teaches yoga, makes jam and leaves lavender soaps, goat's cheeses, organic wine and fresh flowers to welcome you. Perfect for a couple wishing to hike, bike and escape the world – for a magical while.

Price	€450–€580 per week.
Sleeps	2-3.
Rooms	1 double, 1 sofabed in office; 1 shower room, 1 separate wc.
Closed	Never.

Marie Freslon
Rochegude, Gard

Tel	+33 (0)4 66 72 93 16
Fax	+33 (0)4 66 72 93 16
Email	chanu2@wanadoo.fr

Entry 311 Map 16

Maison des Cerises

This village cottage seduces all. Britta is a gifted artist with an eye for light, harmony and spotting the potential in bric-a-brac finds. She has restored the three-storey house with sympathy and skill – walls are stone or limewashed, floors warm terracotta, beams darkly aged, colours pure and natural. The ground-floor bedroom, a creamy space of painted wooden furniture and pretty fabrics, opens to a small garden with a very large cherry tree. Its bathroom, equally spacious, is *Country-Living* perfect with a claw-foot bath. The romantic top bedroom, with sparkling shower room, is tucked under the eaves. In between is the light-washed living room – elegantly simple with candlesticks, neutral curtains and wine-dark sofa – and, a few steps up, the rustic dining room/kitchen with pine dresser and thick, cream china. The living is easy here: step out to the baker's and the grocer's, basket in hand. Take the children to the water park at Uzès, swim in the river Cèze, hunt for bargains in village markets, then return to your little garden, and feel at peace with the world. Exceptional.

Price	€500–€850 per week.
Sleeps	4 + cot.
Rooms	2: 1 double, 1 twin/double; 1 bathroom, 1 shower room.
Closed	Never.

Britta Brand
Saint Marcel de Careiret, Gard

Tel	+33 (0)4 66 63 89 40
Mobile	+33 (0)6 75 33 38 19
Email	brittabrand@wanadoo.fr
Web	www.maison-des-cerises.com

2 chemin de la Carcarie

Arlette is the perfect hostess, welcoming but discreet. And cultured: her tortoises have Greek names. You'll meet them in the large wild garden. Her patch is the wonder of the house and Arlette will happily walk you round, passing on the names of the plants and giving you the local gen. Views here take in the pretty village, which has a château. You feel part of local life, yet close to Uzès, one of the most beautiful medieval towns in France (they filmed *Cyrano de Bergerac* there). This 17th-century farmhouse is slightly shabby – all part of the charm – but there are both washing machine and dryer and all linen and towels are included. Upstairs, a big bedroom sleeps four (one very comfy bed, two singles on the mezzanine) so the house is best suited to a couple or a young family – and there's space for football in the garden. Dried garden flowers hang from old beams in the dining room, and you eat on the terrace under a Provençal sun. Arlette lives in part of the house: she is on hand to chat, advise and inform while leaving you all your privacy. No dishwasher, so bring your Marigolds.

Price	€420–€580 per week.
Sleeps	2-4.
Rooms	2: 1 double with child's bed & twin beds on mezzanine; 1 bathroom.
Closed	Never.

Arlette Caccamo-Laniel
Montaren, Gard

Tel	+33 (0)4 66 22 52 14
Email	arlette.laniel@wanadoo.fr

Rue du 4 Septembre

Glorious Uzès, the first Duchy of France, an architectural masterpiece – a town of towers, vaulted stone walkways and twisting streets. The Wars of Religion came but in the 17th century prosperity returned and magnificent houses such as this one were built in the grand style. Step in off the street and travel back a few hundred years to this second-floor apartment up a private spiral staircase. Inside are old terracotta floors, great high ceilings and noble beams. No terrace, but space and light, a magnificent old fireplace and two excellent bathrooms. The kitchen is simple but well-equipped, the dining room displays a long elegant table. The Uzès market is a wonder of the Provençal world and it's on your doorstep – as are concerts, galleries, restaurants and delectable shops. You are also midway between the wild hills of the Cevennes and the Roman Triangle cities of Arles, Avignon and Nîmes. So, a superb place for a family stay, but it would be a pity to limit yourself to the summer holidays: in winter the apartment is blissfully cosy. *Secure parking a five-minute walk. Lock-up for bikes.*

Price	£380–£500. Prices per week.
Sleeps	4 + 1 child.
Rooms	2: 1 double, 1 twin with child's bed; 1 bath, 1 shower, separate wc.
Closed	Never.

	Susie & David Nelson
	Uzès, Gard
Tel	+44 (0)20 7233 1293
Email	davidandsusienelson@btinternet.com

La Terre des Lauriers

The setting – six hectares of bird-filled woodland stretching down to the river – is breathtaking. Let the local canoe-hire folk ferry you up the river, then float back home again via that marvel of Roman engineering, the Pont du Gard. These delightful owners are escapees from Paris; Marianick draws, paints and makes sumptuous jams, Gérard has created a botanic trail down to the river. This 18th-century *bergerie* has been restored with simple elegance: the large, lofty, open-plan space, attractive with fine new furniture and yellow and white counter kitchen, is linked by a white metal staircase to mezzanine bedrooms upstairs. You share the huge grounds, pool and garden with B&B guests and those staying in another cottage but have your own terrace for dining, and views of the private vineyard. The wild and flowering surroundings are full of buzz and flutter; and there's a gym by the pool where you can work off any extra pounds gained in the area's fine restaurants. Magic for families. *Sawday B&B.*

Price	€800–€1,000 per week.
Sleeps	4-6.
Rooms	2: 1 double, 1 twin, 1 sofabed in living room; 1 bathroom, 1 separate wc.
Closed	Never.

Marianick & Gérard Langlois
Remoulins, Gard
Tel   +33 (0)4 66 37 19 45
Fax   +33 (0)4 66 37 19 45
Email   langlois@laterredeslauriers.com
Web   www.laterredeslauriers.com

Rue du Château

Behind the arched blue door lies a restored 15th-century silk mill, its vaulted cellar rooms intact. It is an Aladdin's cave, an intoxicating mix of French, English, Moroccan and Indian treasures. Escape the blistering heat into this cool, calm space; the village is perched in the foothills of the Cévennes and you are in the middle of it. No garden, but a peaceful gravelled courtyard with chairs for dozing, a barbecue, a fountain and a summer shower. Inside, your gaze drifts to mellow yellow-washed walls, tiles – the best of old and new – and lofty ceilings. The sitting room is cavernous but cosy in wintertime: a wood-burning stove, William Morris-covered armchairs, comfy sofas, books, an upright piano. Arched doors lead from the well-equipped kitchen into the courtyard where you may eat. Up a floor and those lofty old silk rooms have magically become bedrooms, one with a dreamy Provençal mural behind the bed, another with a patchwork bedspread. History, big open fields and vineyards await – if you can leave your own little piece of heaven. *July-August: house for 8 with pool also available.*

Price	€450–€1,000 per week.
Sleeps	6.
Rooms	3: 2 doubles, 1 twin; 3 shower rooms.
Arrival	Friday, but flexible.
Closed	Never.

	Caroline Nolder
	Aigremont, Gard
Tel	+33 (0)4 66 24 44 43
Email	carolinenolder@lesabatier.com
Web	www.familynolder.com

Domaine des Clos - Apartments

When David and Sandrine returned to their Beaucaire roots, they found a worthy vessel for their creativity in an 18th-century wine estate. All has been authentically and lovingly restored. There are five apartments here, all in the main house, looking out onto vineyards (two from private terraces) or the courtyard lawn. Beyond are exquisite Italianate gardens and the best of Provence – from among the olive trees, jasmine and bougainvillea, shady stone pergolas emerge. Inside, fine antiques, including a Louis XIII table and some venerable farmhouse pieces. Modern touches have been beautifully added in the form of bold colours and exotic wall hangings. Well-organised kitchens fulfil all cooking needs; sweet dining areas are tucked into inviting nooks. Consider an aperitif (or a booked meal) on the terrace of the old stables; in winter, keep warm by the fireplace in the communal salon, delightful with deep fuchsia walls and ceilings hung with handcrafted fixtures. It is hugely original, wonderfully artistic, and the information booklet includes enough markets to keep the lunch bag brimming. *Sawday hotel. Meals on request.*

Price	€450–€1,500 each per week.
Sleeps	5 apartments for 2-7.
Rooms	Apartment 1: 1 double; 1 bathroom.
	Apartments 2, 3 & 4: 1 double, 1 twin; 1 shower room.
	Apartment 5: 1 double, 2 twins, 1 single; 1 bathroom, 1 shower room.
Closed	Rarely.

Sandrine & David Ausset
Beaucaire, Gard
Tel   +33 (0)4 66 01 14 61
Fax   +33 (0)4 66 01 00 47
Email   contact@domaine-des-clos.com
Web   www.domaine-des-clos.com

Rhône Valley – Alps • Provence – Alps – Riviera

La Ferme du Nant

In summer, you rent one or both of the floors and self-cater; in winter, you have one whole beautiful catered chalet. Floor to ceiling windows span the front of the old house pulling in views that are pure Heidi. Downstairs is a cosily restored living area with a wonderful central fireplace, country dining table and big open kitchen. Upstairs, past a collection of ancient wooden sledges, are pine floors, halogen spotlights illuminating white walls, sandblasted timbers, big blue sofas. Two bedrooms are on the mezzanine – fun for kids – and there's a long, rustic, south-facing balcony to catch the sun. Furniture is a mix of Savoyard and modern with the odd giant pop-art portrait to add a sparkle. Bathrooms are white with mosaics. A trap door leads to a DVD cellar, a sloping garden has been reshaped to take a terrace and heated pool (the old cheese store makes great changing rooms) and the village is a six-minute walk downhill. The owners live on the top floor with their labrador; Susie also owns a horse – the riding is wonderful. *B&B also.*

Price	€840–€1,260 per floor (6-8 people) per week. Minimum 3 days. Catered in winter.
Sleeps	12-16 (or 6-8 + 6-8).
Rooms	Ground floor: 3 twins/doubles; 2 bathrooms, 1 shower room. First floor: 3 twins/doubles; 3 shower rooms. Extra beds available.
Arrival	Saturday in summer, flexible in winter.
Closed	Rarely.

	Susie Ward
	La Chapelle d'Abondance, Haute-Savoie
Tel	+33 (0)4 50 73 40 87
Email	susie@susieward.com
Web	www.susieward.com

Le Château du Bérouze

Probably the finest house in Samoëns, the château is very old – the main part dates back to 1485 – yet it was once on the verge of being demolished. New Zealand journalists Jack and Jane came to the rescue, pouring love and talent into reviving old timbers and stones, then opened the large, extravagantly carved doors to guests. Up the stone steps to a first-floor apartment of elegant proportions, you find an ample, open-plan kitchen, a modern living room, a day room, three big bedrooms and two bathrooms, one with a claw-foot bath. Lofty ceilings are a criss-cross of white-painted beams, lintels are ancient stone, floors rug-strewn, there's a gas-flame stove and big old radiators to keep you warm. The garden is every bit as lovely, with lush lawns, orchards and flowers, terrace and potager. And… the house is partly moated, streams flow in and out, home to ducks and trout. It's a special place in every season: skiing and skating in winter, rafting and riding in summer, high hiking in spring. Unspoilt Samoëns, its restaurants and bars, is a five-minute stroll, and your kind hosts will babysit if you ask them.

Price	£800-£2,000 per week.
Sleeps	8-12.
Rooms	3: 2 twins/doubles, 1 quadruple; 2 bathrooms; 2 sofabeds.
Closed	Never.

Jack & Jane Tresidder
Samoëns, Haute-Savoie

Tel	+33 (0)4 50 34 95 72
Fax	+33 (0)4 50 34 95 91
Email	jane.tresidder@wanadoo.fr
Web	www.chateauduberouze.com

Chalet Amaryllis

Samoëns will seduce you: one of the prettiest French resorts, once an important stone-cutting centre, now an historic monument. A step from your door are a covered grain market and a Gothic church, shops resplendent with pastries and charcuterie, and a linden tree planted in 1483. Sitting in its big garden with fantastic mountain views, the chalet is a mere 60 years, its pale timber frame freshly sandblasted. A lovely lofty living room, corsetted in pine, cosy and homely with rugs, big sofas, posters, paintings and rowing trophies, dominates the interior. The kitchen is clearly the domain of a keen chef: the owners alternate B&B with rentals – super meals all year. Pine-furnished bedrooms are downstairs, so darker, each with CD/MP3 player and en suite bathroom. Samoëns sits at 750m but a new high-speed gondola transports you to the whole of the Grand Massif: 265km of piste and the same view of Mont Blanc as the international, and less charming, Flaine. Superb summer walking, myriad outdoor activities, a hot tub on the terrace – mulled wine under the stars? *Pool planned 2008. B&B also. Meals on request.*

Price	€1,500-€3,900 per week.
Sleeps	14.
Rooms	5: 1 double, 2 twins/doubles, 2 quadruples; 5 bathrooms.
Arrival	Flexible.
Closed	Never.

Mark & Victoria Fangen Hall
Samoëns, Haute-Savoie

Tel	+33 (0)4 50 54 26 61
Mobile	+33 (0)6 89 57 69 29
Email	info@chalet-amaryllis.com
Web	www.chalet-amaryllis.com

Valhalla

A touch of Teutonic mythology in the Chamonix valley, Valhalla was designed by a Norwegian architect just five years ago and is a delightful mix of clean, Nordic lines and soft Savoyard touches; all is contemporary and open plan. The vast picture windows on one side flood the entire chalet with light and give views of the sweeping valley and jagged mountains beyond. At one end, soft leather sofas and an open fire beckon the weary skier in winter, or sink into the hot tub if you prefer; at the other, the long table is perfect for wining and dining on a grand scale. The beautiful kitchen has marble surfaces and will entice even the most amateur of cooks (or go catered and avoid the kitchen altogether) Head up the wide wooden staircase to the galleried landing and peer down on the warm scene below. Bedrooms, too, are bright and stylish with comfortable beds dressed in crisp, striped linen. Some with balconies (and more views), some with little stoves; all have pretty little bathrooms decorated with hand-crafted stone tiles. Fine comfort, wonderful peace, and only a few minutes from the centre.

Price	£2,000-£6,525 per week, from self-catering to fully catered.
Sleeps	10-12.
Rooms	5: 2 doubles, 3 twin/doubles, 2 single beds on mezzanine; 3 bathrooms, 2 shower rooms.
Closed	Never.

Colleen Olianti
Chamonix, Haute-Savoie

Tel	+44 (0)1276 24262
Mobile	+33 (0)6 71 91 20 60
Email	sales@collineige.com
Web	www.collineige.com

Villa Terrier

A grand old 1910 villa in the middle of big, bustling, beautiful Chamonix. Sporting a smart new stone roof with shiny copper pipes, it looks across to Mont Blanc and the vertiginous Chamonix 'needles'. Ceilings are high, old pine spans the floors, original cornicing beautifies the walls. The living room is charming with an elegant mirror above a carved stone fireplace, rose-pink sofas to sink into, grand lamps to read by, delightful curtains to draw across big windows; the kitchen is family big. Up the wide staircase to light, roomy bedrooms, one with a balcony, two with sloping ceilings. Some have huge bathrooms and, although fabulously new, a traditional French feel, with their claw-foot baths, big basins and fat iron radiators. White towels and bathrobes spread the mood of unashamed luxury. There's music and the internet, an indoor play area for children downstairs – an attic space for them under the eaves, too – lifts to the slopes and four-course dinners with wine. Plus sauna and pool. Chamonix is the killer-black-run capital of Europe – and just as popular in summer.

Price	£1,400–£3,000 summer. £2,400–£4,800 winter. Catered £565–£785 p.p. summer; £665–£1,100 p.p. winter. Prices per week.
Sleeps	8-12.
Rooms	5: 2 doubles, 2 twins/doubles, attic room for 4 children; 4 bathrooms, 2 separate wcs.
Closed	Rarely.

Colleen Olianti
Chamonix-Mont Blanc, Haute-Savoie

Tel	+44 (0)1276 24262
Mobile	+33 (0)6 71 91 20 60
Email	sales@collineige.com
Web	www.collineige.com

Entry 322 Map 12

Mazot Les Tines

Shaded by poplars rustling in the wind is this upstairs-downstairs little chalet. As the name implies, it was once a wood store – Colleen's. She is the owner, runs her own ski company, and lives across the garden. All is light and bright and stylishly decorated, with country furniture and modern checks. Downstairs is open plan with a roundly rustic dining table for four, a shower room with bathrobes, a washing machine and a kitchen with pottery and pine. The living area is cosy and charming: colourful textiles and prints grace pine-clad walls, there's a perfect red sofa, a little wood-burning stove, a stereo. The mezzanine is great for kids with its ladder to two single mattresses. A floor-to-ceiling window looks onto the garden, filling the space with light. Up the wooden spiral staircase is the bedroom with its balcony and magnificent mountain views. Outside stairs leads down to the garden where roses clamber up wooden walls, geraniums fill window boxes, creepers weave through a pile of stacked slates. You are on the edge of lovely Les Tines and a bus brings you to even lovelier Chamonix.

Price	£400-£750 per week.
Sleeps	4.
Rooms	2: 1 double, 1 mezzanine for 2; 1 shower room.
Closed	Never.

Colleen Olianti
Chamonix-Mont Blanc, Haute-Savoie
Tel +44 (0)1276 24262
Mobile +33 (0)6 71 91 20 60
Email sales@collineige.com
Web www.collineige.com

Les Mazots

It's a steep road to get here: views over the Mont Blanc ranges soar. In a quiet corner of Chamonix, this 1930s-built chalet is still only on its second careful owner. Charming Colleen has run the house as a B&B for over 15 years and now lets it for self-catering, too. The lovely house has a faded elegance, with much of the furniture left by the original owners: worn leather armchairs, sepia photographs of acrobats on dark panelled walls, shelves on the stairs crammed with old tomes – deeply atmospheric. Bedrooms are a good size, comfortably furnished and traditional; billowing duvets spread themselves on antique iron beds: sound sleep is guaranteed. The excellent modern kitchen has stainless-steel worktops and a large oven. Checked sofas sit under pretty reading lamps, the large wooden fireplace is decorated with candlesticks and French windows open onto the terrace where the hot tub beckons, and then it's down to the sloping garden and fruit trees. World-renowned for its ski domains, which are at your doorstep, Chamonix is also great in summer. *Cook available on request.*

Price	£1,500–£3,000 summer. £2,500–£5,000 winter. Catered £525–£765 p.p. summer; £485–£1,050 p.p. winter. Prices per week.
Sleeps	16.
Rooms	8: 2 doubles, 4 twins/doubles, 2 singles; 5 bathrooms, 1 separate wc.
Arrival	Flexible.
Closed	Never.

Colleen Olianti
Chamonix–Mont Blanc, Haute-Savoie

Tel	+44 (0)1276 24262
Mobile	+33 (0)6 71 91 20 60
Email	sales@collineige.com
Web	www.collineige.com

Chalet Jolyvue

One of the most unspoilt resorts in the French Alps: the architecture is pretty, the locals are friendly, the restaurants are excellent and, if the night life's not wild enough for you, Chamonix is a 25-minute drive. You come to Jolyvue round the back, through a small sloping garden, then up to the first-floor apartment. This may not be grand living but it's light, pretty and cosy – two floors of white walls, cheerful fabrics, down duvets and new pine. You have an open log fire, a flat-screen telly, music with surround sound, even WiFi. The 'master' bedroom is on this floor, the tiny others are tucked under the eaves. Catch the afternoon sun on the balcony and gaze across the valley to Mont Joly – bliss – then trot into town; it's no distance at all. In winter, this is one of the most snow-sure resorts around and great for off-piste skiing. In summer, there's walking, biking, white water rafting. Catch the télécabine to Signal, walk the ridge to Mont Joly (the views to Mont Blanc are stunning), take the tram to Nid d'Aigle, then trek home via the Bionnassay Glacier. Marvellous. *Ski lifts 4-min. drive.*

Price	€400-€1,350 per week.
Sleeps	5-7.
Rooms	3: 1 double, 1 twin, 1 single, 1 sofabed; 1 bathroom, 1 shower room, separate wc.
Closed	Never.

Hugh Gilbert
Les Contamines-Monjoie, Haute-Savoie

Tel	+44 (0)1638 500 144
Mobile	+44 (0)7775 732 839
Email	hugh.gilbert@btinternet.com
Web	www.jolyvue.com

Chalet Gingerbread

Surrounded by young chalets and gardens – which become one big white carpet in winter – Gingerbread is one of the youngest. On the inside, it must also be one of the most splendid: a great cathedral ceiling on the first floor, a home-cinema below (satellite TV on a 1.2m wide flat screen, Bose surround sound – wow!). It's a huge space, seriously swish, three floors of terracotta tiles and timber floors, interior doors panelled and stained, and walls and ceilings white or wood-clad. The dining area leads to a decked south-facing terrace, an open tread staircase invites you to the second level, the sitting area has heaps of smart and coordinated sofas and the kitchen trumpets every new thing. No question this is the bees-knees for winter: logs piled high in the garage, boot warmers in the drying room, the ski lift five minutes by navette. Megève – "the 21st arrondissement of Paris" – has cobbled streets of chic shops and even chic-er people, two summer toboggan trails, 87 lifts, 97 restaurants and a vast outdoor pool. All this is a short hop in the car. Prepare to be spoiled. *1km from ski lift.*

Price	€4,950–€9,950 per week, including daily cleaning.
Sleeps	8-10.
Rooms	5: 2 doubles, 2 twins/doubles, 1 children's room with bunks; 3 bathrooms, 2 separate wcs.
Arrival	Saturday, flexible in summer.
Closed	Never.

Gayle Halstead
Megève, Haute-Savoie

Tel	+44 (0)1204 852 108
Fax	+44 (0)1204 853 828
Email	gh@chaletgingerbread.co.uk
Web	www.chaletgingerbread.co.uk

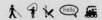

Entry 326 Map 12

Le Boën

Anyone in love with the mountains will be in their element here. Your young Canadian log cabin seems to have stood for ever; you live below, the owners live above. They are a skiing family and know every inch of this terrain, so you are in the best hands. In summer, come for walks and wildflower pastures, golf, tennis and mountain biking. In winter, snowboard or ski: it's within walking distance of the lift that whisks you up to the Megève ski arena. Inside, an L-shaped kitchen/living room, white walls, tiled floors (heated for winter), old-fashioned sofa and armchairs, a table for six. The kitchen is a good size and newly equipped, there are sliding doors to a plastic-furnished terrace, swings and boules in the big garden, yours to share with the family. The main bedroom, with pastel bedding and extra bunks, has sensational views; the second bedroom is darker due to high windows. There's a perfect alpine auberge in the village and others in nearby Prazaly while Megève, with every shop and restaurant you could wish for, bustles stylishly all year. There's even a jazz festival in summer.

Price	€404–€999 per week. Linen not included.
Sleeps	4–6.
Rooms	2: 1 triple, 1 family room for 3; 1 bathroom.
Closed	Never.

Josiane & Christian Bouchage
Praz sur Arly, Haute-Savoie
Tel +33 (0)4 50 21 98 14
Email bouchage.chris@wanadoo.fr

La Marmotte Penthouse

The 1970s chalet-style building was given a facelift by a local architect in 2004 and the duplex penthouse has stacks of style as well as sweeping views. There are soft pale sofas for up to ten and flashes of cushion colour in the generous high-ceilinged living room; more space floods in through vast windows that slide onto the two sunny balconies: watch the village go by at your feet and keep your eye on the pistes. Floors are brushed oak, the kitchen is brilliantly equipped, bathrooms shine. Under chunky rafters, the compact bedrooms are deeply comfortable with built-in wardrobes, fluffy duvets, the best mattresses, wine-red wool carpeting and contemporary curtains. The master bedroom shares an east-facing balcony with the bunk-bedded room and... a stunning view of the National Park; the twin is on a cosy mezzanine looking down onto the living space. You are ideally placed for village shops and bars, a ski-booted hop away from the most sophisticated, far-reaching and interlinked skiing in the Alps and a lithe step from fabulous summer walks. *Ski bus service links Courchevel 1850, 1650 & 1350.*

Price	£950–£1,780 per week.
Sleeps	6–10.
Rooms	3: 1 double, 1 twin & pull-out single on mezzanine, 1 bunk room & pull-out single; two bath/shower rooms, sofabed.
Closed	Rarely.

	Ros & Jeremy Charles
	Courchevel 1650, Savoie
Tel	+44 (0)20 8455 4554
Mobile	+44 (0)7788 741 870
Email	jeremycharles1@hotmail.com
Web	www.rentapent.com

Entry 328 Map 12

La Maroquinerie

The living here is simple, convivial, genuine. Sit on the sunny terrace (you are often above the cloud) with a drink and the post lady may join you, bringing her own bottle, or the neighbour may invite you for an aperitif by his *tonneau*. Or sit alone and look for eagles. Winding your way up the narrow mountain road after dusk, you will probably see deer, wild boar, foxes. Inside the ground floor of this 18th-century mountain village house, the dark rusty-red living room has beams and a huge slate fireplace you can sit in as well as cook in (logs provided), new pine flooring and old pine furniture, clocks, paintings, books and games. Also, a simple kitchen area (when Andrew is upstairs, he will cook for you – very nicely – if you ask). Each large double bedroom has a venerable shower cubicle and basin. Two minutes from cross-country skiing: you can ski back to the door in a good season and ski hire is right there. The mountain walks are wonderful: there are racquets in the house for snow walking, in summer you'll fight your way through the sheep and goats grazing wild. *Occasional table d'hôtes.*

Price	€350 per week.
Sleeps	4.
Rooms	2 doubles; 2 showers, separate wc.
Arrival	Any day by arrangement.
Closed	Never.

Elizabeth & Andrew Bamford
Montpascal, Savoie

Tel	+33 (0)4 79 59 79 60
Fax	+44 (0)207 7515736
Email	information@lesfontaines.com
Web	www.chaletsalpes.com

Souffle de Vent

Down a narrow cobbled street, through an arch that opens off a little pedestrian lane in the historic town centre, then up an impressive stone staircase, and you come to this light-filled townhouse. There are four apartments on two floors, with a small courtyard on the first, each with a fresh, open feel in spite of the 'centre ville' address. Whitewashed walls, parquet floors, glowing terracotta, a mix of pale modern furniture and antiques – an iron bedstead piled with cushions, a painted wardrobe – create a cool, peaceful feel. Bedrooms are simple but cosy with ivory-pale bed linen, some with featherlight muslin drapes; bathrooms are unexpectedly large. The open-plan kitchen and living rooms, all but one with a wood-burning stove (free logs!), have big windows so you can watch the sleepy world go by. This is outdoorsy France; pack a picnic and go hiking, biking, or swimming in the three nearby rivers. Or browse through typical old Barjac with its shops, ateliers and *pétanque* on the square. *Apartments also available as B&B (minimum 3 days).*

Price	€350–€550 per week.
Sleeps	2; 2-3; 2-3; 2-4.
Rooms	4 apartments: 2 for 2-3, 1 for 2-4, 1 for 2; each with 1 bathroom.
Closed	Never.

	Jan Willem Schipper
	Barjac, Ardèche
Tel	+33 (0)4 75 36 56 05
Fax	+33 (0)4 75 36 56 05
Email	info@souffledevent.com
Web	www.souffledevent.com

Entry 330 Map 16

La Filature - Orange & Bleu

A vast building, an ambitious project. This young Dutch family have taken on an old silkworm spinnery built in 1872, and converted it for B&B and gîtes. The old workshop is to open for cultural events and receptions. Eveline and Luc speak perfect English, are full of creative energy and enjoy cooking for guests occasionally: expect a candlelit table under a wisteria-clad pergola, a market-inspired menu, flowing local wines and happy talk. The two apartments have their own entrances and breakfast patios, the living is easy, there's masses of space, you are way off any main road and the children can go barefoot and bare-bum. As for the interiors, they are large, light and charming with white walls, old tile or parquet floors, white duvets on big beds, white throws on sofas, well-equipped kitchens, a cupboard or two and vineyard views. Lovely for families: a little play area on the mezzanine, a big, walled grassy field, a trampoline, ping-pong, a pool – and the loungers are wicker, not plastic. There's a restaurant you can walk to and many more in Barjac and other villages. *Shared pool. B&B also. Meals on request.*

Price	Orange €550–€950. Bleu €350–€750. Prices per week. Cleaning not included.
Sleeps	Orange 4–6. Blue 4. Extra children's beds.
Rooms	Orange: 2 doubles/twins; 1 bathroom, separate wc. Bleu: 1 double, 1 twin; 1 bathroom.
Closed	Never.

Eveline Leopold & Luc Matter
Saint André de Cruzières, Ardèche

Tel	+33 (0)4 75 36 44 40
Email	info@lafilature.eu
Web	www.lafilature.eu

Salivet & La Sousto

Few places have it all but this must be one of them. Breathtaking mountain views, a lovely artistic owner and a fascinating, secluded old farm. Honey-stoned Salivet stands where the oxen sheds and haylofts used to be; the ruins of the original farmhouse are still visible in the garden. Jane, an English artist who specialises in silk screen printing, lives next door; she and her architect partner have restored and furnished the place simply but beautifully with old beams, terracotta floors, whitewashed walls, stone fireplaces and antique furniture. On summer nights you can sleep on the roof terrace; during the day, sit on the terrace under the wisteria, snooze on the lawn under the weeping willow or cool off in the pool. La Sousto is similarly delightful and unspoiled. Jane runs courses on silk decoration to include a 'silk tour', which can be booked in advance. She sells honey, homemade jams and truffles in season, cooks fabulous meals on request (much organic) and will supply walking itineraries, maps and flower guides to this beautiful area. *Shared pool. Meals on request.*

Price	Salivet €750–€1,100. Sousto €450–€600. Prices per week.
Sleeps	Salivet 7-8 + cot. Sousto 2 + 2 children.
Rooms	Salivet: 2 doubles, 1 twin, 1 single, 1 single on mezzanine; 1 bath, 1 shower, 2 separate wcs. Sousto: 1 double, 1 children's twin; 1 bathroom, separate wc.
Arrival	Salivet: Saturday; Sousto: Friday.
Closed	November-April.

	Jane Worthington Truinas, Drôme
Tel	+33 (0)4 75 53 49 13
Mobile	+33 (0)6 99 29 27 78
Email	worthingtonjc@aol.com

Les Mûriers

Come for views, simplicity, peace. And lovely people: Jill is an artist and sculptor, her Danish husband is a raku specialist who runs pottery courses in summer, and they've lived and worked here for 30 years. The grass is unmown to preserve the wild flowers, the trees are full of birds, there are cherries in early June, beehives for honey, herbs in the garden and truffles on the land. And a swimming pool, protected from the wind by a hedge. Your private and secluded gîte has a rose-covered veranda for shade and big ochre floor tiles in the main room, along with a sofa and two wicker armchairs, a big dining table, a country cupboard. The bedrooms have open hanging space, pretty olive curtains, good sculptures by Jill. In the kitchen: a hob, an oven, a pottery clock. Slip down to the bottom of the garden with a glass of something chilled and watch the sun set over the vineyards and the hills. No sound – bar the neighbour's dog at supper time. You're up high here and it's a magical spot. Come in spring for the hiking, in summer for the music at Orange, all year round for the peace. *Shared pool.*

Price	€450-€550 per week.
Sleeps	3-4.
Rooms	2: 1 twin/double, 1 single; 1 shower room, 1 wc.
Closed	Never.

Jill Ratel
Venterol, Drôme
Tel +33 (0)4 75 26 22 08
Email dominique.ratel@wanadoo.fr

L'Amiradou

The name means 'high on the hill with long views' – and you'll be moved by them: every window frames a Cézanne. The drive through the herb-scented hills is out of this world, the familiar white flank of Mont Ventoux is ever present. The builder who helped Susan and Andrew renovate this old cottage thought they'd made a mistake: standing above the main house, it has the better view. Many levels give both house and garden huge character (but make it unsuitable for the very young) and the interior is immaculate. An Indian patchwork hangs in one bedroom, a vast baker's table separates kitchen from living room, there are hand-painted tiles round bathroom mirrors, smart sofas and antique pine. You have a log fire and central heating for winter and a well-equipped kitchen. Susan and Andrew love their adopted land, are delighted to advise you about the best places to visit and otherwise leave you quietly to yourselves. You share their pool; the south-facing pool-house and terrace, scented with lavender and honeysuckle, is all yours. Restaurants and markets abound. *Shared pool.*

Price	€600–€1,100 per week.
Sleeps	4.
Rooms	2: 1 double, 1 twin; 2 bathrooms.
Closed	Winter.

Susan & Andrew Smith
Mérindol les Oliviers, Drôme

Tel	+33 (0)4 75 28 78 69
Fax	+33 (0)4 75 28 78 69
Email	smitha@club-internet.fr
Web	www.lamiradou.com

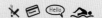

Entry 334 Map 16

L'Amiradou - Tréfouli

An iron gate in a garden wall: enter a small paradise. Built five years ago, Tréfouli stands in perfect keeping with the land that surrounds it – and that land is ravishing. Set on the same hillside as L'Amiradou, it overlooks valleys of orchards and vines and Cézanne's evocative mountain. Inside, a delightful interior of white walls and terracotta, a baker's table dividing dining room from kitchen, luminous bathrooms with generous showers, a fireplace full of logs. Thanks to high ceilings the rooms feel generously big. French windows open to a covered veranda with a Moroccan-tiled table and stylish ironwork chairs… then numerous terraces, nooks and crannies. Big flat slabs of stone curve over the honey-coloured gravel and lead to a blissful pool where the water is warm from mid-May to September. On this steeply terraced site – unsuitable for tinies – the land drops away beneath you into wild oak woods full of songbirds and chirruping cicadas. In an area famous for its Roman sites and Côtes du Rhône villages, you are in the heart of the 'golden triangle' of ancient Vaison la Romaine. Bliss.

Price	€700–€1,400 per week.
Sleeps	4.
Rooms	2 doubles; 1 bathroom, 1 shower room.
Arrival	Thursday.
Closed	Winter.

Susan & Andrew Smith
Mérindol les Oliviers, Drôme

Tel	+33 (0)4 75 28 78 69
Fax	+33 (0)4 75 28 78 69
Email	smitha@club-internet.fr
Web	www.lamiradou.com

Château Colombier

Take the whole house! So wonderful for a big family gathering. But for smaller groups there are endless mix-and-match possibilities: a two-bedroom apartment under the eaves; one bedroom in the tower; a twin room with its own shower on the ground floor. The apartment, with a big salon and a kitchen on the landing, is self-contained; the rest share the big, golden-yellow, beautifully equipped kitchen with its table for 16. Unless you're in one big party, you'll be making new friends. Bedrooms are freshly painted to match their names – Lavender, Verveine, Apricot – and are simply and charmingly furnished: voile curtains, pretty brocante. Bathrooms are spotless and chic. Downstairs, where the walls are a metre thick and the ceilings vaulted, is the living room, cosy with a wood-burning stove, heaps of books, music and piano, a tapestry on the wall. Clare adores her *maison de maître*; it stands in a walled garden on the edge of the village, its views of orchards, woods and mountains changing colour with each hour. No pool but bikes to borrow and the river is five minutes down the lane.

Price	€390-€490 for 2.
	Apartment €990-€1,500.
	Whole house €2,300-€3,500.
	Prices per week.
Sleeps	16-18.
Rooms	1 apartment for 6 (2 family rooms;
	1 single; 2 shower rooms,
	1 bathroom).
	Also: 4 doubles, 1 twin; 1 bathroom,
	5 shower rooms. Sofabeds.
Arrival	Saturday, or by arrangement
Closed	Never.

	Clare Howard
	Condorcet, Drôme
Mobile	+44 (0)7773 800 741
Email	clare.howard@e-coaches.co.uk
Web	www.chateaucolombier.com

Le Vieil Aiglun - Gite du Couchant

Getting here is half the fun, up a steep, windy, well-tarred road, and your arrival at this ancient hilltop village is rewarded with an unforgettable panorama: most of Haute Provence spread out before you. An energetic, creative and very lovely Belgian family opens Le Vieil Aiglun's rustic doors for B&B in a huge barn; a dining room in a vaulted byre; a pool, a play area and these gîtes. Privately separate, your small house has two bedrooms, one up, one down, a well-planned kitchen/diner with a sofabed, a bathroom with two pretty white basins and an enclosed garden in the walls of an old ruin. Plus views of a Romanesque church on a hill, romantically floodlit at night. It's perfectly gorgeous inside: fresh white walls and rafters, plain linen curtains, red and orange bedcovers, Moroccan lights. After a hard day's sunbathing by the fenced pool (open June-September) book in for twice-weekly table d'hôtes. The long glamorous candelabra-lit table – with special low table for tinies – is stunning, and a huge open fire turns bad-weather days into the cosiest nights. *B&B also. Shared pool. Meals on request.*

Price	€550–€950 per week.
Sleeps	5-6.
Rooms	1 twin, 1 triple; 1 bathroom, 1 sofabed in living room.
Closed	Never.

Charles & Annick Speth
Aiglun, Alpes-de-Haute-Provence
Tel   +33 (0)4 92 34 67 00
Email   info@vieil-aiglun.com
Web   www.vieil-aiglun.com

Le Vieil Aiglun - Gîte du Levant

Once again, the local artisans have done a brilliant job. Once again, the interior sings: Annick has a joyous sense of style. Welcome to the Gîte du Levant, a house of comfort, charm and stupendous views. Inside is a large open-plan living space with the palest floor tiles, the softest stone walls and the subtlest fabrics – deep rose and soft grey. French windows fling open to a perfectly lovely terrace stuffed with herbs to delight your nose and palate. Light pours in to illuminate pretty metal dining chairs, modern sofas, a fireplace for the cooler months, touches of brocante. The kitchen is custom made from beech, its latticed cupboards holding pink and grey china, of course. The iron-balustraded staircase takes you up to serene bedrooms: the pale lilac room matches the trees in the garden, the other, spacious and cool, opens to a terrace – watch the sun rise (*le levant* – the east) from your bed. The bathroom is large, bright and welcoming. A pool-with-a-view and a charming play area, plus lots of outdoor space, add up to delights for all the family. *Shared pool. B&B also.*

Price	€950–€1,400 per week.
Sleeps	5.
Rooms	2: 1 double, 1 twin; 1 bathroom, 2 separate wcs. Exra bed.
Closed	Never.

Charles & Annick Speth
Aiglun, Alpes-de-Haute-Provence
Tel   +33 (0)4 92 34 67 00
Email   info@vieil-aiglun.com
Web   www.vieil-aiglun.com

Entry 338 Map 16

Les Granges de Saint Pierre

Everything in this remarkably converted 14th-century barn – once attached to the priory – is stylish and caring. Lavender-infused air, simple iron furniture, modern art, a fine use of colour, an inner terrace where lemons grow – it has a sense of peace and space. Arched doorways with new doors and ancient locks lead to big, light bedrooms with tiled floors and colourwashed walls. Bathrooms are sophisticated in rust-red and white. You have a sunny, lofty, white-beamed living room with cream drapes, canvas directors' chairs and big sofas in front of an even bigger fire. The kitchen is in the corner: terracotta-painted units, old country furniture, stripped floor. Rooms gather round a central terrace filled with geraniums, there's fruit in the orchards and chickens in the pen. Josiane, kind and intelligent, lives with her husband in the château next door where the magical pool half hides in a walled garden. Simiane la Rotonde, once the regional capital of lavender, is a gem: a hilltop village with a 16th-century market place, surrounded by vast purple fields. A heavenly place. *B&B also. Shared pool.*

Price	€670–€980 per week.
Sleeps	6.
Rooms	3: 2 doubles, 1 twin; 3 shower rooms.
Closed	Never.

Josiane Tamburini
Simiane la Rotonde,
Alpes-de-Haute-Provence

Tel	+33 (0)4 92 75 93 81
Fax	+33 (0)4 92 75 93 81
Web	communities.msn.co.uk/ lesgrangesdesaintpierre/home.htm

Chalet La Renardière

Wow! On the far edge of lively Villeneuve, in the heart of Serre Chevalier, a stunning chalet, a house for all seasons. Not only do snowy peaks appear at every well-dressed window but the three-storey house is surrounded by seven private hectares. The garden is enclosed so everyone's safe, there are carpets of colour in springtime, shady spots for summer time and a trout stream running through. Enter a large sunny hallway encased in the palest pine, then step into a vast and lovely light-filled area for reading, dining, lounging, living, its sweet spaces divided by archway, open fire and wood-burner. Add furnishings of chic leather and cushion-tumbled sofa and you have an irresistibly soft, inviting and luxurious interior. The all-pine kitchen is emboldened by chequerboard tiles and splashes of steel, the bathrooms, spa bath and sauna exude mountain warmth, the French windows open to a vast decked terrace, the bedrooms glow with fresh flowers and fabrics, and the pristine furnishings are tempered with alpine antiques. Even the doors are reclaimed. Amazing. *Chef on request. Ski lift three-minute walk.*

Price	€4,500–€9,900 per week.
Sleeps	14.
Rooms	6: 3 doubles, 3 twins; 6 bathrooms, separate wc.
Closed	Never.

Madame Parker
Serre Chevalier, Hautes-Alpes
Tel   +33 (0)6 07 73 71 48
Email   contact@chalet-larenardiere.com
Web   www.chalet-larenardiere.com

Entry 340 Map 12

Snowgums - Apartments One & Two

Next to the apple and pear trees, Pippa has created a lovely level spot in the garden whence you may gawp at the views. But you'll catch them anyway from this charming old farmhouse, whose rustic walls and vaulted ceilings hold two big apartments done with cheerful covers on pale pine beds, cotton rugs on tiled floors, jolly towels in shining showers, lightness, brightness and comfort. The cupboards spill novels and games, there are cots and high chairs for the asking, the Chantemerle cable car is a five-minute walk and Pippa will child-sit if you'd like an evening out. Pippa, a Londoner raised in Australia, has that charming, relaxed manner you would expect and makes a stay here memorable. She has a deep love for the outdoor life and will point you in the direction of most of the area's activities – hiking, biking, rock climbing, parapenting, tobogganing, skiing. She buys local produce for the welcome pack and is totally involved with village life. There are heated floors for cosiness, a drying room for ski gear and a free shuttle bus up and down the valley. Brilliant value. *Chef on request. Cable-car 5 min drive.*

Pippa has been in sustainability for years, campaigning for cycling routes, waste management, arts centres and NGOs. Now, she grows chemical-free fruit on 40 trees, waters the garden with the local irrigation system, laid in... 1350, manures the land with the horse, donkey and sheep who do the mowing. A wildflower meadow attracts butterflies, ladybirds and other useful insects, as does companion planting by the vegetable patch. Renovations are done with hemp insulation and limewash finishes and old is re-used before any new is brought in. She'll encourage you too, with baskets for non-plastic shopping.

Price	£400–£500.
Sleeps	Apartment One: 4-6.
	Apartment Two: 2-4.
Rooms	Apartment One: 1 family room for 4,
	1 sofabed in living room;
	2 shower rooms.
	Apartment Two: I twin, 1 sofabed in
	living room; 1 shower room.
Closed	Never.

	Pippa Curtis
	Briançon, Hautes-Alpes
Tel	+33 (0)4 92 20 44 26
Email	info@alpsholiday.com
Web	www.alpsholiday.com

SPECIAL GREEN ENTRY
see page 18

La Lauzière

For 300 days a year sunshine bathes this staggeringly beautiful land: the setting is spectacular. The delightful 18th-century Provençal farmhouse has rolling views over Côtes du Rhône vineyards to one side, and a sense of space inside. It sits solid to the ground with its large windows framed in sea-green and its honey-toned stone walls. The interior has an unpretentious contemporary Provençal feel: natural eggshell walls, colourful fabrics, original terracotta floors and iron beds. Bedrooms have old-fashioned French-size beds and views of either pool or courtyard while downstairs there is a choice of sitting rooms. Matisse prints hang on the walls; there's an open fireplace in the yellow-walled kitchen. The attractive pool is at the back, wander round the garden and you will discover an orchard of cherry trees. In the typically Provençal village of Puyméras, a five-minute stroll, you will find tennis courts, two bistro-cafés and a restaurant. Close by is medieval Vaison la Romaine with its Roman ruins and popular market. As for the walking – mountain, valley and gorge await you.

Price	€1,525-€2,525 per week.
Sleeps	6.
Rooms	3: 2 doubles, 1 twin, 1 single; 2 bathrooms, 1 separate wc.
Closed	Mid-October to mid-May.

Ralf Maurer
Puyméras, Vaucluse

Tel	+33 (0)1 53 01 09 14
Fax	+33 (0)1 53 01 09 14
Email	mail@provenceliving.com
Web	www.provenceliving.com

Les Romarins - Les Vignes, Le Studio & Côté Jardin

Sit on your terrace overlooking the garden with a glass of something cool to hand as you relish the tantalising aroma of spicy sausages on the barbecue. Then a pleasant stroll or horse ride through the vineyards? An excursion to lovely Vaison la Romaine and its Roman ruins? A night at the opera in Orange's magnificent Roman amphitheatre? Or just a quiet snooze in a shaded garden lounger before an outing to one of the region's many fine restaurants – though perhaps this evening it'll be aperitif on the terrace of your lively hosts, Judy and Jeremy, before sharing a table d'hôtes dinner. You'll be spoilt for choice in this lovely secluded spot, a former wine estate just outside Cairanne, whose fine Côtes du Rhône Villages regularly sweep the honours in wine competitions. There are three comfy, well-furnished apartments here, each with its own private terrace. White-tiled floors and pale walls highlight the clever use of colour (tan, yellow, russet, blue) in bedcovers, wall prints, cushions and kitchen/bathroom tiles. Simple bliss at its best. *Meals on request.*

Price	€200-€560 each per week.
Sleeps	Les Vignes 4.
	Le Studio 2.
	Côté Jardin 2 + child.
Rooms	Les Vignes: 1 double, 1 mezzanine
	double; 2 showers.
	Le Studio: 1 double; 1 shower.
	Côté Jardin: 1 double; 1 shower.
Closed	Never.

	Judy Harrison & Jeremy Rose
	Cairanne, Vaucluse
Tel	+33 (0)4 90 30 77 72
Email	romarins2@wanadoo.fr
Web	www.romarins.net

Entry 343 Map 16

Les Convenents

Pure Provence: the views from your traditional stone mas are of vines, sunflowers and distant pines. Welcoming and warm Sarah, who does B&B next door, stocks the kitchen of the small gîte with basics – fruit, wine, olive oil – and often invites guests next door for a drink. She is also happy for you to share the pretty pool but if you prefer the privacy of your own sitting-out area (with barbecue) that's fine too. Inside, the feel is contemporary, light and bright; there's a dear little living/kitchen area with pale tiled floors, sandy walls, cheery blue and yellow curtains with matching cushions and throws, attractive cane armchairs, pale beams. The kitchen in the corner is cleverly designed to include oven, fridge and freezer. (If you need bigger pots and pans, you can borrow them.) Upstairs are two small but adequate bedrooms whose yellow and blue bedspreads, cushions and curtains echo the furnishings downstairs. There's ping-pong, boules and bikes to borrow, and Vaison la Romaine, with restaurants and Tuesday market, is happily nearby. *Cot & high chair provided. Shared pool. Sawday B&B. Meals on request.*

Price	€600–€800 per week.
Sleeps	4 + cot.
Rooms	2: 1 double, 1 twin; 1 shower room.
Arrival	Friday.
Closed	Never.

Sarah Banner
Uchaux, Vaucluse
Tel   +33 (0)4 90 40 65 64
Fax   +33 (0)4 90 40 65 64
Email sarahbanner@wanadoo.fr
Web   www.lesconvenents.com

La Maison aux Volets Rouges

Step off the street into the 'red-shuttered' house to be wrapped in a warm embrace. Family photographs line the hall and stairs; this is a much-loved home, and its sprawling layout – two staircases to separate parts of the house – makes it ideal for three-generation parties. Rooms are big with tiled floors (rugs in winter), beams, family antiques. The salon, with its open fire, leads to a courtyard while the dining room opens off a farmhouse kitchen, equipped so that cooks may hone their skills. High-beamed bedrooms have good storage and individual touches – a brass bed, an arched window, a baby bed with a teddy bear. Three minutes and you're by the pool – a peaceful distance from the children's frolics. The pool house, surrounded by lawns and shady trees, is almost a second home: kitchen, barbecue, veranda and shower. Borrow a bike, play tennis at the local club (no charge), and be sure to visit glorious Avignon and Aix. Restaurants are a mere stroll. Brigitte, who lived in England for 30 years, is chatty, enthusiastic, wants guests to enjoy her family home and lives in the same village.

Price	€1,800-€2,500 per week. Linen not included.
Sleeps	9 + cots.
Rooms	5: 3 doubles, 1 twin, 1 single; 3 shower rooms, 1 bathroom.
Arrival	Saturday, but flexible out of season.
Closed	Never.

Brigitte Woodward
Uchaux, Vaucluse

Tel	+33 (0)4 90 40 6456/ 6218
Fax	+33 (0)4 90 40 64 56
Email	b.woodward@hotmail.fr

Mas du Clos de l'Escarrat - Studios & Apartments

If more sumptuous décor and glitzy bathrooms have started to pall, try a return to simplicity. This 17th-century stone farmhouse, a complete ruin when the Barails took it on ten years ago, is pleasingly quiet and unassuming. Ignore the approach road winding past an industrial area and lorry park: you'll soon be away from it all among the tulip fields and the vines, gazing on distant mountains. The gîtes are basic but very pleasant, decorated in soft yellow tones. Provençal fabrics and some unexpected features – a marble table, a beautiful pottery bowl – add arresting touches. Kitchens and bathrooms are small but perfectly adequate. In the shared garden a host of trees jostle for space – linden, fig, oleander, bamboo – and the swing in the plane tree will be irresistible to small visitors. The swimming pool is Monsieur's pride and joy – and when he is not tending it, he will take you on a wine tour, followed by a gastronomic dinner at the mas. He and Madame are retired – a warm and charming couple who have travelled extensively in Latin America. *Wine tours organised. Shared pool.*

Price	Studio €465. Apartment 1 €600-€720. Apartment 2 €665-€925. Prices per week. September-June prices per day, on request.
Sleeps	2 studios for 2. Apartment for 2-3. Apartment for 2-4.
Rooms	Studio: 1 double; 1 bathroom. Apartment 1: 1 double, 1 single; 1 bathroom. Apartment 2: 1 double, 1 twin; 1 bathroom.
Arrival	Sat July-August, flexible low season.
Closed	Never.

Charles & Andrée Barail
Jonquières, Vaucluse

Tel	+33 (0)4 90 70 39 19
Mobile	+33 (0)6 61 22 39 19
Email	contact@bed-breakfast-provence.fr
Web	www.bed-breakfast-provence.fr

Mas Garrigue & Jolie Cottage

Near the majestic Dentelles de Montmirail – small mountains crested with delicate fingers of white stone – here is the perfect place for walkers and cyclists. In both houses, strenuous activity could be followed by lazy poolside afternoons or finishing that novel on a sun-dappled terrace. Judith makes sure the basics are there: coffee, tea, wine; the olive oil is from her own trees. Large are the windows of the Mas, long is the view, the terrace gets the sun all day. In the sunken living room: a fireplace for chilly days, sofas for relaxing, big oil paintings for a touch of colour, a handsome stone floor; in the downstairs double: a dressing room; in the little study: a single bed and garden door. Upstairs are a twin room with double exposure, and a double with a romantic little terrace for more amazing views; a cottage immediately behind sleeps a further two. About a mile away is the absurdly romantic one-up one-down Jolie Cottage, an enchanting and secluded hideaway for two just an orchard walk from the owners' fine big pool. Judith can help you plan a trip, find a cook or even a babysitter.

Price	Mas & cottage €1,250–€3,100. Jolie Cottage €600–€750.
Sleeps	Mas & cottage 6-8. Jolie Cottage 2.
Rooms	Mas: 2 doubles, 1 twin; 1 bathroom, 2 shower rooms; adjoining cottage 1 double; 1 shower room. Jolie Cottage: 1 double; 1 shower room.
Closed	Mas & cottage: Never. Jolie Cottage: November-April.

Judith Baker
Saint Hippolyte le Graveyron, Vaucluse

Tel	+33 (0)4 90 62 34 97
Fax	+33 (0)4 90 62 34 97
Email	baker@judith-provence.com

Entry 347 Map 16

La Saga

Stepping out of a narrow, winding street in the heart of Pernes you find yourself in a scene from the Arabian Nights – or might it be Petrarch? An enclosed courtyard holds a spring-fed pool, a wide terrace, greenery galore, a wooden pergola, romantic lighting: poetry that on a warm summer's night would melt the heart of the toughest pragmatist. From here into the 21st century: a cool haven of space with an airy feel, a minimalist décor, earth colours, natural fabrics, and plain good taste. Quirky touches, too. You'll want to stay a while to experience both worlds, the ice-cube lamps against the old stonework, the Art Deco style and the abstract art. Comfortable bedrooms have quiet style, the excellent kitchen has an extraordinary quantity of crockery, cutlery, platters and baskets, and the living area's 30s-style leather sofas open arms to a superior music system; the owner is a professional musician. Just up from the market square yet quieter than the countryside: no tractors, no roosters. Fine dining, festivals great and small, history, art and winegrowers are all around you. *Children over seven welcome.*

Price	£900–£2,600 per week. Linen not included.
Sleeps	10.
Rooms	5: 4 doubles, 1 twin; 1 bathroom, 1 shower room.
Closed	Never.

Peter Beachill
Pernes Les Fontaines, Vaucluse

Tel	+44 (0)870 446 0168
Email	enquiries@la-saga.co.uk
Web	www.la-saga.co.uk

Le Cœur d'Avignon

No exaggeration – this is indeed the heart of Avignon, within the ancient walls, a few minutes' walk from the main square and just round the corner from shops, cafés, restaurants, even an English bookshop/tea room where DVDs can be hired. Bubbly Pam has done great restoration work, aided and abetted by a rare gift for unearthing quirky bits, pieces and prints that make all the difference – sometimes building a whole colour scheme around one of her treasures. Blue-grey, off-white, wine-red tones, a touch of ochre/copper in the café-style kitchen, high-quality natural-fibre linens. Windows on three sides ensure a refreshing breeze even on hot days, and the terrace with barbecue is the place for breakfast, aperitif, or a long, lazy dinner. You have a breath-catching green view from the huge double windows in the master bedroom, a cosy fireplace, a dining space for six. Potter through the Popes' Palace, remembering that the Holy See was once here, dance up a storm on the famed Pont d'Avignon, then relax over dinner on a barge cruise down the Rhône. The Avignon festival? Unmissable. A fun place to stay.

Price	€600-€800 per week.
Sleeps	4.
Rooms	2 doubles; 2 bathrooms.
Arrival	Friday.
Closed	Never.

Pamela Hall-Johnston
Avignon, Vaucluse

Tel	+33 (0)4 90 30 88 40
Mobile	+33 (0)6 14 60 14 83
Email	pam@frenchfolies.com
Web	www.frenchfolies.com/Avignon

Le Mas du Coq - Oliver & Tamaris

A delightful private paradise, separate from the farmhouse across the courtyard but with the same friendly welcome from your hosts, who also do courses. The two semi-detached villas – Oliver and Tamaris – overlook a huge green garden, a glory of shrubs, cypress and palm trees. To one side, a fenced pool with all the right furniture for relaxing. In a far corner, a special kids' domain with slide, swings and sandpit: lots of room for them to let off steam – or for adults wanting a quiet bit of sunbathing and a good book away from the pool. Each villa is well equipped for four to six people, with comfy bedrooms featuring cheery colours in stripes and floral patterns, efficient kitchens (one villa has a second kitchen on the terrace), easy living rooms with fireplaces, tiled floors throughout and big, well-furnished private terraces with barbecues. There are mounds of markets, festivals, excursions, courses, good walking, cycling and horse riding in the area. Or antiques browsing in exquisite Isle-sur-la-Sorgue. And excellent restaurants, of course, wherever you wander. *Shared pool.*

Price	€500-€1,000 per week.
Sleeps	Oliver 4-6. Tamaris 4-6.
Rooms	Oliver: 1 double, 1 twin, sofabed; 1 shower room. Tamaris: 1 double, 1 twin, sofabed; 1 bathroom.
Closed	Never

	Decima Macquisten Cavaillon, Vaucluse
Tel	+33 (0)4 90 71 19 06
Email	guy.decima@wanadoo.fr
Web	provenceaccommodation.com

Le Mas du Coq - Farmhouse

You'll be thoroughly charmed by the beautiful private courtyard, with its two shady pergolas, pool, dining area and refreshing greenery galore. Then walk into Decima and Guy's wonderfully welcoming kitchen/dining room and be charmed all over again! This 18th-century farmhouse has been restored with enormous imagination and respect for the old features and materials used. You'll feel instantly at home. Off the kitchen/diner is the lovely airy sitting room with its plump white sofas and stone fireplace surround; on the other side, a comfy, laid-back study. The first-floor bedrooms, in cool blues and greens blended with white, repeat the spacious, airy feeling. Take time out to admire the 111 pictures/prints that adorn the walls. Then back to the courtyard for a dip in the pool, tea for two under the small pergola, or aperitifs round the table while planning the next day's outings in this particularly charming corner of Provence. A festival, wine tasting, horse riding or a long hike to work off all that good cuisine the area is noted for? Or the Lubéron's picturesque hilltop villages.

Price	€1,200-€2,300 per week.
Sleeps	6-8.
Rooms	4: 2 doubles, 1 twin, 1 sofabed in study, 1 twin in annexe; 2 bathrooms, separate wc.
Closed	Never.

Decima Macquisten
Cavaillon, Vaucluse

Tel	+33 (0)4 90 71 19 06
Email	guy.decima@wanadoo.fr
Web	provenceaccommodation.com

Entry 351 Map 16

L'Ancienne Poste

Perched on a slab of rock overlooking the Lubéron hills, the old Post Office in Ménerbes has wine-red shutters and a crumbling charm. But nothing can prepare you for the dazzling interior: three floors of uncluttered elegance, light-filled spaces and views that become ever more exquisite the higher you climb (the roof terrace is sensational). The owner has incorporated nature into the architecture, the entire back wall has been removed and replaced with glass, and the stratified cliff face gives the courtyard a spectacular edge; a mirror ball projects twinkling light across the space at night. Bare stonework rubs shoulders with clean white walls, light woods with zinc and stainless steel; Moroccan rugs and Nepalese buddhas in niches add personality. Sheets and duvet covers are fine white cotton, one bathroom is in the bedroom and the open kitchen combines minimalism with rusticity. Families who were born and bred in the village made famous by Peter Mayle now share it with a colourful collection of artists, writers and bon vivants. Amazing. *On-street parking. Access to private pool at restaurant 1.3km.*

Price	€2,492–€3,740.
Sleeps	10 + 2.
Rooms	5: 2 doubles, 3 doubles/twins, 1 twin; 3 bathrooms, 1 shower room . Petite Maison: 1 double; 1 shower room, 1 separate wc.
Closed	Never.

Philippe Brown
Ménerbes, Vaucluse

Tel	+44 (0)20 8133 5331
Fax	+1 413 832 6111
Email	philippe@ancienneposte.com
Web	www.ancienneposte.com

Mas Vignes Folles

Outside and in, a very special place. Among lavish lavender fields, cherry orchards and vineyards, set round a beautiful courtyard, these connected houses are, in parts, sculpted into the rock. The main house has exquisite vaulted stone ceilings, masses of warm wood (particularly striking heavy old doors), a stunning period fireplace and views across the vineyard to Mont Ventoux. The soothing burble of the simple (switch-operated) fountain can be heard inside. Rooms in the garden house show the same elegantly easy mix of country antiques, super fabrics and modern touches giving a classic marble-topped French style or a more feminine air. After a battle on the boules pitch, or tennis by the stream, imagine a carefree lunch on the terrace beneath the graceful wisteria, surrounded by delicious landscaped gardens; or a magical dinner in the beautifully set, lantern-lit courtyard. Alison's feel for lighting is exceptional. With so much wood inside, so much greenery outside, the sense of being at one with nature is all-pervading. A lovely sitting room and two good kitchens make this perfect for two families sharing.

Price	€2,000–€6,000 per week. Enquire about renting each house separately.
Sleeps	Main house 4. Garden House 6.
Rooms	Main house: 2 doubles; 1 bathroom, 1 shower room, separate wc. Garden house: 3 twins; 3 shower rooms, separate wc.
Closed	Never.

Alison Vaissiere
Bonnieux, Vaucluse

Mobile	+44 (0)7720 349 272
Email	info@masvignesfolles.com
Web	www.masvignesfolles.com

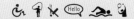

Entry 353 Map 16

Le Mas de Miejour

Yours is the oldest part of this pretty Provençal farmhouse with your own entrance and garden with barbecue. Fred and Emma, craftspeople both, came here to bring up their children. They do B&B in the other half, Fred turns potter in the winter and Emma conjures up leather baby shoes. Passionate about wine, they are qualified sommeliers and can point you to the best vineyards. The farmhouse atmosphere is utterly restful. Well-equipped yet nicely old-fashioned and homely with its little windows and ancient tiles, the kitchen is dominated by an ancient bread oven, perhaps originally pillaged from the 12th-century château nearby. Up steepish steps are the salon, with comfy leather sofa and armchairs, and the bedrooms. The double bed is huge, the white-tiled bathroom is small but fine, the views are over the garden or fields; Mont Ventoux lies beyond. The land here is flat with a high water table so the garden, sheltered by trees and fields of tall maize and sunflowers in summer, is always fresh and green. You are most welcome to share the lovely, fenced pool – and the wine knowledge. *Sawday B&B also. Shared pool.*

Price	€450–€1,000 per week.
Sleeps	5.
Rooms	3: 1 double, 1 twin, 1 single; 1 bathroom.
Closed	November–February.

Frédéric & Emmanuelle Westercamp
Le Thor, Vaucluse

Tel	+33 (0)4 90 02 13 79
Email	frederic.westercamp@wanadoo.fr
Web	www.masdemiejour.com

La Gardiole

The oldest of Bonnieux' two churches, crowning this perfect hilltop village, is surrounded by ancient cedars so huge they can be spotted for miles. Here, on the lower flanks of the hill, is an unexpectedly simple and inexpensive place to stay. Owned by the good people who run the town's small, lofty B&B, Le Clos du Buis, this is perfect for two. Your studio room is in the lower half of a newish stone building, the top floor is occupied but quite separate. Décor is neither stylish nor contemporary but simple and clean with a certain old-fashioned charm. You have a white-walled double room with flowery curtains and comfy beds, a small blue-tiled bathroom, a round dining table, a new sofa, and a small kitchen with shining pans and two rings. Views open wide to the Lubéron and your garden, with a cherry tree for shade, has a delightful private pool. Bonnieux is one of the less touristy 'perched villages', its steep, winding streets numerous enough to get lost in, its restaurants fashionable, its Friday market carnival-like in summer. *Sawday hotel. Two further houses for four & six in nearby Castellet.*

Price	€350–€600 per week. Linen not included.
Sleeps	2-4.
Rooms	1 twin/double; 1 bathroom, sofabed.
Closed	Never.

Monsieur & Madame Maurin
Bonnieux, Vaucluse

Tel	+33 (0)4 90 75 88 48
Fax	+33 (0)4 90 75 88 57
Email	le-clos-du-buis@wanadoo.fr
Web	www.leclosdubuis.com

Jas des Eydins

Among vineyards and cherry orchards, with views to the Lubéron hills, a blissful retreat at the end of a private lane. These 18th-century stone buildings, once a sheepfold and part of a Provençal farm, were restored by their architect owner and his elegant art historian wife. There's a charming simplicity, a soothing, serene mix of country antiques and modern bits and pieces. You have a large, beautifully equipped kitchen and open-plan sitting room and three peaceful bedrooms (one in an adjoining building) shaded by a trellis of Banksia roses. On hot summer days, relax by the heavenly pool, enveloped in the scent of roses and lavender, or enjoy the big garden and revel in distant views of Mont Ventoux. In the evenings, dine on the covered terrace to the chirrup of the cicadas. There's a fabulous outdoor kitchen with chimney and built-in barbecue, too. Shirley and Jan live next door, are family-friendly and on hand if you need them, but leave you to relax in peace – perfect hosts. If you can bear to break away, there are some enchanting hillside villages to discover.

Price	€1,300-€1,950 per week.
Sleeps	6.
Rooms	3: 2 twins/doubles, 1 twin; 2 bathrooms, 1 shower room. On request: extra twin room in main house, with private entrance.
Arrival	Saturday, but flexible in low season.
Closed	November to mid-March.

Shirley & Jan Kozlowski
Bonnieux, Vaucluse

Tel	+33 (0)4 90 75 84 99
Email	jasdeseydins@wanadoo.fr
Web	www.jasdeseydins.com

Château de la Loubière - La Grange, Les Platanes, Sebastian's House

Space, peace and much to explore. Ten acres of parkland surround these three stone-built gîtes, outbuildings of the 16th-century château. While the kids make hay in the sun-drenched grounds, you can slip into the pool or gaze on the Provençal countryside. In a mad moment, you might even play tennis; a court lies hidden among the trees. Nicely separated, each gîte has been renovated by the McDougalls, who live in the château, to keep its Provençal charm intact. Rooms have exposed stonework, terracotta floors and fresh white walls, furnishings are bright and uncluttered and quirky features have been retained – one bathroom has an iron hayrack, another an old feeding trough. The open-plan living areas, some with fireplaces or beams, have sunny terraces for alfresco eating. Kitchens are modern and well-equipped, bedrooms light and breezy with pretty bedcovers and soft lamps. Toss a coin in La Grange for the bedroom with the terrace. There's walking, riding, the Lubéron National Park, festivals in Aix, restaurants in Pertuis. The McDougalls can provide a babysitter.

Price	Grange €1,700–€2,500. Platanes €600–€1,300. Sebastian's €500–€1,200. Prices per week.
Sleeps	La Grange 10. Platanes 4. Sebastian's 6.
Rooms	Grange: 2 doubles, 1 twin, 2 twins/doubles; 3 baths, 4 sep. wcs. Platanes: 1 double, 1 twin/double; 1 bath. Sebastian's: 2 doubles, 1 twin; 1 bath.
Closed	November–March.

Deb & Alec McDougall
Pertuis, Vaucluse

Tel	+33 (0)4 90 09 53 96
Mobile	+33 (0)6 24 51 81 05
Email	info@laloubiere.com
Web	www.laloubiere.com

Ferme de la Platane

The magnificent 12th-century château of Ansouis dominates the skyline, the braided hills surround you, enchantment is in the air. Each of the secluded apartments in the old farmhouse is a delight, each has space. La Cour is reached through a courtyard garden, its terrace and pergola facing west; the approach to La Fenière and La Magnanerie is via an outside stone staircase, their terraces and living spaces (with magical views) are above, their bedrooms below. La Petite Maison is creeper-covered, with blue shutters and cream-coloured stone. Crisp sofas rub shoulders with country armoires, stylish walk-in showers with antique roll-top baths. Old limewashed walls and terracotta floors keep you cool. With the welcome bread and wine comes an information folder so you can plan how lively or laid-back you wish to be. The lazy pool beckons… as do the innumerable festivals, concerts and markets of this part of the Lubéron (at least one for each day of the week). Pad through the vines to medieval Ansouis and that château (15 minutes) or take the car to lively Lourmarin (five). A delightful getaway.

Price	€400-€850 each per week.
Sleeps	4 apartments for 2.
Rooms	Each apartment: 1 twin/double; 1 bathroom.
Arrival	Saturday, but flexible in low season.
Closed	Never.

Rosemary & Peter Fraser
Ansouis, Vaucluse
Tel   +33 (0)4 90 09 80 89
Mobile +33 (0)6 74 52 90 37
Email   fermedelaplatane@yahoo.fr
Web   www.fermedelaplatane.com

Chez Manon

If you yearn to live like the eagles, nesting high up with a breathtaking view, but in an uncharacteristically luxurious nest, then Chez Manon is a must. Overlooking Apt and the soothing green Lubéron hills, with ancient hilltop villages dotted about and soft lights twinkling on as dusk falls… this is the stuff dreams are made of. Dine on the large terrace near the pool and be bewitched. Or relax on the back patio to the tune of the spring that inspired the property's name (from the Provençal film *Manon des Sources*). In between, the superb 17th-century farmhouse: breezy, spacious and exquisitely restored, where old blends with new – a few oriental touches for spice – and where you can enjoy a quiet fireside read (the house has its own library) or entertain guests from a beautifully equipped kitchen with enough tableware to cater for the proverbial army. The décor is good-quality traditional heightened by cheery yellows and warm russets, dark wood and colourful prints and posters. Superb walking and cycling, great markets every day of the week, and some fine dining in these hills.

Price	€2,500-€3,500 per week.
Sleeps	10-12.
Rooms	6: 3 doubles, 1 family (2 double beds), 1 single with trundle, 1 single with trundle (in downstairs library); 3 bathrooms, 3 separate wcs.
Closed	Never.

Pamela Hall-Johnston
Apt, Vaucluse
Tel   +33 (0)4 90 30 88 40
Mobile   +33 (0)6 14 60 14 83
Email   pam@frenchfolies.com
Web   www.chezmanon.com

Entry 359 Map 16

Le Massonnet - Main House

A long drive lined with ancient plane trees brings into focus this large, exquisitely restored 16th-century flour mill. Then, through the wrought-iron gates and round the softly burbling fountain, you find charming hosts Claire and Thierry de Foy waiting to greet you. Everything here is comfort and top hospitality: two cosy green-blue bedrooms (for B&B or your extra family members), one connected to a snug peachy-beige studio for two. Then the big airy apartments, Lavande all in soothing blues, Colombier in warm earth colours, both a blend of old and new, with excellent fabrics and great garden views. Among the many original and quirky touches you will find two high points: the legendary, hand-made Apt wall tiles dotted here and there in their unbelievably beautiful deep blue and turquoise colours; and the massive original wooden flour mill whose top is the focal point of a large shared living room-cum-kitchen that is often used when groups take the whole property. All this just outside Apt, with the entire Lubéron region and its delightful hilltop villages an easy nip away. *Shared pool. B&B also.*

Price	Apartments €200–€730 per week. Extra bedrooms €52–€61 per night.
Sleeps	Cyprès 2. Lavande 2-4. Colombier 2-4.
Rooms	Cyprès: 1 twin; 1 shower, separate wc. Lavande: 1 double, sofabed, 1 bath, separate wc. Colombier: 1 double, sofabed, 1 shower. Two extra bedrooms on ground floor.
Arrival	Saturday July & August, flexible other months.
Closed	Never.

Thierry & Claire de Foy
Apt, Vaucluse

Tel	+33 (0)4 90 04 66 15
Fax	+33 (0)4 90 04 66 15
Email	info@lemassonnet.com
Web	www.lemassonnet.com

Le Massonnet - Garden Wing

The ground-floor, 'garden' wing of the main house has its own special feel. For one thing, the bedroom and two apartments all have their own private, well-furnished terraces with dreamy pergolas and a grandstand view of the huge, tree-studded garden dotted with flowers and shrubs, overlooking the Lubéron hills. The perfect spot for a lazy breakfast, a lively aperitif or a candlelight dinner for two. The apartments have medium-sized living rooms and – as throughout this superb place – a blend of old and new, simple lines, an airy feeling and well-equipped kitchens. Colours run to warm ochre, russet, gold and peach, natural fabrics predominate, and the keyword is quality. After some serious pool-sampling there's lots to get up to in this lovely region: colourful markets in one town or another every day of the week; walking, riding, wine visits, courses (art courses working with colour are a local speciality); festivals in Avignon, Aix en Provence and La Roque d'Anthéron, and many village mini-festivals. Plus fine eating choices everywhere, some just minutes away. *Shared pool. B&B also.*

Price	Apartments €450–€1,155 per week. Extra bedrooms €52–€61 per night.
Sleeps	Églantier 4-6. Noisetier 2-4. Two extra bedrooms on same floor.
Rooms	Églantier: 2 twins, 1 sofabed; 1 bathroom. Noisetier: 1 double, sofabed; 1 bathroom, separate wc.
Arrival	Saturday July & August, flexible other months.
Closed	Never.

	Thierry & Claire de Foy
	Apt, Vaucluse
Tel	+33 (0)4 90 04 66 15
Fax	+33 (0)4 90 04 66 15
Email	info@lemassonnet.com
Web	www.lemassonnet.com

Mas des Genêts

Set among vineyards and lavender fields just below the charming village of Saignon, perched like a fort on turrets of white rock, this one-up-one-down stone cottage is a sweet retreat in the popular Lubéron. Reached by a private drive, the pale-stoned extension (once a tractor shed) is part of an old farmhouse that has been skilfully converted by American-born Stephen and his English wife Meg. They live in the main part of the house and there's a twin-bedded ground-floor apartment for two next door. Each property has its own private terrace and lawn from which to take your fill of birdsong and big mountain views. Inside, original beams, new terracotta tiles, modern pine tables and chairs, books, puzzles and games... even underfloor heating for winter stays. There's a functional kitchenette in one corner and a sunny upstairs bedroom with a big brass bed, sloping beamed ceilings and blue and green floral blinds. Take the footpath to Saignon (25 minutes), or walk in the Lubéron hills: you can hike straight from the door. And don't miss the superb Saturday market in Apt.

Price	€380–€580 per week.
Sleeps	2.
Rooms	1 double; 1 shower room.
Closed	Never.

Meg & Stephen Parker
Saignon, Vaucluse

Tel	+33 (0)4 90 04 65 33
Fax	+33 (0)4 90 74 56 85
Email	masdegenet@aol.com
Web	www.masdesgenets.eu

Bastide du Jas - Four Apartments

There is magic in the air here. In the very heart of delightful Saignon, up a tiny cobbled street, down another, and you reach the surprisingly private Bastide, hidden by vegetation and the lie of the land. Coming down the path, you first see the summer restaurant (three simple menus) with its open kitchen and terrace, then the reception with its antique desk, red taffeta curtains and tall-stick decoration. This chic sophistication sets the atmosphere for the rest of the elegant and beautifully renovated old mas. There are three apartments for two on the ground floor, each with a fireplace for winter and a little terrace for summer, the upper floors have glorious views, over the rooftops and far away. Antique doors on built-in cupboards, richly falling curtains, vintage armchairs and chests of drawers set off by white walls and rust-red tomettes – the mix of ancient and modern is deeply pleasing; bathrooms and kitchens are high-quality chic with all the essentials. These are supremely comfortable holiday apartments and the lovely swimming pool is at your feet. *Restaurant on the premises. Sawday Hotel.*

Price	Apartment for 3 €800.
	Studio for 2 €600. Prices per week.
Sleeps	3; 3; 3; 2.
Rooms	Apartments for 3: 1 double, extra
	single bed; 1 bathroom.
	Studio apartment for 2; 1 shower room.
	On request: 4 doubles, 1 room for 4,
	with bathrooms.
Arrival	Flexible.
Closed	Apartments: rarely. Restaurant & extra
	rooms mid- November-March.

Anne–Cécile & Gerhard Rose
Saignon, Vaucluse

Tel	+33 (0)4 90 74 11 50
Fax	+33 (0)4 90 04 68 51
Email	auberge.presbytere@wanadoo.fr
Web	www.labastidedujas.com

La Grande Bastide - Rosiers, Auvent, Grand Colorado, Petit Colorado

Through the brown iron gates and down the drive fringed with ancient oaks to the grand bastide. The setting is stunning – the hills to the east, the valley to the west – and hikers will be in heaven. You walk, or cycle, out of the house into the multi-coloured landscape of the Colorado range, famous for its ochre pigments. These four gîtes, neat as new pins, separated by thick walls, stand apart from the owners' living quarters in a wing of the old house – and share a huge pool and a walled courtyard garden full of roses with mulberry trees for shade. All is spotless and spacious; there are beams and new terracotta tiles, pale sofas, light-wood tables and chairs, big new beds and linen, and a generous farmhouse table in each pristine kitchen. In contrast, the garden is a joyous multitude of jasmine, honeysuckle, lavender and roses. You are north of Sault, famous for its lavender and nougat, and south of Apt, whose all-day Saturday market is legendary. Peaceful Rustrel, walkable from here, has a shop and a sprinkling of restaurants and bars; and your bread is delivered every morning. *Shared pool.*

Price	Rosiers €800–€1,550.
	Auvent €520–€1,000.
	Grand Colorado €520–€1,100.
	Petit Colorado €450–€650.
	Prices per week.
Sleeps	Rosiers 6. Auvent 4. Grand Colorado 4.
	Petit Colorado 2.
Rooms	Rosiers: 2 doubles, 1 twin; 2 baths.
	Auvent: 1 double, 1 twin; 1 bath.
	Grand Colorado: 2 doubles; 1 bath
	Petit Colorado: 1 double; 1 bath.
Closed	Never.

André & Yangbin Marini
Rustrel, Vaucluse

Tel	+33 (0)1 47 20 98 11
Fax	+33 (0)1 47 20 64 58
Email	bin.yang@wanadoo.fr
Web	www.grande-bastide-provence.com

Château Villa Nova - Apartment

Swan through a blue and white tiled hall, ascend elegant stairs to your quarters and bathe in the golden light; it floods through tall windows as you gaze over the rooftops of history-packed Saint Rémy. You'll soon get used to château living! Cleverly converted with no expense spared, the 19th-century mansion contains two bedrooms and a reception room. All is quiet and tasteful here. The owners fell for the light, the lavender and the sun, bought this house and come often, so the feel is of a well-loved home. Bedroom colours are whites and ivories, furnishings antique and understated – a cream fauteuil here, a chandelier there, perfect for these high-ceilinged rooms. There are large mirrors, marble fireplaces, sweeping oak floors, and shots of colour from cushions, lampshades and mosaic tiles. The place hums with quality. There is no private garden but a charming balcony off the immaculate kitchen, ideal for dinner à deux. Christian looks after you, arranges pick-up from Avignon station, helps organise bikes. There's the Camargue to explore, and fabulous restaurants and shops a short stroll.

Price	€950–€1,750 per week.
Sleeps	4.
Rooms	2: 1 double, 1 twin/double; 2 bathrooms.
Arrival	Saturday, but flexible out of sesaon.
Closed	Rarely.

Irene Duncan
Saint Rémy de Provence,
Bouches-du-Rhône
Tel   +353 (0)1 210 8937
Email   duncan.it@gmail.com
Web   www.vbro.com/79367

Entry 365 Map 16

Mas des Tourterelles

Climb the steps to your veranda and let the views wash over you. All around, peace, greenery, the little pool tucked into the garden – and the bustling centre of Saint Rémy mere minutes away. The Aherns have thrown themselves into their new life in the Alpilles; Richard restoring the farmhouse with its honey-coloured stone, beams and tiles, Carrie adding the light and deceptively simple touches – pale walls, linen curtains, sisal carpets, splashes of colour. Bedrooms – you can 'add on' extra from the adjoining B&B – are restful spaces of white and grey with pretty bedcovers and striking photographs on the walls. Bathrooms are neat, well-planned oases of shiny white. Relax in the elegantly simple sitting room, dine on the veranda. There's also a smart dining table in your cool, *Country Living* kitchen – big range, white sink, pots and pans hanging from the rafters. On some nights you might join Carrie and Richard for supper or wander into town. There's bags to do – the Van Gogh Museum, the Camargue, hiking in the Alpilles. Then return to your perfectly simple retreat. *B&B also. Shared pool. Meals on request.*

Price	€660–€1,700 per week.
Sleeps	2-6.
Rooms	1 double; 1 bathroom. Extra double & twin may be combined.
Closed	Never.

Richard & Carrie Ahern
Saint Rémy de Provence,
Bouches-du-Rhône
Tel/fax   +33 (0)4 32 60 19 93
Email   richard.ahern@wanadoo.fr
Web   www.masdestourterelles.com

Appartement Quatre

A gem in the centre of one of France's loveliest towns – all fountains and leafy squares. The building dates from 1900 and was designed for the Carmelite nuns whose chapel stands next door. Step off a narrow pedestrian shopping street to ascend a wide and gracious stairway, then into to an airy apartment for two. An immaculate façade, an inviting interior: linen curtains billow in the breeze, the scent of lavender fills the air. It feels immensely cool and peaceful up here. There are white tiled floors, shuttered windows, wicker furniture in the bedroom at the back, and a super big bathroom with a wild pink ceiling and a jacuzzi bath. The kitchen comes in green and blue and is well equipped, so it's off to the market in the morning – a three-minute walk – and back for a feast at night. In the living room are a huge white L-shaped linen sofa and a round antique dining table: lots of comfort, no clutter. Gabriele, a designer, is delightful. She will advise on just about anything, from where to get the best croissants to what's on at the opera. Perfect peace and great value for the area.

Price	€650–€850 per week.
Sleeps	2-3.
Rooms	2: 1 double, 1 single on mezzanine (not for children); 1 bathroom.
Closed	Never.

Gabriele Skelton
Aix en Provence, Bouches-du-Rhône
Tel   +33 (0)4 90 75 98 98
Mobile   +33 (0)6 70 51 39 90
Email   aixapartment@orange.fr

Le Bastidon

This is a dinky little house for two. Standing in Monique and Michel's peaceful garden in the shade of the ancient oaks, it is quite delightful, absolutely tiny and deeply restful. The lovely owners are there when you need them; Michel is a graphic designer and the interiors reflect his eye for fresh colour and clean lines. Make no mistake, the gîte is minute! There's a bedroom with mirror, walls and rafters in cool white, a large bed with blue and white duvet and curtains to match, garden views and Michel's watercolours on the wall. The shower room sparkles with sea-green tiles and towels; the kitchenette has style, a small table and chairs. There's no sitting room but outdoor furniture for warm days. There's also *pétanque*, table tennis and a superb pool with teak loungers and views off to Montagne Sainte Victoire. Beyond, but hidden from view, is a golf course – you are a short putt from the sixth hole, and a round or two can easily be arranged. Atmospheric Aix is close by, Cassis and its *calanques* not much further, and you can dine out every day at the auberge down the road, if you choose. *Shared pool.*

Price	€300–€380 per week.
Sleeps	2.
Rooms	1 double; 1 shower room, separate wc.
Arrival	Saturday, flexible in winter.
Closed	July-August (when rented in conjunction with main house).

Monique & Michel Cassagne
Fuveau, Bouches-du-Rhône

Tel	+33 (0)4 42 53 34 38
Mobile	+33 (0)6 09 20 33 18
Email	m-cassagne@wanadoo.fr
Web	www.provencelocationaix.com

Les Bréguières

This is a gentle secret, a place beyond the designer's grasp: authentic, simple, refreshing. Madame is warmly human yet assures your privacy, Monsieur spends his free time in the olive grove. They live in the nearby house and you may occasionally bump into the grandchildren by the pool. Inside the old *cabanon* are simple wood and warm colours. All is homely and delightful – an L-shaped banquette, books, lovely old pine; there are terracotta tiles on the floor, pictures on the walls and French windows to fling open. The kitchen/living area is filled with morning sun; above is the bedroom on the mezzanine – with beams to be ducked. A giant cherry tree bows with fruit in a little piece of garden, vines and hills surround you, there are mountains in the distance, and the backdrop is dominated by the Cengle de Sainte Victoire, a vast wall of white rock that rises mightily into the sky. The pool, all mosaic and terracotta, is reason enough to come. Ping-pong and boules on the spot, riding and golf close by, and Aix for all things Provençal. Come and forget the world. *Shared pool.*

Price	€480–€760 per week.
Sleeps	2-4.
Rooms	2: 1 double on mezzanine, 1 twin; 1 bathroom.
Closed	Never.

	Jean-Pierre & Sophie Babey
	Rousset, Bouches-du-Rhône
Tel	+33 (0)4 42 29 01 16
Fax	+33 (0)4 42 29 01 16
Email	jp.babey@club-internet.fr

Domaine de la Blaque - Les Gîtes

It's that legendary oasis of calm, surrounded by nature at its best – and with guided star-gazing as well. Hard to resist, especially with Caroline's bubbly welcome and Jean-Luc's commitment to the environment and the glittering, unpolluted night sky. The whole outdoors seems to have moved into these three comfy gîtes, with their use of natural materials (stone, old tiles, wood, lime-washed walls, fabrics) and earth tones highlighted by splashes of warm colour – simplicity and old stones, taste and an air of genuine welcome. Walk into La Grange and your breath will catch as you take in all that airy space, the views and the superb fireplace corner – an instant "That's **my** chair" spot. Snug down together in cosy La Glycine; enjoy La Bergerie's rustic split-level charm and two terraces. All have excellent bedding, good trad-modern furniture. Let Jean-Luc introduce you to astronomy in his own observatory (above right). Or turn your hand to pottery (for which Varages is famous), your legs to some great walking, your whole body to horse riding or a spot of golf. *Shared pool & laundry. Sawday B&B.*

The first (and to date only) *Ecogîte* in the Var –
and these delightful, committed people surely
deserve it. With 20 years of organic farming
under their belts, they now use solar panels for
all their hot water and some space heating, the
rest being provided by wood-burning boilers
and fires. They use only natural materials in
renovating and decorating their great
collection of old buildings: hemp insulation,
lime-washed walls, cotton curtains. Electrical
appliances are reduced to essentials: no micro-
waves or kitchen robots here. And their next
challenge is water management.

Price	€145–€810 per week.
Sleeps	Grange 5-6. Bergerie 3-4. Glycine 3.
Rooms	Grange: 2 doubles, 1 room with bunks; 1 bath, separate wc.
	Bergerie: 1 double, 1 room with bunks; 1 bath.
	Glycine 1 triple; 1 bath.
	Extra beds on request.
Closed	Never.

	Caroline & Jean-Luc Plouvier
	Varages, Var
Tel	+33 (0)4 94 77 86 91
Fax	+33 (0)4 94 77 86 91
Email	ploublaque@hotmail.com
Web	www.lablaque.com

SPECIAL
GREEN ENTRY
see page 18

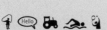

La Maison du Faïencier

Step in from the village square and be catapulted into the early 17th century. Over time, this captivating house has belonged to three master potters; potting ateliers still exist in the village. The living area is a cool sweep of the palest terracotta, the kitchen has a "French Aga", the welcome pack is one of the best we've seen. Beneath a vaulted ceiling, a majestic staircase transports you to huge dreamy bedrooms where white and soft bring instant seduction: sisal floors, pale timbers, delicate ironwork, generous wicker. Some have slanting skylight windows, others overlook the garden. Stonework has been left exposed where possible, old walls stand at jaunty angles, hand basins have been crafted to fit into uneven walls, showers have 'sunflower' heads. Warmly humorous, Fiona and Ron have kept the soul of the place then added a touch of their magic. Stone martins nest in the courtyard, the garden is sweet with lilacs, apricots and figs, the pool resembles a Roman bath and the village offers two markets a week and bikes to hire. Head for the Verdon Gorges and watery adventure! *Meals on request.*

Price	€2,000–€3,500 per week. Additional 70m² salon at extra cost.
Sleeps	10.
Rooms	5 twins/doubles; 1 bathroom, 4 shower rooms. Extra beds available at extra cost.
Closed	Never.

Ron & Fiona Alldridge
Varages, Var
Tel   +33 (0)4 94 77 81 01
Mobile   +33 (0)6 19 96 58 82
Email   alldridge@wanadoo.fr
Web   www.lamaisondufaiencier.com

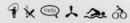

Pimaquet - La Magnanerie

Tucked into the hillside, two old stone houses. Their owner, Mimi, once a university lecturer, now a painter, lives in one of them. La Magnanerie – the rock on which it was built still visible indoors – did indeed house silkworms when the industry flourished. It climbs the hill in four half storeys, each level with a terrace under the shade of a majestic oak. Bedrooms have valley views and a gentle mix of old furniture, bathrooms are bright and beautiful with handmade tiles, the kitchen is charming and nicely equipped. In winter, a log fire adds a cosy glow; in summer, the large main terrace is the perfect spot for enjoying an angelic chorus of birdsong, a spectacular sunset, then a brilliant, star-studded sky. Behind the house is a Roman irrigation canal, fast-flowing and pristine, for the use of which Mimi pays 18 a year. A protected valley, a dreamy place to laze on languid summer days in lush gardens shady with mulberry trees. Then down to the cooling trout stream across the field to swim, paddle or read. Find shops, markets, restaurants in old Carcès and Entrecasteaux. *Fully child-friendly.*

Price	£100-£500 per week.
	Linen not included.
Sleeps	6 + cot.
Rooms	3: 2 doubles, 1 twin; 3 bathrooms.
Closed	Never.

June Watkins
Entrecasteaux, Var
Tel   +44 (0)20 8891 2656
Email   junewatkins@lineone.net

1 rue des Maréchaux

The views will move you – reaching across the village, the vineyards, the forests, all the way to the smoky blue hills of Saint Tropez, filling every little room of this four-storey house with a dose of the outdoors. The old blacksmith's forge is a typical, rustic-French village house whose characterfully steep lopsided stairs – best taken at a leisurely pace – lead to a suntrap of a terrace with a table for four at the top. Inside, all is snug: the sitting/dining room with its charming whitewashed fireplace, wine-coloured sofa for two and lovely Provençal chairs, the kitchen stuffed with pots, pans and crockery, the four-poster bedroom on the second floor, the twin room on the third. Beams are painted French grey, polished old tomettes are decked with rugs, there's a bathroom up and a shower room down. Right outside is a tiny square but for those of stout heart and good back it's an easy walk down to Cotignac's delightful centre, with its soothing fountains and quaint little corners, its terraced cafés, shops and stunning Tuesday market. *Children over 12 welcome. Parking 2 min. walk.*

Price	£480-£680 per week. Linen not included.
Sleeps	4-5.
Rooms	3: 1 double, 1 twin; 2 bathrooms, 1 shower room. Extra bed in hall.
Arrival	Saturday, but flexible.
Closed	Never.

Rosemary Stobart
Cotignac, Var

Tel	+44 (0)1661 886 776
Mobile	+44 (0)7850 375 535
Email	rosemary.stobart@btinternet.com
Web	www.marechaux-cotignac.co.uk

Bastidon Saint Benoît

Pine, rosemary, thyme and lavender fill the air in this corner of the Var. With the olive trees, oaks and broom that range around this sunny one-storey house, they bring welcome relief from hot summers. The fresh, light interiors sing with Provençal colour; there are cool terracotta floors, large picture windows and Anne Marie's joyous stencil work – sprinkled on walls, bedhead and lampshades – to add to the breezy feel. Kitchen and bathroom are roomy and modern while the large sitting/dining room – log fire for cooler months – opens to the terrace; shaded by a pine tree and roll-down awning, this is a lovely spot for dining and lounging. It sits above a neat garden that manages to squeeze in a lawn, an exotic palm and a children's swing. There are also shared boules, ping-pong and pool, but please avoid using the pool at meal times; the owners, former Sawday B&B hosts, are a warm, welcoming couple. Perfectly pitched, half-way between the Verdon Canyon and the Îles du Levant, close to the beaches and water sports of Lac de Sainte Croix, you are brilliantly placed. *Shared pool.*

Price	€500–€700 per week.
Sleeps	2-4.
Rooms	1 double, 1 sofabed in sitting room; 1 shower room.
Closed	Never.

Jean & Anne Marie Pinel Peschardière
Flassans sur Issole, Var

Tel	+33 (0)4 94 04 01 04
Fax	+33 (0)4 94 04 01 04
Email	bastidonsaintbenoit@wanadoo.fr
Web	www.giterural-provence.com

Entry 374 Map 16

Bastide des Hautes Moures - Gîte Anis

A track deep in the Var forest leads to this exquisite 1780s *bergerie*. Attached to the main house, it stands in a hollow amid 14 acres of gnarled scrub oak surrounded by cypresses, roses and lavender. Birds sing, butterflies shimmer. The cottage has been brought back to life in spectacular fashion, a monument to Catherine's flamboyant style and her love of colour; she is also an assiduous seeker of antique and brocante finds. You have a vast, lofty, open-plan kitchen/living room, and an enchantingly pretty bedroom with floral canopied bed and yellow Provençal quilt. The bathroom is charming, the kitchen superb. Antoine was a restaurateur so if you don't want to cook, he will: stuffed vegetables, bass, foie gras, fine breads and jams. You can breakfast with the B&B guests if you prefer, for a small extra charge. Outside is your own little stone terrace with white wrought-iron tables and chairs. It's an easy drive to Aix where there's masses to do – once you've raised yourself from the teak loungers that flank the big saltwater pool. *Sawday B&B. Meals on request. Shared pool. 3rd gîte available for two.*

Price	€600–€950 per week.
Sleeps	2.
Rooms	1 double; 1 shower room. Extra bed available.
Closed	Never.

Catherine & Antoine Debray
Le Thoronet, Var

Tel	+33 (0)4 94 60 13 36
Fax	+33 (0)4 94 60 13 36
Email	infos@bastidedesmoures.com
Web	www.bastidedesmoures.com

Bastide des Hautes Moures - Lodge Kaomi

The old pool house has been spectacularly converted into a discreet, single-storey refuge for two. From a concealed terrace, your views are to the saltwater pool, a piece of beautifully landscaped garden and the wooded hills. Step into the stone-flagged living area and be happy; the owners have gathered some wonderful things on their travels giving an 'out of Africa' feel. Sofas, a low table and a wrought-iron screen divide the cosy dining corner from the kitchen which, with its stone sink set into a white lava worktop and its wide window drawing the eye to the distant hills, is one of most delectable we've seen. Muslin curtains round the four-poster bed float softly in the breeze, the linen is crisp, the bed wide and firm, the shower room has an antique console embracing its basin. Catherine, young and soignée, looks after B&B and gîte guests with imagination and warmth, chef Antoine knows about the eateries in the area and the whole place could scarcely be more peaceful. All this, and the wondrous Abbey of Le Thoronet almost next door. *Sawday B&B. Meals on request. Shared pool. 3rd gîte available for two.*

Price	€700–€990 per week.
Sleeps	2.
Rooms	1 double; 1 shower room. Extra bed.
Closed	Never.

Catherine & Antoine Debray
Le Thoronet, Var

Tel	+33 (0)4 94 60 13 36
Fax	+33 (0)4 94 60 13 36
Email	infos@bastidedesmoures.com
Web	www.bastide-des-moures.com

Villa Les Oliviers

Given wings, you could launch yourself from the terraced garden and drift over the rooftops of Bargemon. The villa hangs above the village with views to forested hills and, on a good day, the sparkle of the bay of Saint Tropez. Its terraces of vines, fruit trees and lavender are interspersed with shady corners, eating areas and a balustraded pool with pool house. Behind, a steep path climbs to a studio – perfect for writing, or an extra guest. With more steps outside, the house has been furnished inside with taste and an intimate atmosphere. When not travelling, the owners, he a diplomat and writer, she an art dealer, live here. The living area, with its fireplace and welcoming sofas, has a dining table overlooking those stunning views; the lovely Provençal kitchen opens onto a terrace furnished with a Raj tent; antique beds and modern art fill the bedrooms (the single is very small); there are books and art everywhere. The owners are not always around but leave a generous welcome pack. Ideal for coast or mountains, exploring hilltop villages or medieval Bargemon's galleries and restaurants.

Price	£800-£1,900 per week.
Sleeps	7-8.
Rooms	4: 3 doubles, 1 single; 1 bathroom, 3 shower rooms, 2 separate wcs.
Closed	Never.

Frédérique Neuville
Bargemon, Var

Tel	+41 (0)2 27 00 46 19
Email	provencemagique@msn.com
Web	www.provencemagique.com

La Maison Blanche

You're hard by one of the prettiest, most fashionable villages of east Provence but here you are secluded. Cradled by pine-clad mountains, this immaculate farmhouse stands among lawns, flower-filled meadows and orchards. In spring you'll hear nightingales and smell wild narcissi; in summer the fruit trees spill apricots, cherries and figs; in autumn, apples – feel free to gather. Keeping the old beams and lovely honeycomb floor tiles, the new English owners have completely redecorated the house in a restful palette and lots of mirrors to pull the light in. Furniture is a mixture of dark-oak antique and new traditional French with spanking new beds, distressed cream woodwork and fine pale fabrics. The charming end bedroom, once the hayloft, has a vine-clad balcony from which you can pluck grapes in the autumn. As bedrooms are reached by two staircases, the house is perfect for families holidaying together. The village, with a lively weekly market, is a short walk up the hill. Then back for lunch on the generous terrace under the shade of the lime trees and a dip in the gorgeous pool. *Fully child-friendly.*

Price	£850–£2,500 per week.
Sleeps	10.
Rooms	5: 3 doubles, 2 twins; 3 bathrooms, 1 shower room, 1 separate wc.
Closed	Never.

Joyce Hibell
Bargemon, Var
Tel +44 (0)1625 617 758
Email joycehibell@aol.com
Web www.lamaisonblanche.co.uk

Number One - 1st & 2nd Floors

Again, in the four middle-floor apartments of this marvellous ensemble, we have aristocratic old bones dressed in cleancut modern fashions and bathed in the eternal light of Provence. The lovely original wrought-iron banister leads up, and up, the many wide stairs to the four doors. Inside, original terracotta covers the floors, there is space, light and the same gracious minimalism founded on total respect for the building's fine classical proportions. Living areas are lit by the elegance of the high 19th-century windows overlooking the pretty square while bedrooms, crisp and quiet, are behind, set back from the sleepy bustle down below. Design and quality are keywords here: kitchens are quietly superb, bathrooms, large or small, are works of art in themselves. Creative contemporary furniture and local antiques blend with original beams and fireplaces, decorative touches are just a couple of pots, a tribal mask, a few pebbles. The surprise of such stylish urban comfort in a little old Provençal village is vastly stimulating. *Tennis at owner's house, 10-minute drive.*

Price	€400-€1,100 per week.
Sleeps	4 apartments for 2-4.
Rooms	Each apartment: 1 twin/double, 1 double sofabed; 1 bath or shower room. The two apartments on each floor can connect.
Closed	Never.

Arja Suddens
Mons, Var

Tel   +33 (0)4 94 76 35 15
Email   arja.suddens@wanadoo.fr
Web   www.numberonemons.com

Number One - Ground & Top Floors

If you long for the unexpected, the sudden jolt of contrast, this is for you; if you love undemonstrative luxury, it's for you too. Elegant 17th-century architecture and gentle all-white interiors hold suave leather furniture, a few choice pieces placed just so – a giant vase, a piece of antique textile, an old Provençal triple settee – and always, quantities of restful space. Step in from the sights and shapes of timeless Provence to what could be 21st-century Milan. On the ground floor, coloured furniture and a working fireplace glow against the white walls, tall windows give onto the plane tree and the light of the square, bold Italian-style furniture, utterly contemporary and deeply comfortable, enhances the space; the bedroom seems humble in contrast. The lofty top-floor apartment under the eaves has a big fabulous terrace looking across Mons to the endless hills and the sea. Come back inside to a bright, luxurious living space for two where you may want to stay for ever. Kitchens and bathrooms are, of course, in sleek modern harmony with the rest. *Ground-floor meeting/reception room for 12.*

Price	€400–€1,100 per week.
Sleeps	Ground Floor 2. Top Floor 2.
Rooms	Each apartment: 1 twin/double; 1 bathroom.
Closed	Never.

Arja Suddens
Mons, Var

Tel +33 (0)4 94 76 35 15
Email arja.suddens@wanadoo.fr
Web www.numberonemons.com

Provence – Alps – Riviera

Les Mérelles - Studio

Wrapped in jasmine, wisteria and roses, this house is straight out of a story book. Snug amid two hectares of Mediterranean gardens, it is private yet enjoys the benefits of the main house: swimming pool, shady or sunny garden spots, views to the mountains, woodland to explore, herbs from Regina's organic garden. Step through French windows into a large, elegant space, both bedroom and living room. With rocking chairs, pale walls and green quilting, views to garden or forest, muslin drifting at the windows, it's an enchanting haven. The kitchen, a pearl of creative practicality, is ingeniously hidden by curtains; the shower room is classy and big. Another pretty room acts as bedroom or study. Eat outside – there's a covered patio – or at a choice of nearby restaurants, or join your hosts for a Provençal meal. Charming and cultured Germans with excellent English, they will also do your laundry. Walk or cycle – bicycles to borrow – from the grounds, explore alpine foothills or coastal towns, enjoy markets and summer festivals. A relaxing den for two. *Shared pool. Meals on request.*

Price	€900 per week.
Sleeps	3.
Rooms	2: 1 twin/double, 1 single; 1 shower room.
Closed	Never.

Peter & Regina Westrick
Callian, Var
Tel +33 (0)4 94 47 72 21
Fax +33 (0)4 94 76 53 25
Email regina.westrick@wanadoo.fr

La Ferme de Guillandonne

This enchanting 200-year-old farmhouse is the height of country-hideaway chic. Earthy, stylish, magical, it stands under the sprawling embrace of an ancient oak (one of many) and is bordered on one side by a stream. You are wrapped in ten acres of countryside. Rows of lavender run along one side of the pool while on the other a tunnel of wisteria leads down to a sun-trapping terrace. The interior is equally satisfying. Walls are washed in traditional colours – cool yellows, cosy reds, pale greens. There are old beams and a big arched window gives onto the terrace. One of the bedrooms has a magnificent high ceiling and a window that looks out onto a Chinese mulberry tree, another an original open fireplace and views over the pool. Marie-Joëlle, a former English teacher, and her husband, an architect, have renovated with a happy respect for the spirit of the place, for its history and the landscape that envelops it. You are in one of the loveliest parts of the Var and villages here have musical events running throughout the summer. This is a *bona fide* classic, a very special place. Don't miss it. *Sawday B&B.*

Price	€1,000–€2,300 per week.
Sleeps	6-7 + cot.
Rooms	3: 2 doubles, 1 twin; 2 bathrooms, 2 shower rooms (1 with separate entrance). Extra bed.
Closed	Never.

Marie-Joëlle Salaün
Tourrettes, Var

Tel	+33 (0)4 94 76 04 71
Mobile	+33 (0)6 24 20 73 09
Fax	+33 (0)4 94 76 04 71
Email	guillandonne@wanadoo.fr

Entry 382 Map 16

557 Chemin des Hautes Cottes

Committed Francophiles, the Yorkes have lavished quantities of TLC on their big 'neo-Provençal' house and terraced garden. It's a seductive hideaway in a cocoon of luxuriant vegetation, like a balcony hanging over the glorious scenery. Inside there is space and an almost palpable sense of calm. Artist Morag has a flair for colour and impeccable, unpretentious taste: gold, turquoise, blue, brick-red and white are married with Indian cottons, local antiques (a wedding cupboard is proudly dated 1832), good kilims and personal mementoes – the house of a family you would like to know better. Her enchanting and colourful paintings decorate the walls, the lime-green sofa before the open fireplace is almost edible, there are all the books on Provence you may need. Plus fine big bedrooms, pretty Salernes-tiled bathrooms, a perfect family kitchen to prepare for the stupendously gleaming antique refectory table. Then choose the pool or a secret corner in the luscious garden, or go for water sports of every description on Lac de Saint Cassien, or walking in the hills behind Callian. *10-minute walk to village.*

Price	£800–£2,100 per week.
Sleeps	8 + cots.
Rooms	4: 2 doubles, 2 twins; 3 bathrooms, 1 shower room, separate wc.

Robert & Morag Yorke
Callian, Var

Tel	+44 (0)1403 790 311
Mobile	+44 (0)7860 559 445
Email	robert.yorke@btinternet.com
Web	www.callian.co.uk

Château Petitpierre

You have seen people, on programmes such as Grand Designs, getting their dream houses built, with helpers and hinderers of many professions: it takes time and money, toil and tears. This secret château in its secret garden-in-the-making is a dream, too, but the little Count and Countess built every bit of it with their own fair hands, laying stone on stone, tile on tile, in one week of pure childlike pleasure. The fortress-like architecture, so utterly in keeping with the wild landscapes and rough climate of these hills, hides an astonishingly modernist treatment of the interior. The walls are moveable partitions, curtains on rods can be placed wherever you create doorways and, apart from a few family antiques from the renowned Dollie workshops, the furniture is easy-build flat-pack elements that you may paint any colour you like – as long it's primary. At last, a holiday home designed for some of the most psychologically challenged of us all: those who never grow up. Rental comes with the pleasure of building and daubing for days on end, on condition you help with the still-virgin garden.

Price	Less than you think.
Sleeps	306.
Rooms	153 miniature doubles.
Arrival	Under cover of darkness.
Closed	Whenever grown-ups are around.

Comte & Comtesse Secrets de Bébé
Bébéville sous Bois, Var
Email   primary@hiddendream.works

Le Madison

From first-floor windows, an expanse of sky. Below, green fairways, trees and distant hills. The communal pool is out of sight, the motorway a distant hum, the golf course beckons... here is peacefulness, light and space. Your three-bedroom apartment in this gated, pink and white 'village' is probably one of the largest and surely the most immaculate. Slip a CD into the state-of-the-art music centre, slide open the glass doors to the almost wraparound balcony, roll down the electric shade, unfurl on a white-cushioned lounger. The owners have employed the most talented artisans and have decorated to their own design. The result is a spare, sweeping, luxurious décor with a red and cream theme and oriental touches. Everything is crisply, perfectly new: the pale quarry tiles, the creamy drapes, the Turkish carpet, the de Dietrich oven, the huge TV (plus videos for kids). And when you've tired of the fine linens and the silk cushions, there's the sea two miles away, and Nice, Mougins, Saint Tropez. Not forgetting three tennis clubs and innumerable golf courses... the nearest lapping at your feet. *Shared pool.*

Price	€1,500–€2,100 (£1,000–£1,400) per week.
Sleeps	6.
Rooms	3 twins/doubles; 2 bathrooms, 1 shower room, 1 separate wc.
Closed	Rarely.

Ennis & Barry Bartman
Mandelieu, Alpes-Maritimes
Tel +44 (0)1582 769 728
Mobile +44 (0)7831 636 644
Email mandelieu@bdbartman.co.uk
Web www.rivieragolf.info

Les Princes d'Orange

Longing to do it as the French do? This is exactly the sort of place that Parisians hope to escape to for the month of August, a modern Riviera apartment on a gated estate set in manicured grounds with well-clipped lawns and beds of sweet-scented flowers. It is pretty, spotless and conveniently positioned but the highlight is the vast balcony and its magnificent views down the Côte d'Azur with alpine foothills rising behind – you can see Italy on a good day. It is a perfect spot, one that encourages great sloth, and it faces south-east, so expect to breakfast lazily in the sun, under the awning if it gets too hot. The interior swims with light from full-height windows, you live with fabulous views, big old-gold sofas, a glass dining table on marble floors, white walls, a queen-size bed dressed in pure cotton. The beach and the old town are both within walking distance (about 15 minutes), though buses pass frequently if you prefer. The old town is a must: café culture, a maze of narrow streets, a covered market, pretty squares, a cathedral and a château. Exceptional.

Price	£375–£550 per week.
Sleeps	2.
Rooms	1 double; 1 bathroom.
Arrival	Saturday, but flexible out of season.
Closed	Never.

	Sian & James Wroe
	Antibes, Alpes-Maritimes
Tel	+33 (0)6 09 46 04 89
	+33 (0)6 23 68 16 72
Email	james.wroe@orange.fr
Web	www.orangedazur.co.uk

Villa Ackermann

Hedges enfold the large garden, the high front gate is always closed, you are a few suburban streets away from the bay and can spy the sea from the top terrace. You won't meet the owners but they have gone to impressive lengths to make this a calm, comfortable, inviting place to stay. The villa was built 30 years ago in open and airy Provençal style: walls are white, floors tiled, terraces shaded, kitchen and bathrooms are in mint condition. Exotica from far-flung travels – Ethiopia, India, Bolivia – strew the spacious open-plan ground floor: a plump rattan sofa and armchairs softened by cushions, two pretty baskets hanging on a wall. Elegant wrought-iron beds are deliciously draped with mosquito nets and each upper-floor bedroom drifts into a terrace. Tempting to spend all day here curled up with a novel but, if you tire of the palms and the pool, you can set off for the lake or for Cannes (a short drive), sandy beaches (a short stroll), the small Picasso Museum in Vallauris, the larger one in Antibes, and restaurants whose prices range from reasonable to stratospheric.

Price	€880–€1,380 per week.
Sleeps	6.
Rooms	3: 2 doubles, 1 twin; 1 bathroom, 1 shower, separate wc.
Closed	Never.

Uwe & Christiane Ackermann
Vallauris, Alpes-Maritimes
Tel	+49 6151 41107
Fax	+49 6151 41752
Email	uackermann@yahoo.de
Web	home.ferienwohnungen.de/ackermann

Villa Gardiole

'Twixt Cannes and Nice: a protected, gated hideaway. This two-hectare, hillside paradise – built in the 1950s – includes the owners' house, your charming villa and one other… and all rooms lead to the garden, it seems. Wisely: this is a glorious expanse of grass, trees, landscaped bushes and potager (yours to poach), a discreet lake-like pool, a wooden pergola, a serene all-glass weights room (that opens up in warm weather), swings, slides, treehouse, hammocks and bamboo forest. And your dining courtyard. Inside, rustic terracotta floors, a polished country dresser, a regiment of copper pans, a touch of trompe l'œil – the feel is immaculate Provençal. Downstairs, a pale green-check sofa, a working chimney and an open country kitchen; upstairs, a gaily canopied bed and an en suite terrace. Madame Severgnini can arrange a maid, a cook, a yoga teacher, a personal trainer, a gardening course with an expert, Italian cookery with her. The Brague National Park starts from the back door and there are so many cultural and sporty ways in which you may fill your hours. Fabulous! *Shared pool.*

Price	€2,000–€4,000 per week.
Sleeps	7.
Rooms	3: 2 doubles, 1 twin, 1 single; 4 bathrooms.
Arrival	Flexible.
Closed	Never.

	Ignazia Severgnini
	Biot, Alpes-Maritimes
Tel	+33 (0)4 93 65 55 08
Fax	+33 (0)4 93 65 50 44
Email	severgnin@aol.com
Web	www.villagardiole.com

Provence – Alps – Riviera

Domaine de Pierrefeu - Apartment

Valbonne is a lively village with restaurants, shops, galleries and heaps of Provençal charm. There's a weekly Friday market for great food and – on the first Sunday of the month – antiques and brocante. Here is a modern house in its own vast grounds, at the end of a quiet cul de sac set back from the road, with a garden to roam and a good pool – yours during the day while the charming owner is at work. Your ground-floor apartment is small but cosy, with white walls, floral curtains, a sofa with a throw and French windows opening to a covered terrace and delightful mosaic-tiled table. Lovely in summer; and you have all you need to knock up a meal in the kitchen, pretty with its creamy pink tiles. The bedroom is traditionally furnished, the bathroom is large and lovely, with plenty of space to fit your things. This would be a delightfully cool apartment even in the height of summer, and the pool area is surrounded by loungers, flowering shrubs and palm trees for shade… all you hear is birdsong. So peaceful, and the village just a seven-minute walk.

Price	€450–€650 per week. Two-day bookings out of season.
Sleeps	2.
Rooms	1 double; 1 bathroom.
Arrival	Flexible out of season.
Closed	Never.

Caroline Duval-Flahault
Valbonne, Alpes-Maritimes
Tel   +33 (0)4 93 12 90 47
Email   cduvalflahault@wanadoo.fr

La Bergerie & Le Cabanon

The soft stone walls of these two sweet cottages keep you cool in the hottest weather. In the sheepfold, enjoy your morning coffee at the old manger – now a breakfast bar – or on the terrace, and watch the sun come up over high-perched Bar sur Loup, a 20-minute walk away. Surrounded by grass, oaks, olives, pines and rocky-peaked mountains, this is a blissfully peaceful place. Sylvie, an actress, and sporty Pascal (they met hang-gliding), have restored and decorated in a stylish but informal way. Floors are bleached wood, timber ceilings are painted, there are simple, charming touches and the Bergerie bedroom has fabulous views. The Cabanon has the extra seductions of washing machines – and a piano. The owners and their three children make you feel warmly at home but don't intrude. Come for cherries in May, fireflies in June: a spring and summer paradise. It's a short hop to the coast if you fancy the snazziness of the Riviera; gentler forays might include visits to the stunning hilltop villages of the area. There is another slightly more up-to-date cottage 50 metres away, which sleeps two plus child.

Price	€350–€650 per week.
Sleeps	Bergerie 2-3. Cabanon 3.
Rooms	Bergerie: 1 double, sofabed in dining room; 1 shower room. Cabanon: 1 double, 1 small child's room, shower room.
Closed	Never.

Sylvie & Pascal Delaunay
Le Bar sur Loup, Alpes-Maritimes

Tel   +33 (0)4 93 42 50 08
Email   chemindelachenaie@hotmail.com
Web   www.chemindelachenaie.com

Entry 390 Map 16

La Maison

One of the loveliest places in this book, utterly authentic and sure of itself, with that special air that attracts the artist and the writer. It is a place to chance upon, as if the house were too modest to seduce you in advance. The lucky ones who do will find an old Provençal stone farmhouse standing beneath the protective gaze of Le Baou, a sugar-loaf mountain. You are surrounded by peace and Laurence's luscious terraced garden; beyond are the suburbs of Vence and distant road hum. Your top-floor apartment is reached via open stone steps and a super private terrace, shaded by an ancient olive tree. Laurence, warm, cultured and full of life, lives on the ground floor, her equally delightful son lives above her. Bedrooms are simple and cosy, beds dressed in fine linen. One has whitewashed walls and a beautiful 18th-century 'built-in' cupboard, the other an antique desk and views through trees. There's a long refectory dining table in the kitchen with rush-seated chairs, and a tiny but adorable sitting room. Stroll down to the waterfalls and swimming holes of the Cagne river. *Parking on road.*

Price	€400–€550 per week.
Sleeps	4 + 1 child.
Rooms	2: 1 double, 1 twin, child's bed available; 1 bathroom.
Closed	Never.

Laurence Thiebaut
Vence, Alpes-Maritimes
Tel   +33 (0)4 93 58 13 95
Mobile   +33 (0)6 24 62 76 35
Email   lamaisondelaurence@hotmail.com
Web   www.lamaisondelaurence.com

Noble Apartments

From a flower-filled balcony, high up in an 18th-century apartment block on the Place du Justice, you can scan the rooftops of Old Nice. (Stand on tip-toes and you can see the sea.) Off the street, between cafés where the lawyers and their clients meet, is an elegant wrought-iron and glass door with a brass plaque. Enter the hall and let the lift transport you to the fourth floor. Kara Noble and Pam Demacon have renovated Fresco (named after the gorgeous old fresco on its ceiling) and Carrera (named after the marble on the bathroom floor) in such a way that they interlink for two parties. Each apartment is filled with light: romantic Fresco, with its old honeycomb tiles, cosy sofa and scatter cushions, and homely but luxurious Carrera, with its full kitchen and antique pieces. Expect crisp cotton on very comfortable beds, air conditioning for summer nights, double glazing for quiet, books, magazines, art, brocante. Pam is gardienne and is charming. Step out of the door: the flower and veg market is up the road; walk straight ahead: you find promenade, beach and glittering sea. A special address.

Price	Fresco: €500–€600. Carrara: €700–€800. Together: €1,100–€1,400. Prices per week.
Sleeps	Fresco 2. Carrara 4.
Rooms	Fresco: 1 twin/double; 1 shower room. Carrara: 2 twins/doubles; 2 bathrooms. Apartments connect to create Frescarra for 6.
Arrival	Flexible.
Closed	Never.

Kara Noble
Nice, Alpes-Maritimes
Tel   +33 (0)6 25 89 69 53
Email   pam@nobleapartments.com
Web   www.nobleapartments.com

Les Cloîtres

Overlooking Sospel's 600-year-old cathedral, this historic building was probably one of the original monastic or university buildings clustered round the bishop's throne, and your big bright apartment must be one of the most extraordinary you will find. All the walls, all the ceilings are frescoed, a 20th-century local artist's two-year labour of love. The rooms – two bedrooms (one with French windows to the courtyard), library/sitting and dining rooms – are vast with soaring ceilings, polished wood and honeycomb tile floors. With the Hollands' antique furnishing, the atmosphere is old-style grand yet comfortable and totally undaunting. The excellent kitchen has a door onto the wide terrace for cool dining. When Sospel, a wonderful leafy backwater in the hills, was an Italian town it was favoured by the clergy – and their wealth. It is still lively, in a civilised way (good choice of restaurants), and a great base for fabulous walking, kayaking, fishing and paragliding. The fleshpots of the coast beckon from below and the huge and famous Friday market in Vintimiglia is just a 25-minute drive. *Children over 10 welcome.*

Price	€350–€550 per week.
Sleeps	5.
Rooms	2: 1 double, 1 family room for 3; 1 bathroom, 1 shower room.
Arrival	Flexible.
Closed	Never.

Brett & Caroline Holland
Sospel, Alpes-Maritimes

Tel	+33 (0)4 93 91 44 23
Mobile	+33 (0)6 24 86 77 96
Email	brett.holland@bpb.barclays.com

armoire wardrobe, cupboard

bastide can be a stronghold, a small fortified village or, in Provence, another word for *mas*

bateau mouche river boat for sightseeing cruises

bergerie sheepfold, sheep shed, shepherd's hut/house

brocante secondhand furniture, objects, fabric, hats, knick-knacks

cabanon cabin, chalet or, in Provence, cottage

calanques deep coastal creeks

cave cellar, wine cellar

chambre d'hôtes B&B

charcuterie pork butcher's shop, delicatessen produce sold in same

chartreuse charterhouse

château mansion or stately home built for aristocrats between the 16th and 19th centuries.

château fort castle, with fortifications

châtelain/e lord/lady of the manor

dégustation wine-, food-tasting

dépendance outbuilding of château, farm etc

domaine viticole wine-growing estate

donjon keep (of medieval castle)

épicerie grocer's shop

fauteuil armchair

foire fair

four à pain bread oven

gardien warden, caretaker

gîte d'étape overnight dormitory-style hut/house, often run by the local village or municipality, for cyclists or walkers (often with optional meals)

lavoir washing place or wash house

longère a long, low farmhouse or outbuilding

magnanerie silkworm farm

maison bourgeoise/maison de maître big, comfortable house standing in quite large grounds, built for member of the liberal professions, captain of industry, trade

maison paysanne country cottage

mas in Provence, a country house, usually long and low with old stone walls, pantiled roof and painted shutters; in Languedoc, a stone hut or shelter in a vineyard or field

maison vigneronne tiny vine-worker's cottage or a comfortable house owned by the estate manager or proprietor

mazot hut, another word for *mas*, used in the Rhône Valley – Alps region

mairie town hall

marché au gras market where you can buy foie gras and other delights

moulin mill

œil de boeuf literally bull's eye window, ie. small circular or oval window

pétanque game of bowls or *boules* played originally in south of France

pineau alcoholic aperitif from the Charentes region made from wine and cognac

pigeonnier pigeon-house or dovecote

pommeau alcoholic drink made from apples

potage vegetable soup

potager vegetable garden

pressoir wine, cider press

puys Auvergnat dialect for 'peak'

salle d'accueil reception room

salle d'eau shower room

salle de séjour living room

table d'hôtes dinner at communal table, usually with the owners of the house

tomette hexagonal terracotta floor tile

tonneau barrel

Biologique & Organic
Produce called 'organic' in English is known as *de culture biologique* in French, bio for short. If you talk about *organique*, people may think you are having trouble with your organs.

Biscuit & Gâteau
Biscuit literally means 'twice cooked' and originally meant dehydrated army rations or the base for some sticky puddings. Sweet biscuits are usually called *gâteaux secs* or *petits gâteaux*; savoury biscuits are *gâteaux d'apéritif*. At breakfast, *gâteau maison* will probably be a simple sponge-cake with jam or a French-style fruit cake, also called *cake* (pronounced cack).

Tourte: French for a pie with pastry on top, it only applies to savoury dishes.

Tarte: An open tart or flan.

Flan: Baked custard.

Tartine: Breakfast food. Usually, half a baguette sliced lengthwise and buttered; can be toasted before buttering, when it becomes a *tartine grillée*.

Une pie: Magpie.

Un pis: (same pronunciation as pie) is an udder of any milking animal.

Scotch: Either adhesive tape or whisky – context is all.

Mousse: Mousse, as in chocolate; or foam, lather, froth, as on sea, soap, beer; or foam rubber; or moss.

Marmelade: Well-stewed   fruit. 'Marmalade' is *confiture d'oranges amères* (jam made with bitter oranges).

Pomme de pin: Fir cone. 'Pineapple' is *ananas*.

Pamplemousse is 'grapefruit'.

Grappe: Bunch, cluster. *Grappe de raisins* – bunch of grapes.

Raisin: Generic term for the fruit of the vine: the grape. One 'grape' is *un grain de raisin*. Steinbeck's book translates as *Les Raisins de la Colère*.

Raisins de Corinthe: currants (you can hear the etymology); *raisins de Smyrne* – sultanas; *raisins secs* – raisins!

Prune: Fresh plum; *pruneau* – prune.

Verger: Orchard. Many a greengrocers' shop is called *Aux Fruits du Verger*.

Trouble: Cloudy, murky – you can send that bottle of wine back.

Troublé: Troubled, disturbed.

The French have 11 annual national holidays. In May there can be a holiday nearly every week depending upon the dates of the 'moveable feasts' (see below). So be prepared for stores, banks and museums to shut their doors for days at a time. Booking hotels in advance becomes essential.

1 January	New Year's Day (*Jour de l'an*)
1 May	Labour Day (*Fête du premier mai*)
8 May	WWII Victory Day (*Fête de la Victoire*)
14 July	Bastille Day
15 August	Assumption of the Blessed Virgin (*Assomption*)
1 November	All Saints Day (*La Toussaint*)
11 November	Armistice Day (*Jour d'armistice*)
25 December	Christmas Day (*Noël*)
26 December	2nd day of Christmas (Alsace Lorraine only)

Moveable feasts	2008	2009
Good Friday (Alsace Lorraine only)	21 March	10 April
Easter (*Pâques*)	23 March	12 April
Easter Monday	24 March	13 April
Ascension (*l'Ascencion*)	1 May	21 May
Pentecost (*la Pentecôte*)	11 May	31 May

When a holiday falls on a Tuesday or Thursday, many people may make a longer break by including Monday or Friday (*faire le pont*). This is not official and does not apply to institutions such as banks but is sufficiently commonplace to cause difficulties in booking rooms or travelling.

With over 60,000 km of clearly marked long distance footpaths, or *sentiers de Grande Randonnée* (GRs for short), and a fantastic variety of landscapes and terrains, France is a superb country in which to walk. Hike in the snow-topped glaciers of the Northern Alps, walk through the lush and rugged volcanic 'moonscapes' of the Auvergne, or amble through the vineyards of Burgundy, Alsace or Provence.

Stroll for an afternoon, or make an odyssey over several months. Some long-distance walks have become classics, like the famous GR65, the pilgrim path to Santiago de Compostela, the Tour du Mont Blanc, or the 450-km long GR3 *Sentier de la Loire*, which runs from Ardèche to the Atlantic. Wild or tamed, hot or temperate, populated or totally empty: France has it all.

Photo: istockphoto

Wherever you are staying, there will almost certainly be a GR near you. You can walk a stretch of it, then use other paths to turn it into a circular walk. As well as the network of GRs, marked with red and white parallel paint markings, there's a network of *Petites Randonnées* (PRs), usually signalled by single yellow or green paint stripes. In addition, there are *sentiers de Grande Randonnée de Pays* (GRPs), marked by a red and yellow stripe, and any number of variants of the original GR route which eventually become paths in their own right. Paths are evolving all the time.

The paths are lovingly waymarked and maintained by the Fédération Française de la Randonnée Pédestre (FFRP), which was founded in 1947 under another name. The federation is also responsible for producing the topo-guides, books for walkers containing walking directions and maps (see under Books). For further information, consult www.ffrp.asso.fr

The great reward for walkers is that you'll penetrate the soul of rural France in a way you never could from a car. You'll see quaint ruined châteaux, meet country characters whom you'll never forget and you'll encounter a dazzling variety of flora and fauna if you look for it. France has a remarkably rich natural heritage, including 266 species of nesting birds, 131 species of mammals, and nearly 5,000 species of flowering plants.

Look out for golden eagles, griffon vultures and marmots in the Alps and Pyrenees, red kites and lizard orchids in the Dordogne, and fulmars and puffins off the rocky Brittany coast. There's no room for complacency, however, as hundreds of species are threatened with extinction: 400 species of flora are classed as threatened and about 20 species of mammals and birds are vulnerable or in danger of extinction.

When to go

The best months for walking are May, June, September and October. In high mountain areas, summers are briefer and paths may be free of snow only between July and early September. In the northern half of France, July and August are also good months; southern France is ideal for a winter break, when days are often crisp and clear.

Code du Randonneur

(The Walking Code)
• Love and respect nature
• Avoid unnecessary noise
• Destroy nothing
• Do not leave litter
• Do not pick flowers or plants
• Do not disturb wildlife
• Shut all gates behind you
• Protect and preserve the habitat
• No smoking or fires in the forests
• Stay on the footpath
• Respect and understand the country way of life and the country people
• Think of others as you think of yourself

Maps

The two big names for maps are IGN (Institut Géographique National) and Michelin. IGN maps are likely to be of most use for walkers. A useful map for planning walks is the IGN's France: Grande Randonnée sheet No. 903 which shows all the country's long distance footpaths. For walking, the best large-scale maps are the IGN's 1:25,000 Série Bleue and Top 25 series. Also look out for IGN's 1:50,000 Plein Air series which includes GRs and PRs, plus hotels and campsites. Unfortunately they cover only limited areas.

Books

The FFRP produces more than 180 topo-guides — guidebooks for walkers which include walking instructions and IGN maps (usually 1:50,000). Most of these are now translated into English so it's worth buying the ones you need before you leave.

Clothing and equipment

This obviously depends on the terrain, the length of the walk and the time of year, but here's a suggested checklist:

boots, sunhat, suncream and lip salve, mosquito repellent, sunglasses, sweater, stick, water bottle, gaiters, change of clothing, phrase book, maps, compass, field guides to flora and fauna, waterproof daypack, camera and spare film, Swiss Army knife, whistle (for emergencies), spare socks, binoculars, waterproof jacket and trousers, emergency food, first-aid kit, torch.

Two and a half times the size of Great Britain, France offers rich rewards to the cyclist: plenty of space, a superb network of minor roads with little traffic, and a huge diversity of landscapes, terrains and smells. You can chose the leafy forests and gently undulating plains of the north, or the jagged glacier-topped mountains of the Alps. Pedal through wafts of fermenting grapes in Champagne, resinous pines in the Midi, or spring flowers in the Pyrenees. Amble slowly, stopping in remote villages for delicious meals or a café au lait, or pit yourself against the toughest terrains and cycle furiously.

You will also be joining in a national sport: bikes are an important part of French culture and thousands don their lycra and take to their bikes on summer weekends. The country comes to a virtual standstill during the three-week Tour de France bike race in July and the media are dominated by talk of who is the latest *maillot jaune* (literally 'yellow jersey' – the fellow in the lead). Cycling stars become national heroes and heroines with quasi-divine status.

Mountain bikes are becoming more and more popular. They are known as VTTs (*vélos tout terrain*) and there is a well-developed network of VTT trails, usually marked in purple.

When to go

Avoid July and August, if possible, as it's hot and the roads are at their busiest. The south is good from mid-March, except on high ground which may be snow-clad until the end of June. The north, which has a similar climate to Britain's, can be lovely from May onwards. Most other areas are suitable from April until October.

Getting bikes to and through France

If you are using public transport, you can get your bicycle to France by air, by ferry or via the Channel Tunnel. Ferries carry bikes for nothing or for a small fee. British Airways and Air France take bikes free if you don't exceed their weight allowance. If you are travelling by Eurostar, you should be able to store your bike in one of the guards' vans which have cycle-carrying hooks, with a potential capacity of up to eight bikes per train. To do this you need to book and 'buy your bike a ticket'.

Some mainline and most regional trains accept bikes, sometimes free of charge, most for a fee. Some have dedicated bike spaces, others make room in the guard's van. Information is contradictory on timetables and ticket agents may not have up-to-date information. Trains indicated by a small bike symbol in the timetable may no longer accept bikes, some without the symbol do. To be sure, check out the train at the station the day before you set off. Insist on a ticket *avec réservation d'un emplacement vélo*. If you are two or more make sure the reservation is multiple. In the Paris area, you can take bikes on most trains except during rush hours and at certain central RER stations.

Maps

The two big names are Michelin and the Institut Géographique National (IGN). For route-planning, IGN publishes a map of the whole of France showing mountain-biking and cycle tourism (No. 906). The best on-the-road reference maps are Michelin's Yellow 1:200,000 Series. IGN publishes a Green Series to the scale of 1:100,000. For larger scale maps, go for IGN's excellent 1:25,000 Top 25 and Blue Series (which you will also use for walking).

A new map of Paris showing bike routes, one-way streets, bus sharing lanes, rental facilities, weekend pedestrian and bike only streets is available at some bookshops. Or order it online at: www.media-cartes.fr

Repairs and spare parts

Bike shops are at least as numerous as in Britain and you should be able to get hold of spare parts, provided you don't try between noon and 2pm.

Some useful contacts

• Fédération Française de la Randonnée Pédestre (FFRP), the leading organisation for walkers and ramblers. Many of their guide books have been translated into English. www.ffrp.asso.fr
• Fédération Française de Cyclotourisme For cyclists and mountain bikers. www.ffct.org
• SNCF (French Railways) www.voyages-sncf.com

Photo: istockphoto

Bike rental

We advise you to consult the owners of your gîte about local bike rental, how to go about it and what quality to expect.

New in Paris: Vélib'

The city council has just launched its new short-ride bike rental scheme with 750 'stations' strategically placed throughout Paris, each holding a dozen or more solidly-built bikes that you can rent after subscribing by credit card at one of the central registration points (1 for a day, 5 for a week, 29 for a year). To encourage users to hire for short periods, the first half hour of each new rental period will be included in the subscription, an extra charge will be levied thereafter. For full information, consult www.velib.paris.fr

In Lyon, France's second city, this system has been operating for some time, with great success.

General de Gaulle signed the initial legislation for the creation of France's national and regional parks in 1967. Forty national and regional nature parks now represent 11% of the country's landmass. Most are off the beaten track and are often missed by the foreign visitor. The motorway network is such that one swishes by huge patches of beautiful countryside without even realising it.

The National and Regional Nature Parks charter promotes:
• Protection and management of natural and cultural heritage
• Participation in town and country planning and implementation of economic and social development
• Welcoming and informing the public, raising environmental awareness.

There is a ban on hunting, camping, building and road construction in the six national parks: Cévennes, Écrins, Mercantour, Port-Cros, Pyrénées and Vanoise. Access can be difficult but the rewards are considerable. There are regional parks to be found, for example, in the mountains of Queyras (Hautes Alpes), the plains of Vexin (Île de France), along the coast of Camargue (Provence), in the woodlands in the Northern Vosges (Alsace-Lorraine), in the wetlands of Brière (Western Loire) and off-shore in Port-Cros (Côte d'Azur).

All are ideal for rambles. Serious walkers can choose from the many *sentiers de Grande Randonnée* (GRs for short) which range through the parks, and all park offices can provide maps of local walks.

There are grottoes and museums to visit, along with animal parks with roaming bison, yak, greater kudu and a pack of wolves, plus bikes, canoes and kayaks to rent. Other activities include horse riding, canal boating, sailing, fishing, spa treatments, wine tours, bathing, rock climbing, hang-gliding, ballooning. There are packhorses in Livradois-Forez (Auvergne) and donkeys for hire in Haut Languedoc. Many activities are ideal for children and a multitude of crafts can be observed: clog making, silk weaving, glass working, stone working in the Morvan (Burgundy), cheese making and pipe making in the Haut Jura (Franche Comté).

The central website below links to all the parks and has a useful summary in English:
www.parcs-naturels-regionaux.tm.fr

Photo: istockphoto

1. Armorique
2. Marais du Cotentin et du Bessin
3. Boucles de la Seine Normande
4. Caps et Marais d'Opale
5. Scarpe-Escaut
6. Avesnois
7. Vexin français
8. Montagne de Reims
9. Lorraine
10. Vosges du Nord
11. Normandie-Maine
12. Perche
13. Haute Vallée de Chevreuse
14. Gâtinais français
15. Forêt d'Orient
16. Ballons des Vosges
17. Brière
18. Loire-Anjou-Touraine
19. Brenne
20. Morvan
21. Haut Jura
22. Périgord-Limousin
23. Volcans d'Auvergne
24. Livradois-Forez
25. Pilat
26. Chartreuse
27. Massif des Bauges
28. Landes de Gascogne
29. Causses du Quercy
30. Monts d'Ardèche
31. Chartreuse
32. Queyras
33. Grands Causses
34. Camargue
35. Lubéron
36. Verdon
37. Haut-Languedoc

As I write, swallows are nesting in our wood-pellet store, the fountain plays in the pond, tall grasses bend before a gentle breeze, and the solar panels heat water too hot to touch — even during a very dull summer. We have, to our delight, created an inspiring and serene place.

The roof was lifted to allow us to fix thick insulation panels beneath the tiles. More panels were fitted between the rafters and as a separate internal wall, and underfloor heating was laid. We are insulated for the Arctic, and almost totally airtight; we open windows for natural ventilation. A very economical Austrian heating boiler sucks in wood-pellets and slowly and cleanly consumes them. Rainwater is channelled to a 6000-litre underground tank and then, filtered, flushes loos and fills basins. Sun-pipes funnel the daylight into dark corners and double-glazed Velux windows pour it into every office. Our electricity consumption is extraordinarily low: we have attractive background lighting, and individual 'task' lights are used only as needed.

We built a green-oak barn between two old barns, and this has become the heart of the offices, warm, light and beautiful. Wood plays a major role: our simple oak desks were made by a local carpenter, my office floor is of oak, and there is oak panelling. Even the carpet tiles tell a story — they are made from the wool of Herdwick sheep from the Lake District. The hill farmers there suffered dreadfully

We began in the early 90s in a small terraced house in Bristol and then, straining at the seams, decamped to a farm five miles away in the countryside. Beautiful as they were, our new offices leaked heat, flooded whole rooms with light to illuminate one person, and were not ours to alter. We failed our eco-audit in spite of using recycled cooking oil in one car and gas in another, and recycling everything we could.

So we leapt at the chance to buy some old barns closer to Bristol, to create our own eco-offices and start again. Our accountants thought we were mad and there was no time for proper budgeting. The back of every envelope bore the signs of frenzied calculations, and then I shook hands with the farmer and went off on holiday. Two years later we moved in.

Photo left: Quentin Craven
Photo right: Tom Germain

during the Foot and Mouth outbreak and the National Trust, landlords to many of them, sought other sources of income for their tenants. The tough wool of the Herdwicks makes great carpet. The choice of other materials, too, was a focus: we used non-toxic paints and finishes and, however difficult they were to apply, they have proved to be gentle and beautiful to live with.

'Events' blew our budget apart, but we have a building of which we are proud and which helped us win two national awards in 2006. Architects and designers are fascinated and we work with a renewed commitment to our environmental policies. Best of all, we are now in a position to encourage our owners and readers to take 'sustainability' more seriously. It has been satisfying to see how much other people enjoy coming to the offices, and it is more and more the case that people applying to us for jobs are doing so because of where and how we work.

I end by answering an obvious question: our office carbon emissions will be reduced by about 75%. Our bills are low and, as time goes by, will be relatively lower – and lower. I am embarrassed to confess that we have not yet completed a new environmental audit, so I cannot report on exact savings. But we subscribe fully to the peak oil theory: that the rate of oil extraction has peaked, or is about to very soon, and we should all be pursuing ways of reducing our dependency on the stuff.

Cynics – and there are still plenty – tell me that there might have been better ways of spending our reserves than by putting them in to an eco-office. But it has been worth every penny and every ounce of effort. Becoming 'green' is a journey and, although we began long before most companies, we still have a long way to go. We would like to be a major influence on our owners, all 5,500 of them, and on our readers and web-users in the reduction of their own ecological footprints.

We need to be as loyal to our convictions as we are to our clients. We are not just a travel publisher. Like every other business, we are part of the community and have a wide responsibility.

Alastair Sawday

A whole week self-catering in Britain with your friends or family is precious, and you dare not get it wrong. To whom do you turn for advice and who on earth do you trust when the web is awash with advice from strangers? We launched Special Escapes to satisfy an obvious need for impartial and trustworthy help — and that is what it provides. The criteria for inclusion are the same as for our books: we have to like the place and the owners. It has, quite simply, to be 'special'. The site, our first online-only publication, is featured on www.thegoodwebguide.com and is growing fast.

Cosy cottages • Sumptuous castles • Tipis • Hilltop bothies • City apartments and more

www.special-escapes.co.uk

Alastair
Sawday's

Self-catering in Britain

The Little Food Book   £6.99

"This is a really big little book. It is a good read and it will make your hair stand on end"
Jonathan Dimbleby

"…lifts the lid on the food industry to reveal some extraordinary goings-on"
John Humphrys

The Little Money Book   £6.99

"Anecdotal, humorous and enlightening, this book will have you sharing its gems with all your friends"
Permaculture Magazine

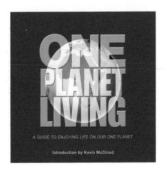

One Planet Living   £4.99

"Small but meaningful principles that will improve the quality of your life."
Country Living

"It is a pleasure to pick up and learn essential facts from."
Organic Life

To order any of the books in the Fragile Earth series call 01275 395431 or visit www.fragile-earth.com

THE

BIG

"Time is running out.
Don't despair. Do get angry.
Do get active. And do buy
'The Big Earth Book' to get
all that in perspective."
Jonathon Porritt, Forum for the Future

EARTH

BOOK

IDEAS AND SOLUTIONS FOR A PLANET IN CRISIS

James Bruges

We all know the Earth is in crisis. We should know that it is big enough to sustain us if we can only mobilise politicians and economists to change course now. Expanding on the ideas developed in *The Little Earth Book,* this book explores environmental, economic and social ideas to save our planet. It helps us understand what is happening to the planet today, exposes the actions of corporations and the lack of action of governments, weighs up new technologies, and champions innovative and viable solutions. Tackling a huge range of subjects – it has the potential to become the seminal reference book on the state of the planet – it's the one and only environmental book you really need.

James Bruges's *The Little Earth Book* has sold over 40,000 copies and has been translated into eight languages.

Praise for *The Big Earth Book*:
"Time is running out. Don't despair. Do get angry. Do get active. And do buy *The Big Earth Book* to get all that in perspective." Jonathon Porritt, *Forum for the Future*

"This is a wonderful book – really informative but written in a very clear, easy-to-read way." Patrick Holden, *The Soil Association*

RRP £25.00 To order at the Reader's Discount price of £20 (plus p&tp) call 01275 395431 and quote 'Reader Discount BEB FSC'.

Have you enjoyed this book? Why not try one of the others in the Special Places to Stay series and get 35% discount on the RRP *

British Bed & Breakfast (Ed 12)	RRP £14.99	Offer price £9.75
British Bed & Breakfast for Garden Lovers (Ed 4)	RRP £14.99	Offer price £9.75
British Hotels & Inns (Ed 9)	RRP £14.99	Offer price £9.75
Pubs & Inns of England & Wales (Ed 4)	RRP £14.99	Offer price £9.75
French Bed & Breakfast (Ed 10)	RRP £15.99	Offer price £10.40
French Holiday Homes (Ed 4)	RRP £14.99	Offer price £9.75
French Hotels (Ed 4)	RRP £14.99	Offer price £9.75
Paris Hotels (Ed 6)	RRP £10.99	Offer price £7.15
Spain (Ed 7)	RRP £14.99	Offer price £9.75
Italy (Ed 4)	RRP £14.99	Offer price £9.75
Portugal (Ed 4)	RRP £11.99	Offer price £7.80
Croatia (Ed 1)	RRP £11.99	Offer price £7.80
Greece (Ed 1)	RRP £11.99	Offer price £7.80
Turkey (Ed 1)	RRP £11.99	Offer price £7.80
Ireland (Ed 6)	RRP £12.99	Offer price £8.45
Morocco (Ed 2)	RRP £11.99	Offer price £7.80
India (Ed 2)	RRP £11.99	Offer price £7.80
Green Places to Stay (Ed 1)	RRP £13.99	Offer price £9.10

*postage and packing is added to each order

To order at the Reader's Discount price simply phone 01275 395431 and quote 'Reader Discount FSC'.

If you have any comments on entries in this guide, please tell us. If you have a favourite place or a new discovery, please let us know about it. You can return this form or visit www.sawdays.co.uk.

Existing entry

Property name: _____

Entry number: _____ Date of visit: _____

New recommendation

Property name: _____

Address: _____

_____

Tel: _____

Your comments

What did you like (or dislike) about this place? Were the people friendly? What was the location like?

_____

_____

_____

_____

_____

Your details

Name: _____

Address: _____

_____

_____ Postcode: _____

Tel: _____ Email: _____

Please send completed form to:
FSC, Sawday's, The Old Farmyard, Yanley Lane, Long Ashton, Bristol BS41 9LR, UK

Wheelchair-accessible

At least one bedroom and bathroom accessible for wheelchair users. Phone for details.

Limited mobility

At least one bedroom and bathroom accessible without steps.

Quick reference indices

WiFi
Wireless internet access
available for guests.

Waterside
Not more than 500 metres
from the sea, a lake or a
river.

1 Midi – Pyrénées

Caussé

Nothing is too much trouble for Sue and Robert, eager that your stay be perfect. The pretty little studio apartment just below their own 300-year old cottage has been thoughtfully and generously fitted out – small indoors, enormous outside. Traditionally restored, it has a cool tiled floor, exposed stone and yellow plaster walls, very comfortable beds – a double plus bunks – and excellent linen. There's a small corner kitchen with some charming crockery and French windows that open to a private terrace overlooking the 17-acre garden, resplendent with fruit trees and potager (you're welcome to help yourself) and enticing spots, sunny or shady, in which to settle with a drink and a book. It's a great-value place to stay and Robert and Sue are infinitely kind – and flexible about arrangements. They'll provide breakfast at a small extra charge, or a picnic lunch; they'll even, on occasion, babysit or cook dinner. Robert's pâté is excellent, especially if he has been listening to Verdi! (Mozart, apparently, provides a less inspiring background for pâté production.) *Shared pool. B&B also. Meals on request.*

2

3

Price	€350–€476 per week. Shorter stays welcome: enquire about rates (minimum 3 days).
Sleeps	2-4.
Rooms	Studio apartment:1 double & adult-size bunks; 1 shower room.
Arrival	Flexible.
Closed	Rarely.

4

5

6

7

8

Sue & Robert Watkins
Saint Paul d'Espis, Tarn-et-Garonne

Tel	+33 (0)5 63 29 14 22
Fax	+33 (0)5 63 29 14 22
Email	causse.stpaul@orange.fr

9

11 Entry 233 Map 14

10